THE AMERICAN NEGRO
HIS HISTORY AND LITERATURE

THOUGHTS
ON
AFRICAN COLONIZATION

Wm. Lloyd Garrison

ARNO PRESS and THE NEW YORK TIMES

NEW YORK 1968

General Editor
WILLIAM LOREN KATZ

EARLIEST RESPONSES
OF AMERICAN NEGROES AND WHITES
TO AFRICAN COLONIZATION*

In 1832 PUBLICATION OF WILLIAM LLOYD GARRISON'S *Thoughts on African Colonization* marked a significant reversal in the policies of the young abolitionist movement. For many years those opposed to slavery, including Garrison himself, had accepted the argument that the emancipation of Negro slaves should be followed by their removal from the United States, preferably to Africa. The man most influential in convincing Garrison to reject the idea of sending American Negroes to Africa was James Forten, a wealthy black sailmaker and inventor, and a leader in his Philadelphia community. In all probability Forten also assisted Garrison in securing the collection of Negro anti-colonization writings that form an important part of his book. By including these documents Garrison sought to establish that Negroes had always opposed African colonization.

Garrison was apparently unaware, as were many later historians, that Negro enthusiasm and effort actually predated white interest in African colonization. Significantly, James Forten never told Garrison about the great interest he and other Negro leaders had had as early as 1816 in promoting African resettlement for American Negroes,

* Portions of this introduction were read by the author at the Annual Meeting of the Association for the Study of Negro Life and History at Greensboro, North Carolina, October 13, 1967.

i

and from 1832 until now no historian has said simply and clearly that for some time before 1817 the most important Negro leaders favored and were working for Negro colonization in Africa. Yet the evidence on this point is unassailable and is corroborated by documents citing the words of Forten himself and Bishop Richard Allen of Philadelphia. Their views were strikingly similar to those expressed by black separatists a century and a half later. Relevant to feelings and events of today, the story of early Negro interest in African colonization and the total rejection of the idea by the Negro masses in 1817, also casts new light on the past.

The logical starting point for this story is the career of Captain Paul Cuffee, a wealthy New Bedford Negro shipowner. After an 1811 visit to the Sierra Leone colony in Africa, Cuffee opened negotiations with the African Institution of London, an organization of British businessmen whose interest in the colony mixed philanthropy with economic gain.[1] Cuffee persuaded the merchants that their colony needed "good, sober, steady characters" and, at a personal financial loss of thousands of dollars, brought thirty-eight black volunteer settlers from America to Sierra Leone in 1815.

However, more significant than his first transplanting of black Americans to Africa, was Paul Cuffee's influence for colonization among his fellow Americans, black and white. When he returned to the United States he successfully prevailed upon the most influential Negro leaders of the time to form branches of the African Institution; his recruits included Reverend Peter Williams in New York, Reverend Daniel Coker in Baltimore, and James Forten, Bishop Richard Allen, and Reverend Absalom Jones in Philadelphia, the fountainhead of Negro thought at the time.[2] Obviously the most prominent leaders of the largest black ghettos, north and south, viewed Negro colonization in Africa as a viable solution to the problems they faced in the United States.

Many of these leaders had lived through, and some had fought in, the American Revolution only to see its promises unfulfilled for black people. James Forten, a volunteer in the American navy, had been captured and held aboard a British prison ship but had rejected a British offer to defect. Though Northern states were in the process of abolishing slavery by 1817, the Northern Negro was not truly free or equal in rights to the lowliest white. In 1787, the very month after the conclusion of the Constitutional Convention in Philadelphia, respectable Negro worshippers, including Richard Allen and Absalom Jones, were pulled from their knees while at prayer in a white church and expelled—an act which led them to form the first Negro church in the United States. In 1812 Paul Cuffee, who had sailed his brig *Traveller* to Sierra Leone and back the year before, was accorded rude treatment on a public conveyance between Washington and Baltimore and was denied service in a restaurant in Baltimore.[3]

The anti-Negro feeling in Philadelphia was vividly recalled by James Forten's accomplished granddaughter, Charlotte L. Forten: "There was no Northern city in which colored people were so badly treated as in that 'City of Brotherly Love.' In some parts of the city their lives were in constant danger; they were mobbed, insults of all kinds were heaped upon them. . . ."[4]

The fear of kidnappers from the slave states hung over every Philadelphia Negro family. In mid-January 1817 the Quakers had gathered in their Arch Street meeting house to hear from a delegation they had dispatched to meet with leading members of the Congress and Senate in Washington to secure legislation to protect free Negroes from kidnapping. The memorial the delegation carried to Congress painted a grim and frightening picture:

> Men, women and children legally set free and peaceably enjoying the comforts of domestic life, become prey to a set of hardened, unprincipled men, who, cautiously masking the nature of their designs, go prowling thro the neighborhoods where black people reside, and from secret observation and enquiry, obtain such a knowledge of the features, size, etc. of the persons marked for their plunder, as will if required, be sufficient for a statement of pretended ownership.

A week later the Philadelphia branch of the Pennsylvania Abolition Society held a special meeting to demand legal redress for "the outrages on the rights of the People of Colour." It is interesting to note that Bishop Richard Allen was himself the victim of a kidnapper who swore that he had recently purchased him as a slave; unlike many other black people, Allen was able to summon so many witnesses who knew him that the perjurer was himself jailed.[5]

The heavy burdens of poverty and discrimination as well as the terrors of kidnapping hung over the black ghettos of the North. But even wealthy Negroes, such as James Forten, who had amassed a small fortune by inventing a useful sailing device, felt the weight of oppression. Charlotte Forten recalled: ". . . my grandfather was obliged to send his sons away to school and to go to the expense of employing private teachers for his daughters. The wrongs of his people weighed heavily upon his mind; and as old age came, and the prospect did not seem to brighten, he became at times deeply discouraged."[6]

It would have been strange indeed if in this period, as in others throughout the black man's history in America, the realities of oppression did not turn Negro leaders toward the hope of better tomorrows in Africa. Thus, the most significant black leaders of the time united in the African Institution to urge free Negroes to emigrate to Africa.

But at the time Paul Cuffee was returning from his 1815 expedition to Sierra Leone, white men, whose motives mixed genuine philanthropy with calculated selfishness, were also considering the removal of the American free Negro population to Africa. Reverend Robert Finley, pastor of the Basking Ridge Presbyterian Church in New Jersey, became increasingly aware that in his region both the number of free Negroes "and their wretchedness, too" increased each year. Toward the end of November 1816 the minister left Basking Ridge for Washington with his plan for African colonization. Five days after his arrival in the Capital he dispatched a letter to Paul Cuffee seeking his support.

Cuffee's reply was encouraging.[7] In a whirlwind campaign lasting the month of December, Finley discussed his plan for shipping free Negroes to Sierra Leone with leading government officials including fellow-Princetonian President James Madison. Finley's way was well prepared by his brother-in-law, Elias B. Caldwell, Clerk of the United States Supreme Court and a prominent Washingtonian; the *National Intelligencer* printed a vast amount of the minister's pro-colonization propaganda and allowed him to use its offices as a headquarters. On December 21 and 28 Finley's efforts were crowned with success when prominent government officials, ministers, and important Washingtonians met at the Davis Hotel to form "The American Society for Colonizing the Free People of Color of the United States." Bushrod Washington agreed to serve as president and the list of vice-presidents included Henry Clay, Daniel Webster, John Randolph, Francis Scott Key, and General Andrew Jackson.[8]

The speeches of Henry Clay and John Randolph, re-
printed in New York and Philadelphia newspapers, made
it abundantly clear that the Society had no intention of
interfering with slavery and maintained, on the contrary,
that the removal of free Negroes from the land would
substantially reduce the problem of slave control. Although the Society always referred respectfully to the
pioneer efforts in colonization inaugurated by Paul Cuffee
and asserted that concern for Negroes motivated their
actions, anti-Negro sentiments were inevitably used to
attract the support of slaveholders and other whites.[9]

By New Year's Day 1817 Finley had completed his
business in Washington and left for home by way of
Philadelphia, intending to meet with the Negro leadership; his writings indicate he was aware of their participation in the African Institution and their great interest
in colonization in Sierra Leone. Though it received no
notice in the Philadelphia newspapers, his arrival coin-
cided with massive newspaper coverage of his efforts in
Washington and the release of many of his propaganda
pieces from the *National Intelligencer.* In New York the
editor of the *Courier* predicted that although whites
might be indifferent to the colonization idea, "Negroes
will open their eyes wide enough, we suspect, at this
proposal." He then posed a few questions to the new
Society:

> Why was not something proposed for the *enslaved*
> blacks? Why not send *them* to Africa. That would
> indeed look a little like humanity and disinterested-
> ness. But the free blacks are a dangerous mixture
> with the enslaved blacks. Aye—there's the rub—
> and there the occasion of all this unexpected, unsub-
> stantial tenderness and humanity towards them.

Two weeks later this editor wrote a piece that was
given prominent space in a leading Philadelphia news-

paper on January 15. Writing in a mock Negro dialect and signing himself as "Sambo," he suggested that if colonization was such a fine idea why didn't Henry Clay return to England or wherever his ancestors came from; he also suggested that Negroes remain in the United States and whites sail to Africa, and even proposed that Negroes form an organization to facilitate the white exodus. It was in this highly charged atmosphere of claim and counter-claim that Finley, founder of the American Colonization Society, met with Philadelphia's Negro leaders.[10]

It is not possible to state with certainty whether the private meeting with Finley took place before or after a massive Negro meeting at the Bethel Church. However, an analysis of statements made to Finley by James Forten and Bishop Richard Allen lead this writer to conclude that the meeting took place before the mass meeting. Forten notes that the private meeting took place at the church of Reverend Absalom Jones and Finley's biographer states that it consumed "nearly an hour." Only the statements of James Forten and Bishop Allen were recorded by Finley, who tells us that Forten, speaking on colonization,

> . . . was animated on the subject. He said their people would become a great nation: he pointed to Hayti, and declared it as his opinion that their people could not always be detained in their present bondage; he remarked on the peculiarly oppressive situation of his people in our land—observing that neither riches nor education could put them on a level with the whites, and the more wealthy and the better informed any of them became, the more wretched they were made; for they felt their degradation more acutely. *He* gave it as his decided opinion that Africa was the proper place for a colony. He observed to those present, that should they settle anywhere in the vicinity of the whites,

their condition must become before many years as it now is, since the white population is continually rolling back, and ere long they must be encompassed again with whites.

Bishop Richard Allen was next recorded by Finley, and he

. . . spoke with warmth on some oppression which they suffer from the whites, and spoke warmly in favor of colonization in Africa—declaring that were he young he would go himself. He spoke of the advantages of the colony of Sierra Leone, and highly of Paul Cuffee. He considered the present plan of colonization as holding out great advantages for the blacks who are now young.[11]

It was probably a short time after the initial meeting with Finley that at least 3,000 Negro men assembled at the Bethel Church to discuss the colonization question. It is apparent that the Negro leaders who summoned them had not planned a denunciation of the American Colonization Society but a serious consideration of its colonization plans. Their words as reported by Finley, their involvement with the African Institution, and their relationship with Paul Cuffee indicate that the Negro leadership maintained a lively interest in colonization in general and the plans of the American Colonization Society in particular.[12]

The clearest view of the meeting's origins and the beliefs of its sponsors is preserved in a letter from its chairman, James Forten, to Paul Cuffee. Besides briefly describing the leaders' associations with the African Institution and with Finley, it provides a fleeting glimpse of early Negro separatism. Despite its historic significance, this letter has never been quoted adequately before. Wrote Forten to his "esteemed friend" on January 25, 1817:

The African Institution met at the Rev. R. Allens the very night your letter came to hand. I red that part to them that wished them a happy New Year, for which they desired me to return you many thanks. I must now mention to you that the whole continent seems to be agitated concerning the Colonising the People of Colour. You mention to me that a gentleman from Washington has written you on the subject of your opinion. I suppose it must have been the Rev. Robert Finley from the State of New Jersey. He convinced us to gather the other night at the Rev. A. Jones, on this interesting subject. He mentioned his intention of writing you. Indeed the People of Colour, here was very much fritened at first. They were afrade that all the free people would be compeled to go, particularly in the southern States. We had a large meeting of Males at the Rev. R. Allens Church the other evening. Three thousand at least attended, and there was not one sole that was in favour of going to Africa. They think that the slave holders want to get rid of them so as to make their property more secure. However it appears to me that if the Father of all mercies, is in this interesting subject (for it appears that they all think that something must and aut to be done but do not know where nor how to begin) the way will be made strate and clear. We however have agreed to remain silent, as the people here both the white & colour are decided against the measure. My opinion is that they will never become a people until they com out from amongst the white people, but as the majority is decidedly against me I am determined to remain silent, except as to my opinion which I freely give when asked. . . .

> I remain very affectionately
> Yours unalterably,
> James Forten[13]

This incomplete record of the meeting indicates how totally the Negro men of Philadelphia rejected the idea of colonization, the white society formed to promulgate the concept, and the beliefs of their own leadership. It does not reveal, nor is there any documentary information now available that reveals, whether or not leadership and membership clashed. Unfortunately no Philadelphia newspaper announced the meeting nor reported its results despite the fact that the attendance represented virtually all of the city's Negro adult male population.[14]

The meeting created a crisis for the Negro leadership of Philadelphia and Forten admitted that "We however have agreed to remain silent." His personal integrity is shown in his comment that although he has refrained from public controversy, his private views "I freely give when asked." His "Yours unalterably" closing to Paul Cuffee and his black separatist sentiment "My opinion is that they will never become a people until they com out from amongst the white people" underscores his firm belief that the 3,000 Negroes were in error.[15]

Some time between January 25, when Forten wrote his letter to Paul Cuffee, and another giant anti-colonization meeting six and a half months later, Forten and the Philadelphia Negro leadership reversed their position. In the meeting of August 10, 1817 James Forten and Russell Parrott, selected as chairman and secretary respectively, issued "on behalf of the meeting" an address that denounced colonization and rejected participation in any project connected with it. Garrison included this address in his book immediately after the January resolution.[16]

For the rest of his life Forten crusaded against all plans to remove American Negroes from their adopted homeland. He convinced Garrison that colonization did nothing but divert American Negroes from the struggle for a better life in America and keep whites from facing their responsibilities to all citizens regardless of race or color. The white abolitionist leader's acceptance of Forten's premise led to the denunciation of colonization embodied in *Thoughts on African Colonization.* Those Negro and white historians who followed Garrison with far more evidence at hand than he had, continued to present a simplistic view of the Bethel Church mass meeting. In 1842 Reverend Robert Purvis, son-in-law of meeting chairman James Forten, delivered an oration that maintained that Forten, Bishop Allen, Reverend Jones, and the other Philadelphia Negro leaders had always opposed African colonization and had called the Bethel Church meeting to denounce "the evil tendencies and effects" of the American Colonization Society. Obviously, and on both counts, nothing could have been further from the truth.[18]

William Lloyd Garrison's *Thoughts on African Colonization* pointed white abolitionists in the direction the Negro masses of Philadelphia had chosen for themselves in 1817. It had a profound effect upon many of the white antislavery advocates who had joined the American Colonization Society and been led away from the fight against slavery. With cogent reasoning and documentation from the Society's publication *The African Repository,* Garrison destroyed the ideological foundation of the American Colonization Society and proved its underlying anti-Negro intent. His volume is one of the inspired documents of the antislavery struggle, a turning point in the movement its author led.

William Loren Katz

NOTES

¹ *Edinburgh Review*, August 1811; *Niles Weekly Register*, March 21, April 4, June 6, and June 29, 1816; P. J. Staudenraus, *The African Colonization Movement, 1816–1865* (New York, 1961) pp. 9–11; Henry Noble Sherwood, "Paul Cuffee," *Journal of Negro History*, VIII (April 1923) pp. 61–64; *History of Prince Lee Boo* (Dublin, 1822) pp. 165–168.

² "Discourse of Peter Williams on the Death of Capt. Paul Cuffee," *The Third Annual Report of the American Society for Colonizing the Free People of Colour of the United States* (Washington, 1820) pp. 115–117; Staudenraus, *African Colonization*, pp. 9–11; James Forten to Paul Cuffee, January 25, 1817, Paul Cuffee Papers, New Bedford Public Library.

³ Robert Purvis, *Remarks on the Life and Character of James Forten, Delivered at Bethel Church, March 30, 1842* (Philadelphia, 1842) pp. 4–13; Paul Cuffee, *Journal* entry for May 5, 1812, Paul Cuffee Papers; Richard Allen, *The Life, Experience and Gospel Labors of the Rt. Rev. Richard Allen* (Philadelphia, 1887) pp. 14–15; Leon F. Litwack, *North of Slavery* (Chicago, 1961) pp. 3–4; Robert G. Harper to American Colonization Society, August 20, 1817 in *First Annual Report of the American Society for Colonizing the Free People of Colour of the United States* (Washington, 1818) p. 15.

⁴ Charlotte Forten Grimke, "Personal Recollections of Whittier," *The New England Magazine*, VIII pp. 468–469.

⁵ Pennsylvania Abolition Society, *Minutes 1800–1824*, Special Meeting, January 25, 1817, ms. collection, Pennsylvania Historical Society; Philadelphia Yearly Meeting (Arch Street), Meeting for Sufferings, *Minutes 1802–1834*, pp. 247–248, ms. collection, Society of Friends, Department of Records, Philadelphia; Edward Raymond Turner, "The First Abolition Society in the United States," *Pennsylvania Magazine of History and Biography* XXXVI (1912) p. 96.

⁶ Grimke, "Personal Recollections," pp. 468–469.

⁷ Robert Finley to John P. Mumford, February 14, 1816, Robert Finley to Paul Cuffee, December 5, 1816, Paul Cuffee to Robert Finley, January 6, 1816 in Isaac Van Arsdale Brown, *Biography of Robert Finley* (Philadelphia, 1819) pp. 83, 88, 93, 104; *Niles Weekly Register*, December 14, 1816; *National Intelligencer*, December 14, 1816; Staudenraus, *African Colonization*, pp. 24–26.

⁸ *National Intelligencer*, December 24, 31, 1816; E. B. Caldwell to Rev. Isaac V. A. Brown, July 8, 1818 in Brown, *Biog-*

raphy (1857 edition) p. 104; Staudenraus, *African Colonization,* pp. 26–31.

9 Brown, *Biography* (1857 edition) pp. 102–104; *Niles Weekly Register,* December 28, 1816; *Poulson's American Daily Advertiser* (Philadelphia) January 2, 3, 4, 1817.

10 Brown, *Biography* (1819 edition) pp. 88, 102; *Poulson's,* January 2, 3, 4, 8, 10, 13, 15, 1917; *Weekly Aurora* (Philadelphia) January 27, 1817; *Aurora General Advertiser* (Philadelphia) January 18, 1817; *New York Courier, January* 1, 13, 1817; *The Democratic Press* (Philadelphia) January 18, 1817; *United States Gazette* (Philadelphia) January 7, 21, 1817.

11 Brown, *Biography* (1819 edition) pp. 99–102, (1857 edition) pp. 121–124; James Forten to Paul Cuffee, January 25, 1817, Cuffee Papers. The Brown biography of Finley maintains he met with the Philadelphia Negro leadership after the Bethel Church meeting but provides no date for either meeting. It does state that Finley was back in New Jersey by the middle of January. The 1819 edition asserts that the Negro leaders whose words Finley transcribed were "J. F. and R. A." and the 1857 edition identifies them as "John Foster and Richard Allen." Neither *Robinson's Original Annual Directory for 1817* nor *Paxton's Philadelphia Directory for 1818* list a Negro named John·Foster. Those who prepared the latter edition must have meant to say James Forten; the similarity of views expressed in the interview and in his January 25, 1817 letter to Cuffee substantiate this.

12 James Forten to Paul Cuffee, January 25, 1817, Cuffee Papers, Brown *Biography* (1819 edition) pp. 99–102.

13 James Forten to Paul Cuffee, January 25, 1817, Cuffee Papers; Henry Noble Sherwood, "Paul Cuffee," *Journal of Negro History,* VIII (April, 1923) pp. 64–65 has the only reference to the Forten letter found in the literature.

14 *1810 Census,* pp. 33, 33a; James Mease, *The Picture of Philadelphia* (Philadelphia, 1811) p. 53; W. E. B. DuBois, *The Philadelphia Negro* (Philadelphia, 1899) p. 23; James Forten to Paul Cuffee, January 25, 1817, Paul Cuffee Papers, New Bedford Library. Since this letter refers to the Bethel Church meeting as taking place "the other evening," it undoubtedly preceded the Richmond, Virginia meeting of January 24, 1817 and therefore is the first known Negro protest meeting on American soil. An August 27, 1967 interview with Leonard F. Williams, Bethel Church historian, established that only males twenty-one and over had voting rights in the Church in 1817

xiv

and that Church records began with the year 1822. These points explain why only males were invited to the January meeting and why no record of the exact evening of the meeting exists in the Bethel files. A careful search of Philadelphia newspapers and Quaker records has failed to uncover any mention of the meeting or its date.

¹⁵ James Forten to Paul Cuffee, January 25, 1817, Cuffee Papers.

¹⁶ William Lloyd Garrison, *Thoughts on African Colonization,* pp. 10–13; Carter G. Woodson, *Negro Orators and Their Orations* (Washington, 1925) pp. 52–55.

¹⁷ Purvis, *Discourse,* pp. 4–17; Billington (ed.) *The Journal,* pp. 8–10; Samuel J. May, *Some Recollections of Our Antislavery Conflict* (Boston, 1869) pp. 286–288; James Forten to W. L. Garrison, December 31, 1830, *Journal of Negro History,* XXIV (April, 1939) pp. 199–200.

¹⁸ Ray Allen Billington (ed.) *The Journal of Charlotte L. Forten* (New York, 1953) pp. 8–9; William C. Nell, *The Colored Patriots of the American Revolution* (Boston, 1855) pp. 177–178; G. B. Stebbens, *Facts and Opinions Touching the Real Origin, Character and Influence of the American Colonization Society* (Boston, 1853) pp. 194–196; Robert Purvis, *Remarks on the Life and Character of James Forten Delivered at Bethel Church, March 30, 1842* (Philadelphia, 1842) pp. 14–15.

THOUGHTS

ON

AFRICAN COLONIZATION

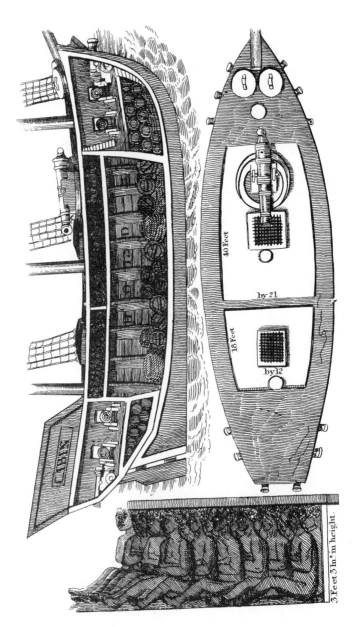

SECTION OF A SLAVE SHIP.

3 Feet 3 in : m height.

40 Feet

18 Feet

by 21

by 12

From Walshs Notes of Brazil

THOUGHTS

ON

AFRICAN COLONIZATION:

OR

AN IMPARTIAL EXHIBITION

OF THE

DOCTRINES, PRINCIPLES AND PURPOSES

OF THE

American Colonization Society.

TOGETHER WITH THE

RESOLUTIONS, ADDRESSES AND REMONSTRANCES

OF THE

FREE PEOPLE OF COLOR.

'Out of thine own mouth will I condemn thee.'
'Prove all things; hold fast that which is good.'

BY WM. LLOYD GARRISON.

BOSTON:
PRINTED AND PUBLISHED BY GARRISON AND KNAPP,
NO. 11, MERCHANTS' HALL.

1832.

PREFACE.

I DEDICATE this work to my countrymen, in whose intelligence, magnanimity and humanity I place the utmost reliance. Although they have long suffered themselves to be swayed by a prejudice as unmanly as it is wicked, and have departed widely from the golden rule of the gospel, in their treatment of the people of color, to suppose that they will always be the despisers and persecutors of this unfortunate class is, in my opinion, to libel their character. A change in their feelings and sentiments is already visible—a change which promises, ere long, to redeem their character from the bloody stains which slavery has cast upon it, and to release the prisoner from his chains. May they be ashamed to persist in a mean and thievish course of conduct, and afraid to quarrel with the workmanship of God ! May a righteous indignation be kindled in their breasts against a combination which is holding them up, for the scorn and contempt of other nations, as incorrigible oppressors, whom neither self-respect, nor the opinions of mankind, nor the fear of God, can bring to repentance ! Their duty is plain, and it may easily be done. Slavery must be overthrown either by their own moral strength, or by the physical strength of the slaves. Let them imitate the example of the people of Great Britain, by seeking the immediate overthrow of the horrid system. Let a National Anti-Slavery Society be immediately organized, the object of which shall be, to quicken and consolidate the moral influence of the nation, so that Congress and the State Legislatures may be burdened with petitions for the removal of the evil—to scatter tracts, like rain-drops, over the land, on the subject of slavery—to employ active and eloquent agents to plead the cause incessantly, and to form auxiliary societies—to encourage planters to cultivate their lands by freemen, by offering large premiums ; to promote education and the mechanical arts among the free people of color, and to recover their lost rights. Religious professors, of all denominations, must bear unqualified testimony against slavery. They must not support, they must not palliate it. No slaveholder ought to be embraced within the pale of a christian church ; consequently, the churches must be purified ' as by fire.' Slavery in the District of Columbia is sustained in our national capacity : it ought, therefore, to be prostrated at a blow. The clause in the Constitution should be erased, which tolerates, greatly to the detriment and injustice of the non-slaveholding States, a slave representation in Congress. Why should property be represented at the impoverished south, and not at the opulent north ?

To impair the force of this exposition, the ardent advocates of the Colonization Society will undoubtedly attempt to evade the ground of controversy, and lead uncautious minds astray in a labyrinth of sophistry. But the question is not, whether the climate of Africa is salubrious, nor whether the mortality among the emigrants has been excessive, nor whether the colony is in a prosperous condition, nor whether the transportation of our whole colored population can be effected in thirty years or three centuries, nor whether any slaves have been emancipated on condition of banishment ; but whether the doctrines and principles of the Society accord with the doctrines and principles of the gospel, whether slaveholders are the just proprietors of their slaves, whether it is not the sacred duty of the nation to abolish the system of slavery now, and to recognise the people of color as brethren and countrymen who have been unjustly treated and covered with unmerited shame. *This is the question—and the only question.*

With such a mass of evidence before them, of the pernicious, cruel and delusive character of the American Colonization Society, I leave the patriot, the philanthropist and the christian to judge of the fitness of the following inflated and presumptuous assertions of its advocates :— ' The plan is of heavenly origin, against which the gates of hell shall never prevail '—' a circle of philanthropy, every segment of which tells and testifies to the beneficence of the whole '— ' addressing its claims alike to the patriot, and the christian, it being emphatically the cause of liberty, of humanity, of religion ' *—' so full of benevolence and the hallowed impulses of Heaven's own mercy, that one might, with the propriety of truth, compare its radiant influences to a rainbow, insufferably bright, spanning the sombre clouds of human wrong, that have accumulated on the horizon of our country's prosperity, and beating back, with calm and heavenly power, the blackening storm that always threatens, in growling thunders, a heavy retribution ' †—' that citizen of the United States who lifts a finger to retard this institution, nay, that man who does not use his persevering efforts to promote its benevolent object, fails, in our opinion, to discharge his duty to his God and his country' ‡ (1)—' nothing but a distinct knowledge and a calm consideration of the facts in the case, is wanting to make every man of common intelligence, common patriotism, and common humanity, the earnest friend of the Colonization Society ' ! ! §

There is one important consideration, which, owing to the contractedness of my limits, I have omitted to enforce in this work. It is this : the serious injury which our interests must inevitably suffer by the removal of our colored population. Their labor is indispensably necessary and extremely valuable. By whom shall the plantations at the south be cultivated but by them ? It is universally conceded that they can resist the intensity of a southern sun, and endure the fatigues attendant on the cultivation of rice, cotton, tobacco and sugar-cane, better than white laborers : at least, their bodies are now inured to this employment. I do not believe that any equivalent would induce the planters to part with their services, or white laborers to occupy their places. In the great cities, and in various parts of the southern States, free persons of color constitute a laborious and useful class. In a pecuniary point of view, the banishment of one-sixth of our population,—of those whom we specially need,—would be an act of suicide. The veriest smatterer in political economy cannot but perceive the ruinous tendency of such a measure.

---

* African Repository.　　　　† Rev. Mr Maffit's ' Plea for Africa.'
‡ Western Luminary.　　　　§ Christian Spectator.

(1) The clerical gentleman who presumes to utter this opinion is the same who has also the hardihood to assert that ' many of the best citizens of our land are holders of slaves, and hold them *in strict accordance with the principles of humanity and justice* ' ! !

THOUGHTS

ON

AFRICAN COLONIZATION.

PART I.

INTRODUCTORY REMARKS.

IN attacking the system of slavery, I clearly foresaw all that
has happened to me. I knew, at the commencement, that my
motives would be impeached, my warnings ridiculed, my person
persecuted, my sanity doubted, my life jeoparded : but the
clank of the prisoner's chains broke upon my ear—it entered
deeply into my soul—I looked up to Heaven for strength to sustain me in the perilous work of emancipation—and my resolution
was taken.

In opposing the American Colonization Society, I have also
counted the cost, and as clearly foreseen the formidable opposition which will be arrayed against me. Many of the clergy
are enlisted in its support : their influence is powerful. Men
of wealth and elevated station are among its contributors :
wealth and station are almost omnipotent. The press has been
seduced into its support : the press is a potent engine. Moreover, the Society is artfully based upon and defended by *popular
prejudice :* it takes advantage of wicked and preposterous opinions, and hence its success. These things grieve, they cannot

[PART I.]   1

deter me. ' Truth is mighty, and will prevail.' It is able to make falsehood blush, and tear from hypocrisy its mask, and annihilate prejudice, and overthrow persecution, and break every fetter.

I am constrained to declare, with the utmost sincerity, that I look upon the colonization scheme as inadequate in its design, injurious in its operation, and contrary to sound principle ; and the more scrupulously I examine its pretensions, the stronger is my conviction of its sinfulness. Nay, were Jehovah to speak in an audible voice from his holy habitation, I am persuaded that his language would be, ' Who hath required this at your hands ?'

It consoles me to believe that no man, who knows me personally or by reputation, will suspect the honesty of my skepticism. If I were politic, and intent only on my own preferment or pecuniary interest, I should swim with the strong tide of public sentiment instead of breasting its powerful influence. The hazard is too great, the labor too burdensome, the remuneration too uncertain, the contest too unequal, to induce a selfish adventurer to assail a combination so formidable. Disinterested opposition and sincere conviction, however, are not conclusive proofs of individual rectitude ; for a man may very honestly do mischief, and not be aware of his error. Indeed, it is in this light I view many of the friends of African colonization. I concede to them benevolence of purpose and expansiveness of heart ; but in my opinion, they are laboring under the same delusion as that which swayed Saul of Tarsus—persecuting the blacks even unto a strange country, and verily believing that they are doing God service. I blame them, nevertheless, for taking this mighty scheme upon trust ; for not perceiving and rejecting the monstrous doctrines avowed by the master spirits in the crusade ; and for feeling so indifferent to the moral, political and social advancement of the free people of color in this their only legitimate home.

In the progress of this discussion I shall have occasion to use very plain, and sometimes very severe language. This would be an unpleasant task, did not duty imperiously demand its application. To give offence I am loath, but more to hide or modify the truth. I shall deal with the Society in its collective form—as one body—and not with individuals. While I shall be necessitated to marshal individual opinions in review, I protest, *ab origine*, against the supposition that indiscriminate censure is intended, or that every friend of the Society cherishes similar views. He to whom my reprehension does not apply, will not receive it. It is obviously impossible, in attacking a numerous and multiform combination, to exhibit private dissimilarities, or in every instance to discriminate between the various shades of opinion. It is sufficient that exceptions are made. My warfare is against the AMERICAN COLONIZATION SOCIETY. If I shall identify its general, preponderating and clearly developed traits, it must stand or fall as they shall prove benevolent or selfish.

I bring to this momentous investigation an unbiassed mind, a lively sense of accountability to God, and devout aspirations for the guidance of the Holy Spirit. Unless He ' in whom there is no darkness at all,' pours light upon my path, I shall go astray. I have taken Him at His word : ' If any man lack wisdom, let him ask of God, and it shall be given him.' Confessing my own foolishness, I have sought that knowledge which cannot err.

I would premise, that, like many others, I formerly supposed the Colonization Society was a praiseworthy association, although I always doubted its efficiency. This opinion was formed for me by others, upon whom I placed implicit confidence : it certainly was not based upon any research or knowledge of my own, as I had not at that time perused a single Report of the Society, nor a page in its organ, the African Repository. My approval was the offspring of credulity and ignorance. I am explicit on this point, because my opponents have accused me of inconsistency—though it ought not surely to disgrace a man, that, discovering himself to be in error, he promptly turns to the embrace of truth. As if opinions, once formed, must be as irrevocable as the laws of the Medes and Persians ! If this were so, accountability would lose its hold on the conscience, and the light of knowledge be blown out, and reason degenerate into brutish instinct. Much stress has been laid upon the fact, that, in 1828, I delivered an address in **Park-street** meeting-house on the Fourth of July, on which occasion a collection was made in behalf of the American Colonization Society. It is true—but whereas I was then blind, now I see. My address, however, was far from being acceptable to the friends of colonization who were present, not only on account of my denunciation of slaveholders, but because I inserted only a single sentence in favor of the Society. In all my writings, I have never commended this combination in as many sentences as I have used in making this explanation. So much for my marvellous apostacy !

It is only about two years since I was induced to examine the claims of the Colonization Society upon the patronage and confidence of the nation. I went to this examination with a mind biassed by preconceived opinions favorable to the Society, and rather for the purpose of defending it against opposition than of bringing it into disrepute. Every thing, apart from its principles, was calculated to secure my friendship. Nothing but its revolting features could have induced me to turn loathingly away from its embrace. I had some little reputation to sustain ; many of my friends were colonizationists ; I saw that eminent statesmen and honorable men were enlisted in the enterprise ; the great body of the clergy gave their unqualified support to it ; every fourth of July the charities of the nation were secured in its behalf ; wherever I turned my eye in the free States, I saw nothing but unanimity ; wherever my ear caught a sound, I heard nothing but excessive panegyric. No individual had ventured to blow the trumpet of alarm, or exert his energies to counteract the influence of the scheme. If an assailant had occasionally appeared, he had either fired a random shot and retreated, or found in the inefficiency of the Society the only cause for hostility. It was at this crisis, and with such an array of motives before me to bias my judgment, that I resolved to make a close and candid examination of the subject.

I went, first of all, to the fountain head—to the African Repository and the Reports of the Society. I was not long in discovering sentiments which seemed to me as abhorrent to humanity as contrary to reason. I perused page after page, first

with perplexity, then with astonishment, and finally with indignation. I found little else than sinful palliations, fatal concessions, vain expectations, exaggerated statements, unfriendly
representations, glaring contradictions, naked terrors, deceptive assurances, unrelenting prejudices, and unchristian denunciations. I collected together the publications of auxiliary
societies, in order to discern some redeeming traits ; but I found
them marred and disfigured with the same disgusting details. I
courted the acquaintance of eminent colonizationists, that I
might learn how far their private sentiments agreed with those
which were so offensive in print ; and I found no dissimilarity
between them. I listened to discourses from the pulpit in favor
of the Society ; and the same moral obliquities were seen in
minister and people.

These discoveries affected my mind so deeply that I could
not rest. I endeavored to explain away the meaning of plain
and obvious language ; I made liberal concessions for good
motives and unsuspicious confidence ; I resorted to many expe-
dients to vindicate the disinterested benevolence of the Society ;
but I could not rest. The sun in its mid-day splendor was not
more clear and palpable to my vision, than the anti-christian
and anti-republican character of this association. It was evident to me that the great mass of its supporters at the north did
not realise its dangerous tendency. They were told that it was
designed to effect the ultimate emancipation of the slaves—to
improve the condition of the free people of color—to abolish
the foreign slave trade—to reclaim and evangelize benighted
Africa—and various other marvels. Anxious to do something
for the colored population—they knew not what—and having no
other plan presented to their view, they eagerly embraced a
scheme which was so big with promise, and which required of
them nothing but a small contribution annually. Perceiving the
fatality of this delusion, I was urged by an irresistible impulse
to attempt its removal. I could not turn a deaf ear to the cries
of the slaves, nor throw off the obligations which my Creator
had fastened upon me. Yet in view of the inequalities of the
contest, of the obstacles which towered like mountains in my
path, and of my own littleness, I trembled, and exclaimed in

the language of Jeremiah,—' Ah, Lord God ! behold I cannot speak : for I am a child.' But I was immediately strengthened by these interrogations : ' Is any thing too hard for the Lord ?' Is Error, though unwittingly supported by a host of good men, stronger than Truth ? Are Right and Wrong convertible terms, dependant upon popular opinion ? Oh no ! Then I will go forward in the strength of the Lord of Hosts—in the name of Truth—and under the banner of Right. As it is not by might nor by power, but by the Spirit of God, that great moral changes are effected, I am encouraged to fight valiantly in this good cause, believing that I shall ' come off conqueror, and more than conqueror '—yet not I, but Truth and Justice. It is in such a contest that one shall chase a thousand, and two put ten thousand to flight. ' The Lord disappointeth the devices of the crafty, so that their hands cannot perform their enterprise. He taketh the wise in their own craftiness ; and the counsel of the froward is carried headlong.' ' Because the foolishness of God is wiser than men ; and the weakness of God is stronger than men.'

Little boldness is needed to assail the opinions and practices of notoriously wicked men ; but to rebuke great and good men for their conduct, and to impeach their discernment, is the highest effort of moral courage. The great mass of mankind shun the labor and responsibility of forming opinions for themselves. The question is not—what is true ? but—what is popular ? Not—what does God say ? but—what says the public ? Not—what is my opinion ? but—what do others believe ? If people would pin their faith upon the bible, and not upon the sleeves of their neighbors, half of the heresies in the world would instantly disappear. If they would use their own eyes, their own ears, their own understandings, instead of the eyes, and ears, and understandings of others, imbecility, credulity and folly would be as rare as they are now common in community. But, unhappily, to borrow the words of Ganganelli, a large majority of mankind are ' mere abortions :' calling themselves rational and intelligent beings, they act as if they had neither brains nor conscience, and as if there were no God, no accountability, no heaven, no hell, no eternity.

' My minister,' says one, ' is a most worthy man. He supports this Society : therefore it is a good institution.' ' Christians of all denominations are enlisted in this enterprise,' says another : ' therefore it cannot be wrong.' ' Do you think,' says a third, ' that honest, godly men would countenance a scheme which is not really benevolent ?' But it is unwise for beings, who are accountable only to God, to reason in this manner. All the good men upon earth cannot make persecution benevolence, nor injustice equity ; and until they become infallible, implicit reliance upon their judgment is criminal. Ministers and christians, a few years since, were engaged in the use and sale of ardent spirits ; *but they were all wrong*, and they now acknowledge their error. At the present day, a large proportion of the professed disciples of the Prince of Peace maintain the lawfulness of defensive war, and the right of the oppressed to fight and kill for liberty ; but they hold this sentiment in direct opposition to the precepts of their Leader—' I say unto you which hear, Love your enemies, do good to them which hate you, bless them that curse you, and pray for them which despitefully use you.' Surely ' the time is come that judgment must begin at the house of God.'

I must pause, for a moment, and count the number of those with whom I am about to conflict. If I had to encounter only men-stealers and slaveholders, victory would be easy ; but it is not the south alone that is to be subdued. The whole nation is against me. Church after church is to be converted, and the powerful influence of the clergy broken. The friendship of good men is to be turned into enmity, and their support into opposition. It is my task to change their admiration into abhorrence ; to convince them that their well-meant exertions have been misdirected, and productive of greater evil than good ; and to induce them to abandon an institution to which they now fondly cling.

To those who neither fear God nor regard man—who have sworn eternal animosity to their colored countrymen, and whose cry is, ' Away with them, we do not want them here ! '—I make no appeal. Disregarding as they do that divine command, ' Thou shalt love thy neighbor as thyself,' it would be idle for me to direct my arguments to them. I address myself to high-minded and honorable men, whose heads and hearts are susceptible to the force of sound logic. I appeal to those, who have been redeemed from the bondage of sin by the precious blood of Christ, and with whom I hope to unite in a better world in ascribing glory, and honor, and praise to the Great Deliverer for ever. If I can succeed in gaining their attention, I feel sure of convincing their understandings and securing their support.

Besides the overwhelming odds which are opposed to me, I labor under other very serious disadvantages. My efforts in the cause of emancipation have been received as if they were intended to bring chaos back again, and to give the land up to pillage and its inhabitants to slaughter. My calls for an alteration in the feelings and practices of the people toward the blacks have been regarded as requiring a sacrifice of all the rules of propriety, and as seeking an overthrow of the established laws of nature ! I have been thrust into prison, and amerced in a heavy fine. Epithets, huge and unseemly, have been showered upon me without mercy. I have been branded as a fanatic, a madman, a disturber of the peace, an incendiary, a cut-throat, a monster, &c. &c. &c. Assassination has been threatened me in a multitude of anonymous letters. Private and public rewards to a very large amount, by combinations of individuals and by legislative bodies at the south, have been offered to any persons who shall abduct or destroy me. ' Yea, mine own familiar friend, in whom I trusted, which did eat of my bread, hath lifted up his heel against me.' This malignity of opposition and proximity of danger, however, are like oil to the fire of my zeal. I am not deliriously enthusiastic—I do not covet to be a martyr ; but I had rather die a thousand deaths, than witness the horrible oppression under which more than two millions of my countrymen groan, *and be silent.* No reproaches, no dangers shall deter me. At the north or the south, at the east or the west,—wherever Providence may call me,—my voice shall be heard in behalf of the perishing slave, and against the claims of his oppressor. Mine is the frank avowal of the excellent WILBERFORCE :—I can admit of no compromise when the commands of equity and philanthropy are so imperious. I wash my hands of the blood that may be spilled. I protest against the system, as the most flagrant violation of every principle of justice and humanity. I NEVER WILL DESERT THE CAUSE. In my task it is impossible to tire : it fills my mind with complacency and peace. At night I lie down with composure, and rise to it in the morning with alacrity. I NEVER WILL DESIST FROM THIS BLESSED WORK.

Now that the concentrated execration of the civilized world is poured upon those who engage in the foreign slave trade, how mild and inefficient, comparatively speaking, seem to have been the rebukes of Pitt, and Fox, and Wilberforce, and Clarkson ! Yet these rebukes were once deemed fanatical and outrageous by good men—yea, like flames of fire, threatening a universal conflagration ! So the denunciations which I am now hurling against slavery and its abettors,—which seem to many so violent and unmerited,—will be considered moderate, pertinent and just, when this murderous, soul-destroying system shall have been overthrown.

Fanaticism has been the crime alleged against reformers in all ages. 'These,' it was said of the apostles, ' that have turned the world upside down, come hither also.' Luther was a madman in his day : what is he now in the estimation of the friends of civil and religious liberty ? One of

> ' Those starry lights of virtue, that diffuse
> Through the dark depths of time their vivid flame.'

That base and desperate men should thus stigmatize those who endure the cross as good soldiers, and walk as pilgrims and strangers here, is not wonderful; but that the professed followers of Jesus Christ should join in this hue-and-cry is lamentable. Singular enough, I have been almost as cruelly aspersed by ministers of the gospel and church members, as by any other class of men. Unacquainted with me, and ignorant of my sentiments, they have readily believed the accusations of my enemies. The introduction of my name into conversation has elicited from them contemptuous sneers or strong denunciations. I have a right to complain of this treatment, and I do strongly protest against it as unchristian, hurtful and ungenerous. To prejudge and condemn an individual, on vague and apocryphal rumors, without listening to his defence or examining evidence, is tyranny. Perhaps I am in error—perhaps I deserve unqualified condemnation ; but I am at least entitled to a privilege which is granted to the vilest criminals, namely, the privilege of a fair trial. I ask nothing more. To accuse me of heresy, madness and sedition, is one thing ; to substantiate the accusation, another.

Should this work chance to fall into the hands of those who have thus ignorantly reprobated my course, I appeal to their sense of rectitude whether they are not bound to give it a candid and deliberate perusal ; and if they shall find in my writings nothing contrary to the immutable principles of justice, whether they ought not to be as strenuous in my defence as they have been hitherto in seeking my overthrow.

To show that I do not vacate any pledge which I have given to the public, I shall here insert all the specifications, which, from time to time, I have brought against the American Colonization Society. In ' The Liberator ' of April 23, 1831, is the following serious compend :

' I am prepared to show, that those who have entered into this CONSPIRACY A GAINST HUMAN RIGHTS are unanimous in abusing their victims ; unanimous in their mode of attack ; unanimous in proclaiming the absurdity, that our free blacks are natives of Africa ; unanimous in propagating the libel, that they cannot be elevated and improved in this country ; unanimous in opposing their instruction ; unanimous in exciting the prejudices of the people against them ; unanimous in apologising for the crime of slavery ; unanimous in conceding the right of the planters to hold their slaves in a limited bondage ; unanimous in their hollow pretence for colonizing, namely, to evangelize Africa ; unanimous in their *true motive* for the measure—a terror lest the blacks should rise to avenge their accumulated wrongs. It is a conspiracy to send the free people of color to Africa under a benevolent pretence, but really that the slaves may be held more securely in bondage. It is a conspiracy based upon fear, oppression and falsehood, which draws its aliment from the prejudices of the people, which is sustained by duplicity, which really upholds the slave system, which fascinates while it destroys, which endangers the safety and happiness of the country, which no precept of the bible can justify, which is implacable in its spirit, which should be annihilated at a blow.

' These are my accusations ; and if I do not substantiate them, I am willing to be covered with reproach.'

The following is copied from an editorial article of July 9, 1831 :

'The superstructure of the Colonization Society rests upon the following pillars :

'1st. *Persecution.* It declares that the whole colored population must be removed to Africa ; but as the free portion are almost *unanimously* opposed to a removal, it seems to be the determination of the Society to make their situations so uncomfortable and degraded here, as to compel them to migrate : consequently it discourages their education and improvement in this their native home. This is persecution.

2d. *Falsehood.* It stigmatises our colored citizens as being natives of Africa, and talks of sending them to their native land ; when they are no more related to Africa than we are to Great Britain.

3d. *Cowardice.* It avows as a prominent reason why colored citizens ought to be removed, that their continuance among us will be dangerous to us as a people ! This is a libel upon their character. Instead of demanding justice for this oppressed class, the Society calls for their removal !

4th. *Infidelity.* It boldly denies that there is power enough in the gospel to melt down the prejudices of men, and insists, that, so long as the people of color remain among us, *we must be their enemies !*—Every honest man should abhor the doctrine.'

In ' The Liberator ' of July 30, 1831, alluding to the present work, I used the following language :

' I shall be willing to stake my reputation upon it for honesty, prudence, benevolence, truth and sagacity. If I do not prove the Colonization Society to be a creature without heart, without brains, eyeless, unnatural, hypocritical, relentless, unjust, then nothing is capable of demonstration—then let me be covered with confusion of face.'

The following paragraph is extracted from ' The Liberator ' of November 19, 1831 :

' It is the enemy of immediate restitution to the slaves ; it courts and receives the approbation of notorious slave owners ; it deprecates any interference with slave property ; it discourages the improvement of the colored population, except they are removed to the shores of Africa ; it is lulling the country into a fatal sleep, pretending to be something when it is nothing ; it is utterly chimerical, as well as intolerant, in its design ; it serves to increase the value of the slaves, and to make brisk the foreign and domestic slave trade ; it nourishes and justifies the most cruel prejudices against color ; it sneers at those who advocate the bestowal of equal rights upon our colored countrymen ; it contends for an indefinite, dilatory, far-off emancipation ; it expressly declares that it is more humane to keep the slaves in chains, than to give them freedom in this country ! In short, it is the most compendious and best adapted scheme to uphold the slave system that human ingenuity can invent. Moreover, it is utterly and irreconcileably opposed.to the wishes and sentiments of the great body of the free people of color, repeatedly expressed in the most public manner, but cruelly disregarded by it.'

The following passages are taken from my Address to the People of Color, delivered in various places in June, 1831 :

' Let me briefly examine the doctrines of colonizationists. They generally agree in publishing the misstatement, that you are strangers and foreigners. Surely they know better. They know, that, as a body, you are no more natives of Africa, than they themselves are natives of Great Britain. Yet they repeat the absurd charge ; and they do so, in order to cover their anti-republican crusade. But suppose you were foreigners : would such an accident justify this persecution and removal ? And, if so, then all foreigners must come under the same ban, and must prepare to depart. There would be, in that case, a most alarming deduction from our population. Suppose a philanthropic and religious crusade were got up against the Dutch, the French, the Swiss, the Irish, among us, to remove them to New Holland, to enlighten and civilize her cannibals ? Who would not laugh at the scheme—who would not actively oppose it ? Would any one blame the above classes for steadfastly resisting it ? Just so, then, in regard to African colonization. But our colored population are not aliens ; they were born on our soil ; they are bone of our bone, and flesh of our flesh ; their fathers fought bravely to achieve our independence during the revolutionary war, without immediate or subsequent compensation ; they spilt their blood freely during the last war ; they are entitled, in fact, to every inch of our southern, and much of our western territory, having worn themselves out in its cultivation, and received nothing but wounds and bruises in return. Are these the men to stigmatize as foreigners ?

' Colonizationists generally agree in asserting that the people of color cannot be elevated in this country, nor be admitted to equal privileges with the whites. Is not this a libel upon humanity and justice—a libel upon republicanism—a libel upon the Declaration of Independence—a libel upon christianity ? " All men are born equal, and endowed by their Creator with certain inalienable rights—among which are life, liberty, and the pursuit of happiness." What is the meaning of that declaration ? That *all* men possess these rights—whether they are six feet five inches high, or three feet two and a half—whether they weigh three hundred or one hundred pounds—whether they parade in broadcloth or flutter in rags—whether their skins are jet black or lily white—whether their hair is straight or woolly, auburn or red, black or gray—does it not ? We, who are present, differ from each other in our looks, in our color, in height, and in bulk ; we have all shades, and aspects, and sizes. Now, would it not be anti-republican and anti-christian for us to quarrel about sitting on this seat or that, because this man's complexion is too dark, or that man's looks are too ugly ?· and to put others out of the house, because they happen to be ignorant, or poor, or helpless ? To commit this violence would be evidently wrong : then to do it in a large assemblage—in a community, in a state, or in a nation. it is equally unjust. But is not this the colonization principle? Who are the individuals that applaud, that justify, that advocate this exclusion? Who are they that venture to tell the American people, that they have neither honesty enough, nor patriotism enough, nor morality enough, nor religion enough, to treat their colored brethren as countrymen and citizens? Some of them—I am sorry to say—are professedly ministers of the gospel; others are christian professors; others are judges and lawyers; others are our Senators and Representatives; others are editors of newspapers. These ministers and christians dishonor the gospel which they profess; these judges and lawyers are the men spoken of by the Saviour, who bind heavy burdens and grievous to be borne, and lay them on men's shoulders; but they themselves will not move them with one of their fingers. These Senators and Representatives ought not to receive the suffrages of the people. These editors are unworthy of public patronage.

' Colonizationists too generally agree in discouraging your instruction and elevation at home. They pretend that ignorance is bliss; and therefore 't is folly to be wise. They pretend that knowledge is a dangerous thing in the head of a colored man; they pretend that you have no ambition; they pretend that you have no brains; in fine, they pretend a thousand other absurd things—they are a combination of pretences. What tyranny is this! Shutting up the human intellect—binding with chains the inward man—and perpetuating ignorance. May we not address them in the language of Christ? "Wo unto you, scribes and pharisees, hypocrites! for ye shut up the kingdom of heaven against men: for ye neither go in yourselves, neither suffer ye them that are entering to go in! Ye pay tithe of mint and anise and cummin, and have omitted the weightier matters of the law, judgment, mercy and faith."

' Colonizationists generally agree in apologising for the crime of slavery. They get behind the contemptible subterfuge, that it was entailed upon the planters. As if the continuance of the horrid system were not criminal! as if the robberies of another generation justify the robberies of the present! as if the slaves had not an inalienable right to freedom! as if slavery were not an individual as well as a national crime! as if the tearing asunder families, limb from limb,—branding the flesh with red hot irons,—mangling the body with whips and knives,—feeding it on husks and clothing it with rags,—crushing the intellect and destroying the soul,—as if such inconceivable cruelty were not chargeable to those who inflict it!

' As to the effect of colonization upon slavery, it is rather favorable than injurious to the system. Now and then, indeed, there is a great flourish of trumpets, and glowing accounts of the willingness of planters to emancipate their slaves on condition of transportation to Africa. Now and then a slave is actually manumitted and removed, and the incident is dwelt upon for months. Why, my friends, hundreds of worn-out slaves are annually turned off to die, like old horses. No doubt their masters will thank the Colonization Society, or any one else, to send them out of the country; especially as they will gain much glorification in the newspapers, for their *disinterested* sacrifices. Let no man be deceived by these manœuvres.

' My time is consumed—and yet I have scarcely entered upon the threshold of my argument. Now, what a spectacle is presented to the world!—the American people, boasting of their free and equal rights—of their abhorrence of aristocratical distinctions—of their republican equality ; proclaiming on every wind, " that all men are born *equal,* and endowed with certain inalienable *rights,*" and that this land is an asylum for the persecuted of all nations ; and yet as loudly proclaiming that they are determined to deprive millions of their own countrymen of every political and social right, and to send them to a barbarous continent, because the Creator has given them a sable complexion. Where exists a more rigorous despotism ? What conspiracy was ever more cruel ? What hypocrisy and tergiversation so enormous ? The story is proclaimed in our pulpits, in our state and national assemblies, in courts of law, in religious and secular periodicals,—among all parties, and in all quarters of the country,— that there is a *moral incapacity* in the people to do justly, love mercy, and to walk uprightly—that they must always be the enemies and oppressors of the colored people—that no love of liberty, no dictate of duty, no precept of republicanism, no dread of retribution, no claim of right, no injunction of the gospel, can possibly persuade them to do unto their colored countrymen, as they would that they should do unto them in a reversal of circumstances. Now, to these promulgators of unrighteousness, with the Declaration of Independence in one hand, and the Bible in the other, I fearlessly give battle. Rich and mighty and numerous as they are, by the help of the Lord I will put them to open shame. They shall not libel me, they shall not libel my country, with impunity. They shall not make our boasted republicanism a by-word and a hissing among all nations, nor sink the christian religion below heathen idolatry ; and if they persist in publishing their scandalous proclamations, they shall be labelled as the enemies of their species and of the republic, and treated accordingly.

‘ The Colonization Society, therefore, instead of being a philanthropic and religious institution, is anti-republican and anti-christian in its tendency. Its pretences are false, its doctrines odious, its means contemptible. If we are to send away the colored population because they are profligate and vicious, what sort of missionaries will they make ? Why not send away the vicious among the whites, for the same reason and the same purpose ? If ignorance be a crime, where shall we begin to select ? How much must a man know to save him from transportation ? How white must he be ? If we send away a mixed breed, how many will be left ? If foreigners only, then the people of color must remain—for they are our countrymen. Would foreigners submit ? No—not for an instant. Why should the American people make this enormous expenditure of life and money ? Why not use the funds of the Society to instruct and elevate our colored population at home ? This would be rational and serviceable. Instead of removing men from a land of civilization and knowledge—of schools, and seminaries, and colleges—to give them instruction in a land of darkness and desolation—would it not be wiser and better to reverse the case, and bring the ignorant here for cultivation ?’

The foregoing accusations are grave, weighty, positive—involving a perilous responsibility, and requiring ample and irrefragable proof. They are expressed in vehement terms : but to measure the propriety of language, we must first examine the character of the system, or the nature of the object, against which it is directed. If we see a person wilfully abusing the goods of an individual, we may reprehend him, but with comparative mildness. If we see him maiming, or in any way maltreating another man's cattle, we may increase the severity of our rebuke. But if we see him violating all the social and sacred relations of life,—daily defrauding a number of his fellow creatures of the fruits of their toil, calling them his property, selling them for money, lacerating their bodies, and ruining their souls, —we may use the strongest terms of moral indignation. Nor is plain and vehement denunciation of crime inconsistent with the most benevolent feelings towards the perpetrators of it. We are sustained in these positions by the example of Christ, and the apostles, and the prophets, and the reformers.

So, also, if there be an institution, the direct tendency of which is to perpetuate slavery, to encourage persecution, and to invigorate prejudice,—although many of its supporters may be actuated by pure motives,—it ought to receive unqualified condemnation.

It is proper to call things by their right names. What does the law term him who steals your pocket-book, or breaks into your dwelling, or strips you on the highway ? A robber ! Is the charge inflammatory or unjust ? or will it please the villain ? The abuse of language is seen only in its misapplication. Those who object to the strength of my denunciation must prove its perversion before they accuse me of injustice.

Probably I may be interrogated by individuals,—' Why do you object to a colony in Africa ? Are you not willing people should choose their own places of residence ? And if the blacks are willing to remove, why throw obstacles in their path or deprecate their withdrawal ? All go *voluntarily* : of what, then, do you complain ? Is not the colony at Liberia in a flourishing condition, and expanding beyond the most sanguine expectations of its founders ?'

Pertinent questions deserve pertinent answers. I say, then, in reply, that I do not object to a colony, *in the abstract*—to use the popular phraseology of the day. In other words, I am

entirely willing men should be as free as the birds in choosing
the time when, the mode how, and the place where they shall
migrate. The power of locomotion was given to be used at
will ; as beings of intelligence and enterprise,

> ' The world is all before them, where to choose
> Their place of rest, and Providence their guide.'

The emigration from New-England to the far West is constant
and large. Almost every city, town or village suffers annually
by the departure of some of its adventurous inhabitants. Companies have been formed to go and possess the Oregon territory
—an enterprise hazardous and unpromising in the extreme.
The old States are distributing their population over the whole
continent, with unexampled fruitfulness and liberality. But why
this restless, roving, unsatisfied disposition ? Is it because those
who cherish it are treated as the offscouring of all flesh, in the
place of their birth ? or because they do not possess equal
rights and privileges with other citizens ? or because they are
the victims of incorrigible hate and prejudice ? or because
they are told that they must choose between exilement and perpetual degradation ? or because the density of population renders it impossible for them to obtain preferment and competence here ? or because they are estranged by oppression and
scorn ? or because they cherish no attachment to their native
soil, to the scenes of their childhood and youth, or to the institutions of government ? or because they consider themselves
as dwellers in a strange land, and feel a burning desire, a fever-
ish longing to return home ? No. They lie under no odious
disabilities, whether imposed by public opinion or by legislative
power ; to them the path of preferment is wide open ; they
sustain a solid and honorable reputation ; they not only can rise,
but have risen, and may soar still higher, to responsible stations
and affluent circumstances ; no calamity afflicts, no burden de-
presses, no reproach excludes, no despondency enfeebles them ;
and they love the spot of their nativity almost to idolatry. The
air of heaven is not freer or more buoyant than they. Theirs
is a spirit of curiosity and adventurous enterprise, impelled by
no malignant influences, but by the spontaneous promptings of

the mind. Far different is the case of our colored population. Their *voluntary* banishment is *compulsory*—they are *forced* to turn *volunteers*, as will be shown in other parts of this work.

The following proposition is self-evident : The success of an enterprise furnishes no proof that it is in accordance with justice, or that it meets the approbation of God, or that it ought to be prosecuted to its consummation, or that it is the fruit of disinterested benevolence.

I do not doubt that the Colony at Liberia, by a prodigal expenditure of life and money, will ultimately flourish ; but a good result would no more hallow that persecution which is seeking to drag the blacks away, than it would if we should burn every distillery, and shut up in prison every vender of ardent spirits, in order to do good and to prevent people from becoming drunkards. Because Jehovah overrules evil for good, shall we therefore continue to do evil ?

If ten thousand white mechanics, farmers, merchants, &c. &c. were to emigrate to Africa, does any man doubt whether permanent good would result from the enterprise—good to that benighted continent, which would counterbalance all the sacrifices and sufferings attending it ? And yet is there a single mechanic, farmer or merchant, who feels it to be his duty, or would be willing to go ? Suppose the people of color should get the power into their hands to-morrow, and should argue that the whites must not be admitted to equal privileges with themselves ; but that, having so long plundered Africa, and oppressed her children, justice demanded that they should be sent to that desolate land to build up colonies, and carry the light of civilization and knowledge, as a sort of reparation—and that, having superior instruction in literature and science, they were peculiarly qualified for such a mission—how would this doctrine relish ? ' It is a poor rule that will not work both ways,' says the proverb. Yet this logic would be more sound than is our own with regard to the colonization of the blacks.

On this point, deception is practised to a great extent. The advocates of the Colonization Society are constantly aiming to divert public attention from the only proper subject of inquiry, namely, ' Is it based upon benevolence and justice ?'—to the success of the colony. Granting all that they assert, it proves nothing ; but of this success I shall have occasion, doubtless, to speak hereafter. Fine stories are trumpeted all over the country, of the happiness, intelligence, industry, virtue, enterprise and dignity of the colonists ; and changes, absolutely miraculous, are gravely recorded for the admiration and credulity of community. ' The simple,' says Solomon, ' believeth every word : but the prudent man looketh well to his going.'

The doctrine, that the ' end sanctifies the means,' belongs, I trust, exclusively to the creed of the Jesuits. If I were sure that the Society would accomplish the entire regeneration of Africa by its present measures, my detestation of its principles would not abate one jot, nor would I bestow upon it the smallest modicum of praise. Never shall the fruits of the mercy and overruling providence of God,—ever bringing good out of evil and light out of darkness,—be ascribed to the prejudice and sin of man.

It is certain that many a poor native African has been led to embrace the gospel, in consequence of his transportation to our shores, who else had lived and died a heathen. Is the slave trade therefore a blessing ? Suppose one of those wretches who are engaged in this nefarious commerce were brought before the Supreme Court, and being convicted, should be asked by the Judge, whether he had aught to say why sentence of death should not be pronounced upon him ? And suppose the culprit should espy some of his sable victims in court, whom he knew had made a profession of faith, and he should boldly reply—' May it please your Honor, I abducted these people away from their homes, it is true ; but they were poor, miserable, benighted idolators, and must have inevitably remained as such unto the hour of their death, if I had not brought them to this land of christianity and bibles, where they have been taught a knowledge of the true God, and are now rejoicing in hope of a glorious immortality. I therefore offer as a conclusive reason why sentence should not be pronounced, *that I have rescued souls from perdition*, and thus enlarged the company of the saints in light.' Would the villain be acquitted, and, instead of a halter, receive the panegyric of the Court for his conduct ?

Our pilgrim fathers, not being able to worship God according to the dictates of their own consciences in the mother country, were compelled by ecclesiastical despotism to seek a refuge in this rude and barbarous continent. Wonderful have been the fruits of their expulsion ! A mighty republic established—the freest, the wisest, the most religious on earth !—influencing the world by its example, and exciting the emulation of all nations ! Now suppose we should occasionally find in the pages of the Edinburgh or Quarterly Review, or in the columns of the English newspapers, not only a full justification of this oppressive treatment in view of its astonishing consequences, but a claim to approbation on account of its exercise. Would not such effrontery amaze us ? Would not an honest indignation burn within us ? Should we look with a more complacent aspect upon the bigots who kindled those fires of persecution around the Puritans, which, but for the interposition of Heaven, had consumed them to ashes ?

The death of our Lord Jesus Christ was essential to the salvation of the world. Suppose Judas, at the judgment day, should build upon this fact in extenuation of his dreadful crime. What would be the decision of the assembled universe ? Yea, what was the condemnation passed upon him by the Illustrious Sufferer ? ' Wo to that man by whom the Son of man is betrayed ! good were it for that man if he had never been born !'

Let not, then, any imaginary or real prosperity of the settlement at Liberia lead any individual to applaud the Colonization Society, reckless whether it be actuated by mistaken philanthropy, or perverted generosity, or selfish policy, or unchristian prejudice.

I should oppose this Society, even were its doctrines harmless. It imperatively and effectually seals up the lips of a vast number of influential and pious men, who, for fear of giving offence to those slaveholders with whom they associate, and thereby leading to a dissolution of the compact, dare not expose the flagrant enormities of the system of slavery, nor denounce the crime of holding human beings in bondage. They dare not lead. to the onset against the forces of tyranny ; and if *they* shrink from the conflict, how shall the victory be won ? I do

not mean to aver, that, in their sermons, or addresses, or private conversations, they never allude to the subject of slavery ;
for they do so frequently, or at least every Fourth of July.
But my complaint is, that they content themselves with representing slavery as an evil,—a misfortune,—a calamity which has
been entailed upon us by former generations,—*and not as an
individual* CRIME, embracing in its folds robbery, cruelty, oppression and piracy.   *They do not identify the criminals ;* they
make no direct, pungent, earnest appeal to the consciences of
men-stealers ; by consenting to walk arm-in-arm with them, they
virtually agree to abstain from all offensive remarks, and to aim
entirely at the expulsion of the free people of color ; their
lugubrious exclamations, and solemn animadversions, and re-
proachful reflections, are altogether indefinite ; they ' go about,
and about, and all the way round to nothing ; ' they generalize,
they shoot into the air, they do not disturb the repose nor wound
the complacency of the sinner ; ' they have put no difference
between the holy and profane, neither have they shewed difference between the unclean and the clean.' Thus has free inquiry
been suppressed, and a universal fear created, and the tongue
of the boldest silenced, and the sleep of death fastened upon
the nation.   ' Truth has fallen in the streets, and equity cannot
enter.' The plague is raging with unwonted fatality ; but no
cordon sanitaire is established—no adequate remedy sought.
The tide of moral death is constantly rising and widening ; but
no efforts are made to stay its desolating career. The fire of
God's indignation is kindling against us, and thick darkness
covers the heavens, and the hour of retribution is at hand ; but
we are obstinate in our transgression, we refuse to repent, we
impiously throw the burden of our guilt upon our predecessors, we affect resignation to our *unfortunate* lot, we descant
upon the mysterious dispensations of Providence, we deem ourselves objects of God's compassion rather than of his displeas-
ure. ' Shall I not visit for these things ? saith the Lord. Shall
not my soul be avenged on such a nation as this ?'

Were the American Colonization Society bending its energies directly to the immediate abolition of slavery ; seeking to
enlighten and consolidate public opinion, on this momentous

subject ; faithfully exposing the awful guilt of the owners of slaves ; manfully contending for the bestowal of equal rights upon our free colored population in this their native land ; assiduously endeavoring to uproot the prejudices of society ; and holding no fellowship with oppressors ; my opposition to it would cease. It might continue to bestow its charities upon those who should desire to seek another country, and at the same time launch its thunders against the system of oppression. But, alas ! it looks to the banishment of the free people of color as the only means to abolish slavery, and conciliate the feelings of the planters.

The popularity of the Society is not attributable to its merits, but exclusively to its congeniality with those unchristian prejudices which have so long been cherished against a sable complexion. It is agreeable to slaveholders, because it is striving to remove a class of persons who they fear may stir up their slaves to rebellion ; all who avow undying hostility to the people of color are in favor of it ; all who shrink from acknowledging them as brethren and friends, or who make them a distinct and inferior caste, or who deny the possibility of elevating them in the scale of improvement here, most heartily embrace it. Having ample funds, it has been able to circulate its specious appeals in every part of the country ; and to employ active and eloquent agents, who have glowingly described to the people the immense advantages to be reaped from the accomplishment of its designs. With this entire preoccupancy of the ground, and these common though unworthy dispositions in its favor, the wonder is, that it is not more popular.

Much cleverness is not requisite to tell a fine story ; and a fine story is always agreeable to a credulous listener. An agent of the Society goes into a place, and finds no difficulty in procuring a pulpit from which to address a congregation. The benevolent pastor, who, perhaps, has had neither time nor opportunity to examine the principles of the Society, readily officiates on the occasion, and, in the fulness of his heart, believing that he is not asking amiss, supplicates the benediction of Heaven upon the object of the meeting. This co-operation of the pastor with the agent makes an impression decidedly fa-

vorable to the latter upon the minds of the audience, and pre-
pares them to receive his statements with confidence. He first
dwells upon the miserable condition of Africa—desolated with
civil wars—the prey of kidnappers—given up to idolatry—full
of intellectual darkness and spiritual death—and bleeding at
every pore. He next depicts the horrors of the slave trade,
and shows how inefficient have been the laws enacted for its
suppression. He finally expatiates upon the evils and dangers
of slavery ; and is particularly minute in describing the degradation of the free people of color, which he declares to be
irreclaimable in this land of gospel light. ' Now, my christian
brethren and friends,' he continues, ' the object of the American
Colonization Society is to stay the effusion of blood, to give
light to them who sit in darkness, and to make reparation for
the wrongs which have been inflicted upon the sable sons of
Africa. As the people of color must evidently be a distinct
and degraded class while they reside in this country, and as they
are threatened with universal proscription, the Society benevolently proposes to send them back *to their native country*, by
their own *voluntary* consent, together with those slaves who may
be emancipated for this purpose, where they may enjoy equal
rights and privileges, nor longer retain any sense of inferiority
to the whites. Every emigrant will go as a missionary to reclaim the poor natives from their barbarism, and to spread the
tidings of salvation throughout the African continent. By forming a chain of colonies along the coast, a speedy check will be
given to the accursed slave trade,—a trade which cannot be
destroyed in any other manner. Who does not desire to see
Africa civilized and evangelized ? Whose heart does not leap
in view of the suppression of the slave trade ? Who does not
pray for deliverance from the evils of slavery ? Who does not
wish to behold the free people of color,—cursed with ineffectual freedom here,—*recalled from their banishment*, and placed
where no obstacles will impede their march to affluence, preferment and honor ? The Colonization Society, then, powerfully commends itself to the christian, the philanthropist and
the patriot—to every section of our country and to all denominations of men.'

Exquisite ! The picture is crowded with attractions, delightful to the eye. The story is skilfully told, and implicitly believed ; but, like every other story, it has two sides to it. So complete is the delusion, however, that many good people are ready to class those who denounce the Colonization Society, among the opposers of foreign missions, bible and tract societies, and the other benevolent operations of the age !

Far be it from me to accuse the agents of the Society of intentionally perverting the truth or deliberately imposing upon the credulity of the public. Some—perhaps all of them, are men of sincerity and probity ; but, deluded themselves, they help to delude others. Their vision is imperfect ; and ' if the blind lead the blind,' we may expect to find them in the same ditch together.

Great complacency has been manifested on various occasions, by the advocates of the Society, on the ground that it was at first suspected of sinister designs, both at the north and the south, but is now receiving the countenance of both. This exultation is premature. The opposition formerly manifested to the Society by the holders of slaves, grew out of their ignorance of its purpose ; but a very large majority of them now perceive that it is their devoted servant, crouching down at their feet, shielding them from reproach, dragging those away whom they dread, allowing them to sin with impunity, and generously granting them and their children whole centuries in which to repent, and to surrender what they have stolen ! It dissuades them from emancipating their slaves faster than they can be transported to Africa ; and thus regards their persistance in robbery and oppression as evidence of wisdom, benevolence and sanity ! It is natural, that, discovering their mistake, they should now rally in a body around the Society ; and, consequently, we find that the legislatures of the several slaveholding States are passing encomiums upon it, and in some instances appropriating sums of money to be paid over to it by instalments.

The people of the north have been shamefully duped by this scheme ; but, like the slaveholders, they begin to discover their error. Unlike them, however, they are withdrawing their support, in obedience to the injunction of the Apostle : 'Be ye not unequally yoked together with unbelievers : for what fellowship hath righteousness with unrighteousness ? and what communion hath light with darkness ? and what concord hath Christ with Belial ? Wherefore come out from among them, and be ye separate, saith the Lord, and touch not the unclean thing ; and I will receive you.'

To Africa this country owes a debt larger than she is able to liquidate. Most intensely do I desire to see that ill-fated continent transformed into the abode of civilization, of the arts and sciences, of evangelical piety, of liberty, and of all that adds to the dignity, the renown, and the temporal and eternal happiness of man. Shame and confusion of face belong to the Church, that she has so long disregarded the claims of Africa upon her sympathies, and prayers, and liberality—claims as much superior as its wrongs to those of any other portion of the globe. It is indeed most strange that, like the Priest and the Levite, she should have ' passed by on the other side,' and left the victim of thieves to bleed and sicken and die. As the Africans were the only people doomed to perpetual servitude, and to be the prey of kidnappers, she should have long since directed almost her undivided efforts to civilize and convert them,—not by establishing colonies of ignorant and selfish foreigners among them, who will seize every opportunity to overreach or oppress, as interest or ambition shall instigate,—but by sending intelligent, pious missionaries ; men fearing God and eschewing evil—living evidences of the excellence of christianity—having but one object, not the possession of wealth or the obtainment of power or the gratification of selfishness, but *the salvation of the soul.* Had she made this attempt, as she was bound to have made it by every principle of justice and every feeling of humanity, a century ago, Africa would have been, at the present day, ' redeemed, regenerated, and disenthralled,' and the slavery of her children brought to an end. No pirates would now haunt her coast to desolate her villages with fire and sword, in order to supply a christian people with hewers of wood and drawers of water. How much has been needlessly lost to the world by this criminal neglect !

The conception of evangelizing a heathenish country by sending to it an illiterate, degraded and irreligious population, belongs exclusively to the advocates of African colonization. For absurdity and inaptitude, it stands, and must forever stand, without a parallel. Of all the offspring of prejudice and oppression, it is the most shapeless and unnatural. But more of this hereafter.

History is full of instruction on the subject of colonization. The establishment of colonies, in all ages, with scarcely an exception, has resulted either in their subversion by the vices or physical strength of the natives, or by a fatal amalgamation with them ; or else in the rapid destruction of the natives by the superior knowledge and greedy avarice of the new settlers. It is presumption to suppose that the colony at Liberia, composed of the worst materials imaginable, will present an example of forbearance, stability and good faith, hitherto unwitnessed in the world.

Soon after its establishment, the colony narrowly escaped a bloody extirpation, and was the cause of a murderous warfare in which several of the colonists and a large number of the natives were slain. The steady growth of the colony excited the jealousy and alarm of some of the neighboring tribes ; and, accordingly, a consultation was held, at which Kings George, Governor, and all the other head men, contended that ' The Americans were strangers *who had forgot their attachment to the land of their fathers ;* for if not, why had they not renounced their connexion with white men altogether, and placed themselves under the protection of the kings of the country ? King George had already been under the necessity of removing from his town, and leaving the Cape in their hands. This was but the first step of their encroachments. If left alone, they must, in a very few years, master the whole country. And as all other places were full, their own tribe must be without a home, and cease any longer to remain a nation.'* This appeal (which evinces an intimate acquaintance with human nature and much foresight) induced the attack to which allusion has been made. A

---

* Memoir of American Colonists—vide ' The African Repository,' vol. 2, p. 174.

single paragraph from the Rev. Mr Ashmun's account of the battle with the natives may suffice to give the reader an idea of its destructiveness :

' A few musketeers with E. Johnson at their head, by passing round upon the enemy's flank, served to increase the consternation which was beginning to pervade their unwieldy body. In about twenty minutes after the settlers had taken their stand, the front of the enemy began to recoil. But from the numerous obstructions in their rear, the entire absence of discipline, and the extreme difficulty of giving a reversed motion to so large a body, a small part only of which was directly exposed to danger, and the delay occasioned by the practice of carrying off all their dead and wounded, rendered a retreat for some minutes longer, impossible. The very violence employed by those in the front, in their impatience to hasten it, by increasing the confusion, produced an effect opposite to that intended. The Americans perceiving their advantage, now regained possession of the western post, and instantly brought the long nine to rake the whole line of the enemy. Imagination can scarcely figure to itself a throng of human beings in a more capital state of exposure to the destructive power of the machinery of modern warfare ! Eight hundred men were here pressed shoulder to shoulder, in so compact a form, that a child might easily walk upon their heads from one end of the mass to the other, presenting in their rear a breadth of rank equal to twenty or thirty men, and all exposed to a gun of great power, raised on a platform, at only thirty to sixty yards distance ! *Every shot literally spent its force in a solid mass of living human flesh !* Their fire suddenly terminated. A savage yell was raised, which filled the dismal forest with a momentary horror. It gradually died away; and the whole host disappeared. At 8 o'clock, the well known signal of their dispersion and return to their homes was sounded, and many small parties seen at a distance, directly afterwards, moving off in different directions. One large canoe, employed in reconveying a party across the mouth of the Montserado, venturing within the range of the long gun, was struck by a shot, and several men killed.'*

The above (which cannot be perused without a thrill of horror) is one of the legitimate fruits of foreign colonization. Subsequent to this bloody affair, another battle took place, which resulted in the defeat of the natives and the loss of many lives. It is true, the colony since that period has received little molestation, and has succeeded, moreover, in making some amicable treaties with the natives ; but in proportion to its means of defence and numerical force will be its liability to encroach upon the rights of the Africans, and thus to provoke hostilities. If this prophecy should not be fulfilled, history will

---

* African Repository, vol. 2, p. 179.

have spoken in vain, and human nature experienced a total regeneration.

No man of refined sensibility can contemplate the fate of the aborigines of this country, without shuddering at the consequences of colonization ; and if *they* melted away at the presence of the pilgrims and their descendants, like frost before the meridian blaze of the sun,—if *they* fell to the earth, like the leaves of the forest before the autumnal blast, by the settlement of men reputedly humane, wise and pious, in their vicinage,— what can be our hope for the preservation of the Africans, associated with a population degraded by slavery, and, to a lamentable extent, destitute of religious and secular knowledge ? The argument, that the difference of complexion between our forefathers and the aborigines (which is not a distinctive feature between the settlers at Liberia and the natives) was the real cause of this deadly enmity, is more specious than solid. *Conduct*, not *color*, secures friendship or excites antipathy, as it happens to be just or unjust. The venerated William Penn and his pacific followers furnish a case in point.

I avow it—the natural tendency of the colony at Liberia excites the most melancholy apprehensions in my mind. Its birth was conceived in blood, and its footsteps will be marked with blood down to old age—the blood of the poor natives—unless a special interposition of Divine Providence prevent such a calamity. The emigrants will be eager in the acquisition of wealth, ease and power ; and, having superior skill and discernment in trade, they will outwit and defraud the natives as often as occasion permits. This knavish treatment once detected,— as it surely will be, for even an uncivilized people may soon learn that they have been cheated,—will provoke retaliation, and stir up the worst passions of the human breast. Bloody conflicts will ensue, in which the colonists will be victorious. This success will serve to increase the enmity of the natives, and to perpetuate the murderous struggle. The extirpation of one generation may put the colonists in undisputed possession of the land.

This is not a fancy sketch—it is not improbable : on the contrary, it is the obvious and hitherto certain consequence of bringing hastily together large bodies of civilized men with unlettered barbarians.

Jealousy will be another fruitful source of contention. The population of Africa is divided into a vast number of tribes, governed by petty kings,—sometimes indeed united by an amicable league, but commonly distinct and independent. Some of these tribes will form alliances with the colonists, either to obtain protection from their more formidable rivals or from motives of fear, curiosity or selfishness. In this manner, tribe will be arrayed against tribe throughout that vast continent ; the tide of commotion, gathering fresh impetuosity in its headlong career, will rush from the mountains down to the ocean, devastating all that is beautiful, and swiftly defacing that which will require the labors of centuries to restore to its pristine excellence ; there will be wars and rumors of wars, succeeded by deceitful and unstable treaties ratified only to be broken at a favorable moment ; and these collisions will not cease until the colonists obtain an undisputed mastery over the natives.

Would to Heaven these fears might prove to be but the offspring of a distracted mind ! May the colonists be so just in their intercourse with the Africans, as never to impeach their own integrity ; so pacific, as to disarm retaliation and perpetuate good will ; so benevolent, as to excite gratitude and diffuse joy wherever their names shall be known ; and so holy, as to exalt the christian religion in the eyes of an idolatrous nation ! But he must be grossly ignorant of human nature, or strangely infatuated, who believes that they will always, or commonly, exhibit this unexceptionable conduct.

It is my sober conviction, that no contrivance or enterprise could possibly be planned more fatally calculated to obstruct the progress of christianity in a heathenish country, than the establishment of a colony, or colonies, of selfish, ignorant, or even intelligent and high-minded men, on its shores. In every settlement of this kind,—no matter how choice the original materials,—vice will soon preponderate over virtue, intemperance over sobriety, knavery over honesty, oppression over liberty, and impiety over godliness. The natives will see just enough of christianity to hate and shun it ; finding that its fruits are generally bad—that it has no restraining influence upon the mass of its nominal professors,—they will not easily comprehend the utility of abandoning their own idolatrous worship ; looking only to the pernicious examples of the intruders, they will spurn with contempt the precepts of the gospel. Their confidence will be abused—their lands craftily trafficked for nought —their ignorance cheated—their inferiority treated oppressively ; and then what must naturally follow ? Why—WAR—*a war of retaliation.* All the vices, and few of the virtues, of the instructers, will be faithfully copied ; and thus barriers will be erected against the progress of the christian religion, not absolutely insurmountable, it is true, but sufficiently tall and strong to retard its noble career—barriers not only of superstition and ignorance, but of hatred and revenge. These reflections might be extended to the size of a volume ; but they are probably sufficient to convince every unprejudiced, discerning mind, that the establishment of foreign colonies in a barbarous land is the surest way to prevent its speedy evangelism and civilization.

In reply to this reasoning, some of the advocates of African colonization may argue, that schools and houses of worship, multiplying with the growth of the settlement at Liberia, will check the evil propensities and passions of the emigrants, and qualify them to act as missionaries or instructers among the natives ; and thus great good will be bestowed upon Africa. This is at least a summary, if not a sure mode of obviating these difficulties.

In the first place, it is by no means certain—nay, it is not probable, especially if the number of emigrants annually exported to Liberia swell from hundreds to thousands, (and this increase of transportation is positively promised by the Parent Society, and absolutely necessary to cause a perceptible diminution in the annual enlargement of our colored population)—I say, it is neither certain nor probable that the multiplication of literary and religious privileges will keep pace with the unnatural and enormous growth of the colony. Nine years after the first settlement of Liberia, it appears by the following extract of a letter from a highly respectable colored emigrant, (the Rev. George M. Erskine,) there was but the ' remnant of a school' left! This letter is dated ' *Caldwell, Liberia, April 3, 1830.*'

' Sir, the state of things, with regard to schools, is truly lamentable. *The only school in the Colony at this time, is a remnant of one at the Cape.* Among the present emigrants, there are seventeen out of forty-eight that can read the Holy Scriptures, *leaving thirty-one that cannot.* Now, Sir, suppose each company of emigrants to this place bring a like proportion of illiterate persons into the Colony, then what state, think you, it must be in ? But again, Sir : I am greatly mistaken if this Colony is not, for several years yet to come, mostly to be peopled with slaves sent out by their present owners, without any education themselves, and without means and very little desire to have their children instructed ; and add to the above, that this people is planted in the midst, and are daily conversant with, a people that are not only heathen, but a people extremely partial in favor of their grovelling superstition. My dear Sir, this being the case, *whether is it probable that they will come over to us, or we go down to them ?* To me the latter is the most likely, *as it is the very essence of human nature to seek the lowest depth of degradation.* Permit me to say, Sir, there must be a great revolution in this Colony before it can have a salutary influence on the surrounding natives ; that is, before it can have a moral influence over them.' *

Subsequent accounts, I am happy to state, present a better aspect in relation to the education of this outcast and persecuted people : their wants, however, are only partially supplied.

The annual increase of the free colored and slave population in the United States is variously estimated from sixty to seventy-five thousand. The American Colonization Society proposes the annual removal of this vast body,—and more, if it be possible,—provided the energies and patronage of the General Government be enlisted in this expulsive crusade. Now, suppose the entire transportation effected, let any candid man decide how extremely difficult, not to say impracticable, it would be to discipline and instruct such an overwhelming mass of ignorance, or any considerable portion of it—and how pernicious must be the consequences to the colony and the natives, if it should not receive immediate culture !

Secondly. It is neither certain nor probable that, allowing all that is assumed by colonizationists, the influence of secular and religious instruction would be sufficient to restrain the selfish desires and knavish propensities of those whose main object is,

---

* African Repository, vol. 6, p. 121.

not to evangelize the natives, but to secure, by a summary process, competence and power for themselves. Indeed, their juxtaposition with the natives would be eminently calculated to induce the fever of avarice, and to generate the lust of dominion. It is well known that so eager are the colonists to acquire a rapid accumulation of wealth, by trafficking their paltry beads and poisonous rum and tobacco for ivory, camwood and gold dust, it is with the utmost difficulty any considerable portion of them are persuaded to cultivate the soil and engage in agricultural pursuits. Thus we are presented with the disgraceful, if not singular spectacle of a rivalry in cunning and trickishness between a colony of *soi-disant* missionaries (really avaricious and unscrupulous foreigners) and the tribes who are to come under their pious pupilage. If equal dexterity in trade is not apparent, each party is equally pleased with its successful attempts at deception, and both renew the fraudulent commerce with fresh alacrity—the one to gain a new triumph, and the other to retrieve an old defeat. And this is the mode of colonizationists to evangelize Africa ! and this their mode to suppress the slave trade ! and this their mode to elevate the free people of color ! and this their mode to emancipate the slaves! It combines the folly and absurdity of a farce with the solemnity and murderment of a tragedy.

Far be it from me to leave the impression upon the mind of the reader, from these representations, that all the colonists are actuated by the same selfish motives, or that they have exhibited any new and extraordinary traits of character in their commerce with the Africans. Many of them, I believe, are men who fear God and desire the welfare of his creatures : all of them have behaved as honorably, perhaps, and trafficked as equitably, as any other body of men, white or yellow, would have done in the same situation and under the same circumstances. Dishonesty in trade is no prodigy, even in this country. To bring accusations of fraud, cupidity and cunning against human nature, is not libellous. I am persuaded that robbery,—well contrived, deliberately executed robbery,—is perpetrated in every community among ourselves, without any due estimate of its moral turpitude, by reputable merchants and traders upon their cus-

tomers, to a larger extent than all the avowed and heinous thefts
collectively, which are committed against society.   It is lamentable to see how studiously conscience and fair dealing are excluded from the secular business of the world.   If we see,
every day, illustrations of this dishonest conduct, given by men
of refinement, intelligence and good character, what should we
expect from those whose fetters have hardly fallen from their
limbs ; who have been systematically degraded by slavery ; who
have not consequently that lively sense of moral obligation
which accompanies intelligence ; who are beyond the influence
of public sentiment, and surrounded by a barbarous people ?

The establishment of a colony of speculators, then, to evangelize Africa, does not discover much wisdom or promise much
success ; but, on the contrary, exhibits a total blindness of vision and a most unfavorable aspect.

Let it be remembered, however, that *rum* and *tobacco* (two
poisons which are exactly adapted to destroy both soul and
body) are the principal articles given to the natives—because
pertinaciously demanded by them—in exchange for their own.
Their appetite for spirituous liquor, first created by the slave
traders and subsequently excited by the colonists, is insatiate.
Even the justly lamented ASHMUN, if I do not mistake, for I
have not his letter now before me, was so imprudent in one of
his epistles to the Board of Managers as to concede the fatal
necessity of selling rum freely to the natives, in order to maintain a commercial intercourse with them.   Rum they would
have, or nothing ; and rum they obtained then, and do now
obtain.   Any one who will take the trouble to read the adver-
tisements in the Liberia Herald will discover that ardent spirits
form a prominent item in the list of articles offered for sale.
Of the sobriety of the colonists, however, common report
speaks in the most gratifying manner ; but as their number is to
be increased by a redundant importation, we have reason to fear
a declension of morals.

Thirdly.   Colonizationists strenuously contend that our colored population are destined always to remain a degraded class
in this country.   If educated any where, they must be educated
in Africa.   We must take them in their ignorance, and just

released from bondage, and translate them to another continent on the wings of the wind. Delay would be injurious to ourselves, and calamitous to them. They must go in large bodies —by thousands and tens of thousands annually—till the whole be expelled from our shores. For it seems, according to the logic of colonizationists, every individual tainted with black blood must be transported, to insure the regeneration of Africa ! Neither fifty thousand, nor one hundred thousand, nor half a million of these *missionaries* will be able to accomplish the task; but two millions of slaves and four hundred thousand free people of color, and all their descendants in time to come, here— even little babes (pretty prattling reformers !) and children— the maimed, the halt, and the blind—all must be sent off—else alas ! alas ! for poor benighted Africa ! This is no caricature. An ugly face is sure to quarrel with its own likeness. But what is the portrait worth, if it bear no resemblance to the living original ? They who place themselves in a ridiculous attitude must not claim exemption from ridicule.

Let us turn to the picture once more. It is worth our while to contemplate it a few moments longer.

What do we see ? More than one-sixth portion of the American people—confessedly the most vicious, degraded and dangerous portion—crowded on the shores of Africa, by means which are hereafter to be considered, and at an expense which we shall not stop now to calculate, for the purpose of civilizing and evangelizing Africa, and of improving their own condition ! Here, then, are *two* ignorant and depraved nations to be regenerated instead of *one !*—if we may call all the natives that occupy that vast continent a nation—two huge and heterogeneous masses of contagion mingled together for the preservation of each ! One of these nations is so incorrigibly stupid, or unfathomably deep in pollution, (for such is the argument,) that, although surrounded by ten millions of people living under the full blaze of gospel light, and having every desirable facility to elevate and save it, it never can rise until it be removed at least three thousand miles from their vicinage !—and yet it is first to be evangelized in a barbarous land, by a feeble, inadequate process, before it can be qualified to evangelize the other

[PART I.]   5

nation ! In other words, men who are intellectually and morally blind are violently removed from light effulgent into thick
darkness, in order that they may obtain light themselves and
diffuse light among others ! Ignorance is sent to instruct ignorance, ungodliness to exhort ungodliness, vice to stop the progress of vice, and depravity to reform depravity ! All that is
abhorrent to our moral sense, or dangerous to our quietude, or
villanous in human nature, we benevolently disgorge upon Africa for her temporal and eternal welfare ! We propose to build
upon her shores, for her glory and defence, colonies framed of
materials which we discard as worthless for our own use, and
which possess no fitness or durability ! Admirable consistency !
surprising wisdom ! unexampled benevolence ! As rationally
might we think of exhausting the ocean by multiplying the
number of its tributaries, or extinguishing a fire by piling fuel
upon it.

Lastly. Any scheme to proselytize which requires for its
protection the erection of forts and the use of murderous weapons, is opposed to the genius of christianity and radically
wrong. If the gospel cannot be propagated but by the aid of
the sword,—if its success depend upon the muscular power and
military science of its apostles,—it were better to leave the
pagan world in darkness. The first specimen of *benevolence*
and *piety*, which the colonists gave to the natives, was the
building of a fort, and supplying it with arms and ammunition !
This was an earnest manifestation of that ' peace on earth, good
will to man,' which these expatriated *missionaries* were sent to
inculcate ! How eminently calculated to inspire the confidence,
excite the gratitude, and accelerate the conversion of the Africans ! Their ' dread of the great guns of the Islanders,' (to
adopt the language of Mr Ashmun,) must from the beginning
have made a deep and salutary impression upon their minds ;
and when, not long afterward, ' every shot ' from these guns
' *spent its force in a solid mass of living human flesh* '—their
own flesh—they must have experienced a total regeneration.
Bullets and cannon balls argue with resistless effect, and as easily
convert a barbarous as civilized people. One sanguinary conflict was sufficient to spread the glad tidings of salvation among

a thousand tribes, almost with the rapidity of light !—But even irony, though appropriate, is painful. I forbear.

But—says an objector—these reflections come too late. The colony is planted, whatever may be its influence. What do you recommend ? Its immediate abandonment to want and ruin ? Shall we not bestow upon it our charities, and commend it to the protection of Heaven ?

I answer—Let the colony continue to receive the aid, and elicit the prayers of the good and benevolent. Still let it remain within the pale of christian sympathy. Blot it not out of existence. But let it henceforth develope itself naturally. Crowd not its population. Let transportation cease. Seek no longer to exile millions of our colored countrymen. For, assuredly, if the Colonization Society succeed in its efforts to remove thousands of their number annually, it could not inflict a heavier curse upon Africa, or more speedily assist in the entire subversion of the colony.

But—the objector asks—how shall we evangelize Africa ?

In the same manner as we have evangelized the Sandwich and Society Islands, and portions of Burmah, Hindostan, and other lands. By sending missionaries of the Cross *indeed*, who shall neither build forts nor trust in weapons of war ; who shall be actuated by a holy zeal and genuine love ; who shall be qualified to instruct, admonish, enlighten, and proselyte ; who shall not by their examples impugn the precepts, or subject to suspicion the inspiration of the Word of Life ; who shall not be covered with pollution and shame as with a garment, or add to the ignorance, sin and corruption of paganism ; and who shall abhor dishonesty, violence and treachery. Such men have been found to volunteer their services for the redemption of a lost world ; and such men may be found now to embark in the same glorious enterprise. A hundred evangelists like these, dispersed along the shores and in the interior of Africa, would destroy more idols, make more progress in civilizing the natives, suppress more wars, unite in amity more hostile tribes, and convert more souls to Christ, in ten years, than a colony of twenty-thousand ignorant, uncultivated, selfish emigrants in a century. Such a mission would be consonant with reason and com-

mon sense ; nor could it fail to receive the approbation of God.
How simple was the command of our blessed Saviour to his
disciples !—' Go ye forth into all the world, and preach the
gospel to every creature.' Not—' Send out from among yourselves those whom you despise or against whom you cherish a
strong antipathy ; those who need to be instructed and converted themselves ; those who are the dregs of society, made vicious
and helpless by oppression and public opinion ; those who are
beyond the reach of the.gospel in a christian land ; those whose
complexions are not precisely like yours, or who have any personal blemishes whatever that excite your dislike ;—send out
all these to evangelize the nations which sit in darkness and in
the regions of the shadow of death !'

Denham, Clapperton, and Lander, travellers in Afria, represent the natives in a light most favorable for the introduction
of christianity ; as eager to learn and become a civilized and
great people like the Europeans. Excepting the followers of
Mohammed, they are not tenacious of their forms of religious
worship ; and a considerable portion of them are totally indifferent to devotional exercises. It seems apparent, that the
fruits of a mission in Africa would be thrice as numerous as
those of one in India, because the obstacles to be surmounted
are far less formidable.

But—says the objector—the climate of Africa is fatal to
white men.

So is the climate of India. But our missionaries have not
counted their lives dear unto themselves ; and, as fast as one is
cut down, another stands ready to supply his place.

I do not believe that the Creator has immoveably fixed the
habitations of any people within a boundary narrower than the
circumference of the globe. I believe that rapid transitions
from intensity of heat and cold, and cold and heat, are destructive to animal life ; but I also believe that the human body is
easily acclimated, in any region of the world. I believe the time
is swiftly approaching when empires and continents shall as
freely commingle their population as do states and neighborhoods. To limit or obstruct this intercourse, is to impoverish
and circumscribe human happiness. Civilization will remove

those causes which now engender pestilence and death, and neu-
tralize the effects of atmospherical contagion.

Hence it will be seen that I do not assail the Colonization
Society, as many others have done, simply because the settlement at Liberia is unhealthy. It is true, the mortality among
the emigrants has been excessive ; and so it was among the
first settlers of New-England. But the climate of New-England is no longer pestiferous ; and the climate of Africa will
grow sweet and salubrious as her forests disappear, and the
purifying influences of christianity penetrate into the interior.
I expressly contend, however, that it is murderous, indiscriminately to colonize large bodies of men, women and children, in
a foreign land, before the natives are to some extent elevated by
missionary effort : and therefore I consider the Colonization
Society as responsible for the lives of those who have perished
prematurely at Liberia.

But the objection is fallacious. If white missionaries cannot,
black ones can survive in Africa. What, then, is our duty ?
Obviously to educate colored young men of genius, enterprise
and piety, expressly to carry the ' glad tidings of great joy ' to
her shores. Enough, I venture to affirm, stand ready to be
sent, if they can first be qualified for their mission. If our free
colored population were brought into our schools, and raised
from their present low estate, I am confident that an army of
christian volunteers would go out from their ranks, by a divine
impulse and under the guidance of the Holy Spirit, to redeem
their African brethren from the bondage of idolatry and the
dominion of spiritual death.

Whatever may be the result of this great controversy, I shall
have the consolation of believing that no efforts were lacking,
on my part, to uproot the prejudices of my countrymen, to persuade them to walk in the path of duty and shun the precipice
of expediency, to unloose the heavy burdens and let the prisoners go free at once, to warn them of the danger of expelling
the people of color from their native land, and to convince them
of the necessity of abandoning a dangerous and chimerical, as
well as unchristian and anti-republican association. For these
efforts I have hitherto suffered reproach and persecution, and

must expect to suffer till I perish.   This book will doubtless
increase the rage of my enemies ; but no torrent of invective
shall successfully whelm it, no sophistry impair its force, no
activity destroy its influence, no misrepresentation defeat its
usefulness.

I commend it, particularly, to the candid attention of the two
most powerful classes in this country—editors of newspapers
and the clergy.   It is not a light matter for either of them to
propagate false doctrines and excite delusive hopes, on the subject of politics or religion.   Although the press is committed to
a wide extent, I place too much reliance upon the good sense
and liberal patriotism of its conductors to believe that the evidence which is presented in these pages of the inefficiency and
injustice of the colonization scheme, will fail to convince their
understanding.   I cherish still higher expectations of its salutary
influence upon ministers of the gospel.   It may grieve them to
discover that they have been misled themselves, and that they
have unwittingly misled others.   To say to their flocks—'We
have erred in this matter ; we have solicited your charities for
an institution which is built upon prejudice and persecution ; we
have hastily adopted the mistaken opinions of others '—such a
confession may indeed require much grace in the heart, but this
grace, I am persuaded, they will obtain.   As apostles of the
Lord Jesus Christ, sustaining high and awful responsibilities,
and exerting an influence which measurably decides the eternal
destiny of the souls of men, they will not shut their eyes, or
stop their ears, or refuse to examine, or disregard the truth, in
a case involving the temporal and eternal happiness of millions
of their fellow creatures.

SECTION I.

___

THE AMERICAN COLONIZATION SOCIETY IS PLEDGED NOT
TO OPPOSE THE SYSTEM OF SLAVERY.

HAVING concluded my introductory remarks, I now proceed
to substantiate my accusations against the American Colonization Society, by marshalling in review the sentiments of those
who first originated it, and who are its efficient managers
and advocates. It is obvious that, with my limited means,
and in a book designed for a cheap circulation, I shall not be
able to enter into so minute a detail as the present exigency
demands, or make those comments which might serve more
fully to illustrate the character of this association. It should
be stated, moreover, that I have not made any particular effort
to procure materials for this work, being satisfied that those
which have almost accidentally fallen into my hands, contain
ample and conclusive evidence of the unworthiness of the Society. A vast number of the Reports of auxiliary bodies in
various parts of the country, of orations and sermons and essays
in favor of African colonization, are beyond my reach, and must
remain unconsulted. If more proof be demanded, it shall be
given to the public. There is not a sound timber in this great
Babel : from the foundation to the roof, it is rotten and defective.

I shall not stop to interrogate the motives of those who planned the Society. Some of them, undoubtedly, were actuated
by a benevolent desire to promote the welfare of our colored
population, and could never have intended to countenance oppression. But the question is not, whether their motives were
good or bad. Suppose they were all good—would this fact
prove infallibly that they could not err in judgment ? Do we not
almost daily see men running headlong into wild and injurious
enterprises with the very best intentions ? There is a wide

difference between meaning well and doing well. The slave trade originated in a compassionate regard for the benighted Africans ; and yet we hang those who are detected in this traffic. I am willing to concede that Robert Finley and Elias B. Caldwell were philanthropic individuals ; and that a large number of their followers are men of piety, benevolence and moral worth. What then ? Is the American Colonization Society a beneficial institution ? We shall see hereafter.

The history of this Society is familiar to the public. It was organized about the commencement of the year 1817. The first public meeting to consider the expediency of such an organization was held on the 21st of December, 1816, at which the Hon. Henry Clay presided ; but I have never seen its official proceedings. It was addressed by Mr Clay, *Mr Randolph*, Mr Caldwell, and other gentlemen, from whose speeches extracts will shortly be given.

It is my purpose in this section to show, first, the original design of the Society ; secondly, that it is still strictly adhered to ; and, lastly, that the Society is solemnly pledged not to interfere with the system of slavery, or in any manner to disturb the repose of the planters. Upon the rigid observance of this sinful pledge depends its existence ; a single violation of it would be fatal. I want no better reason than this, to wage an uncompromising warfare against it. No man has a right to form an alliance with others, which prevents him from rebuking sin or exposing the guilt of sinners. Every individual is bound to oppose the system of slavery in the most direct, strenuous, unfaltering manner—bound by the ties of brotherhood, by the spirit of christianity, by the genius of republicanism, by the dictates of humanity, by the requirements of justice, by the love of country, by duty to his God. He cannot suppress his voice, nor stop his ears to the groans of the prisoners, and be innocent. If he hide the truth because it may give offence—if he strike hands in amity with a thief—if he leave the needy and oppressed to perish—God will visit him with plagues. Now the language of the non-slaveholding members of the Colonization Society to the owners of slaves is virtually as follows :—
' The free people of color are a nuisance to us, and plotters of

sedition among your slaves. If they be not speedily removed, your *property* will be lost, and your lives destroyed. We therefore do solemnly agree, that, if you will unite with us in expelling this dangerous class from our shores, we will never accuse you of robbery or oppression, or irritate your feelings by asserting the right of the slaves to immediate freedom, or identify any one of you as a criminal ; but, on the contrary, we will boldly assert your innocence, and applaud you as wise and benevolent men for holding your slaves in subjection until you can cast them out of the country.' I say, this is *virtually* their language, as I shall soon indisputably show. Thus we are presented with the strange spectacle of a procession composed of the most heterogeneous materials. There go, arm-in-arm, a New-England divine and a southern kidnapper ; and there an ungodly slaveholder and a pious deacon ; each eyeing the other with distrust, and fearful of exciting a quarrel, both denouncing the poor, neglected, despised free black man as a miserable, good-for-nothing creature, and both gravely complimenting their foresight and generosity in sending this worthless wretch on a religious mission to Africa !

I cannot exhibit the folly and wickedness of this alliance in a clearer light than by inserting the following extract of a letter from Capt. Charles Stuart, of the English Royal Navy, one of the most indefatigable philanthropists in England :

' The American Colonization Society looks abroad over its own country, and it finds a mass of its brethren, whom God has been pleased to clothe with a darker skin. It finds one portion of these free ! another enslaved ! It finds a cruel prejudice, as dark and false as sin can make it, reigning with a most tyrannous sway against both. It finds this prejudice respecting the *free*, declaring without a blush, " We are too wicked ever to love them as God commands us to do—we are so resolute in our wickedness as not even to desire to do so—and we are so proud in our iniquity that we will hate and revile whoever disturbs us in it—We want, like the devils of old, to be let alone in our sin—We are unalterably determined, and neither God nor man shall move us from this resolution, that our free colored fellow subjects never shall be happy in their native land." The American Colonization Society, I say, finds this most base and cruel prejudice, *and lets it alone ;* nay more, it directly and powerfully supports it.

' The American Colonization Society finds 2,000,000 of its fellow subjects most iniquitously enslaved—and it finds a resolution as proud and wicked as the very spirit of the pit can make it against obeying God and letting them go free in their native land. *It lets this perfectly infernal resolution alone,* nay more, it powerfully supports it ; for it in fact says, as a fond and feeble father might say to some overgrown baby before whose obstinate wickedness he quailed, " Never mind, my dear, I don't want to prevent your beating and abusing your brothers and sisters—let that be—but here is a box of sugar plums—do pray give them one or two now and then.'' The American Colonization Society says practically to the slaveholders and the slave party in the United States, '' We don't want to prevent your plundering 2,000,000 of our fellow subjects of their liberty and of the fruits of their toil ; although we know that by every principle of law which does not utterly disgrace us by assimilating us to pirates, that they have as good and as true a right to the equal protection of the law as we have ; and although we ourselves stand prepared to die, rather than submit even to a fragment of the intolerable load of oppression to which we are sub-jecting them—yet never mind—let that be—they have grown old in suffering, and we in iniquity—and we have nothing to do now but to speak *peace, peace* to one another in our sins. But if any of their masters, whether from benevo-lence, an awakened conscience, or political or personal fear, should emancipate any, let us send them to Liberia—that is, in fact, let us give a sugar plum here and there to a few, while the many are living and dying unredressed—and while we are thus countenancing the atrocious iniquity beneath which they are per-ishing.'' In this aspect I find the American Colonization Society declaring itself a substitute for emancipation, and it is in this aspect that I contend with it, and that I proclaim it, *as far as it has this character*, no farther, a bane to the colored people, whether enslaved or free, and a snare and a disgrace to its country.'

The second article of the Constitution of this Society is in the following language :

' The object to which its attention is to be *exclusively* directed, is to pro-mote and execute a plan for colonizing (with their consent) the free people of color residing in our country, in Africa, or such other place as Congress shall deem most expedient.   And the Society shall act, to effect this object, in co-operation with the General Government, and such of the States as may adopt regulations upon the subject.'

The following citations abundantly sustain the charge, that the Society has not swerved from its original design, and does not oppose the system of slavery :

' Whilst he was up, he would detain the Society for a few moments. It was proper again and again to repeat, that it was far from the intention of the Society to affect, *in any manner*, the tenure by which a certain species of property is held.   He was himself a slaveholder ; *and he considered that kind of prop-erty as inviolable as any other in the country.* He would resist as soon, and with as much firmness, encroachments upon it as he would encroachments upon any other property which he held.   Nor was he disposed even to go as far as the gentleman who had just spoken, (Mr Mercer) in saying that he would emancipate his slaves, if the means were provided of sending them from the country.'—[Speech of Henry Clay.—First Annual Report.]

' It was proper and necessary distinctly to state, that he understood it consti-tuted no part of the object of this meeting, to touch or agitate in the slightest degree, a delicate question, connected with another portion of the colored pop-ulation of our country. It was not proposed to deliberate upon or consider at all, any question of emancipation, or that which was connected with the aboli-tion of slavery. It was upon that condition alone, he was sure, that many gen-tlemen from the South and West, whom he saw present, had attended, or could be expected to co-operate. It was upon that condition only, that he himself had attended.'—[Speech of Mr Clay before the Society, Jan. 1, 1818.—Second Annual Report.]

' It had been properly observed by the chairman, as well as by the gentlemen from this District (Messrs Clay and Caldwell) that there was nothing in the proposition submitted to consideration which in the smallest degree touched another very important and delicate question, which ought to be left as much out of view as possible, (Negro slavery.)   *   *   *   Mr R. concluded by saying, that he had thought it necessary to make these remarks, being a slaveholder himself, to shew, that, so far from being connected with the abolition of slavery, *the measure proposed would prove one of the greatest securities to enable the master to keep in possession his own property.'*—[Speech of John Randolph at the same meeting.]

' Your committee would not thus favorably regard the prayer of the memorialists, if it sought to impair, *in the slightest degree,* the rights of private property, or the yet more sacred rights of personal liberty, secured to every description of freemen in the United States.

' The resolution of the legislature of Virginia, the subsequent acts and declarations, as well as the high character of the memorialists themselves, added to the most obvious interest of the states who have recently sanctioned the purpose, or recognized the existence of the American Colonization Society, exclude *the remotest apprehension of such injustice and inhumanity.'*
—[Report of the committee of the House of Representatives of the United States, on the memorial of the President and Board of Managers of the Colonization Society.—Second Annual Report.]

' An effort for the benefit of the blacks, in which all parts of the country can unite, of course *must not have the abolition of slavery for its immediate object.* NOR MAY IT AIM DIRECTLY AT THE INSTRUCTION OF THE BLACKS. In either case, the *prejudices* and *terrors* of the slaveholding States would be excited in a moment ; and with reason too, for it is a well-established point, that *the public safety forbids either the emancipation or the general instruction of the slaves.'*   *   *   * ' It [African Colonization] is an enterprise in which *all parts of the country can unite.* The grand objection to every other effort is, that it excites the *jealousies* and *fears* of the south. But here is an effort in which the southern people are the first to engage, and which numbers many of their most distinguished men among its advocates and efficient supporters.'—[Review of the Reports of the Society, from the Christian Spectator.—Seventh Annual Report.]

' It will be seen at home and abroad, that the American Colonization Society, while it *properly enough* stands aloof from the question of slavery, and the abolition of slavery,' &c.—[Report of William McKenney.—Eighth Annual Report.]

' The objects of this institution are well known to the world ; for no concealment whatever has ever been intended. The Society aims at the removal of free persons of color ; *it interferes, in no way whatever, with the rights of property.'*—[Speech of G. W. Custis, Esq.—Ninth Annual Report.]

' We are reproached with doing mischief by the agitation of this question. The Society goes into no household to disturb its domestic tranquillity ; it addresses itself to no slaves to weaken their obligations of obedience. *It seeks to affect no man's property.'*—[Speech of Mr Clay.—Tenth Annual Report.]

' The Committee to whom was referred the memorial of the American Colonization Society, have had the subject under consideration, and now report :

' That upon due consideration of the said memorial, and from all other information which your committee has obtained, touching that subject, they are fully satisfied that no jealousies ought to exist, on the part of this or any other slaveholding State, respecting the objects of this Society, or the effects of its labors.
—[Report of a committee of the Legislature of Delaware, Feb. 8th, 1827.]

‘ The Society has reiterated the declaration that it has no ulterior views diverse from the object avowed in the constitution ; and having declared that it is in nowise allied to any Abolition Society in America or elsewhere, is ready whenever there is need TO PASS A CENSURE UPON SUCH SOCIETIES IN AMERICA.’—[Speech of Mr Harrison of Virginia.—Eleventh Annual Report.]

‘ We have the same interests in this subject with our southern brethren—the same opportunity of understanding it, and of knowing with what *care* and *prudence* it should be approached.　What greater pledge can we give for the moderation and safety of our measures than our own interests as slaveholders, and the ties that bind us to the slaveholding communities to which we belong ?’—[Speech of Mr Key.—Same Report.]

‘ The second objection may be resolved into this ; that the Society, under the specious pretext of removing a vicious and noxious population, is secretly undermining the rights of private property.　This is the objection expressed in its full force, and if your memorialists could for a moment believe it to be true in point of fact, they would never, *slaveholders as they are*, have associated themselves together for the purpose of co-operating with the Parent Society ; and far less would they have appeared in the character in which they now do, before the legislative bodies of a slaveholding State.　And, if any instance could be now adduced, in which the Society has ever manifested even an intention to depart from the avowed object, for the promotion of which it was originally instituted, none would with more willingness and readiness withdraw from it their countenance and support.　But, from the time of its formation, down to the present period, all its operations have been directed exclusively to the promotion of its one grand object, namely, the colonization in Africa of the free people of color of the United States.　It has always protested, and through your memorialists it again protests, that *it has no wish to interfere* with the delicate but important subject of slavery.　It has never, in a solitary instance, addressed itself to the slave.　It has never sought to invade the tranquillity of the domestic circle, nor the peace and safety of society.’—[Memorial of the Auxiliary Colonization Society of Powhatan, to the Legislature of Virginia.—Twelfth Annual Report.]

‘ Therefore she looked, and well might she look, to colonization and to colonization alone.　To abolition *she could not look*, and need not look.　Whatever that scheme may have done, heretofore, in the States now free, it had done nothing and could do nothing in the slave States for the cause of humanity.　This subject he rejoiced to know was now better understood, and all began to see that it was *wiser* and *safer* to remove, by colonization, a great and otherwise insuperable impediment to emancipation, *than to act upon the subject of emancipation itself*.’—[Speech of Mr Key.—Thirteenth Annual Report.]

‘ Our Society has nothing to do directly with the question of slavery.’ * * * ‘ Whilst the Society protests that it has no designs on the rights of the master in the slave—or the property in his slave, which the laws guarantee to him,’ &c.— [Speech of Gerrit Smith, Esq.—Fourteenth Annual Report.]

‘ Its primary object now is, and ever has been, to colonize, with their own consent, free people of color on the coast of Africa, or elsewhere, as Congress may deem expedient.　And, Sir, I am unwilling to admit, under any circumstances, and particularly in this Hall, that it ever has swerved from this cardinal object.’—[Speech of Mr Benham.—Fourteenth Annual Report.]

‘ Something he must yet be allowed to say, as regarded the object the Society was set up to accomplish.　This object, if he understood it aright, *involved no intrusion on property*, NOR EVEN UPON PREJUDICE.’—[Speech of Mr Archer of Virginia.—Fifteenth Annual Report.]

'That the effort made by the Society should be such as to unite all parts of the country—such as to be in any degree ultimately successful, it was necessary to *disclaim all attempts for the immediate abolition of slavery, or the instruction of the great body of the blacks.* Such attempts would have excited alarm and jealousy, would have been inconsistent with the public safety, and defeated the great purposes of the Society.' * * * 'It is pleasing to learn that the Friends, who at first were not favorable to the Society, *having been inclined to the immediate abolition of slavery*, are coming into what we deem the *more wise policy* of encouraging emancipation by colonization.' —[Speech of Harmanus Bleecker, Esq. at the Second Anniversary Meeting of the New-York Colonization Society, April 14, 1831.]

'The plan of colonization seems *the only one entitled to the least consideration.*'—[Speech of M. C. Paterson, Esq. on the same occasion.]

'Nor will their brethren of the North desire to interfere with their constitutional rights, or rashly to disturb a system interwoven with their feelings, habits, and prejudices. A golden mean will be pursued, which, at the same time that it *consults the wishes*, and *respects the prejudices* of the South, will provide for the claims of justice and Christianity, and avert the storm of future desolation.'—[Speech of Lucius Q. C. Elmer, Esq.—First Annual Report of the New-Jersey Colonization Society.]

'Views are attributed to us, that were never entertained, and our plan is tortured *into a design to emancipate the Slaves of the South.* We are made to disregard this description of property, and to touch without reserve the rights of our neighbors. We are said to tread this almost forbidden ground with firm step, and a hardihood of effort is imputed to us, which, if true, might well excite the indignation of our southern citizens.—But, Sir, our Society and the friends of colonization wish to be distinctly understood upon this point. From the beginning they have *disavowed*, and they do yet *disavow*, that their object is *the emancipation of the slaves.* They have no wish, *if they could*, to interfere in the smallest degree with what they deem the most interesting and fearful subject which can be pressed upon the American public.' * * * 'There is no people that treat their slaves with so much kindness and with so little cruelty. Nor can I believe that we shall meet with any serious opposition from that quarter, when our object is distinctly understood—when it is known that our operations are confined exclusively to the free black population. That this is our *sole* object, I appeal with entire confidence to the constitution of our Society and to the constitution and Annual Reports of the Parent Institution.' * * * 'We again repeat—that our operations are confined to the free black population, and that there is no ground for fear on the part of our southern friends. We hold their slaves as we hold their other property, SACRED. Let not then this slander be repeated.'—[Speech of James S. Green, Esq. on the same occasion.]

'Nothing has contributed more to retard the operations of the Colonization Society than the mistaken notion that it interferes directly with slavery. This objection is rapidly vanishing away, and many of the slaveholding States are becoming efficient supporters of the national society. In the Senate of Louisiana during its last session, resolutions were adopted expressive of the opinion that the object of this Society was deserving the patronage of the general government. An enlightened community now see, that this Society infringes upon no man's rights, that its object is noble and benevolent—to remedy an evil which is felt and acknowledged at the north and south—to give the free people of color the privileges of freemen.'—[From a Tract issued by the Massachusetts Colonization Society in 1831, for gratuitous distribution.]

'This institution proposes to do good by a single specific course of measures. Its direct and specific purpose *is not the abolition of slavery*, or the relief of pauperism, or the extension of commerce and civilization, or the enlargement of science, or the conversion of the heathen. The single object which its constitution prescribes, and to which all its efforts are necessarily directed, is, African colonization from America. It proposes only to afford facilities for the voluntary emigration of free people of color from this country to the country of their fathers.'—[Review on African Colonization.—Christian Spectator for September, 1830.]

' It interferes in nowise with the right of property, and hopes and labors for the gradual abolition of slavery, by the voluntary and gradual manumission of slaves, when the free persons of color shall have first been transferred to their aboriginal climate and soil.'—[G. W. P. Custis, Esq.—African Repository, vol. i. p. 39.]

' Does this Society wish to meddle with our slaves as our rightful property? I answer *no*, I think not.'—[African Repository, vol. ii. p. 13.]

' They have been denounced by some as fanatical and visionary innovators, pursuing without regard to means or consequences, an object destructive of the rights of property, and dangerous to the public peace.' * * * ' The sole object of the Society, as declared at its institution, and from which it can never be allowed to depart, is ' to remove with their own consent, to the coast of Africa, the free colored population, now existing in the United States, and such as hereafter may become free.' * * * ' In pursuing their object, therefore, (although such consequences may result from a successful prosecution of it,) the Society cannot be justly charged with aiming to disturb the rights of property or the peace of society. Your memorialists refer with confidence to the course they have pursued, in the prosecution of their object for nine years past, to shew that it is possible, without danger or alarm, to carry on such an operation, notwithstanding its supposed relation to the subject of slavery, and that they have not been regardless, in any of their measures, of what was due to the state of society in which they live. They are, themselves, chiefly slaveholders, and live, with all the ties of life binding them to a slaveholding community. They know when to speak and when to forbear upon topics connected with this painful and difficult subject. They put forth no passionate appeals before the public, seek to excite no feeling, and avoid, with the most sedulous care, every measure that would endanger the public tranquillity.' * * * ' The managers could, with no propriety, depart from their original and avowed purpose, *and make emancipation their object.* And they would further say, that if they were not thus restrained by the terms of their association, they would still consider any attempts to promote the increase of the free colored population by manumission, *unnecessary, premature,* and *dangerous.*' * * * ' It seems now to be admitted that, whatever has any bearing upon that question, must be managed with the utmost consideration ; that the peace and order of society must not be endangered by indiscreet and ill-timed efforts to promote emancipation ; and that a true regard should be manifested to the feelings and the fears, and even the *prejudices* of those, whose co-operation is essential.'—[Memorial of the Society to the several States.—A. R. vol. ii. pp. 57, 58, 60.]

' To found in Africa an empire of *christians and republicans ;* to reconduct the blacks to their native land, without disturbing the order of society, the laws of property, or the rights of individuals ; rapidly, but legally, *silently, gradually,* to drain them off ; these are the noble ends of the colonization scheme.'—[African Repository, vol. ii. p. 375.]

' Nor have I ever been able to see, for my part, why the patronage of Congress to a benevolent and patriotic Society, which, without interfering, in the smallest degree, with that *delicate interest*, only aims to remove what we all consider as a great evil—our free people of color—(and which evil *does* inter-

fere with that interest,) should excite the jealousy or spleen of our most watchful and determined advocates of state rights.'—[Idem, p. 383.]

' Recognising the constitutional and legitimate existence of slavery, it seeks
not to interfere, either directly or indirectly, with the rights which it creates.
*Acknowledging the necessity by which its present continuance and the
rigorous provisions for its maintenance are justified*, it aims only at furnishing the States, in which it exists, the means of immediately lessening its
severities, and of ultimately relieving themselves from its acknowledged evils.'—
[Opimius in reply to Caius Gracchus.—African Repository, vol. iii. p. 16.]

' *It is no abolition Society ;* it addresses as yet *arguments to no master*,
and disavows with horror the idea of offering temptations to any slave. IT DE-
NIES THE DESIGN OF ATTEMPTING EMANCIPATION, EITHER PAR-
TIAL OR GENERAL ; it denies, with us, that the General Government have
any power to emancipate ; and declares that the States have exclusively the
right to regulate the whole subject of slavery. The scope of the Society is
large enough, but it is in nowise mingled or confounded with the broad sweeping
views of *a few fanatics* in America, who would urge us on to the sudden
and total abolition of slavery.' * * * ' The first great material objection is
that the Society does, in fact, in spite of its denial, meditate and conspire the
emancipation of the slaves. To the candid, let me say that there are names on
the rolls of the Society too high to be rationally accused of the duplicity and insidious falsehood which this implies ; farther, the Society and its branches are
composed, in by far the larger part, of *citizens of slaveholding States*, who
cannot gravely be charged with a design so perilous to themselves. To the un-
candid disputant, I say, let him put his finger on one single sentiment, declaration or act of the Society, or of any person, with its sanction, which shows such
to be their object : there is in fact no pretext for the charge.' * * * ' Let
me repeat, the *friends* of the Colonization Society, three-fourths of them are
SLAVEHOLDERS ; the legislatures of Maryland, Georgia, Kentucky and Tennessee, all slaveholding States, have approved it ; *every member* of this auxiliary Society is, *either in himself, or his nearest relatives, interested in
holding slaves.*' * * * ' Once more ; this Society is no way connected
with certain Abolition Societies in the country. To these the Colonization Society would say, " Your object is unattainable, your zeal dangerous, and nothing can give it the right direction or the right temperature, but your surrendering
your plan to ours : be convinced, that if the blacks are ever to be removed
from us, it will be by the free will of the owners, and by means of the opportunity which our *innocent* plan of an asylum for such as may be sent will afford." '—[' The Col. Society Vindicated.'—Idem, pp. 197, 200, 202, 203.]

' They can impress upon the southern slaveholder, by the strength of facts,
and by the recorded declarations of honest men, that the objects of the Colonization Society are altogether pure and praiseworthy, and *that it has no intention
to open the door to universal liberty*, but only to cut out a channel, where
the merciful providence of God may cause those dark waters to flow off.'—
[Idem, vol. iv. p. 145.]

' About twelve years ago, some of the wisest men of the nation, (*mostly
slaveholders*,) formed, in the city of Washington, the present American Colonization Society. Among them were men high in office, who had spent many
years in studying the interests of their country, and who could not, therefore,
be suspected of short-sighted enthusiasm, or any secret design of disturbing the
rights or the safety of our southern citizens.' * * * ' You will observe,
first, that *there is to be no intermeddling with property in slaves.* THE
RIGHTS OF MASTERS ARE TO REMAIN SACRED IN THE EYES OF
THE SOCIETY. The tendency of the scheme, and one of its objects, is to
secure slaveholders, and the whole southern country, against certain evil

consequences, growing out of the three-fold mixture of our population.'—[Address of the Rockbridge Col. Society.—Idem, p. 274.]

' It is true, their operations have been confied to the single object, colonization.—They do nothing directly to effect the manumission of slaves.—They think nothing can be advantageously done in favor of emancipation, but by means of colonization, of which emancipation will be a certain consequence that may be safely and quietly awaited.'—[Mr Key's Address.—Idem, p. 303.]

' The Colonization Society, as such, have renounced wholly the name and the characteristics of abolitionists. On this point they have been unjustly and injuriously slandered. They need no such barrier to restrict them, as the sentiment of Mr Harrison, for their operations are entirely in a different department. INTO THEIR ACCOUNTS THE SUBJECT OF EMANCIPATION DOES NOT ENTER AT ALL.'—[' N. E.'—Idem, p. 306.]

' Being, chiefly, slaveholders ourselves, we well know how it becomes us to approach such a subject as this in a slaveholding state, and in every other. If there were room for a reasonable jealousy, we among the first should feel it ; being as much interested in the welfare of the community, and having as much at heart, as any men can have, the security of ourselves, our property and our families.' * * * ' Our object is, not to prevail upon the master to part with his slave, for that we leave to his own reflection and CONVENIENCE ; but to afford to those masters who have determined, or may determine, to manumit their slaves ; provided they can be removed from this country, the means of removing them to a place where they may be really free, virtuous, respectable and happy. —Nothing can be more innocent and less alarming.'—[Review of Mr Tazewell's Report.—Idem, p. 341.]

' The American Colonization Society has, at all times, solemnly disavowed any purpose of interference with the institutions or rights of our Southern communities.'—[Idem, vol. v. p. 307.]

' From its origin, and throughout the whole period of its existence, it has constantly disclaimed all intention whatever of interfering, in the smallest degree, with the rights of property, or the object of emancipation, gradual or immediate. *It is not only without inclination*, but it is without power, to make any such interference. It is not even a chartered or incorporated company ; and it has no other foundation than that of Bible Societies, or any other christian or charitable unincorporated companies in our country. It knows that the subject of emancipation belongs exclusively to the several States in which slavery is tolerated, and to individual proprietors of slaves in those States, under and according to their laws.' * * * ' The Society presents to the American public *no project of emancipation.*' * * * ' Its exertions have been confined exclusively to the free colored people of the United States, and to those of them who are willing to go. It has neither *purpose* nor power to extend them to the larger portion of that race held in bondage. Throughout the whole period of its existence, this disclaimer has been made, and incontestible facts establish its truth and sincerity. It is now repeated, in its behalf, that the spirit of misrepresentation may have no pretext for abusing the public ear.'—[Mr Clay's Speech.—African Repository, vol. vi. pp. 13, 17, 19.]

' The Society, from considerations like these, whilst it disclaims the remotest idea of ever disturbing the right of property in slaves, conceives it to be possible that the time may arrive, when, with the approbation of their owners, they shall all be at liberty ; and, with those already free, be removed, with their own consent, to the land of their ancestors.'—[African Repository, vol. vi. p. 69.]

' *It is not the object of this Society to liberate slaves, or touch the rights of property.* TO SET THEM LOOSE AMONG US WOULD BE AN EVIL

MORE INTOLERABLE THAN SLAVERY ITSELF. It would make our situation insecure and dangerous.'—[Report of the Kentucky Col. Soc.—Idem, p. 81.]

' It contemplates no purpose of abolition : it touches no slave until his fetters have been voluntarily stricken off by the hand of his own master.'—[Speech of John A. Dix, Esq.—Idem, p. 165.]

' What has awakened that spirit of suspicion and enmity which is now manifested by these men in every form of open and active hostility ? Can it be attributed to any departure of the Society from its avowed original design and principles ? We maintain that it cannot ; we maintain that the character of the Society has from the commencement been uniformly the same, and that its proceedings have been consistent with its character. Were or are the design and principles of the Society hostile to the rights and interest of the Southern States ? We maintain that they were and are not ; but on the contrary, are worthy to be cherished by the citizens of these States, and to be sustained with all their energies as means of their political and moral strength.' * * * ' The *free* people of color alone are to be colonized by the Society, and whether the benefits of its scheme are ever to be extended to *others*, is a question referred to those to whom it pertains as a matter of right and duty to decide.' * * * ' The Colonization Society would be the last Institution in the world to disturb the domestic tranquillity of the South.'—[Defence of the Society.—Idem, pp. 197, 207, 209.]

' This Society, here in the outset, most explicitly disclaims all intention to interfere in the smallest degree with the slave population. It is with the free colored population alone, and that too, with their own consent, that this Society proposes to act.'—[Address of the Maryland State Colonization Society to the People of Maryland.]

' To the slaveholder, who had charged upon them the wicked design of interfering with the rights of property under the specious pretexts of removing a vicious and dangerous free population, they address themselves in a tone of conciliation'and sympathy. We know your rights, say they, and we respect them— we know your difficulties, and we appreciate them. *Being mostly slaveholders ourselves*, having a common interest with you in this subject, an equal opportunity of understanding it, and the same motives to prudent action, what better guarantee can be afforded for the just discrimination, and the safe operation of our measures ? And what ground for apprehension that we, who are bound to you by the strongest ties of interest and of sympathy, should intrude upon the repose of the domestic circle, or invade the peace and security of society ? Have not the thirteen years' peaceful, yet efficient, operations of our Society attested the *moderation of our views* and the safety of our plans ? We have protested from the commencement, and during our whole progress, and we do now protest, that we have never entertained the purpose of intermeddling with the private property of individuals. We know that we have not the power, even if we had the inclination, to do so. Your rights, as guarantied by the Constitution, are held sacred in our eyes ; and we should be among the foremost to resist, as a flagrant usurpation, any encroachment upon those rights. Our only object, as at all times avowed, is to provide for the removal to the coast of Africa, with their own consent, of such persons of color as are already free, and of such others as the humanity of individuals, or the laws of the different states, may hereafter liberate. Is there any thing, say they, in this proposition at war with your interest, your safety, your honor, or your happiness ? Do we not all regard this mixed and intermediate population of free blacks, made up of slaves or their immediate descendants, as a mighty and a growing evil, exerting a dangerous and baneful influence on all around them ? '—[Address of Cyrus Edwards, Esq. of Illinois.—African Repository, vol. vii. p. 100.]

' It was never the intention of the Society to interfere with the rights of the proprietors of slaves ; nor has it at any time done so.'—[Address of R. J. Breckenridge of Kentucky.—Idem p. 176.]

' The specific object to which the entire funds of the Institution are devoted, is simple and plainly unexceptionable in this respect, that it interferes with no rights of individuals, and with no law of the land.' * * * ' It embraces in its provisions only the free. It does not interfere—it desires not to interfere, in any way, with the rights or the interests of the proprietors of slaves. *It condemns no man because he is a slaveholder ;* it seeks to quiet all unkind feelings between the sober and virtuous men of the North and of the South on the subject of slavery ; it sends abroad no influence to disturb the peace, and endanger the security and prosperity of any portion of the country.'—[Character and Influence of the Colonization Society.—African Repository, vol. vii. pp. 194, 200.]

' Can it be a ruthless scheme of political speculation, which would trample, with rude and unhallowed step, upon the rights of property, to gratify the visionary and fanatical projects of its authors ? No : this is impossible. Yet such is the language of intemperate opposition, with which this Society has been assailed by its enemies.' * * * ' Equally absurd and false is the objection, that this Society seeks indirectly to disturb the rights of property, and to interfere with the well-established relation subsisting between master and slave. The man who avows such monstrous purposes as these, and seeks to shelter himself under the sanction and authority of the American Colonization Society, is a base traitor to the cause which it seeks to advance—AN ENEMY OF THE WORST AND MOST DANGEROUS STAMP, because he assumes the specious garb of a friend and coadjutor. Let him stand, or let him fall, by the verdict of an insulted and outraged community—but do not make liable for his acts a great Institution, whose real friends will be the first to reject and discountenance him, and to mark upon his forehead in indelible characters, '' This is a traitor to the cause of his country and the cause of humanity.''—It is true that the friends of the American Colonization Society have permitted themselves to entertain the high and exalted hope, that, by its influences, ultimate and remote, the burdens which are incident to slavery may be greatly mitigated, and possibly the evil itself at some future day be entirely removed. But mark, Mr President, and mark well, ye hearers, the grounds upon which this hope is founded. It could not be sustained by any effort, direct or indirect, to invade the rights of the slaveholding community, for the plain and palpable reason, that the effort itself would furnish the most certain means of defeating the object in view, even supposing the friends of the Society reckless enough to entertain it. It would denote on the part of those who made it, an extremity of madness and folly, wholly unprecedented in the history of the world, and if persevered in, would dissolve the government into its original elements, even though the principle of union which holds it together were a thousand-fold stronger than it is.' * * * ' Surely the friends of the Colonization Society have done nought either to alarm the honest fears of the patriot, or excite the morbid sensibilities of the slaveholder.'—[Address delivered before the Lynchburg Auxiliary Colonization Society, August 18, 1831.]

' While, therefore, *they determined to avoid the question of slavery,* they proposed the formation of a colony on the coast of Africa, as an asylum for free people of color.' * * * ' The emancipation of slaves or the amelioration of their condition, with the moral, intellectual, and political improvement of people of color within the United States, *are subjects foreign to the powers of this Society.*'—[Address of the Board of Managers of the American Colonization Society to its Auxiliary Societies.—African Repository, vol. vii. pp. 290, 291.]

'The American Colonization Society was formed with special reference to the *free* blacks of our country. With the *delicate subject* of slavery it presumes not to interfere. And yet doubtless from the first it has cherished the hope of being in some way or other a medium of relief to the entire colored population of the land. Such a hope is certainly both innocent and benevolent. And so long as the Society adheres to the object announced in its constitution, as it hitherto has done, the master can surely find no reasonable cause of anxiety. And it is a gratifying circumstance that the Society has from the first *obtained its most decided and efficient support from the slaveholding States.*'—— [Sermon, delivered at Springfield, Mass., July 4th, 1829, before the Auxiliary Colonization Society of Hampden County, by Rev. B. Dickinson.]

'The American Colonization Society in no way directly meddles with slavery. It disclaims all such interference.'—[Correspondent of the Southern Religious Telegraph.]

' This system is sanctioned by the laws of independent and sovereign states. Congress cannot constitutionally pass laws which shall tend directly to abolish it. If it ever be abolished by legislative enactments, it must be done by the respective legislatures of the States in which it exists. It never designed to interfere with what the laws consider as the rights of masters—it has made no appeals to them to release their slaves for colonization, nor to their slaves to abandon their masters. With this delicate subject, the Society has avowedly nothing to do. Its ostensible object is necessarily the removal of our free colored population.'—[Middletown (Connecticut) Gazette.]

' With slaves, however, the American Colonization Society has *no concern* whatever, except to transport to Africa such as their owners may liberate for that purpose.'—[Oration delivered at Newark, N. J., July 4th, 1831, by Gabriel P. Disosway, Esq.]

' It disclaims, and always has disclaimed, all intention whatever, of interfering in the smallest degree, direct or indirect, with the rights of slaveholders, the right of property, *or the object of emancipation, gradual or immediate. It knows that the owners of slaves are the owners, and no one else—it does not, in the most remote degree, touch that delicate subject.* Every slaveholder may, therefore, remain at ease concerning it or its progress or objects.'— [An advocate of the Society in the New-Orleans Argus.]

It were needless to multiply these extracts. So precisely do they resemble each other, that they seem rather as the offspring of a single mind, than of many minds. A large majority of them come in the most official and authoritative shape, and their language is explicit beyond cavil.

Here, then, is a combination, embracing able and influential men in all parts of the country, pledging itself not only to respect the system of slavery, but to frown indignantly upon those who shall dare to assail it. And what is this system which is to be held in so much reverence, and avoided with so much care? It is a system which has in itself no redeeming feature, but is full of blood—the blood of innocent men, women and children ; full of adultery and concupiscence ; full of darkness, blasphemy and wo ; full of rebellion against God and treason against the

universe ; full of wrath—impurity—ignorance—brutality—and
awful impiety ; full of wounds and bruises and putrefying sores ;
full of temporal suffering and eternal damnation.   It is, says
Pitt, a mass, a system of enormities, which incontrovertibly bid
defiance to every regulation which ingenuity can devise, or
power effect, but a total extinction ; a system of incurable injustice, the complication of every species of iniquity, the greatest practical evil that ever has afflicted the human race, and
the severest and most extensive calamity recorded in the history of the world.   Fox calls it a most unjust and horrible
persecution of our fellow creatures.   The Rev. Dr. Thomson
declares it is a system hostile to the original and essential rights
of humanity—contrary to the inflexible and paramount demands
of moral justice—at eternal variance with the spirit and maxims
of revealed religion—inimical to all that is merciful in the heart,
and holy in the conduct—and on these accounts, necessarily
exposed and subject to the curse of Almighty God.   It is, says
Rowland Hill, made up of every crime that treachery, cruelty
and murder can invent.   Wilberforce says, it is the full measure of pure, unmixed, unsophisticated wickedness ; and scorn-
ing all competition or comparison, it stands without a rival in
the secure, undisputed possession of its detestable pre-eminence.
In this country, slavery is a system which leaves the chastity of
one million females without any protection ! which condemns
more than two millions of human beings to remediless bondage !
which authorises their sale at public vendue in company with
horses, sheep and hogs, or in a private manner, at the pleasure
of their owners ! which, under penalty of imprisonment, and
even death, forbids their being taught the lowest rudiments of
knowledge ! which, by the exclusion of their testimony in courts,
subjects them to worse than brutal treatment ! which recog-
nizes no connubial obligations, ruthlessly severs the holiest relations of life, tears the scarcely weaned babe from the arms of
its mother, wives from their husbands, and parents from their
children !   But who is adequate to the task of delineating its
horrors, or recording its atrocities, in full ?   Who can number
the stripes which it inflicts, the groans and tears and impreca-
tions which it extorts, the cruel murders which it perpetrates ?

or who measure the innocent blood which it spills, or the degradation which it imposes, or the guilt which it accumulates ? or
who reveal the waste of property, the perversion of intellect, the
loss of happiness, the burial of mind, to which it is accessary ?
or who trace its poisonous influence and soul-destroying tendency back for two hundred years down to the end of time ?
None—none but God himself ! It is corrupt as death—black as
perdition—cruel and insatiate as the grave. To adopt the ner-
vous language of another :—The thing I say is true. I speak
the truth, though it is most lamentable. I dare not hide it, I
dare not palliate it ; else the horror with which it covereth me
would make me do so. Wo unto such a system ! wo unto the
men of this land who have been brought under its operation !
It is not felt to be evil, it is not acknowledged to be evil, it is
not preached against as evil ; and, therefore, it is only the more
inveterate and fearful an evil.* *It hath become constitutional.*
IT IS FED FROM THE STREAM OF OUR LIFE, and it will grow
more and more excessive, until it can no longer be endured by
God, nor borne with by man.

And this is the system, with which, as the reader has seen,
the American Colonization Society is resolved not to interfere ;
and with the upholders of which, ministers of the gospel and
professors of religion of all denominations have made a treaty
of peace ! Tell it not abroad—publish it not in the capitals of
Europe—lest the despots of the old world take courage, and
infidelity strengthen its stakes !

If men who are reputedly wise and good—if religious teachers and political leaders, those whose opinions are almost implicitly adopted, and whose examples are readily followed by
the mass of the people—if such men suppress their voices on
this momentous subject, and turn their eyes from its contemplation, and give the right hand of fellowship to the buyers and
sellers of human flesh, is there not cause for lamentation and
alarm ? The pulpit is false to its trust, and a moral paralysis

---

* The term evil is used here in a criminal sense. I know that colonizationists
regard slavery as an evil ; but an evil which has been *entailed* upon this land,
for the existence of which we are no more to blame than for the prevalence
of plague or famine.

has seized the vitals of the church.   The sanctity of religion is thrown, like a mantle, over the horrid system.   Under its auspices, robbery and oppression have become popular and flourishing.   The press, too, by its profound silence, or selfish neutrality, or equivocal course, or active partizanship, is enlisted in the cause of tyranny—the mighty press, which has power, if exerted aright, to break every fetter, and emancipate the land. If this state of things be not speedily reversed, ' we be all dead men.'   Unless the pulpit lift up the voice of warning, supplication and wo, with a fidelity which no emolument can bribe, and no threat intimidate ; unless the church organise and plan for the redemption of the benighted slaves, and directly assault the strong holds of despotism ; unless the press awake to its duty, or desist from its bloody co-operation ; as sure as Jehovah lives and is unchangeable, he will pour out his indignation upon us, and consume us with the fire of his wrath, and our own way recompense upon our heads.   ' Ah, sinful nation, a people laden with iniquity, a seed of evil doers, children that are corrupters !   When ye spread forth your hands, I will hide mine eyes from you ;   yea, when ye make many prayers, I will not hear : *your hands are full of blood.*   Wash you, make you clean ; put away the evil of your doings from before mine eyes ;   cease to do evil ; learn to do well ; *seek judgment, relieve the oppressed,* judge the fatherless, plead for the widow. If ye be willing and obedient, ye shall eat the good of the land : but if ye refuse and rebel, ye shall be devoured with the sword : *for the mouth of the Lord hath spoken it.*'

I know the covert behind which colonizationists take refuge. They profess to be—and, doubtless, in many instances are— aiming at the ultimate emancipation of the slaves ;   but they are all for *gradual* abolition—all too courteous to give offence—too sober to be madmen—too discreet to adopt *rash* measures. But I shall show, in the progress of this work, that they not only shield the holders of slaves from reproach, (and thus, by assuring them of their innocence, destroy all motives for repentance,) but earnestly dissuade them from emancipating their slaves without an immediate expulsion.   Fine conceptions of justice !   Enemies of slavery, with a vengeance !

Suppose a similar course had been pursued by the friends of Temperance—when would have commenced that mighty reformation which has taken place before our eyes—unparalleled in extent, completeness and rapidity ? Suppose, instead of exposing the guilt of trafficking in ardent spirits, and demanding instant and entire abstinence, they had associated themselves together for the exclusive purpose of colonizing all the drunkards in the land, as a class dangerous to our safety and irremediably degraded, on a spot where they could not obtain the poisonous alcohol, but could rise to respect and affluence—how would such an enterprise have been received ? Suppose they had pledged themselves not to ' meddle ' with the business of the traders in spirituous liquors, or to injure the 'property' of distillers, and had dwelt upon the folly and danger of ' immediate' abstinence, and had denounced the advocates of this doctrine as madmen and fanatics, and had endeavored, moreover, to suppress inquiry into the lawfulness of rum-selling—how many importers, makers and venders of the liquid poison would have abandoned their occupation, or how many of the four hundred thousand individuals, who are now enrolled under the banner of entire abstinence, would have been united in this great enterprise ? Suppose, further, that, in a lapse of fifteen years, this association had transported two thousand drunkards, and the tide of intemperance had continued to rise higher and higher, and some faithful watchmen had given the alarm and showed the fatal delusion which rested upon the land, and the Society should have defended itself by pointing to the two thousand sots who had been saved by its instrumentality—would the public attention have been successfully diverted from the *immense evil* to the *partial good ?* Suppose, once more, that this Society, composed indiscriminately of rum-sellers and sober, pious men, on being charged with perpetuating the evils of intemperance, with removing only some of the fruits thereof instead of the tree itself, should have indignantly repelled the charge, and said—' We are as much opposed to drunkenness, and as heartily deprecate its existence, as any of our violent, fanatical opposers ; but the holders of ardent spirit have invested their capital in it, and to destroy its sale would invade the right of *property* ; policy at least, bids us not to assail their conduct, as otherwise we might exasperate them, and so lose their aid in colonizing the tipplers.' What would have been accomplished ? But no such logic was used : the duty of immediate reform was constantly pressed upon the people, and a mighty reform took place.

Colonizationists boast inordinately of having emancipated three or four hundred slaves by their scheme, and contemptuously inquire of abolitionists, ' What have *you* effected ?' Many persons have been deceived by this *show* of success, and deem it conclusive evidence of the usefulness of the Colonization Society.   But, in the first place, it is very certain that none of these slaves were liberated in consequence of the faithful appeals of the Society to the consciences of the masters ; for it has never troubled their consciences by any such appeals.   Secondly, it is obvious that these manumissions are the fruits of the uncompromising doctrines of abolitionists ; for they are calculated to bring slaveholders to repentance, and they will yet liberate other slaves to be caught up and claimed by the Society as trophies of its success.   Thirdly, it has been shown that while this Society (allowing it the utmost that it claims) is effecting very little and very doubtful good, it is inflicting upon the nation great and positive evil, by refusing to arraign the oppressors at the bar of eternal justice, and by obstructing the formation of abolition societies.   It rivets a thousand fetters where it breaks one.   It annually removes, on an average, two hundred of our colored population, whereas the annual increase is about seventy thousand.   It releases some scores of slaves, and says to the owners of more than two millions—' Hold on ! do n't emancipate too fast !'

What have the abolitionists *done* ? They have done more, during the past year, to overthrow the system of slavery, than has been accomplished by the gradualists in half a century. They have succeeded in fastening the attention of the nation upon its enormities, and in piercing the callous consciences of the planters.   They are reforming and consolidating public opinion, dispelling the mists of error, inspiring the hearts of the timid, enlightening the eyes of the blind, and disturbing the slumbers of the guilty. Colonizationists gather a few leaves which the tree has cast off, and vaunt of the deed : abolitionists ' lay the axe at once to its roots, and put their united nerve into the steel '—nor shall their strokes be in vain—for soon shall ' this great poison-tree of lust and blood, and of all abominable and heartless iniquity, fall before them ; and law and love, and God and man, shout victory over its ruin.'

Has the reader duly considered the fatal admissions of the advocates of the colonization scheme, presented in the preceding pages ? Some of them it may be serviceable to the cause of truth and justice to recapitulate.

1. *The Society does not aim directly at the instruction of the blacks: their moral, intellectual and political improvement within the United States, is foreign to its powers.*

2. *The public safety forbids either the emancipation or the general instruction of the slaves.*

3. *The Society properly enough stands aloof from the question of slavery.*

4. *It is ready to pass censure upon abolition societies.*

5. *It involves no intrusion on property, nor even upon prejudice.*

6. *It has no wish, if it could, to interfere in the smallest degree with the system of slavery.*

7. *It acknowledges the necessity by which the present continuance of the system and the rigorous provisions for its maintenance are justified.*

8. *It denies the design of attempting emancipation either partial or general : into its accounts the subject of emancipation does not enter at all : it has no intention to open the door to universal liberty.*

9. *The rights of masters are to remain sacred in the eyes of the Society.*

10. *It condemns no man because he is a slaveholder.*

Each of these particulars deserves a volume of comments, but I am compelled to dismiss them in rotation with a single remark.

1. One reason assigned by the Society for refusing to promote the education of our colored population, is, a dread of exciting ' the *prejudices* and *terrors* of the slaveholding States '! Is it credible ? As far, then, as this Society extends its influ-

ence, more than two millions of ignorant, degraded beings in this boasted land of liberty and light have nothing to hope : their moral, intellectual and political improvement is foreign to its powers ! Cruel neglect ! barbarous coalition ! A sinful fear of rousing the prejudices of oppressors outweighs the claims of the contemned blacks, the requirements of the gospel, the dictates of humanity, and the convictions of duty. Will this plea avail aught at the bar of God ? Millions of our countrymen purposely kept in darkness, although we are able to pour daylight upon their vision, merely to gratify and protect their buyers and sellers !

2.   There never was a more abominable or more absurd heresy propagated, than the assumption that the public safety would be jeoparded by an immediate compliance with the demands of justice : yet it has obtained among all orders of society.   Even ministers of the gospel, who are bound to cry aloud, and spare not,—to lift up their voices like a trumpet, and show this guilty nation its sins,—to say to the holders of slaves, ' Loose the bands of wickedness, undo the heavy burdens, let the oppressed go free, *and break every yoke,*'—even they fly to this subterfuge, and deprecate a general emancipation.   On this subject, ' they know not what they do ;' they reason like madmen or atheists ; they advance sentiments which unhinge the moral government of the universe, and directly encourage the commission of the most heinous crimes.   How long would any one of their number retain his situation, if he were to preach in explicit terms to his congregation as follows ?—' My dear hearers, if any among you are daily oppressing the weak, or defrauding the poor, do not cease from your robbery and cruelty at once, as you value your own happiness and the welfare of society ! Relax your tyrannous grasp gradually from the throat of your neighbor, and steal not quite so much from him this year as you did the last !'—But they emphatically hold this language whenever they advise slaveholders not to repent *en masse,* or too hastily.   The public safety, they say, forbids emancipation ! or, in other words, the public safety depends upon your persistance in cheating, whipping, starving, debasing your slaves ! Nay, more—many of them, horrible to tell, are traffickers in human flesh ! ' For this thing which it cannot bear, the earth is

disquieted. The gospel of peace and mercy preached by him who steals, buys and sells the purchase of Messiah's blood !— rulers of the church making merchandize of their brethren's souls ! —and Christians trading the persons of men ! ' *

3. The system of slavery is full of danger, outrage, desolation and death—' a volcano in full operation '—a monster that is annually supplied with sixty thousand new victims, devoured as soon as born—and yet the Colonization Society ' properly enough stands aloof ' from it !! It utters no lamentations— makes no supplications—gives no rebukes—presents no motives for repentance !

4. The Society is not only ready to pass, but it is constantly bestowing its censure upon abolition societies. It represents their members as guided by a visionary, wild and fanatical spirit, as invaders of rights which are sacred, incendiaries, disturbers of the peace of society, and enemies to the safety and happiness of the planters. Determining itself to avoid the question of emancipation—to leave millions of human beings to pine in bondage without exposing the guilt of the oppressors —it endeavors to prevent any other association agitating the subject. Hence between colonization and abolition societies there is no affinity of feeling or action ; and hence arises the

---

* ' If the most guilty and daring transgressor be sought, he is a Gospel Minister, who solemnly avows his belief of the Presbyterian Confession of Faith, or the Methodist Discipline, and notwithstanding himself is a Negro Pedler, who steals, buys, sells, and keeps his brethren in slavery, or supports by his taciturnity, or his smooth prophesying, or his direct defence, the Christian professor who unites in the kidnapping trade. Truth forces the declaration, that every church officer, or member, who is a slaveholder, records himself, by his own creed, a hypocrite !' * * ' To pray and kidnap ! to commune and rob men's all ! to preach justice, and steal the laborer with his recompense ! to recommend mercy to others, and exhibit cruelty in our own conduct ! to explain religious duties, and ever impede the performance of them ! to propound the example of Christ and his Apostles, and declare that a slaveholder imitates them ! to enjoin an observance of the Lord's day, and drive the slaves from the temple of God ! to inculcate every social affection, and instantly exterminate them ! to expatiate upon bliss eternal, and preclude sinners from obtaining it ! to unfold the woes of Tophet, and not drag men from its fire ! are the most preposterous delusion, and the most consummate mockery.' * * * ' The Church of God groans. It is the utmost Satanic delusion to talk of religion and slavery. Be not deceived : to affirm that a slaveholder is a genuine disciple of Jesus Christ, is most intelligible contradiction. A brother of Him who went about doing good, and steal, enslave, torment, starve and scourge a man because his skin is of a different tinge ! Such Christianity is the Devil's manufacture to delude souls to the regions of wo.'—REV. GEORGE BOURNE.

cause, inexplicable to many, why they cannot pursue their objects amicably together.

5.   The attempt of the Society to conciliate the holders of slaves must result either in disappointment, or in an abandonment of the path of duty.   If they are guilty of robbery and oppression, they must be arraigned as criminals, or they never will reform : for why should honest, benevolent men change their conduct ? If, through a false delicacy of feeling or cringing policy, their wickedness be covered up, alas for the slaves, and alas for the regeneration of the south ! all hope is lost.

6.   The Society has no wish, *if it could*, to interfere with the system of slavery !   Monstrous indifference, or barbarous cruelty !   And yet it presumes to occupy the whole ground of the controversy, and to direct the actions of the friends of the blacks throughout the land ! By the phrase ' *interfere*,' is meant no desire to contest the claims of the planters to their bondmen, or to kindle the indignation of the people against their atrocious practices.

7.   It appears that all those terrible enactments which have been made for the government of the slaves—such, for example, as forbid their learning to read under the penalty of stripes, and even death—are acknowledged by the Society to be necessary for the maintenance of order ! What a concession !

8.   Sometimes we are told that the Society is aiming at the liberation of all the slaves, and then that it has no design of attempting either partial or general emancipation : so contradictory are its assurances !   It is manifest that it does not mean to touch the question of slavery ; and hence the imperious necessity of forming abolition societies.

9.   The rights of masters are to remain sacred in the eyes of the Society ! What rights ? Those by which the intelligent creatures of God are bought and sold and used like cattle ? those which are founded upon piracy, cruelty and outrage ?* Yes ! This, then, is an abandonment of the ground of right and justice, and ends the controversy between truth and error.

---

* ' We are told not to meddle with vested rights : I have a sacred feeling about vested rights ; but when vested rights become vested wrongs, I am less scrupulous about them.'—*Speech of Rev. Mr. Burnett, of England.*

10.   It condemns no man because he is a slaveholder ! Certainly, then, it allows that slaveholders are upright men—not guilty of fraud—not oppressors—not extortioners ! and that the slaves are truly and justly their property—not entitled to freedom—not better than cattle—not conscious of evil treatment—not worthy of remuneration for their toil—not rational and accountable beings !

SECTION II.

THE AMERICAN COLONIZATION SOCIETY APOLOGISES FOR SLAVERY AND SLAVEHOLDERS.

My charges against the American Colonization Society acquire breadth and solemnity as I progress in my task.   I have fairly and abundantly sustained my first,—*that the Society is not the enemy of the slave-system* ; and I now proceed to prove my second,—*that it apologises for slavery and slaveholders.*

‘ There is a golden mean, which all who would pursue the solid interest and reputation of their country may discern at the very heart of their confederation, and will both advocate and enforce—a principle, of justice, conciliation and humanity—a principle, sir, which is not inconsistent with itself, and yet can sigh over the degradation of the slave, *defend the wisdom and prudence of the South against the charge of studied and pertinacious cruelty,*’ &c.—[Address of Robert F. Stockton, Esq. at the Eighth Annual Meeting of the Parent Society.]

‘ It is a fact, given us on the most unquestionable authority, that there are now in the southern States of our union, hundreds, and even thousands of proprietors, who would gladly give liberty to their slaves, but are deterred by the apprehension of doing injury to their country, and perhaps to the slaves themselves.’—[Discourse by the Rev. Dr. Dana.—African Repository, vol. i. p. 145.]

‘ Guarding that system, the existence of which, though *unfortunate,* THEY DEEM NECESSARY.’—[African Repository, vol. i. p. 227.]

‘ We all know from a variety of considerations which it is unnecessary to name, and in consequence of the policy which is obliged to be pursued in the southern States, that it is extremely difficult to free a slave, and hence the enactment of those laws *which a fatal necessity seems to demand.*’—[African Repository, vol. ii. p. 12.]

‘ They are convinced, that there are now hundreds of masters who are so only from *necessity.*’—[Memorial of the Society to the several States.—A. R. vol. ii. p. 60.]

'*I do not condemn,* let me be understood, *their detention in bondage* under the circumstances which are yet existing.'—['The Colonization Society Vindicated.'—Idem, vol. iii. p. 201.]

'A third point in which the first promoters of this object were united, is, that few individual slaveholders can, in the present state of things, emancipate their slaves if they would. There is a certain relation between the proprietor of slaves and the beings thus thrown upon him, which is far more complicated, and far less easily dissolved, than a mind unacquainted with the subject is ready to imagine. The relation is one which, where it exists, grows out of the very structure of society, and for the existence of which, the master is ordinarily as little accountable as the slave.'

'He [the planter] looks around him and sees that the condition of the great mass of emancipated Africans is one *in comparison with which the condition of his slaves is enviable ;*—and he is convinced that if he withdraws from his slaves his authority, his support, his protection, and leaves them to shift for themselves, he turns them out to be vagabonds, and paupers, and felons, and to find in the work-house and the penitentiary, the home which they ought to have retained on his paternal acres.—Hundreds of humane and Christian slaveholders retain their fellow-men in bondage, because *they are convinced that they can do no better.*'—[Address of the Managers of the Colonization Society of Connecticut.—Af. Rep. vol. iv. pp. 119, 120.]

'I AM NOT COMPLAINING OF THE OWNERS OF SLAVES ; they cannot get rid of them.—*I do not doubt that masters treat their slaves with kindness,* nor that the slaves are happier than they could be if set free in this country.'—[Address delivered before the Hampden Col. Soc., July 4th, 1828, by Wm. B. O. Peabody, Esq.]

'*Policy,* and even *the voice of humanity* forbade the progress of manumission ; and the *salutary hand of law* came forward to co-operate with our convictions, and to arrest the flow of our feelings, and the ardor of our desires.'—[Review of the Report of the Committee of Foreign Relations.—Af. Rep. vol. iv. p. 268.]

'When an owner of slaves tells me that he will freely relinquish his slaves, or even that he will relinquish one-half of their value, *on condition that he be compensated for the other half,* and provision be made for their transportation, I feel that he has made a generous proposal, and *I cannot charge him with all the guilt of slavery,* though he may continue to be a slaveholder.'—[Af. Rep. vol. v. p. 63.]

'Even slavery must be viewed as a great national calamity ; a public evil entailed upon us by untoward circumstances, *and perpetuated for the want of appropriate remedies.*'—[Idem, vol. v. p. 89.]

'Slavery is an evil which is entailed upon the present generation of slaveholders, which they must suffer, *whether they will or not.*'—[Idem, p. 179.]

'Our brethren of the South, have the same sympathies, the same moral sentiments, the same love of liberty as ourselves. By them as by us, slavery is felt to be an evil, a hindrance to our prosperity, and a blot upon our character. But it was in being when they were born, and has been forced upon them by a previous generation.'—[Address of Rev. Dr. Nott.—Idem, p. 277.]

'With a writer in the Southern Review we say, "the situation of the people of these States was not of their choosing. When they came to the inheritance, it was subject to this mighty incumbrance, and it would be criminal in them to ruin or waste the estate, to get rid of the burden at once." With this writer we add also, in the language of Captain Hall, that the " slaveholders ought not (immediately) to disentangle themselves from the obligations which have devolved upon them, as the masters of slaves." We believe that a master *may* sustain his relation to the slave, with as little criminality as the slave sustains his relation to the master.' * * * ' Slavery, in its mildest form, is an evil of the darkest character. Cruel and unnatural in its origin, no plea can be urged in justification of its continuance but the plea of *necessity.*'—[Af. Rep. vol. v. pp. 329, 334.]

' How much more consistent and powerful would be our example, but for that population within our limits, whose condition (*necessary* condition, I will not deny) is so much at war with our institutions, and with that memorable national Declaration—" that all men are created equal." '—[Fourteenth Ann. Report.]

' *It* [the Society] *condemns no man because he is a slaveholder.*' * * * ' They [abolitionists] confound the *misfortunes* of one generation with the *crimes* of another, and would sacrifice both individual and public good to an *unsubstantial theory of the rights of man.*'—[A. R. vol. vii. pp. 200, 202.]

' Many thousand individuals in our native State, you well know, Mr President, are restrained, said Mr Mercer, from manumitting their slaves, as you and I are, by the melancholy conviction, that they cannot yield to the suggestions of humanity, without manifest injury to their country.' * * * ' The laws of Virginia now discourage, and very wisely, perhaps, the emancipation of slaves.' —[Speech of Mr Mercer.—First Annual Report.]

' We are ready even to grant, for our present purpose, that, so far as mere animal existence is concerned, the slaves have no reason to complain, and the friends of humanity have no reason to complain for them.' * * * ' There are men in the southern states, who long to do something effectual for the benefit of their slaves, and would gladly emancipate them, did not *prudence* and *compassion* alike forbid such a measure.'—[Review of the Reports of the Society, from the Christian Spectator.—Seventh Annual Report.]

' Such unhappily is the case ; but there is a *necessity* for it, [for oppressive laws,] and so long as they remain amongst us will that necessity continue.'— [Ninth Annual Report.]

' I MAY BE PERMITTED TO DECLARE THAT I WOULD BE A SLAVE-HOLDER TO-DAY WITHOUT SCRUPLE.'—[Fourteenth Annual Report.]

' For the existence of slavery in the United States, those, and those only, are accountable who bore a part in originating such a constitution of society. The bible contains no explicit prohibition of slavery. There is neither chapter nor verse of holy writ, which lends any countenance to the fulminating spirit of universal emancipation, of which some exhibitions may be seen in some of the newspapers.' * * * ' The embarrassment which many a philanthropic proprietor has felt in relation to his slaves, has been but little known at the north, and has had but little sympathy. He finds himself the lord of perhaps a hundred human beings ; and is anxious to do them all the good in his power. He would emancipate them ; but if he does, their prospect of happiness can hardly be said to be improved by the change. Some half a dozen, perhaps, in the hundred, become industrious and useful members of society ; and the rest are mere vagabonds, idle, wicked, and miserable.' —[Review on African Colonization.—Vide the Christian Spectator for September, 1830, in which the reader will find an elaborate apology for the system of slavery, and this, too, by a clergyman !]

' The existence of slavery among us, though not at all to be objected to our southern brethren as a *fault*, is yet a blot on our national character, and a mighty drawback from our national strength.'—[Second Annual Report of the N. Y. State Col. Soc.]

' Entertaining these views of this fearful subject, why should our opponents endeavor to prejudice our cause with our southern friends ? And we are the more anxious on this point, for we sincerely entertain exalted notions of their sense of right, of their manliness and independence of feeling—of their dignity of deportment—of their honorable and chivalric turn of thought, which spurns a mean act as death. And if I was allowed to indulge a personal feeling, I would say that there is something to my mind in the candor, hospitality and intelligence of the South, which charms and captives, which wins its way to the heart and gives assurance of all that is upright, honorable, and humane. There is no people that treat their slaves with so little cruelty and with so much kindness. There is nothing in the condition of slavery more congenial with the feelings of the South than with the feelings of the North. Philanthropy and benevolence flourish with as much vigor with them as with us—their hearts are as warm as ours—they feel for the distresses of others with as much acuteness as we do—their ears are as open to the calls of charity as ours—they as deeply regret as we do the existence of slavery—and oh ! how their hearts would thrill with delight, if the mighty incubus could be removed without injury or destruction to every thing around them.'—[Speech of James S. Green, Esq. on the same occasion.]

' Many of the best citizens of our land are holders of slaves, and hold them IN STRICT ACCORDANCE WITH THE PRINCIPLES OF HUMANITY AND JUSTICE.'—[Rev. Thomas T. Skillman, editor of the Western Luminary, an ardent supporter of the Col. Soc.]

'It is a very common impression that a principal evil of the condition of the southern blacks, is the severity of their treatment. THIS IS AN ERROR. It is almost every where disreputable to treat slaves with severity ; and though there are indeed exceptions, yet in most cases in the South, even tyranny itself could not long withstand the reproaches of public opinion. A STILL GREATER AND MORE DANGEROUS EVIL, IS THE VERY REVERSE. It is *indulgence;* not only in such things as are proper and innocent, but in indolent habits and vicious propensities.'
—[From an address prepared for the use of those who advocate the cause of the African Education Society at Washington—a Society which educates none but those who consent to remove to Liberia.]

' How should a benevolent Virginian, in view of the fact, that out of thirty-seven thousand free people of color in his State, only two hundred were proprietors of land, how should he be in favor of general emancipation ? But, show him, that if he will emancipate his slaves, there is a way in which he can without doubt improve their condition, while he rids himself of a grievous burden, and he will promptly obey the demands of justice—he will then feel that his generous wishes can with certainty be fulfilled. While he knows that scarcely any thing is done to meliorate the condition of those now free, and reflects on the many obstacles in the way of doing it in this land, he feels bound by a regard to what he owes himself—his children—his country, and even his slaves themselves, not to emancipate them. For he is sure, that, by emancipation, he will only add to the wretchedness of the one, and at the same time put at imminent hazard the dearest interests of the other. Thus he is forced to refrain from manumission, and not only so, but against all his benevolent inclinations, he is forced to co-operate with his fellow-citizens in sustaining the present system of slavery. He would most cheerfully follow the impulse of his noblest feelings —he would remove the curse which the short-sighted policy of his fathers entailed upon him ; but he cannot disregard the first law of nature ; especially not, when, were he to do it, he would render the *curse* still more calamitous in its consequences.'—[An advocate of the Colonization Society in the Middletown (Connecticut) Gazette.]

'Slavery is indeed a curse; and bitter is the lot of him who is born with slaves on his hands. And now, instead of denouncing as inhuman and unmerciful monsters and tyrants, those who are thus *unfortunate,* I say, let the commiseration and pity of every good citizen and christian in the land be excited, and let fervent prayers be offered in their behalf, and that God would direct the whole American mind to the adoption of the most effectual measures for the accomplishment of the total abolition of slavery.'—[New-Haven Religious Intelligencer for July 16, 1831.]

'Special reference will also be had to the condition and wishes of the slave States. In most of them it is a prevailing sentiment, that it is not safe to furnish slaves with the means of instruction. Much as we lament the reasons for this sentiment, and the *apparent necessity* of keeping a single fellow creature in ignorance, we willingly leave to others the consideration and the remedy of this evil, in view of the overwhelming magnitude of the remaining objects before us. —[Address of the Board of Managers of the African Education Society of the United States.]

'And when we [of New-England] did emancipate our slaves, we were driven to the measure by the force of example ; and we did not do it until it was found quite convenient ; and then what provision was made for the poor blacks ? Let our State Prison records answer the question. Our Southern brethren have been *more kind :* they will not emancipate them until they send them where they can enjoy *liberty,* more than in name. As a Northern man I feel it my duty, and I take pleasure in giving the *meed of praise* to my Southern brethren.'— [Speech of Rev. Mr Gallaudet, at a colonization meeting in New-York city.]

'The slave works for his master, who feeds and clothes him, defends him from harm, and takes care of him when he is sick. The free colored man works for himself, and has nobody to take care of him but himself.' —[From a little colonization work, published in Baltimore in 1828, 'for the use of the African Schools in the United States' ! ! ˉ entitled 'A Voice from Africa.']

'The slaveholder will tell you, that he did not take liberty from the African— he was a slave when he found him, and he is no more than a slave yet. The man who owns one hundred acres of land more than he can cultivate himself, is as much a slaveholder as he who owns a slave.'—[An advocate of colonization in the Richmond (Indiana) Palladium for Oct. 1, 1831.]

'I DO NOT MEAN TO SPEAK OF SLAVERY AS A SYSTEM OF CRUELTY AND OF SUFFERING. On this point I am free to say, from personal observation and occasional residences for some years at the South, there has been much misapprehension among our fellow-citizens of the North. And I rejoice to add, that *the condition of the slaves generally is such as the friends of humanity have no reason to complain of.'*—[Oration delivered at Newark, N. J. July 4th, 1831, by Gabriel P. Disosway, Esq.]

'Slavery, it is true, is an evil—a national evil. Every laudable effort to exterminate it should be encouraged. And we presume that nine-tenths of the slaveholders themselves, would rejoice at the event, could it be accomplished, of the entire freedom from the country of every person of color, and would willingly relinquish every slave in their possession. But the slaves *are* in their possession—they are entailed upon them by their ancestors. And can they set them free, and still suffer them to remain in the country ? Would this be policy ? Would it be safe ? No. When they can be transported to the soil from whence they were derived—by the aid of the Colonization Society, by Government, by individuals, or by any other means—then let them be emancipated, and not before.'—[Lowell (Mass.) Telegraph.]

It is a self-evident proposition, that just so far as you alleviate the pressure of guilt upon the consciences of evil doers, you weaken the power of motive to repent, and encourage them to sin with impunity. To descant upon the wrongs of the slave-system, and yet exonerate the supporters of it from reprehension, is to deal in absurdities : we might preach in this manner until the crack of doom, and never gain a convert. Paradoxes may amuse, but they never convince the mind.

Now, I defy the most ingenious advocates of perpetual slavery to produce stronger arguments in its favor than are given in the foregoing extracts. What better plea could they make ? what higher justification could they need ? Nay, these apologies of colonizationists represent oppression not merely as innocent, but even commendable—as a system of benevolence, upheld by philanthropists and sages !

' I do not condemn the detention of the slaves in bondage under the circumstances which are yet existing,' says an advocate ; by which consolatory avowal we are taught that the criminality of man-stealing depends upon *circumstances*, and not upon the fact that it is a daring violation of the rights of man and the laws of God.

' The planter sees that the condition of the great mass of emancipated Africans is one, in comparison with which the condition of his slaves is *enviable*,' assert the Board of Managers !—a concession which transforms robbery into generosity, cruelty into mercy, and leads the slaveholder to believe that, instead of deserving censure, his conduct is really meritorious ! —a concession which is at war with common sense, and contrary to truth.

' I am not complaining of the owners of slaves—I do not doubt that the slaves are happier than they could be if set free in this country,' declares an apologist, even in Massachusetts ! Stripes and servitude would doubtless soon alter his opinion. With him, to sell human beings at public auction, and to separate husbands and wives, and children and parents, is not a subject of complaint ! and to be a slave, to be fed upon a peck of corn per week, unable to possess property, liable to be torn from the partner of his bosom and children at a moment's warn-

ing, mal-treated worse than a brute, &c. &c. &c. is more desirable than to be a free man, able to acquire wealth, unrestricted
in his movements, from whom none may wrest his wife or children, and who can find redress for any outrage upon his person
or property !

' Policy, and even *humanity,*' cries another, 'forbid the progress of manumission ' ! Indeed ! But is it right to hold our
fellow creatures as chattels, and to perpetuate their ignorance
and servitude ? O no ! this is *wrong*, but it would be a greater
wrong to emancipate them ! Is this folly or villany ? To oppress our brother is wrong, but to cease from oppressing him
would not be right !

' I would be a slaveholder to-day without scruple,' says
another advocate.

' Many owners of slaves,' another declares, ' hold them
in strict accordance with the principles of humanity and justice ' ! ! ! Yes, to deprive men of their inalienable rights is to
do unto them as we would have them do unto us !

Finally, another boldly declares that the slaves are treated
too indulgently !—The laws which regard them as beasts, but
punish them for the commission of crime as severely as if they
possessed the knowledge of angels, he must suppose are too
lenient. Their allowance of corn is too liberal ; they ought not
to wear any raiment ; to sleep in their wretched huts is calculated to make them effeminate—the open field is a more suitable place for cattle ; no religious instruction should be granted
even orally to them ! The slaves, as a body, too kindly treated !
The Lord have compassion upon any of their number who shall
come under the control of him who holds this opinion !

Sentiments, like these, act upon the consciences of slave
owners like opiates upon the body, lulling them into a slumber
as profound and fatal as death. It were almost as hopeless a
task to attempt to arouse, alarm and animate them, so long as
they repose under the stupefying effects of this poison, as to
raise the dead. This must not be. Slaveholders are the enemies of God and man ; their garments are red with the blood
of souls ; their guilt is aggravated beyond the power of language
to describe ; and they must be made to see and realise their

awful condition.   Truth must send its arrows into their consciences, and Terror rouse them to exertion, and Conviction
bring them upon their knees, and Repentance propitiate the anger
of Heaven, or they perish by the sword.   The slaves must be
free ;   and He who is no respecter of person is now holding out
to us this alternative—either to wait until they burst their chains
and wade through a river of blood to freedom, or to liberate
them willingly ourselves.   Can we hesitate in our choice ?   Be
this our only reply to those who apologise for the oppressors,
and fix the standard of policy higher than that of duty : ' Wo
unto them that call evil good, and good evil ; that put darkness
for light, and light for darkness ; that put bitter for sweet, and
sweet for bitter !   Wo unto them that are wise in their own
eyes, and prudent in their own sight !' which justify the wicked
for reward, and take away the righteousness of the righteous
from him !'

———

SECTION III.

THE AMERICAN COLONIZATION SOCIETY RECOGNISES SLAVES AS PROPERTY.

THE heresies of this combination are flagrant and numerous.
A larger volume than this is needed to define and illustrate them
all.   Much important evidence, and many pertinent reflections,
I am compelled to suppress.

My next allegation against it is, *that it recognises slaves as
property*.   This recognition is not merely technical, or strictly
confined to a statutable interpretation.   I presume the advocates of the Society will attempt to evade this point, by saying
that it never meant to concede the moral right of the masters to
possess human beings ; but the evidence against them is full and
explicit.   The Society, if language mean any thing, does unequivocally acknowledge property in slaves to be as legitimate
and sacred as any other property, of which to deprive the owners either by force or by legislation, without making restitution,
would be unjust and tyrannical.   Here is the proof :

' It interferes in no wise with the *rights of property.*' * * 'It is utterly opposed to any measures which might infringe upon the *rights of property.*' * * 'We hold their slaves *as we hold their other property,* SACRED.'— [African Repository, vol. i. pp. 39, 225, 283.]

' Does this Society wish to meddle with our slaves as our *rightful property*? I answer *no,* I think not.' * * 'The Society cannot be justly charged with aiming to disturb the *rights of property* or the peace of society.' * * 'It seeks to affect no man's *property.*' * * 'To found in Africa, an empire of *christians and republicans;* to reconduct the blacks to their native land, without disturbing the order of society, the *laws of property,* or the rights of individuals,' &c.—[African Repository, vol. ii. pp. 13, 58, 334, 375.]

' They are also convinced, that the Society have conducted their operations with so much prudence, as to give no cause of alarm to the holders of slaves, for the security of *this property.*'—[African Repository, volume iii. p. 341.]

' The rights of masters are to remain sacred in the eyes of the Society.'—[African Repository, vol. iv. p. 274.]

' The Society has never interfered, and has no disposition to interfere with the rights of private property.' * * 'The alarm for the rights of property appears to have subsided, and the Society is no longer charged with any sinister or insidious design. It has constantly disclaimed any intention of disturbing the rights of others; and its conduct entitles its declaration to credit.' * * 'The American Colonization Society has, at all times, solemnly disavowed any purpose of interference with the institutions or rights of our Southern communities.' * * 'Our friends, who are cursed with this greatest of human evils (slavery) deserve our kindest attention and consideration. Their *property* and safety are both involved.'—[African Repository, vol. v. pp. 215, 241, 307, 334.]

' It has constantly disclaimed all intention whatever of interfering, in the smallest degree, with the rights of property.' * * 'The Society, from considerations like these, whilst it disclaims the remotest idea of ever disturbing the *right of property* in slaves,' &c. * * 'It is not the object of this Society to liberate slaves, or touch the rights of *property.*' * * 'Honorable instances might be adduced of *disinterested benevolence* on the part of the owners of slaves, and of their *sacrificing property* to a large amount, in their enfranchisement and restoration to the land of their ancestors.' * * 'The American Society has disclaimed from the first moment of its institution, all intention of interfering with *rights of property.*' * * 'The federal government has no control over this subject : it concerns rights of property secured by the federal compact, upon which our civil liberties mainly depend ; it is a part of the same collection of political rights ; and *any invasion of it would impair the tenure by which every other is held.*' * * 'It is equally plain and undeniable, that the Society in the prosecution of this work, has never interfered or evinced even a disposition to interfere in any way with the *rights of proprietors of slaves.*' * * 'The slaveholder, so far from having just cause to complain of the Colonization Society, has reason to congratulate himself, that in this Institution a channel is opened up, in which the public feeling and public action can flow on, without doing violence to his *rights.*'—[African Repository, vol. vi. pp. 13, 69, 81, 153, 165, 169, 205, 363.]

' It was proper again and again to repeat, that it was far from the intention of the Society to affect, in any manner, the tenure by which a certain *species of property* is held. He was himself a slaveholder ; *and he considered that kind of property as inviolable as any other in the country.*'—[Speech of Henry Clay.—First Annual Report.]

' Your committee would not thus favorably regard the prayer of the memorialists, if it sought to impair, *in the slightest degree,* the *rights of private property.*'—[Report of the committee of the House of Representatives of the United States, on the memorial of the President and Board of Managers of the Colonization Society.—Second Annual Report.]

' The Society has at all times recognised the constitutional and LEGITIMATE existence of slavery.'—[Tenth Annual Report.]

' The Society protests that it has no designs on the rights of the master in the slave—or the property in his slave, which the laws guarantee to him.'—[Fourteenth Annual Report.]

' Something he must yet be allowed to say, as regarded the object the Society was set up to accomplish. This object, if he understood it aright, *involved no intrusion on property,* NOR EVEN UPON PREJUDICE.'—[Fifteenth Annual Report.]

' To the slaveholder, who had charged upon them the wicked design of interfering with the RIGHTS OF PROPERTY under the specious pretext of removing a vicious and dangerous free population, they address themselves in a tone of conciliation and sympathy. We know your rights, say they, *and we respect them.*' * * ' Equally absurd and false is the objection, that this Society seeks indirectly to disturb the rights of property, and to interfere with the well established relation subsisting between master and slave.'—[African Repository, vol. vii. pp. 100, 228.]

' I repeat, that though not a slaveholder, yet I think that every man ought to be protected in his property, and as the laws of our country have decreed that negroes are property, every person that holds a slave, according to these laws, ought to be protected.'—[' A new and interesting View of Slavery.' By Humanitas, a colonization advocate. Baltimore, 1820.]

' We are made to disregard this description of *property,* and to touch without reserve the *rights* of our neighbors.'—[Proceedings of the First Annual Meeting of the New-Jersey Colonization Society.]

Thus the American Colonization Society shamelessly surrenders the claims of justice, and leaves the enemies of oppression weaponless ! Hence it rejects the proposition, that *man cannot hold property in man ;* and we are called upon to prove that which is self-evident. No accidental differences of condition or complexion—no vicissitudes of fortune—no reprisal or purchase or inheritance, can justly make one individual the slave of another. When God created man, he gave him dominion over the fowls of the air and the beasts of the field ; but not over his fellow man. ' All men are born free and equal,' and are ' made of one blood.' Shall we look to wealth as giving one a title to the labor and freedom of another ? Wealth is the creature of circumstances, and not an arbitrary law of nature. It takes to itself wings, and flies away ; and he who is an opulent tyrant to-day, may on this principle be an impoverished slave to-morrow. Does physical strength make valid this claim ? This, too, is evanescent : sickness and age would ultimately degrade the most muscular tyrants to servitude ; and mankind would be composed of but two parties—the strong and the weak. Can high birth annul the rights of the lower classes ? There is no difference at their birth, between the children of the beggar and those of the king. ' We brought nothing into this world,' says an inspired apostle, ' and it is certain we can carry nothing out.'

Man is created a rational being ; and therefore he is a subject of moral government, and accountable. Being rational and accountable, he is bound to improve his mind and intellect. With this design, his Creator has outstretched the heavens, and set the sun in his course, and hung out the burning jewels of the sky, and spread abroad the green earth, and poured out the seas, that he might steadily progress in knowledge.

The slaves are men ; they were born, then, as free as their masters ; they cannot be property ; and he who denies them an opportunity to improve their faculties, comes into collision with Jehovah, and incurs a fearful responsibility. But we know that they are not treated like rational beings, and that oppression almost entirely obliterates their sense of moral obligation to God or man.

I fully coincide in opinion with the authoress of a work entitled, ' IMMEDIATE, NOT GRADUAL ABOLITION,' that the holder of a slave, whether he obtained him by purchase or by inheritance, is as guilty as the original thief.* The wretch who stole him could by no possible means acquire or transmit the right to make a slave of him, or to keep him in slavery. *He has a right to his liberty :*—through whatever number of transfers the usurpation of it may have passed, the right is undiminished.

---

* The owners of slaves are licensed robbers, and not the just proprietors of what they claim : freeing them is not depriving them of property, but restoring it to the right owner ; it is suffering the unlawful captive to escape. It is not wronging the master, but doing justice to the slave, restoring him to himself. Emancipation would only take away property that is its own property, and not ours ; property that has the same right to possess us, as we have to possess it ; property that has the same right to convert our children into dogs and calves and colts, as we have to convert theirs into these beasts ; property that may transfer our children to strangers, by the same right that we transfer theirs.— *Rice.*

No man, says Algernon Sidney, can have a right over others, unless it be by them granted to him : That which is not just, is not law ; and that which is not law, ought not to be in force : Whosoever grounds his pretensions of right upon usurpation and tyranny, declares himself to be an usurper and a tyrant—that is, an enemy to God and man—and to have no right at all : *That which was unjust in its beginning, can of itself never change its nature :* He who persists in doing injustice, aggravates it, and takes upon himself all the guilt of his predecessors : The right to be free is a truth planted in the hearts of men, and acknowledged so to be by all who have hearkened to the voice of nature, and disproved by none but such as through wickedness, stupidity, or baseness of spirit, seem to have degenerated into the worst of beasts, and to have retained nothing of men but the outward shape, or the ability of doing those mischiefs which they have learnt from their master the devil.

The following is the indignant, emphatic, eloquent language of Henry Brougham, on the subject of slave property :

'*Tell me not of rights—talk not of the property of the planter in his slaves.* I deny the right—I acknowledge not the property. The principles, the feelings of our common nature, rise in rebellion against it. Be the appeal made to the understanding or to the heart, the sentence is the same that rejects it. In vain you tell me of the laws that sanction such a claim ! There is a law above all the enactments of human codes—the same throughout the world, the same in all times—such as it was before the daring genius of Columbus pierced the night of ages, and opened to one world the sources of power, wealth and knowledge ; to another, all unutterable woes ;— such it is at this day : it is the law written by the finger of God on the heart of man ; and by that law, unchangeable and eternal, while men despise fraud, and loathe rapine, and abhor blood, they shall reject with indignation the wild and guilty fantasy, that man can hold property in man ! In vain you appeal to treaties, to covenants between nations. The covenants of the Almighty, whether the old or the new, denounce such unholy pretensions. To those laws did they of old refer, who maintained the African trade. Such treaties did they cite, and not untruly ; for by one shameful compact, you bartered the glories of Blenheim for the traffic in blood. Yet, in despite of law and of treaties, that infernal traffic is now destroyed, and its votaries put to death like other pirates. How came this change to pass ? Not assuredly by parliament leading the way ; but the country at length awoke ; the indignation of the people was kindled ; it descended in thunder, and smote the traffic, and scattered its guilty profits to the winds. Now, then, let the planters beware—let their assemblies beware—let the government at home beware—let the parliament beware ! the same country is once more awake,—awake to the condition of negro slavery ; the same indignation kindles in the bosom of the same people ; the same cloud is gathering that annihilated the slave trade ; and, if it shall descend again, they, on whom its crash shall fall, will not be destroyed before I have warned them ; but I pray that their destruction may turn away from us the more terrible judgments of God !'

Is this the language of fanaticism ? Is Henry Brougham a madman ?

The following extracts must close the evidence in support of my third allegation, that the Colonization Society disregards the fundamental principle of human liberty and equality, that man cannot hold *property* in man :

' Let me ask, who can wish under existing circumstances that the constitution should be altered, when it must bring with it a *violation* of *property*—and when that violation of private property must engender such hostility of feelings, and elicit such bitter vituperation ? The whole Union would feel a concussion, and no one can count the costs of the contest.' * * * ' By means of our colony, they may remove their slaves and restore them to freedom—and at the same time no way jeopardize the safety of themselves or their *property*.'—[Proceedings of the First Annual Meeting of the New-Jersey Colonization Society.]

' The establishment of our colony will afford facilities to proprietors for completing in Africa the exercise of the *right which can only be partially exercised in this country, of disposing of our property, in our own way, without injury to the community.*'—[Fourteenth Annual Report.]

What audacity do those advocates of the Society exhibit, who use, in reference to beings made a little lower than the angels, language like this—' disposing of *our property* in *our own way* '—' we hold their *slaves*, as we hold their other *property*, sacred ' ! ! * If they really mean and believe what they say, it is something more heinous than impertinence to urge the planters to dispossess themselves of their property by colonization ; and if the slaves belong *of right* to them,—are on a par with goods and chattels,—how idle, how supremely ridiculous it is to mourn over their *wretched condition*, to sigh for their emancipation, to declaim against the evil and wickedness of slavery, or even to denounce the slave trade ! But the unfortunate blacks are not now, and never can be, the property of the planters ; consequently the claims of their pretended owners are no better than those of the pirate or highway robber.

---

* Is there no difference between a vested interest in a house or a tenement, and a vested interest in a human being ? No difference between a right to bricks and mortar, and a right to the flesh of man—a right to torture his body and to degrade his mind at your good will and pleasure ? There is this difference,— the right to the house originates in law, and is reconcilable to justice ; the claim (for I will not call it a right) to the man, originated in robbery, and is an outrage upon every principle of justice, and every tenet of religion.'—*Speech of Fowell Buxton in the British Parliament.*

SECTION IV.

THE AMERICAN COLONIZATION SOCIETY INCREASES THE VALUE OF SLAVES.

I come now to my fourth charge,—which, although not more serious or consequential than any of the foregoing, may possibly create more surprise,—namely, that the Society *increases the value of slaves, and adds strength and security to the system of slavery.* It is the discovery of this fact that is so wonderfully, and to many superficial observers so inexplicably, increasing the popularity of the Society at the south. It would require more pages of this work than its necessarily contracted limits permit, to sum up minutely the evidence on this point, and to give those illustrations which might serve more clearly to establish its validity. The most common, as it is the most potent, argument used by colonization agents among slave owners, to secure their patronage, is,—' The successful prosecution of our scheme will remove the chief source of danger to yourselves, and enable you to hold your property in greater security : the presence of free persons of color among your slaves is eminently calculated to make them insubordinate, and to procure their violent emancipation.' This argument, I say, is introduced into every conversation, and every public address, and every essay ; and whoever carefully consults the numbers of the African Repository, through seven volumes, will find it repeated in almost every appeal to the south.

I choose to consider the testimony of southern men, in regard to the invigorating effects of the colonization enterprise upon the system of slavery, conclusive. Here is a very small portion of it: more may be found under the sixth section of this work.

' The object of the Colonization Society commends itself to every class of society. The landed proprietor may ENHANCE THE VALUE OF HIS PROPERTY by assisting the enterprise.'—[African Repository, vol. i. p. 67.]

' But is it not certain, that should the people of the Southern States refuse to adopt the opinions of the Colonization Society, [relative to the gradual abolition of slavery,] and continue to consider it both just and politic to leave, untouched, a system, for the termination of which, we think the whole wisdom and energy of the States should be put in requisition, that they will CONTRIBUTE MORE EFFECTUALLY TO THE CONTINUANCE AND STRENGTH OF THIS SYSTEM, by removing those now free, than by any or all other methods which can possibly be devised ? Such has been the opinion expressed by Southern gentlemen of the first talents and distinction.   Eminent individuals have, we doubt not, lent their aid to this cause, in expectation of at once accomplishing a generous and noble work for the objects of their patronage and for Africa, and GUARDING THAT SYSTEM, the existence of which, though *unfortunate,* they deem *necessary,* by separating from it those, whose disturbing force augments its inherent vices, and darkens all the repulsive attributes of its character. In the decision of these individuals, as to the effects of the Colonization Society, *we perceive no error of judgment :* OUR BELIEF IS THE SAME AS THEIRS.'—[Idem, p. 227.]

'THE EXECUTION OF ITS SCHEME WOULD AUGMENT INSTEAD OF DIMINISHING THE VALUE OF THE PROPERTY LEFT BEHIND.' —[Idem, vol. ii. p. 344.]

'The removal of every single free black in America, would be productive of nothing but safety to the slaveholder, nor would the emancipation of as many as the benevolence of individual masters would send off, as far as I can see, be productive of disaffection among the remainder, more than the example of such as are every day set free, and sent to the Ohio or elsewhere ; and if so large a part should ever be set free as to create discontent among the remainder, (and nothing but the emancipation of a great majority can do this,) yet that remainder must then, from the terms of the proposition, be so much diminished, as to be easily kept down by superior numbers.'—[Idem, vol. iii. p. 202.]

'The tendency of the scheme, and one of its objects, is to *secure slaveholders and the whole Southern country,* against certain evil consequences, growing out of the present threefold mixture of our population.'—[Idem, vol. iv. p. 274.]

'We all know the effects produced on our slaves by the fascinating, but delusive appearance of happiness, exhibited in persons of their own complexion, roaming in idleness and vice among them.   By removing the most fruitful source of discontent from among our slaves, we should render them more industrious and attentive to our commands ; and by rendering them more industrious and obedient, we should naturally secure their better treatment—we should ameliorate their condition.   Our enemies have admitted that good would result from the removal of this class.   Caius Gracchus declares, that if the Society could attain " this single object in good faith, (the removal of the free people of color) he should, perhaps, be among the last citizens in the commonwealth—who would raise his voice against it," and the author of the CRISIS (who is doubtless regarded as authority in South Carolina) acknowledges, " that there is no doubt but that if we in the South, were relieved of this population, it would be better for our southern cities, where they principally reside."   Nothing can be more plain then, than that the Colonization Society, in its efforts to remove the free people of color, is accomplishing a work to which the citizens of the South, whether friends or foes to the Society, have given their decided approbation.'— [Idem, vol. vi. p. 205.]

'If, as is most confidently believed, the colonization of the free people of color will render the slave who remains in America more obedient, more faithful, more honest, and, consequently, *more useful to his master,'* &c.—[Second Annual Report.]

' There was but one way, [to avert danger,] but that might be made effectual, fortunately ! It was to PROVIDE AND KEEP OPEN A DRAIN FOR THE EXCESS BEYOND THE OCCASIONS OF PROFITABLE EMPLOYMENT. Mr Archer had been stating the case in the supposition, that after the present class of free blacks had been exhausted, by the operation of the plan he was recommending, others would be supplied for its action, in the proportion of the excess of colored population it would be necessary to throw off, by the process of voluntary manumission or sale. This effect must result inevitably from the depreciating value of the slaves ensuing their disproportionate multiplication. *The depreciation would be relieved and retarded at the same time, by the process.* The two operations would aid reciprocally, and sustain each other, and both be in the highest degree beneficial. It was on the ground of interest, therefore, the most indisputable *pecuniary interest*, that he addressed himself to the people and Legislatures of the slaveholding States.'—[Speech of Mr Archer.—Fifteenth Annual Report.]

' Every motive which operates on the minds of slaveholders, tending to make the colonization of the free blacks an object of *interest* to them, should operate in an equal degree to secure the hearty co-operation of the government of every slaveholding State.'—[African Repository, vol. vii. p. 176.}

' None are obliged to follow our example ; AND THOSE WHO DO NOT, WILL FIND THE VALUE OF THEIR NEGROES INCREASED BY THE DEPARTURE OF OURS.'—[An advocate of colonization in the Western (Ky.) Luminary.]

' So far from its having a dangerous tendency, when properly considered, it will be viewed as AN ADDITIONAL GUARD TO OUR PECULIAR SPECIES OF PROPERTY.'—[An advocate of the Society in the New-Orleans Argus.]

' The slaveholder, who is in danger of having his slaves contaminated by their free friends of color, will not only be relieved from this danger, but THE VALUE OF HIS SLAVE WILL BE ENHANCED.'—[A new and interesting View of Slavery. By Humanitas, a colonization advocate. Baltimore, 1820.]

It is perfectly obvious, that whatever tends to weaken and depress the present system, must render the holding of slaves less desirable, and the prospect of emancipation more auspicious. Cherishing this conviction, thousands of individuals in this country, and tens of thousands in Great Britain, are led by conscientious motives to abstain from the use of productions raised by slave labor, and to prefer those only which are the fruits of the toil of freemen. They believe in the soundness of the axiom, that ' the receiver is as bad as the thief ;' and knowing that the slaves are held in bondage not on the ground of benevolence, or because their liberation would endanger the public safety, but *because they are profitable to their owners*, they also believe that the consumers of slave goods contribute to a fund for supporting slavery with all its abominations ; that they are the Alpha and the Omega of the business ; that the slave-trader, the slave-owner, and the slave-driver, are virtually the agents of the consumer, for by holding out the temptation, he is the original cause, the first mover in the horrid process ; that we are imperiously called upon to refuse those articles of luxury, which are obtained at an absolute and lavish waste of the blood of our fellow men ; that a merchant, who loads his vessel with the proceeds of slavery, does nearly as much in helping forward the slave trade, as he who loads his vessel in Africa with slaves—they are both twisting the same rope at different ends ; that our patronage is putting an immense bribe into the hands of the slaveholders to kidnap, rob and oppress ; that, were it not for this, they would be compelled by sheer necessity to liberate their slaves—for as soon as slave labor becomes unprofitable, the horrid system cannot be upheld.

None of these scruples, to my knowledge, are entertained by colonizationists : their only aim and anxiety seem to be, ' to prune and nourish the system,—not to overthrow it ; to increase the avarice of the planters by rendering the labor of their bondmen more productive,—not to abridge and starve it ; to remove the cause of those apprehensions which might lead them to break the fetters of their victims,—not to perpetuate it ; ' to provide (I quote the confession of the last distinguished proselyte to the Society, Mr Archer of Virginia) and to keep open a drain for the *excess of increase beyond the occasions of* PROFITABLE EMPLOYMENT,'—not to make slave labor ruinous to the planters.

By removing whatever number of slaves it be, from this country, the number which remains must be diminished—and the more the number which remains is diminished, the more helpless will they become, the less will be the hope of their ever recovering their own liberty, and the more and the longer they will be trampled upon.

The greater the number of slaves transported, *the greater will be the value of the labor of those who remain ;* the more valuable their labor is, *the greater will be the temptation to over-labor them, and the more, of course, they will be oppressed.**

---

* Stuart's Circular.

The increase of the free colored population disturbs the security of the planters, and forces many to manumit their slaves through sheer terror.   The expatriation of this class, therefore, manifestly tends to quiet the apprehensions of the oppressors, to rivet more firmly the chains of the slaves, to make their services in higher demand, and to render even their gradual emancipation impracticable.

Thus the American Colonization Society is the *apologist*, the *friend*, and the *patron* of SLAVEHOLDERS and SLAVERY !

SECTION V.

THE AMERICAN COLONIZATION SOCIETY IS THE ENEMY OF IMMEDIATE ABOLITION.

It follows, as a necessary consequence, that a Society which is not hostile to slavery, which apologises for the system and for slaveholders, which recognises slaves as rightful property,* and which confessedly increases their value, is *the enemy of immediate abolition.*   This, I am aware, in the present corrupt state of public sentiment, will not generally be deemed an objectionable feature ; but I regard it with inexpressible abhorrence and dismay.

----

* The slaves, they say, are their *property*. Once admit this, and all your arguments for interference are vain, and all your plans for amelioration are fruitless. The whole question may be said to hang upon this point. If the slaves are not property, then slavery is at an end. The slaveholders see this most clearly ; they see that while you allow these slaves to be their *property*, you act inconsistently and oppressively in intermeddling, as you propose to do, with what is theirs as much as any other of their goods and chattels : you must proceed, therefore, in your measures for amelioration, as you call it, with ' hesitating steps and slow ;' and there is nothing you can do for restraining punishment, for regulating labor, for enforcing manumission, for introducing education and Christianity, which will not be met with the remonstrance, undeniably just by your own concessions, that you are encroaching on the sacred rights of property,—the slaveholders see all this, and they can employ it to paralyse and defeat all your efforts to get at emancipation, and to prepare for it. It is on this account, that I wish it settled in your minds, as a fixed and immutable principle, that there is and can be no property of man in man. Adopt this principle, and give it that ascendency over your minds to which it is entitled ;—and slavery is swept away.— *Speech of Rev. Dr Thomson of Edinburgh.*

Since the deception practised upon our first parents by the old serpent, there has not been a more fatal delusion in the minds of men than that of the gradual abolition of slavery. *Gradual* abolition ! do its supporters really know what they talk about ? Gradually abstaining from what ? From sins the most flagrant, from conduct the most cruel, from acts the most oppressive ! Do colonizationists mean, that slave-dealers shall purchase or sell a few victims less this year than they did the last ? that slave-owners shall liberate one, two or three out of every hundred slaves during the same period ? that slave-drivers shall apply the lash to the scarred and bleeding backs of their victims somewhat less frequently ? Surely not—I respect their intelligence too much to believe that they mean any such thing. But if any of the slaves should be exempted from sale or purchase, why not all ? if justice require the liberation of the few, why not of the many ? if it be right for a driver to inflict a number of lashes, how many shall be given ? Do colonizationists mean that the practice of separating the husband from the wife, the wife from the husband, or children from their parents, shall come to an end by an almost imperceptible process ? or that the slaves shall be defrauded of their just remuneration, less and less every month or every year ? or that they shall be under the absolute, irresponsible control of 'their masters ? Oh no ! I place a higher value upon their good sense, humanity and morality than this ! Well, then, they would immediately break up the slave traffic—they would put aside the whip—they would have the marriage relations preserved inviolate—they would not separate families—they would not steal the wages of the slaves, nor deprive them of personal liberty ! This is abolition—*immediate abolition.* It is simply declaring that slave owners are bound to fulfil—now, without any reluctance or delay—the golden rule, namely, to do as they would be done by ; and that, as the right to be free is inherent and inalienable in the slaves, there ought now to be a disposition on the part of the people to break their fetters. All the horrid spectres which are conjured up, on this subject, arise from a confusion of the brain, as much as from a corruption of the heart.

I utterly reject, as delusive and dangerous in the extreme, every plea which justifies a procrastinated and an indefinite emancipation, or which concedes to a slave owner the right to hold his slaves as *property* for any limited period, or which contends for the gradual preparation of the slaves for freedom ; believing all such pretexts to be a fatal departure from the high road of justice into the bogs of expediency, a surrender of the great principles of equity, an indefensible prolongation of the curse of slavery, a concession which places the guilt upon any but those who incur it, and directly calculated to perpetuate the thraldom of our species.

Immediate abolition does not mean that the slaves shall immediately exercise the right of suffrage, or be eligible to any office, or be emancipated from law, or be free from the benevolent restraints of guardianship.   We contend for the immediate personal freedom of the slaves, for their exemption from punishment except where law has been violated, for their employment and reward as free laborers, for their exclusive right to their own bodies and those of their own children, for their instruction and subsequent admission to all the trusts, offices, honors and emoluments of intelligent freemen.   Emancipation will increase and not destroy the value of their labor ; it will also increase the demand for it.   Holding out the stimulus of good treatment and an adequate reward, it will induce the slaves to toil with a hundred fold more assiduity and faithfulness.   Who is so blind as not to perceive the peaceful and beneficial results of such a change ?   The slaves, if freed, will come under the watchful cognizance of law ;   they will not be idle, but *avariciously* industrious ; they will not rush through the country, firing dwellings and murdering the inhabitants ; for freedom is all they ask—all they desire—the obtainment of which will transform them from enemies into friends, from nuisances into blessings, from a corrupt, suffering and degraded, into a comparatively virtuous, happy and elevated population.

Nor   does immediate abolition mean that any compulsory power, other than moral, should be used in breaking the fetters of slavery.   It calls for no bloodshed, or physical interference ; it jealously regards the welfare of the planters ; it simply demands an entire revolution in public sentiment, which will lead to better conduct, to contrition for past crimes, to a love instead of a fear of justice, to a reparation of wrongs, to a healing of breaches, to a suppression of revengeful feelings, to a quiet, improving, prosperous state of society !

Now see with what earnestness and inveteracy the friends of the Colonization Society oppose immediate abolition !

' It appears, indeed, to be the only feasible mode by which we can remove that stigma as well as *danger* from among us. Their sudden and entire freedom would be a fearful, and perhaps dreadful experiment, destructive of all the ends of liberty, for which their condition would unfit them, and which they would doubtless greatly abuse. Even their release, at apparently proper intervals, but uncontrolled as to their future habits and location, would be a very hazardous charity. Their gradual emancipation, therefore, under the advantages of a free government, formed, in their native land, by their own hands, offering all the rewards usual to industry and economy, and affording the means of enjoying, in comfort, a reputable and free existence, is the only rational scheme of relieving them from the bondage of their present condition.' * * * ' To eradicate or remove the evil *immediately*, is impossible ; nor can any law of conscience govern necessity.'—[Af. Rep. vol. i. pp. 89, 258.]

' Vaunt not over us, dear brethren of the north, we inherited the evil from our forefathers, and we really do not think you do your brethren any good, or that you serve the interests of the people of color, when you recommend and enforce premature schemes of emancipation.' * * * ' The operation, we were aware, must be—and, for the interests of our country, ought to be gradual.' * * * ' According to one, (that rash class which, without a due estimate of the fatal consequence, would forthwith issue a decree of general, immediate, and indiscriminate emancipation,) it was a scheme of the slaveholder to perpetuate slavery.'—[Idem, vol. ii. pp. 12, 254, 336.]

' Slavery, in its mildest form, is an evil of the darkest character. Cruel and unnatural in its origin, no plea can be urged in justification of its continuance, but the plea of necessity—not that necessity which arises from our habits, our prejudices, or our wants ; but the necessity which requires us to submit to existing evils, rather than substitute, by their removal, others of a more serious and destructive character. It was this which produced the recognition of slavery in the constitution of our country ; it is this which has justified its continuance to the present day; and it is in this only that we can find a palliation for the rigors of our laws, which might otherwise be considered as the cruel enactments of a dark and dismal despotism. There have not, I am aware, been found wanting individuals to deny both the existence and the obligations of such a necessity. There are men, actuated in some instances, by a blind and mistaken enthusiasm, and in others, by a spirit of mischievous intent, loudly calling on us, in the names of justice and humanity, for the immediate and unqualified emancipation of our slaves. To men of this description, it is in vain to point out the inevitable effects of such a course, as well on the objects of their real or pretended solicitude, as on the community in which they exist. It is in vain to assure them, that while the preservation of the latter would require a policy even more rigorous than pertains to slavery itself, the short-lived and nominal freedom of the former must end in their ultimate and utter extinction. All this is of no consequence. Provided slavery be abolished in name, it matters not what horrors may be substituted in its room.' * * * ' The scope of the Society is large enough, but it is in no wise mingled or confounded with the broad sweeping views of a *few fanatics* in America, who would urge us on to the sudden and total abolition of slavery.'—[Af. Rep. vol. iii. pp. 15, 197.]

' What is to be done ? Immediate and universal emancipation will find few, if any advocates, among judicious and reflecting men.' * * * ' There is a portion of our brethren, who have been laboring for many years, with the most benevolent intentions, but, as I conceive, with erroneous views, in the cause of abolition.' * * * ' The Colonization Society, as such, have renounced wholly the name and the characteristics of abolitionists.' * * * INTO THEIR ACCOUNTS THE SUBJECT OF EMANCIPATION DOES NOT ENTER AT ALL.' * * * ' Here, that race is in every form a curse, and if the system, so long contended for by the uncompromising abolitionist, could prevail, its effect would be to spread discord and devastation from one end of the Union to the other.'—[Idem, vol. iv. pp. 202, 303, 306, 363.]

' With a writer in the Southern Review we say, " the situation of the people of these States was not of their own choosing. When they came to the inheritance, it was subject to this mighty incumbrance, and it would be criminal in them to ruin or waste the estate, to get rid of the burden at once." With this writer we add also, in the language of Capt. Hall, that the " slaveholders ought not (immediately) to disentangle themselves from the obligations which have devolved upon them, as the masters of slaves." We believe that a master *may* sustain his relation to the slave, with as little criminality as the slave sustains his relation to the master. But we feel little sympathy for those who, in the language of Mr Harrison of Virginia, " still look upon their slaves in the light in which most men regarded them when the slave trade was legitimate. Of those, wherever they are, who hold their slaves with that same sentiment which impelled the kidnapper when he forcibly bore them off, I know not how morality can distinguish them from the original wrong-doers, pirates by nature, and pirates by civilized law." That the system of slavery must exist temporarily in this country, we as firmly believe, as that for its existence a single moment, there can be offered justly no plea but necessity. Were the very spirit of angelic charity to pervade and fill the hearts of all the slaveholders in our land, it would by no means require that all the slaves should be instantaneously liberated.'—[Af. Rep. vol. v. p. 329.]

' The long established habits of the South, the attachments which are frequently found subsisting between the proprietor and his servants, together with the difficulty of substituting at once white for slave labor, and the derangement which would ensue in the domestic concerns of life, would not merely make general emancipation at once inexpedient, but the attempt would denote the extremity of madness and folly, and convulse this government to its centre.'— [Idem, vol. vi. p. 291.]

' The Society, meeting the objections of the *abolition enthusiast*, in a like spirit of mildness and forbearance, assures him of their equal devotion to the pure principles of liberty and the powerful claims of humanity. We know, say they, and we deplore the evil of slavery as the deadliest curse to our common country. We see, and we lament its demoralizing effects upon the children of our affections, from the budding innocence of infancy, to the full maturity of manhood. But, we have not, we do not, and *we will not* interfere with this delicate, this important subject. There are rights to be respected, prejudices to be conciliated, fears to be quelled, and safety to be observed in all our operations. And we protest, *most solemnly protest*, against the adoption of your views, as alike destructive of the ends of justice, of policy, and of humanity. No wild dream of the wildest enthusiast was ever more extravagant than that of turning loose upon society two millions of blacks, idle and therefore worthless, vicious and therefore dangerous, ignorant and therefore incapable of appreciating and enjoying the blessings of freedom. Could *your* wishes be realized, your gratulation would be quickly changed into mourning, your joy into grief, and your labor of love into visits of mercy to our jails and our penitentiaries, to the abodes of vice and the haunts of poverty. Come, ye abolitionists, away with your *wild enthusiasm*, your *misguided philanthropy*.'—[African Repository, vol. vii. p. 101.]

' The Colonization Society is removing the greatest obstacles in the way of emancipation ; but none, we think, who is acquainted with the circumstances and condition of our southern States, *and who has any conscience or humanity,* would deem it expedient or christian to dissolve instantaneously all the ties which unite masters and slaves.'—[Idem, vol. vii. p. 186.]

' It is not right that men should be free, when their freedom will prove injurious to themselves and others.' * * ' He has encountered determined opposition from several individuals, who are so reckless and fanatical as to require the instantaneous remedying of an acknowledged evil, which may be remedied gradually, with safety, but which cannot be remedied immediately without jeopardizing all the interests of all parties concerned.'—[Idem, p. 202, 280.]

' He was quite sure that in the Northern States, there was no opinion generally prevailing, that immediate, absolute, and universal emancipation was desirable. There might be, said Mr Storrs, some who are actuated by pure motives and benevolent views, who considered it practicable ; but he might say with confidence, that very few, if any, believed that it would be truly humane or expedient to turn loose upon the community more than a million, of persons, totally destitute of the means of subsistence, and altogether unprepared in every moral point of view, to enjoy or estimate their new privileges. Such a cotemporaneous emancipation of the colored population of the Southern States could only bring a common calamity on all the States, and the most severe misery on those who were to be thus thrown upon society, under the most abject, helpless and deplorable circumstances.'—[Speech of Hon. Mr Storrs.—Twelfth Annual Report.]

' The condition of a slave suddenly emancipated, and thrown upon his own resources, is very far from being improved ; and, however laudable the feeling which leads to such emancipation, its policy and propriety are at least questionable.'—[Report of the Pennsylvania Colonization Society.]

' We may, therefore, fairly conclude the object of immediate universal emancipation wholly unattainable, or, if attainable, at too high a price.'—[Mathew Carey's Essays.]

' Observation has fully convinced them that emancipation has often proved injurious to both : consequently laws have been enacted in several of the States to discourage, if not to prevent it. The public safety and interest, as well as individual happiness, seemed to require of legislatures the adoption of such a measure. For, it appeared highly probable that the manumitted would not only be poor and wretched, but likewise a public nuisance ; and perhaps at some future day, form the nucleus of rebellion among those unhappy persons still in slavery.' —[A colonization advocate in the Middletown (Connecticut) Gazette.]

' To our mind, it is clearly the doctrine of the Bible, that there may be circumstances, in which the immediate and universal emancipation of slaves is not a duty. Demanding instantaneous and universal emancipation, and denouncing every instance of *holding* slaves as a crime, is not the way to bring it to pass. If such a course proceeds from a right spirit, it is from a right spirit misinformed.'—[Vermont Chronicle.]

' When the writer visited England from the colonies, he was constantly astonished to find the Wilberforceans, or saints, as they were called, influenced by the *wildest enthusiasm* upon the sublime theory of liberty ; urging *immediate emancipation* of the slave, and yet totally uninformed as to its destructive consequences to their future welfare, in their present uneducated condition, without some provision being made to so enlighten them that they may be enabled to estimate religious obligations and distinguish between right and wrong ; oth-

erwise it would be indispensable to have strong military posts and constant martial law to preserve order, and prevent a murderous anarchy and lawless confusion. It is not anticipated that this state of things could ever be consummated in the United States ; but it may afford a very salutary lesson in guiding our consideration of similar occurrences that may take place.'
—[From a colonization pamphlet, entitled ' Remarks upon a plan for the total abolition of slavery in the United States. By a Citizen of New-York.]

' We do not wish to be understood, as sanctioning the measures now pursued with respect to the subject of slavery, by some misguided enthusiasts in the northern and eastern sections of the United States. Were the measures they advocate with so much heat, to be adopted, a heavier curse could hardly fall upon our country. Their operation, we feel fully satisfied, would work the ruin of those, whom these imprudent advocates of instant and total emancipation, wish primarily to benefit. We have always regarded these advocates for the instantaneous abolition of slavery, in all cases, as doing more injury to our colored population than any other class of men in the community. The slaves of this country cannot be at once emancipated. It is folly, it is madness to talk of it. From the very nature of the case, in justice to that deeply injured class, in justice to ourselves, the work must be gradual.' * * * ' We cannot doubt the ultimate success of the American Colonization Society. And however much some of the clamorous advocates of instant, immediate abolition may vent their rage against this noble institution, it will prosper, it will flourish. Our intelligent community are beginning to see that the American Colonization Society presents *the only door of hope* to the republic.'—[Western Luminary.]

' But *what* shall be done ? Some—and their motives and philanthropic zeal are worthy of all honor—plead for immediate emancipation. But Mr Ladd had seen enough to know that *that* would be a curse to all parties. He acknowledged a difficulty here ; *but it is a difficulty that often occurs in morals.* When we have gone far in a wrong road, it often happens that we cannot in a moment put ourselves in the right one. One penalty of such a sin is, that it clings to us, and cannot be shaken off at once with all its bitter consequences by a mere volition.'—[Speech of William Ladd, Esq.]

' The warmest friend to the abolition of slavery, while he deplores the existence of the evil, must admit the necessity of cautious and gradual measures to remove it. The inhabitants of the South cannot, and ought not, suddenly to emancipate their slaves, to remain among them free. Such a measure would be no blessing to the slaves, but the very madness of self-destruction to the whites. In the South, the horrid scenes that would too certainly follow the liberation of their slaves, are present to every imagination, to stifle the calls of justice and humanity. A fell spirit of avarice is thus invigorated and almost justified, by the plea of necessity.'—[First Annual Report of the New Jersey Col. Soc.]

' The impropriety and impolicy of manumitting slaves, *in any case*, in our country, one would suppose, must be apparent to all. It is not a little astonishing that individuals acquainted with the facts, and the evils brought upon society by the free black population, should persist in declaring that duty and humanity call upon us to give the slaves their freedom. It really appears to me that there is entirely too much " namby pamby sentimentality " and affected feeling exhibited respecting the condition of slaves. Do these individuals believe that benevolence and humanity command us to turn loose upon society a set of persons who confessedly only serve to swell the amount of crime, while they add nothing to the industry, to the wealth, or the strength of the country ? Because abstractedly considered, man has no right to hold his fellow man in bondage, shall we give up our liberty, and the peace of society, in order that this principle may not be violated ? The fact is, *the negroes are happier when kept in bondage.* In their master they find a willing and efficient protector, to guard them

from injury and insult, to attend to them when sick and in distress, and to provide for their comfort and support, when old age overtakes them. When in
health, they are well fed and clothed, and by no means, in common cases, are
they hardly worked.'—[A warm advocate of African Colonization in the Alex-
andria Gazette.]

'But there are other difficulties in the way of immediate emancipation. We
believe that no one, who has taken charge of an infant, and made a cripple of
him, either in his feet, his hands, or his mind, so that when he is of mature age,
he is unable to take care of himself, has a right to turn him out of doors, to
perish or destroy himself, and call it, giving him his liberty. After having reduced him to this condition, he is bound to afford him the support and protection, which he has rendered necessary.

'This appears to us to be the true relation of the southern planters to their
slaves. Not that the southern planters have generally been guilty of personal
cruelty ; but such has been the general result of the system acted upon, and such
the relation growing out of it. The slaves have grown up, under the eye of
their masters, unable to take care of themselves ; and their masters, for whose
comfort and convenience this has been done, are bound to provide for them.

'Nor do we think that the exhortation, to "do right and trust Providence,"
applies at all to this case ; for the very question is, "what is right ?" Would it
be right for the slave merchant, in the midst of the Atlantic, to knock the man-
acles from his prisoners and throw them overboard, and call this, giving them
their liberty and trusting Providence with the result ? But how else could he
reduce the doctrine of immediate and complete emancipation to practice ?'—
[Vermont Chronicle.]

The miserable sophistry contained in the foregoing extracts
scarcely needs a serious refutation. 'To say that immediate
emancipation will only increase the wretchedness of the slaves,
and that we must pursue a system of *gradual* abolition, is to
present to us the double paradox, that we must continue to do
evil, in order to cure the evil which we are doing ; and that we
must continue to be unjust, and to do evil, that good may
come.' The fatal error of *gradualists* lies here : They talk as
if the friends of abolition contended only for the emancipation
of the slaves, without specifying or caring what should be done
with or for them ! as if the planters were invoked to cease from
one kind of villany, only to practise another ! as if the manumitted slaves must necessarily be driven out from society into
the wilderness, like wild beasts ! This is talking nonsense : it
is a gross perversion of reason and common sense. Abolition-
its have never said, that mere manumission would be doing justice to the slaves : they insist upon a remuneration for years
of unrequited toil, upon their employment as free laborers, upon
their immediate and coefficient instruction, and upon the exercise of a benevolent supervision over them on the part of their
employers. They declare, in the first place, that to break the

fetters of the slaves, and turn them loose upon the country, without the preservative restraints of law, and destitute of occupation, would leave the work of justice only half done ; and, secondly, that it is absurd to suppose that the planters would be wholly independent of the labor of the blacks—for they could no more dispense with it next week, were emancipation to take place, than they can to-day. The very ground which they assume for their opposition to slavery,—that it necessarily prevents the improvement of its victims, —shows that they contemplate the establishment of schools for the education of the slaves, and the furnishing of productive employment, immediately upon their liberation. If this were done, none of the horrors which are now so feelingly depicted, as the attendants of a sudden abolition, would ensue.

But we are gravely told that education must *precede* emancipation. The logic of this plea is, that intellectual superiority justly gives one man an oppressive control over another ! Where would such a detestable principle lead but to practices the most atrocious, and results the most disastrous, if carried out among ourselves ? Tell us, ye hair-splitting sophists, the exact quantum of knowledge which is necessary to constitute a freeman. If every dunce should be a slave, your servitude is inevitable ; and richly do you deserve the lash for your obtuseness. Our white population, too, would furnish blockheads enough to satisfy all the classical kidnappers in the land.

The reason why the slaves are so ignorant, is because they are held in bondage ; and the reason why they are held in bondage, is because they are so ignorant ! They ought not to be freed until they are educated ; and they ought not be educated, because on the acquisition of knowledge they would burst their fetters ! Fine logic, indeed ! How men, who make any pretensions to honesty or common sense, can advance a paradox like this, is truly inexplicable. ' I never met with a man yet,' says an able writer in Kentucky, ' who impliedly admits the enslaving of human beings as consistent with the exercise of christian duties, who could talk or write ten minutes on the subject, without expressing nonsense, or contradicting himself, or advancing heresy which would expose him to censure on any other subject.' In this connexion, I make the following extract from the Report of the DUBLIN NEGRO'S FRIEND SOCIETY, of which WILBERFORCE is President, and CLARKSON Vice President :

'They do not recognize the false principle, that education, as a preparation for freedom, must precede emancipation ; or that an amelioration of the slaves' condition should be a substitute for it : on the contrary, THEY INSIST UPON UNPROCRASTINATED EMANCIPATION, as a right which is unrighteously withheld, and the restoration of which is, in their opinion, the first and most indispensable step to all improvement, and absolutely essential to the application of the only remedy for that moral debasement, in which slavery has sunk its victims.'

I cannot portray the absurdity of the doctrine of gradual abolition, and the danger and folly of attempting to mitigate the system of slavery, more strikingly, than by presenting the following eloquent extracts from a speech of the Rev. Dr. Thomson of Edinburgh, one of the most learned and able divines in Great Britain, whose sudden death was recorded in the newspapers a few months since :

'The word *immediate* may no doubt be considered as a strong word ; but you will observe that it is used as contrasted with the word *gradual*. And were I to criticise the term *gradual* as certain opponents have treated the term *immediate*, I could easily, by the help of a little quibbling, bring you to the conclusion, that as hitherto employed it means that the abolition is never to take place, and that, by putting it into their petition, they are to be understood as deprecating rather than asking the emancipation of the slaves. "*Immediate*," they argue, "evanishes as soon as you utter it ; it is gone before your petition reaches parliament." How absurd ! If I should say to my servant while engaged in work, "You must go to the south side of the town with a message for me *immediately*," is it indeed implied in the order I have given him, that he could not fulfil it, unless he set off without his hat, without his coat, without his shoes, without those habiliments which are requisite for his appearing decently in the streets of Edinburgh, and executing the task that I had assigned him ? The meaning of the word as used by us is perfectly clear, and cannot be misapprehended by any one : it is not to be made a subject of metaphysical animadversion : it is to be considered and understood under the direction of common sense, and especially as modified and expounded by those statements with which it is associated both in our resolutions and in the petition ; and viewed in that light, *immediate abolition* is not merely an intelligible phrase, but one that does not warrant a particle of the alarm which some have affected to take at it, and is not liable to any one of those objections which some have been pleased to make to it.

'To say that we will come out of the sin by degrees—that we will only forsake it slowly, and step by step—that we will pause and hesitate and look well about us before we consent to abandon its gains and its pleasures—that we will allow another age to pass by ere we throw off the load of iniquity that is lying so heavy upon us, lest certain secularities should be injuriously affected—and that we will postpone the duty of "doing justly and loving mercy," till we have removed every petty difficulty out of the way, and got all the conflicting interests that are involved in the measure reconciled and satisfied ;—to say this, is to trample on the demands of moral obligation, and to disregard the voice which speaks to us from heaven. The path of duty is plain before us ; and we have nothing to do but to enter it at once, and to walk in it without turning to the right hand or to the left. Our concern is not with the result that may follow our obedience to the divine will. Our great and primary concern is to obey that will. God reigns over his universe in the exercise of infinite perfection : he commands us to let the oppressed go free, and to break every yoke ; and submitting, without procrastination, and without any attempts at compromise, to that command, we may be assured that he will take care of all the effects that can be produced by compliance with his authority, and give demonstration to the truth that obedience to his behests is our grand and only security for a prosperous lot.

‘ We are by no means indifferent to the expediency of the case. On the contrary, we think ourselves prepared to prove, by fair reasoning and by ascertained fact, that the expediency of the thing is all on our side ; that immediate abolition is the only secure and proper way of attaining the object which we all profess to have in view ; that to defer the measure to a distant period, and to admit the propriety of getting at it by a course of mitigation, is the surest mode of frustrating every hope we might otherwise entertain, and giving over the slaves to interminable bondage.’   *   *   *

‘ I do not deny, Sir, that the evils of practical slavery may be lessened. By parliamentary enactments, by colonial arrangements, by appeals to the judgment and feelings of planters, and by various other means, a certain degree of melioration *may* be secured. But I say, in the first place, that, with all that you can accomplish, or reasonably expect, of mitigation, you cannot alter the nature of slavery itself. With every improvement you have superinduced upon it, you have not made it less debasing, less cruel, less destructive, in its essential character. The black man is still the *property* of the white man. And that one circumstance not only implies in it the transgression of inalienable right and everlasting justice, but is the fruitful and necessary source of numberless mischiefs, the very thought of which harrows up the soul, and the infliction of which no superintendence of any goverment can either prevent or control. Mitigate and keep down the evil as much as you can, still it is there in all its native virulence, and still it will do its malignant work in spite of you. The improvements you have made are merely superficial. You have not reached the seat and vital spring of the mischief. You have only concealed in some measure, and for a time, its inherent enormity. Its essence remains unchanged and untouched, and is ready to unfold itself whenever a convenient season arrives, notwithstanding all your precaution, and all you vigilance, in those manifold acts of injustice and inhumanity, which are its genuine and its invariable fruits. You may white-wash the sepulchre,—you may put upon it every adornment that fancy can suggest,— you may cover it over with all the flowers and evergreens that the garden or the fields can furnish, so that it will appear beautiful outwardly unto men. But it is a sepulchre still,—full of dead men’s bones and of all uncleanness. Disguise slavery as you will,—put into the cup all the pleasing and palatable ingredients which you can discover in the wide range of nature and of art,—still it is a bitter, bitter draught, from which the understanding and the heart of every man, in whom nature works unsophisticated and unbiassed, recoils with unutterable aversion and abhorrence. Why, Sir, slavery is the very Upas tree of the moral world, beneath whose pestiferous shade all intellect languishes, and all virtue dies. And if you would get quit of the evil, you must go more thoroughly and effectually to work than you can ever do by any or by all of those palliatives, which are included under the term “ mitigation.” The foul sepulchre must be taken away. The cup of oppression must be dashed to pieces on the ground. The pestiferous tree must be cut down and eradicated ; it must be, root and branch of it, cast into the consuming fire, and its ashes scattered to the four winds of heaven. It is thus you must deal with slavery. You must annihilate it,—annihilate it now,—and annihilate it for ever.

‘ Get your mitigation. I say in the second place, that you are thereby, in all probability farther away than ever from your object. It is not to the Govern-

ment or the Parliament at home that you are to look—neither is it to the legislatures and planters abroad that you are to look—for accomplishing the abolition
of negro slavery. Sad experience shows that, if left to themselves, they will do
nothing efficient in this great cause. It is to the sentiments of the people at
large that you are to look, to the spread of intellectual light, to the prevalence
of moral feeling, to the progress, in short, of public opinion, which, when resting on right principles and moving in a right direction, must in this free and
Christian country prove irresistible. But observe, Sir, the public mind will not
be sufficiently affected by the statement of abstract truths, however just, or by
reasonings on the tendencies of a system, however accurate. It must be more
or less influenced by what is visible, or by what is easily known and understood
of the actual atrocities which accompany slavery, wherever it is left to its own
proper operation. Let it be seen in its native vileness and cruelty, as exhibited
when not interfered with by the hand of authority, and it excites universal and
unqualified detestation. But let its harsher asperities be rubbed off; take away
the more prominent parts of its iniquity; see that it look somewhat smoother and
milder than it did before; make such regulations as ought, if faithfully executed,
to check its grosser acts of injustice and oppression; give it the appearance of
its being put under the humanizing sway of religious education and instruction;
do all this, and you produce one effect at least,—you modify the indignation of a
great number of the community; you render slavery much less obnoxious; you
enable its advocates and supporters to say in reply to your denunciations of its
wickedness, "O, the slaves are now comfortable and happy; they do not suffer
what they did; they are protected and well treated," and in proof of all this,
they point to what are called "mitigations." But mark me, Sir; under these
mitigations, slavery still exists, ready at every convenient season to break forth
in all its countless forms of inhumanity; meanwhile the public feeling in a great
measure subsides; and when the public feeling—such an important and indispensable element in our attempts to procure abolition—is allowed to subside, tell me,
Sir, when, and where, and by what means it is again to be roused into activity. I
must say, for one, that though I sympathize with my sable brethren, when I hear
of them being spared even one lash of the cart-whip; yet when I take a more enlarged view of their condition—when I consider the nature of that system under
which they are placed, and when I look forward to their deliverance, and the
means by which alone it is to be effected, I am tempted, and almost if not altogether persuaded, to deprecate that insidious thing termed "mitigation," because it directly tends to perpetuate the mighty evil, which will by and by throw
off the improvements by which it is glossed over as quite unnatural to it, will
ultimately grow up again into all its former dreadfulness, and continue to wither
and crush beneath it, all that is excellent and glorious in man.'

'But if our rulers and legislators will undertake to emancipate the slaves, and
do it as it ought to be done, immediately, I beg those who set themselves against
such a a measure, to point out the danger, and to prove it. The *onus* lies upon
them. And what evidence do they give us? Where is it to be found? In what
circumstance shall we discover it? From what principles and probabilities shall
we infer it? We must not have mere hypothesis—mere allegations—mere fancied horrors, dressed up in frightful language. We must have proof to substantiate, in some good measure, their theory of rebellion, warfare, and blood. If
any such thing exists, let them produce it. * * * But if you push me, and
still urge the argument of insurrection and bloodshed, for which you are far more
indebted to fancy than to fact, as I have shown you, then I say, be it so. I repeat that maxim, taken from a heathen book, but pervading the whole Book of
God, *Fiat justitia—ruat cœlum.* Righteousness, Sir, is the pillar of the universe. Break down that pillar, and the universe falls into ruin and desolation. But
preserve it, and though the fair fabric may sustain partial dilapidations, it may
be rebuilt and repaired—it *will* be rebuilt, and repaired, and restored to all its
pristine strength, and magnificence, and beauty. If there must be violence, let
it even come, for it will soon pass away—let it come and rage its little hour,
since it is to be succeeded by lasting freedom, and prosperity and happiness. Give

me the hurricane rather than the pestilence. Give me the hurricane, with its thunder, and its lightning, and its tempest ;—give me the hurricane, with its partial and temporary devastations, awful though they be ;—give me the hurricane, with its purifying, healthful, salutary effects ;—give me that hurricane, infinitely rather than the noisome pestilence, whose path is never crossed, whose silence is never disturbed, whose progress is never arrested, by one sweeping blast from the heavens ; which walks peacefully and sullenly through the length and breadth of the land, breathing poison into every heart, and carrying havoc into every home, enervating all that is strong, defacing all that is beautiful, and casting its blight over the fairest and happiest scenes of human life—and which, from day to day, and from year to year, with intolerant and interminable malignity, sends its thousands and its tens of thousands of hapless victims into the ever-yawning and never-satisfied grave !'

It is said, by way of extenuation, that the present owners of slaves are not responsible for the origin of this system. I do not arraign them for the crimes *of their ancestors*, but for the constant perpetration and extension of similar crimes. The plea that the evil of slavery was entailed upon them, shall avail them nothing : in its length and breadth it means that the robberies of one generation justify the robberies of another ! that the inheritance of stolen property converts it into an honest acquisition ! that the atrocious conduct of their fathers exonerates them from all accountability, thus presenting the strange anomaly of a race of men incapable of incurring guilt, though daily practising the vilest deeds ! Scarcely any one denies that blame attaches somewhere : the present generation throws it upon the past—the past, upon its predecessor—and thus it is cast, like a ball, from one to another, down to the first importers of the Africans ! ' Can that be *innocence* in the temperate zone, which is the *acme of all guilt* near the equator ? Can that be *honesty* in one meridian of longitude, which, at one hundred degrees east, is the *climax of injustice ?*' Sixty thousand infants, the offspring of slave-parents, are annually born in this country, and doomed to remediless bondage. Is it not as atrocious a crime to kidnap these, as to kidnap a similar number on the coast of Africa ?

It is said, moreover, that we ought to legislate prospectively, on this subject ; that the fetters of the present generation of slaves cannot be broken ; and that our single aim should be, to obtain the freedom of their offspring, by fixing a definite period after which none shall be born slaves. But this is inconsistent, inhuman and unjust. The following extracts from the speech of the Rev. Dr. Thomson are conclusive on this point :

' In the first place, it amounts to an indirect sanction of the continued slavery of all who are now alive, and of all who may be born before the period fixed upon. This is a renunciation of the great moral principles upon which the demand for abolition proceeds. It consigns more than 800,000 human beings to bondage and oppression, while their title to freedom is both indisputable and acknowledged. And it is not merely an inconsistency on the part of the petitioners, and a violation of the duty which they owe to such a multitude of their fellow-men, but it weakens or surrenders the great argument by which they enforce their application for the extinction of colonial slavery.

' Besides, it is vain to expect that the planters will acquiesce in such a prospective measure, any more than in the liberation of the existing slaves, for the progeny of the existing slaves must be considered by them as much a part of their property as these slaves themselves. And they would regard it equally unjust to deprive them of what is hereafter to be produced from their own slave stock, as it would be to deprive a farmer, by an anticipating law of all the foals and of all the calves that might be produced in his stable and in his cow-house, after a given specified date.

' We must be true to our own maxims, which are taken from the word of God ; and ask for all that we are entitled to have on the ground of justice and humanity, and be contented with nothing less.

' In the second place, the plan objected to is not merely an acquiescence in the continuance of crime, it is a violation of the best feelings of our nature. For, let any man but reflect on the circumstance of children being born to slavery, merely because they came into the world the last hour of December 1830, instead of the first hour of January 1, 1831—and of children in the same family, brothers and sisters—some of them destined to bondage for life, and others gifted with freedom, for no other reason than that the former were born before, and the latter after, a particular day of a particular year—and of parents being unjustly and inhumanly flogged in the very sight of their offspring arbitrarily made free, while they are as arbitrarily kept slaves—let any man but reflect on these things, and unless the sensibilities of his heart be paralysed even to deadness, he must surely revolt at such a cruel and cold blooded allotment in the fortune of those little ones, and be satisfied with nothing short of the emancipation of the whole community, without a single exception.

' In the third place, supposing all children born after January 1, 1831, were declared free, how are they to be educated ? That they may be prepared for the enjoyment of that liberty with which you have invested them, they must undergo a particular and appropriate training. So say the *gradualists*. Very well ; under whom are they to get this training ? Are they to be separated from their parents ? Is that dearest of natural ties to be broken asunder ? Is this necessary for your plan ? And are not you thus endeavoring to cure one species of wickedness by the instrumentality of another? But if they are to be left with their parents and brought up under their care, then either they will be imbued with the faults and degeneracies that are characteristic of slavery, and consequently be as unfit for freedom as those who have not been disenthralled : or they will be well nurtured and well instructed by their parents, and this implies a confession that their parents themselves are sufficiently prepared for liberty, and that there is no good reason for withholding from them, the boon that is bestowed upon their children.

' Whatever view, in short, we take of the question, the prospective plan is full of difficulty or contradictions, and we are made more sensible than ever that there is nothing left for us, but to take the consistent, honest, uncompromising course of demanding the abolition of slavery with respect to the present, as well as to every future generation of the negroes in our colonies.'

We are told that ' it is not right that men should be free, when their freedom will prove injurious to themselves and others.' This has been the plea of tyrants in all ages. If the immediate emancipation of the slaves would prove a curse, it follows that slavery is a blessing ; and that it cannot be unjust, but benevolent, to defraud the laborer of his hire, to rank him as a beast, and to deprive him of his liberty. But this, every one must see, is at war with common sense, and avowedly doing evil that good may come. This plea must mean, either that a state of slavery is more favorable to the growth of virtue and the dispensation of knowledge than a state of freedom—(a glaring absurdity)—or that an immediate compliance with the demands of justice would be most unjust—(a gross contradiction.)

It is boldly asserted by some colonizationists, that ' *the negroes are happier when kept in bondage,*' and that ' the condition of the great mass of emancipated Africans is one in comparison with which the condition of the slaves is *enviable.*' What is the inference ? Why, either that slavery is not oppression— (another paradox)—or that real benevolence demands the return of the free people of color to their former state of servitude. Every kidnapper, therefore, is a true philanthropist ! Our legislature should immediately offer a bounty for the body of every free colored person ! The colored population of Massachusetts, at $200 for each man, woman and child, would bring at least *one million three hundred thousand dollars.* This sum would seasonably replenish our exhausted treasury. The whole free colored population of the United States, at the same price, (which is a low estimate,) would be worth *sixty-five millions of dollars ! !* Think how many churches this would build, schools and colleges establish, beneficiaries educate, missionaries support, bibles and tracts circulate, railroads and canals complete, &c. &c. &c. ! ! !

The Secretary of the Colonization Society assures us, (*vide* the African Repository, vol. v. p. 330,) that ' *were the very spirit of angelic charity to pervade and fill the hearts of all the slaveholders in our land, it would by no means require that all the slaves should be instantaneously liberated*' ! !—i. e. should the slaveholders become instantaneously metamorphosed into angels, they would still hold the rational creatures of God as their *property*, and yet commit no sin ! Think, for one moment, of an angel in the capacity of a man-stealer—feeding his victims upon a peck of corn per week, or three bushels of corn and a few herrings every ' quarter-day,' as a compensation for their severe labor—flourishing a cowskin over their heads, and applying it frequently to their naked bodies ! Think of him selling parents from children, and children from parents, at private sale or public auction !

Many slaveholders are giving up their slaves from conscientious motives ; they cannot, they dare not longer keep them in servitude ; they believe that the law of God has a higher claim upon their obedience than the laws of their native State. Now suppose all the owners of slaves in our land should be suddenly and simultaneously convicted of sin, and moved to repentance in a similar manner, and should say to their slaves, ' God forbid that we should longer call you our property, or place you on a level with our cattle, or defraud you of your just dues, or sell you or your wives or children to others, or deny you the means of instruction, or lacerate your bodies ! henceforth you are free—but you want employment, and we need laborers—go and work as freemen, and be paid as freemen !'—suppose, I say, a case like this should happen, and a troop of *gradualists* should surround these penitent oppressors, and cry, ' Were the very spirit of angelic charity to pervade and fill your hearts, it would by no means require that all your slaves should be instantaneously liberated—your throats will be cut, your houses pillaged, and desolation will stalk through the land, if you carry your mad purpose into effect—emancipate by a slow, imperceptible process !'—how would this advice sound ? What should be their reply ? Clearly this : ' Whether it be right in the sight of God to hearken unto men more than unto God, judge ye.' Here would be presented a strange spectacle indeed—one party confessing and resolving to forsake their sins, and another urging them to disregard the admonitions of conscience, and to leave off sinning by degrees ! To be sure, a few, a very few, would be *generously* allowed to reform *instanter !*

Those who prophesy evil, and only evil, concerning immediate abolition, absolutely disregard the nature and constitution of man, as also his inalienable rights, and annihilate or reverse the causes and effects of human action.   They are continually fearful lest the slaves, in consequence of their grievous wrongs and intolerable sufferings, should attempt to gain their freedom by revolution ; and yet they affect to be equally fearful lest a general emancipation should produce the same disastrous consequences.   How absurd ! They *know* that oppression must cause rebellion ; and yet they pretend that a removal of the cause will produce a bloody effect ! This is to suppose an effect without a cause, and, of course, is a contradiction in terms.   Bestow upon the slaves personal freedom, and all motives for insurrection are destroyed.   Treat them like rational beings, and you may surely expect rational treatment in return : treat them like beasts, and they will behave in a beastly manner.

Besides, precedent and experience make the ground of abolitionists invulnerable.   In no single instance where their principles have been adopted, has the result been disastrous or violent, but beneficial and peaceful even beyond their most sanguine expectations.   The immediate abolition of slavery in Mexico, in Colombia, and in St. Domingo,* was eminently preservative

---

* The history of the Revolution in St Domingo is not generally understood in this country.   The result of the instantaneous emancipation of the slaves, in that island, by an act of the Conventional Assembly of France in the month of February, 1794, settles the controversy between the *immediatists* and *gradualists.* ' After this public act of emancipation,' says Colonel Malenfant, who was resident in the island at the time, ' the negroes *remained quiet* both in the South and in the West, and *they continued to work upon all the plantations.*' ' Upon those estates which were abandoned, they *continued their labors,* where there were any, even inferior agents, to guide them ; and on those estates, where no white men were left to direct them, they betook themselves to the planting of provisions ; but upon *all the plantations* where the whites resided, the blacks *continued to labor as quietly as before.*' ' On the Plantation Gourad, consisting of more than four hundred and fifty laborers, *not a single negro refused to work ;* and yet this plantation was thought to be under the worst discipline and the slaves the most idle of any in the plain.'   General Lacroix, who published his ' Memoirs for a History of St Domingo,' at Paris, in 1819, uses these remarkable words : ' The colony marched, *as by enchantment,* towards its ancient splendor ; *cultivation prospered ;* every day produced perceptible proofs of its progress.   The city of the Cape and the plantations of the North rose up again visibly to the eye.'   General Vincent, who was a general of a brigade of artillery in St Domingo, and a proprietor of estates in that island, at the same period, declared to the Directory of France, that ' every thing *was going on well in St Domingo.*   The proprietors were in peaceable possession of their estates ; cultivation was making rapid progress ; *the blacks were industrious, and beyond example happy.*'   So much for the horrible concomitants of a general emancipation !   So much for the predicted indolence of the liberated slaves !   Let confusion of face cover all abolition alarmists in view of these historical facts !

and useful in its effects. The manumitted slaves (numbering more than two thousand,) who were settled in Nova Scotia, at the close of our revolutionary war, by the British government, ' led a harmless life,' says Clarkson, ' and gained the character of an industrious and honest people from their white neighbors.' A large number who were located at Trinidad, as free laborers, at the close of our last war, ' are now,' according to the same authority, ' earning their own livelihood, and with so much industry and good conduct, that the calumnies originally spread against them have entirely died away.' According to the Anti-Slavery Reporter for January, 1832, three thousand prize negroes at the Cape of Good Hope had received their freedom— four hundred in one day ; ' but not the least difficulty or disorder occurred : servants found masters, masters hired servants— all gained homes, and at night scarcely an idler was to be seen.'

These and many other similar facts show conclusively the safety of immediate abolition. Gradualists can present, in abatement of them, nothing but groundless apprehensions and criminal distrust. The argument is irresistible.

———

SECTION VI.

THE AMERICAN COLONIZATION SOCIETY IS NOURISHED BY FEAR AND SELFISHNESS.

The reader will find on the fifth page of my introductory remarks, the phrase' ' naked terrors ;' by which I mean, that, throughout all the speeches, addresses and reports in behalf of the Society, it is confessed, in language strong and explicit, that an irrepressible and agonizing fear of the influence of the free people of color over the slave population is the primary, essen-

---

This peaceful and prosperous state of affairs continued from 1794, to the invasion of the island by Leclerc in 1802. The attempt of Bonaparte to reduce the island to its original servitude was the sole cause of that sanguinary conflict which ended in the total extirpation of the French from its soil.—[Vide Clarkson's ' Thoughts on the Necessity of Improving the Condition of the Slaves in the British Colonies,' &c.]

tial and prevalent motive for colonizing them on the coast of Africa—and not, as we are frequently urged to believe, a desire simply to meliorate their condition and civilize that continent. On this point, the evidence is abundant.

' In reflecting on the utility of a plan for colonizing the free people of color, with whom our country abounds, it is natural that we should be first struck by its tendency to confer a benefit on ourselves, by ridding us of a population for the most part idle and useless, and too often vicious and mischievous.' * * * ' Such a class must evidently be a burden and a nuisance to the community ; and every scheme which affords a prospect of removing so great an evil must deserve to be most favorably considered.

' But it is not in themselves merely that the free people of color are a nuisance and burthen. They contribute greatly to the corruption of the slaves, and to aggravate the evils of their condition, by rendering them idle, discontented and disobedient. This also arises from the necessity under which the free blacks are, of remaining incorporated with the slaves, of associating habitually with them, and forming part of the same class in society. The slave seeing his free companion live in idleness, or subsist however scantily or precariously by occasional and desultory employment, is apt to grow discontented with his own condition, and to regard as tyranny and injustice the authority which compels him to labor.*

' Great, however, as the benefits are, which we may thus promise ourselves, from the colonization of the free people of color, by its tendency to prevent the discontent and corruption of our slaves,' &c. * * ' The considerations stated in the first part of this letter, have long since produced a thorough conviction in my mind, that the existence of a class of free people of color in this country is highly injurious to the whites, the slaves and the free people of color themselves : consequently that all emancipation, to however small an extent, which permits the persons emancipated to remain in this country, is an evil, which must increase with the increase of the operation, and would become altogether intolerable, if extended to the whole, or even to a very large part of the black population. I am therefore strongly opposed to emancipation, in every shape and degree, unless accompanied by colonization.'—[General Harper's Letter—First Annual Report, pp. 29, 31,32, 33, 36.]

' The slaves would be greatly benefitted by the removal of the free blacks, who now corrupt them and render them discontented.'—[Second An. Rep.]

' What are these objects ? They are in the first place to aid ourselves, by relieving us from a species of population pregnant with future danger and present inconvenience.'—[Seventh Report.]

' They are dangerous to the community, and this danger ought to be removed. Their wretchedness arises not only from their bondage, but from their political and moral degradation. The danger is not so much that we have a million and a half of slaves, as that we have in our borders nearly two millions of men who are necessarily any thing rather than loyal citizens—nearly two millions of ignorant and miserable beings who are banded together by the very same circumstances, by which they are so widely separated in character and in interest from all the citizens of our great republic.'—[Seventh Annual Report.]

' It may be safely assumed, that there is not an individual in the community, who has given to the subject a moment's consideration, who does not regard the existence of the free people of color in the bosom of the country, as an evil of

---

* How very strange that the slave should ' regard as tyranny and injustice the authority which which compels him to labor ' without recompense ! ! !

immense magnitude, and of a dangerous and alarming tendency. Their abject and miserable condition is too obvious to be pointed out. All must perceive it, and perceiving it, cannot but lament it. But their deplorable condition is not more obvious to the most superficial observer, than is (what is far worse, and still more to be dreaded,) the powerful and resistless influence which they exert over the slave population. While their character remains what it now is, (and the laws and structure of the country in which they reside, prevent its permanent improvement,) this influence must of necessity be baneful and ˜contaminating. Corrupt themselves, like the deadly Upas, they impart corruption to all around them. Their numbers too, are constantly and rapidly augmenting. Their annual increase is truly astonishing, certainly unexampled. The dangerous ascendency which they have already acquired over the slaves, is consequently increasing with every addition to their numbers ; and every addition to their numbers is a subtraction from the wealth and strength, and character, and happiness, and safety of the country. And if this be true, as it unquestionably is, the converse is also true ; the danger of their undue influence will lessen with every diminution of their numbers ; and every diminution of their numbers must add, and add greatly, to the prosperity of the country.'—[Twelfth Annual Report.]

' Another reason is, the pressing and vital importance of relieving ourselves, as soon as practicable, from this most dangerous element in our population.' * *
' We all know the effects produced on our slaves by the fascinating, but delusive appearance of happiness, exhibited in some persons of their own complexion, roaming in idleness and vice among them. By removing the most fruitful source of discontent from among our slaves, we should render them more industrious and attentive to our commands.'—[Fourteenth Annual Report.]

' What is the free black to the slave ? A standing perpetual incitement to discontent. Though the condition of the slave be a thousand times the best—supplied, protected, instead of destitute and desolate—yet, the folly of the condition, held to involuntary labor, finds, always, allurement, in the spectacle of exemption from it, without consideration of the adjuncts of destitution and misery. The slave would have then, little excitement to discontent but for the free black.'—[Fifteenth Annual Report.]

' The evils which arise from the communication of the free people of color with our slaves, must be obvious to every reflecting mind ; and the consequences which may result from this communication at some future day, when circumstances are more favorable to their views, are of a more alarming character. Sir, circumstances must have brought us to the conclusion, if our observation had not enabled us to make the remark, that it is natural for our slaves, so closely allied to the free black population by national peculiarities, and by relationship, to make a comparison between their respective conditions, and to repine at the difference which exists between them. This is a serious evil, and can only be removed *by preventing the possibility of a comparison.*
' By removing these people, we rid ourselves of a lage party who will always be ready to assist our slaves in any mischievous design which they may conceive ; and who are better able, by their intelligence, and the facilities of their communication, to bring those designs to a successful termination.'—[African Repository, vol. i. p. 176.]

' The labors of the Colonization Society appear to us highly deserving of praise. The blacks, whom they carry from the country, belong to a class far more noxious than the slaves themselves. They are free without any sense of character to restrain them, or regular means of obtaining an honest livelihood. Most of the criminal offences committed in the southern States are chargeable to them, and their influence over the slaves is pernicious and alarming.' * * *
' What is the true nature of the evil of the existence of a portion of the African race in our population ? It is not that there are some, but that there are so many

among us of a different caste, of a different physical, if not moral, constitution, who never can amalgamate with the great body of our population. In every country, persons are to be found varying in their color, origin and character, from the native mass. But this anomaly creates no inquietude or apprehension, because the exotics, from the smallness of their number, are known to be utterly incapable of disturbing the general tranquillity. Here, on the contrary, the African part of our population bears so large a proportion to the residue of European origin, as to create the most lively apprehension, especially in some quarters of the Union. Any project, therefore, by which, in a material degree, the dangerous element in the general mass, can be diminished or rendered stationary, deserves deliberate consideration.'—[African Repository, vol. ii. pp. 27, 338.]

' Made up, for the most part, either of slaves or of their immediate descendants ; elevated above the class from which it has sprung, only by its exemption from domestic restraint ; and effectually debarred by the law, from every prospect of equality with the actual freemen of the country ; it is a source of perpetual uneasiness to the master, and of envy and corruption to the slave.' * * ' To remove these persons from among us, will increase the *usefulness*, and improve the moral character of those who remain in servitude, and *with whose labors the country is unable to dispense.* That instances are to be found of colored free persons, upright and industrious, is not to be denied. But the greater portion, as is well known, are a source of malignant depravity to the slaves on the one hand, and of corrupt habits to many of our white population on the other. The arts of subsistence with many of them, are incompatible with the security of property.' * * * ' I am a Virginian—I dread for her the corroding evil of this numerous caste, and I tremble for the danger of a disaffection spreading through their seductions, among our servants.' * * * ' Are they vipers, who are sucking our blood ? we will hurl them from us. It is not sympathy alone,—not sickly sympathy, no, nor manly sympathy either,—which is to act on us ; but vital policy, self-interest, are also enlisting themselves on the humane side in our breasts.'—[African Repository, vol. iii. pp. 10, 67, 197, 201.]

' All must concur in regarding the present condition of the free colored race in America as inconsistent with its future social and political advancement, and, where slavery exists at all, as calculated to aggravate its evils without any atoning good. Among those evils, the most obvious is the restraint imposed upon emancipation by the laws of so many of the slaveholding States : laws, deriving their recent origin from the obvious manifestation which the increase of the free colored population has furnished, of the inconvenience and danger of multiplying their number where slavery exists at all.' * * * ' By the success of this scheme, our country will be enriched. The free blacks constitute a material spoke in that wheel which is crushing down the wealth of our land. The moment we carry this plan into vigorous prosecution, we shall call many of our countrymen to a state of comparative wealth. The removal of the annual increase of our colored population, would give to our mariners a considerable scope of employment, whilst the trade of the Colony would be a source of profit.' * * ' It places the attainment of the grand object in view, that is, to withdraw from the United States annually, so many of the colored population, and provide them a comfortable home and all the advantages of civilization in Africa, *as will make the number here remain stationary.*' * * * ' Let us recur to the principle abovementioned—that every black family occupies the room of a white family. On this principle we are lost, if we suffer the colored population to multiply, unchecked, upon our hands ; because they will increase faster than the whites, and will crowd them out of all the Southern country. But on the same principle we are saved, if by any means of colonization, we can retard the increase of the blacks, and gain ground on them in the South. That we can do with ease, if our people will unite in prosecuting the scheme. Every family taken from the blacks, will add also a family to the whites, and make an actual difference of two families in our favor. This exchange will leave fewer blacks to remove, while it will increase our ability to remove them. Self-interest and self-preservation furnish motives enough to excite our exertions.' * * 'By thus repressing the rapid increase of blacks, the white population would be enabled to reach and soon overtop them. The consequence would be security.'— [African Repository, vol. iv. pp. 53, 141, 271, 276, 344.]

' The existence of a class of men in the bosom of the community, who occupy a middle rank between the citizen and the slave—who encountering every positive evil incident to each condition, share none of the benefits peculiar to either, has been long clearly seen and deeply deplored by every man of observation. The master feels it in the unhappy influence which the free blacks have upon the slave population. The slave feels it in the restless, discontented spirit which his association with the free black engenders.' * * * * 'But, there is yet a more important and alarming view, in which this subject necessarily presents itself to the mind of every Virginian. A community of the character that has been described, with this additional peculiarity, that it differs from the class from which it has sprung, only in its exemption from *the wholesome restraints of domestic authority*, is found in the midst of a numerous and rapidly increasing slave population ; and while its partial freedom, trammelled, as it is, by the necessary rigors of the law, is nevertheless sufficiently attractive, to be a source of uneasiness and dissatisfaction to those who have not attained to its questionable privileges, its exemption from the prompt and efficient inquisition appertaining to slavery, makes it an important instrument in the corruption and seduction of those, who yet remain the property of their masters.' * * * 'Who would not rejoice to see our country liberated from her black population ? Who would not participate in any efforts to restore those children of misfortune to their native shores, and kindle the lights of science and civilization through Africa ? Who that has reflection, does not tremble for the political and moral well-being of a country, that has within its bosom, a growing population, bound to its institutions by no common sympathies, and ready to fall in with any faction that may threaten its liberties ?' * * * ' The existence of this race among us ; a race that can neither share our blessings nor incorporate in our society, is already felt to be a curse ; and though the only curse entailed on us, if left to take its course, it will become the greatest that could befal the nation.
' Shall we then cling to it, and by refusing the timely expedient now offered for deliverance, retain and foster the *alien enemies*, till they have multiplied into such greater numbers, and risen into such mightier consequence as will for ever bar the possibility of their departure, and by barring it, bar also the possibility of fulfilling our own high destiny?' * * 'The object of this Society is two-fold ; for while it immediately and ostensibly directs its energies to the amelioration of the condition of the free people of color, it relieves our country from an unprofitable burden, and which, if much longer submitted to, may record upon our history the dreadful cries of vengeance that but a few years since were registered in characters of blood at St. Domingo.' * * ' It is the removal of the *free* blacks from among us, that is to save us, sooner or later, from these dreadful events foreboded by Mr Jefferson, or from the horrors of St. Domingo. The present number of this unfortunate, degraded, and anomalous class of inhabitants cannot be much short of half a million ; and the number is fast increasing. They are emphatically a mildew upon our fields, a scourge to our backs, and a stain upon our escutcheon. To remove them is mercy to ourselves, and justice to them.'—[African Repository, vol. v. pp. 28, 51, 88, 278, 304, 348.]

' All admit the utility of the separation of the free people of color from the residue of the population of the United States, if it be practicable. It is desirable for them, *for the slaves of the United States*, and for the white race. The vices of this class do not spring from any inherent depravity in their natural constitution, but from their unfortunate situation. Social intercourse is a want which we are prompted to gratify by all the properties of our nature. And as they cannot obtain it in the better circles of society, nor always among themselves, they resort to slaves and to the most debased and worthless of the whites. Corruption, and all the train of petty offences, are the consequences. Proprietors of slaves in whose neighborhood any free colored family is situated, know how infectious and pernicious this intercourse is.' * * * 'Who, if this promiscuous residence of whites and blacks, of freemen and slaves, is for ever to continue, can imagine the servile wars, the carnage and the crimes which will be its probable consequences, without shuddering with horror?' * * 'It were madness to shut our eyes to these facts and conclusions. This rapid increase of the blacks is as certain as the progress of time. The fatal consequences of that increase, if it be not checked, are equally so. Something must be done. The American Colonization Society proposes a remedy—the removal to Africa of the blacks who are free, or shall hereafter become so, with their consent.' * * 'The colored population is considered by the people of Tennessee and Alabama in general, as an immense evil to the country—but the free part of it, by all, as the greatest of all evils. . . . . They feel severely the effects of the deleterious influence which the free negroes exert upon the slaves—and they look, moreover, into futurity, and there they behold an appalling scene—in less than one hundred years, (a short time, we should hope, in the life of this republic,) 16,000,000 of blacks.' * * * * 'Since the recent revolution in the island of St. Domingo, which has placed it in the hands of the African race, it was thought by some that there an asylum might be found for this part of our population. But to that place there were also serious objections, which would prevent its adoption to any considerable extent. The nearness of that Island to our southern borders, and the evil consequences that might result from embodying the free persons of color in the vicinity of those parts of the United States, where slaves are so numerous, forbade the friends of humanity to provide a home for them in that Island.'—[African Repository, vol. vi. pp. 17, 23, 68, 77, 226.]

'The existence, within the very bosom of our country, of an anomalous race of beings, the most debased upon earth, who neither enjoy the blessings of freedom, nor are yet in the bonds of slavery, is a great national evil, which every friend of his country most deeply deplores. They constitute a large mass of human beings, who hang as a vile excrescence upon society—the objects of a low debasing envy to our slaves, and to ourselves of universal suspicion and distrust.' * * 'If this process were continued a second term of duplication, it would produce the extraordinary result of forty white men to one black in the country—a state of things in which we should not only cease to feel the burdens which now hang so heavily upon us, but actually regard the poor African as an object of curiosity, and not uneasiness.' * * 'Enough, under favorable circumstances, might be removed for a few successive years—if young *females* were encouraged to go—to keep the whole colored population in check.'—[African Repository, vol. vii. pp. 230, 232, 246.]

'The existence of such a population among us is a most manifest evil. And every year adds to its threatening aspect. They are more than a sixth of our population ! Their ratio of increase exceeds that of the whites. They have all the lofty and immortal powers of man. And the time must arrive, when they will fearlessly claim the prerogatives of man. They may do it in the spirit of revenge. They may do it in the spirit of desperation. And the result of such a mustering of their energies—who can look at it even in distant prospect without horror ? Almost as numerous are they now, as our whole population when this nation stood forth for freedom in a contest with the mightiest power of the civilized world. And if nothing is done to *arrest their increase*, we shall have in twenty years four millions of slaves ; in forty years eight millions ; in sixty years sixteen millions, and a million of free blacks ;—seventeen millions of people ; seven millions more than our present white population ;—enough for a powerful empire ! And how can they be governed ? Who can foretel those scenes of carnage and terror which our own children may witness, unless a seasonable remedy be applied ? The remedy is now within our reach. *We can stop their increase ;* we can diminish their number.'—[Rev. Baxter Dickinson's Sermon delivered at Springfield, Mass. in 1829.]

' We have a numerous people, who, though they are among us, are not of us ; who are aliens and outcasts in the land of their birth. A people whose condition is degraded and miserable ; who, so far from adding to our national strength, are an element of weakness, and detract from the amount of human effort. A people, whose condition, while it excites our commiseration, must awaken our fears.' * * ' Those persons of color who have been emancipated, are only nominally free ; and the whole race, so long as they remain among us, and whether they be slaves or free, must *necessarily* be kept in a condition full of wretchedness to them and full of danger to the whites. This view of the subject is rendered the more alarming by the rapid increase of this portion of our population.'—[Second Annual Report of the New-York State Colonization Society, pp. 4, 34.]

' We would ask, whence have the troubles, which have taken place among the slaves of Louisiana, originated ? Trace the causes, and we will invariably find them to have proceeded from the suggestions and officious interferences of the free blacks. Their very existence in our limits, enjoying supposed independence, excites the envy and dissatisfaction of the slaves. The latter naturally inquire, why is it, that persons of the same color, are permitted to possess more privileges than they do ? . . . We know the danger to which we are exposed from such a class of beings living in the very heart of our population, and increasing greatly every year.'—[An advocate of the Society in the New-Orleans Argus.]

' Among us the free negroes are multiplying rapidly ; both conscience and religion, as well as propagation, increase them, and, unless instant and decisive steps are taken to prevent their increase, you will soon have 50,000 *determined and vengeful enemies* in the heart of your country, protected there by the constitution, forsooth, by which it seems we are forbidden to expel the free negroes, or to prevent farther importations of this deadly pest in the persons of slaves.'—[Louisville Focus.]

' Will not the people of the United States be induced to do something to remove their colored population ? I refer to their condition, whether bond or free. They are wretched and dangerous, and should be removed. And the danger arises, not because we have thousands of slaves within our borders, but because there are nearly two millions of colored men, who are by necessity any thing rather than loyal citizens.'—[Address by Gabriel P. Disosway, Esq.]

' It is not now a novel or a debateable proposition, that slavery is a great moral and political curse. It is equally clear that its multitudinous evils are greatly increased by the existence among us of a mongrel population, who, freed from the shackles of bondage, yet bear about them the badge of inferiority, stamped upon them indelibly by the hand of nature, and are therefore deprived of those rights of citizenship, without which they must necessarily be a degraded caste—depraved in morals and vicious in conduct, and *exercising a mischievous and dangerous influence over those to whom they are nominally superior.* Their mere existence among the slaves is sufficient, of itself, to excite in the bosoms of the latter a feeling of dissatisfaction with their own condition, apparently worse, because of the coercion to labor which it imposes ; but essentially better, because of the comforts which that labor procures, and of which the idle and dissolute habits of the free negro almost invariably deprive him. The slave, however, is not capable of reasoning correctly, if he reasons at all, on these truths. He envies the free negro his idleness, and his freedom from restraint, with all its attendant disadvantages of poverty and disease, crime and punishment——and hence, he will sometimes indulge the delusive dream of effecting his own emancipation by the murder of those who hold him in bondage. Take away from him this cause of dissatisfaction, and this incentive to insurrection, and then these " impracticable hopes,'' which now sometimes flit before his imagination, will no longer embitter his hours of labor, and urge him to the commission of those horrid deeds of massacre, which, though they may glut a momentary revenge, must result disastrously, not only to the slaves engaged immediately in their perpetration, but to all that unfortunate race. Our true interests require that they shall remove from among us—and no longer be a source of disquietude to the whites, *of envy to the slaves*, and of degradation to themselves.'—[Lynchburg (Va.) Virginian.]

' For the most conclusive reasons this removal should be to Africa. If it be to the West Indies, to Texas, to Canada, then, how strong and various the objections to building up, in the vicinity of our own nation, a mighty empire, from a race of men, *so unlike ourselves* ? But, if the removal be to Africa, then it is to a *happy distance* from us and to their father land. . . . Then let it aid in removing that population, which, under its peculiar relation to the whites, and under its degrading social and civil disabilities, is a most fruitful source of national dishonor, demoralization, weakness and *horrid danger*.'—[Memorial of the New-York State Colonization Society.]

' The males removed should be persons between 16 and 17 years of age ; the females between 13 and 14. Now as a number would be annually removed equal to the whole increase, and as that number would be composed of individuals, of such ages that their removal would affect the future increase of the race in the greatest possible degree, I believe that their numbers would not only not increase, but would diminish. And the number removed might be increased as the proportion of white persons in the State became greater, until the removal reached a point at which all the males who attained the age of sixteen, and all the females who attained the age of fourteen, in any given year, would during that year be removed.'—[Petersburg (Va.) Times.]

' They are well calculated to render the slaves sullen, discontented, unhappy and refractory—and the masters suspicious, fearful of consequences, and disposed to enhance the rigor of the condition of their slaves, in order to avert the dangers that appear to impend over them from the promulgation of the anti-slavery doctrines ; thus, in this case, as in so many others, the imprudent zeal of friends is likely to produce as much substantial injury as the animosity of decided enemies could accomplish.'—[Mathew Carey's Essays.]

' Hatred to the whites is, with the exception in some cases of an attachment to the person and family of the master, nearly universal among the black population. We have then a foe, cherished in our very bosoms—a foe willing to draw our life-blood whenever the opportunity is offered, and, in the mean time, intent upon doing us all the mischief in his power.'—[Southern Religious Telegraph.]

Does the reader wish for any additional proof that the governing motive of the American Colonization Society is fear— undisguised, *excessive* FEAR ? Language is altogether inadequate to express my indignation and contempt, in view of such a heartless and cowardly exhibition of sentiment. There is a deep sense of guilt, an awful dread of retribution, manifested in the foregoing extracts ; but we perceive no evidence of contrition for past or present injustice, on the part of those terror-

stricken plotters. Instead of returning to those, whom they
have so deeply injured, ' with repenting and undissembling
love ; ' instead of seeking to conciliate and remunerate the victims of their prejudice and oppression ; instead of resolving to
break the yoke of servitude and let the oppressed go free ; it
seems to be their only anxiety and aim to outwit the vengeance
of Heaven, and strengthen the bulwarks of tyranny, by expelling
the free people of color from our shores, and effecting such a
diminution of the number of slaves as shall give the white population a triumphant and irresistible superiority ! ' *Check the increase !* ' is their cry—' let us retain in everlasting bondage as
many as we can, *safely ;* but the proportion must be at least ten
millions of ourselves to two millions of our vassals, else we shall
live in jeopardy ! To do justly is not our intention ; we only
mean to remove the surplus of our present stock ; we think we
shall be able, by this prudent device, to oppress and rob with
impunity. Our present wailing is not for our heinous crimes,
but only because our avarice and cruelty have carried us beyond our ability to protect ourselves : we lament, not because
we hold so large a number in fetters of iron, but because we
cannot safely hold more ! '

Ye crafty calculators ! ye hard-hearted, incorrigible sinners !
ye greedy and relentless robbers ! ye contemners of justice and
mercy ! ye trembling, pitiful, pale-faced usurpers ! my soul
spurns you with unspeakable disgust. Know ye not that the reward of your hands shall be given you ? ' Wo unto them that
decree unrighteous decrees, and that write grievousness which
they have prescribed ; to turn aside the needy from judgment,
and to take away the right from the poor, that widows may be
their prey, and that they may rob the fatherless ! And what will
ye do in the day of visitation, and in the desolation which shall
come from far ? to whom will ye flee for help ? and where will
ye leave your glory ? '—' What mean ye that ye beat my people to pieces, and grind the face of the poor ? saith the Lord
God of hosts.'—' Behold, the hire of the laborers which have
reaped down your fields, which is of you kept back by fraud,
crieth ; and the cries of them which have reaped are entered
into the ears of the Lord of Sabaoth.' Repent ! repent !

now, in sackcloth and ashes. Think not to succeed in your
expulsive crusade ; you cannot hide your motives from the.
Great Searcher of hearts ; and if a sinful worm of the dust, like
myself, is fired with indignation at your dastardly behaviour and
mean conspiracy to evade repentance and punishment, how must
the anger of Him, whose holiness and justice are infinite, burn
against you ? Is it not a fearful thing to fall into the hands of
the living God ? You may plot by day and by night ; you may
heap together the treasures of the land, and multiply and enlarge
your combinations, to extricate yourselves from peril ; but *you
cannot succeed.* Your only alternative is, either to redress the
wrongs of the oppressed *now*, and humble yourselves before
God, or prepare for the chastisements of Heaven. I repeat
it—Repentance or Punishment must be yours.

There are several points upon which I wish to fasten the
attention of the reader :

1. The inhumanity and craftiness of these propositions for
the removal of the free people of color.

It will be seen that the conspirators have taxed their ingenuity
to the utmost, to ascertain the exact number of emigrants which
must be transported annually, the amount of money that must be
raised, the persons that must be selected, the number of vessels
that must be employed, &c. &c. It is their determination, if the
necessary means can be obtained, to transport the annual increase
of our colored population ; but in this calculation we find no allowance made for unwillingness or resistance on the part of those
who are the objects of their supervision. It is taken for granted
that all will be induced to go into exile, or must be made willing compulsorily. Nothing else is contemplated but their entire
expulsion. In order to insure a reduction of this ' alarming
increase,' and effectually to check the fruitfulness of generation,
even the unmanly and scandalous proposition is made to remove
principally those of both sexes who are just come to the age of
puberty ! The system of *espionage*, established by Napoleon to
prevent the possibility of a successful conspiracy, was not more
detestable and observant than is this violent and unnatural
project. ' If *young females* were encouraged to go ' !—why,
then they could not propagate here ! Infamous calculation !

2. The principal object avowed for the removal of the free people of color, is, their corruptive and dangerous influence over the slave population.

It is demonstrated, then, beyond disputation, that this removal will infuse new strength into the tottering system of slavery, tighten the grasp of the masters upon the throats of the slaves, lull them into a profound and quiet sleep, postpone the hour of emancipation, and enhance the security and value of slave property. The terror of mind which calls for this separation cannot be benevolence, and the combination which seeks to effect it cannot merit support. It were folly to hope that the owners of slaves will ultimately emancipate them, from conscientious motives. In the first place, they affect to be innocent in holding their victims in servitude ; secondly, they are assured by their colonization brethren that they are not guilty of oppression, but, on the contrary, are watchful guardians ; and lastly, they are obstinate in shutting their eyes upon the light, and kindle into a rage on being arraigned for their tyrannous conduct. Our only ground of hope, then, is in increasing the difficulty of holding their slaves, in multiplying the causes of their apprehensions, in destroying the value of slave labor, and in making their situation full of disquietude and distress. Such a course is not inconsistent with benevolence—such a course we are obligated to pursue, as we value the present and everlasting welfare of the oppressor and the oppressed, and desire to have a conscience void of offence toward God and toward man. It may —it *must* be effected by a scrupulous abstinence from the productions of slavery ; by encouraging planters to cultivate their lands by the hands of free laborers ; by educating our free colored population, and placing them on an equality with ourselves ; and by constantly exhibiting the criminality of holding rational and immortal beings in servile bondage. Thus, and thus only, shall we be able to liberate our enslaved countrymen.

3. Consider the inevitable consequence of these reiterated and malignant statements, with regard to the habits and designs of the free people of color.

First, it deters a large number of masters from liberating their slaves, and hence directly perpetuates the evils of slavery :

it deters them for two reasons—an unwillingness to augment the wretchedness of those who are in servitude by turning them loose upon the country, and a dread of increasing the number of their enemies. It creates and nourishes the bitterest animosity against the free blacks. It has spread an alarm among all classes of society, in all parts of the country ; and, acting under this fearful impulse, they begin to persecute, believing self-preservation imperiously calls for this severe treatment. The legislative enactment of Ohio, which not long since drove many of the colored inhabitants of that State into Upper Canada, was the legitimate fruit of the anathemas of the Colonization Society. A bill has been reported in the same legislature for preventing free people of color from participating in the benefit of the common school fund, in order to hasten their expulsion from the State ! Other States are multiplying similar disabilities, and hanging heavier weights upon their free colored population. The Legislature of Louisiana has enacted that whosoever shall make use of language, in any public discourse, from the bar, the bench, the pulpit, the stage, or in any other place whatsoever shall make use of language, in any private discourses, or shall make use of signs or actions having a tendency to produce discontent among the colored population, shall suffer imprisonment at hard labor, not less than three years, nor more than twenty-one years, or DEATH, at the discretion of the court ! ! It has also prohibited the instruction of the blacks in Sabbath Schools—$500 penalty for the first offence—DEATH for the second ! ! The Legislature of Virginia has passed a bill which subjects all free negroes who shall be convicted of remaining in the commonwealth contrary to law, to the liability of *being sold by the sheriff.* All meetings of free negroes, at any school-house or meeting-house, for teaching them reading or writing, are declared an unlawful assembly ; and it is made the duty of any justice of the peace to issue his warrant to enter the house where such unlawful assemblage is held, for the purpose of apprehending or dispersing such free negroes. A fine is to be imposed on every white person who instructs at such meetings. All emancipated slaves, who shall remain more than twelve months, contrary to law, shall revert to the executors as assets.   Laws have been passed in Georgia and North Carolina, imposing a heavy tax or imprisonment on every free person of color who shall come into their ports in the capacity of stewards, cooks, or seamen of any vessels belonging to the non-slaveholding States.   The Legislature of Tennessee has passed an act forbidding free blacks from coming into the State to remain more than twenty days.   The penalty is a fine of from ten to fifty dollars, and confinement in the penitentiary from one to two years.   Double the highest penalty is to be inflicted after the first offence.   The act also prohibits manumission, without an immediate removal from the State.   The last Legislature of Maryland passed a bill, by which no free negro or mulatto is allowed to emigrate to, or settle in the State, under the penalty of fifty dollars for every week's residence therein ; and if he refuse or neglect to pay such fine, he shall be committed to jail and sold by the sheriff at public sale ; and no person shall employ or harbor him, under the penalty of twenty dollars for every day he shall be so employed, hired or harbored !   It is not lawful for any free blacks to attend any meetings for religious purposes, unless conducted by a *white* licensed or ordained preacher, or some respectable white person duly authorised !   All free colored persons residing in the State, are compelled to register their names, ages, &c. &c. ;   and if any negro or mulatto shall remove from the State, and remain without the limits thereof for a space longer than thirty consecutive days, unless before leaving the State he deposits with the clerk of the county in which he resides, *a written statement of his object in doing so*, and his intention of returning again, or unless he shall have been detained by sickness or coercion, *of which he shall bring a certificate*, he shall be regarded as a resident of another State, and be subject, if he return, to the penalties imposed by the foregoing provisions upon free negroes and mulattoes of another State, migrating to Maryland !   It is not lawful for any person or persons to purchase of any free negro or mulatto any articles, unless he produce a certificate from a justice of the peace, or three respectable persons residing in his neighborhood, that he or they have reason to believe, and do believe, that such free negro or mulatto came honestly and bona fide into possession of any such articles so offered for sale ! A bill has been reported to the Legislature of Pennsylvania, which enacts, that from and after a specified time, no negro or mulatto shall be permitted to emigrate into and settle in that State, without entering into bond in the penal sum of *five hundred dollars*, conditioned for his good behavior. If he neglect or refuse to comply with this requisition, such punishment shall be inflicted upon him as is now directed in the case of vagrants. Free colored residents are not to be allowed to migrate from one township or county to another, without producing a certificate from the Clerk of the Court of Quarter Sessions, or a Justice of the Peace, or an Alderman ! The passage of a similar law has been urged even upon the Legislature of Massachusetts by a writer in the Salem Gazette !

All these proscriptive measures, and others less conspicuous but equally oppressive,—which are not only flagrant violations of the Constitution of the United States, but in the highest degree disgraceful and inhuman,—are resorted to, (to borrow the language of the Secretary in his Fifteenth Annual Report,) ' for the more complete accomplishment of the great objects of the American Colonization Society ' ! !

I appeal to the candor and common sense of the reader, if this grievous persecution be not justly chargeable to the Society ? It is constantly thundering in the ears of the slave States— ' Your free blacks contaminate your slaves, excite their deadliest hate, and are a source of *horrid danger* to yourselves ! They must be removed, or your destruction is inevitable !' What is their response ? Precisely such as might be expected —' We know it ; we dread the presence of this class ; their influence over our slaves weakens our power, and endangers our safety ; they must, *they shall* be expatriated, or be crushed to the earth if they remain !' It says to the free States—' Your colored population can never be rendered serviceable, intelligent or loyal ; they will only, and always, serve to increase your taxes, crowd your poor-houses and penitentiaries, and corrupt and impoverish society !' Again, what is the natural response ?—' It is even so ; they are offensive to the eye, and a pest in community ; theirs is now, and must inevitably be,

without a reversal of the laws of nature, the lot of vagabonds ;
it were useless to attempt their intellectual and moral improvement among ourselves ; and therefore be this their alternative—
either to emigrate to Liberia, or remain for ever a despicable
caste in this country !'

Hence the enactment of those sanguinary laws, to which reference has been made : hence, too, the increasing disposition
which is every where seen to render the situation of the free
blacks intolerable.   Never was it so pitiable and distressing—
so full of peril and anxiety—so burdened with misery, despondency and scorn ; never were the prejudices of society so virulent and implacable against them ; never were their prospects so
dark, and dreary, and hopeless ; never was the hand of power
so heavily laid upon their limbs ; never were they so restricted
in regard to locomotion and the advantages of education, as at
the present time.   Athwart their sky scarcely darts a single ray
of light—above and around them darkness reigns, and an angry
tempest is mustering its fearful strength, and ' thunders are ut-
tering their voices.'   Treachery is seeking to decoy, and violence
to expel them.   For all this, and more than this, and more that
is to come, the American Colonization Society is responsible.
And no better evidence is needed than this : THEIR PERSECU-
TION, TRADUCEMENT AND WRETCHEDNESS INCREASE IN EXACT
RATIO WITH THE INFLUENCE, POPULARITY AND EXTENSION
OF THIS SOCIETY !   The fact is undeniable, and it is conclusive.   For it is absurd to suppose, that as the disposition and
ability of an association to alleviate misery increase, so will the
degradation and suffering of the objects of its charities.

The assertion that the free blacks corrupt the morals of the
slaves, is too ludicrous to need a serious refutation.   Corrupt
the morals of those who are recognized and treated as brutes,
and who know as little of the laws of God as of the laws of the
land !   Immaculate creatures !   The system of slavery is constantly developing new excellencies : it is, we now perceive, the
protector of virtue, the enemy of vice, and a purifier of the soul !

But something more indiscreet and preposterous than this, is
advanced for our admiration.   We are gravely assured, first, by
a New-England clergyman, that, generally, the condition of the

free man of color ' is one in comparison with which the condition of the slave is *enviable* ; ' and, secondly, by the last distinguished convert to the Colonization Society—the Hon. Mr. Archer of Virginia—' the condition of the slave is *a thousand times* the best, [the disparity is wonderful !]—*supplied, protected,* instead of *destitute* and *desolate* ' ! *   Let us draw a brief comparison. The limbs of the free black are fetterless ; he is controlled by no brutal driver ; he bleeds not under the lash ; he is his own master ; his wife and children cannot be torn from his arms ; he enjoys the fruits of his own labor ; he can improve his own mind, make his own bargains, manage his own business, go from place to place, and assert his own rights.   The situation and privileges of the slave are exactly the reverse.   Reader, are they ' enviable '—' a thousand times the best '—in comparison with those of the former ?   I do not mean to say that there are no instances in which the slave fares as well as the free man of color ; but the argument of these apologists implies that a state of slavery is superior to a state of freedom, or it is worthless.

4. It appears, from the quotations that have been given, that the only reason why the free blacks are not colonized in the ' far West,' or in Canada, or Hayti, or Mexico, is, because their proximity to the slave States might prove detrimental.   If they could be sent to any or to all these places, without any danger to ourselves, why then all objections would cease.   This confession places the hypocrisy of this Society in bold relief.   It pretends to be anxious to evangelize benighted Africa, and stop the slave trade ; but only assure it that the blacks may be safely colonized nearer home, and Africa might still continue to grope in darkness, and the slave trade to increase in enormity, and its bowels of compassion would speedily cease to yearn !— Hence it is that the rapid enlargement of the Wilberforce Settlement in Upper Canada so disturbs the repose of the advocates of African colonization ; and many of them would rejoice at its overthrow.

---

* Paupers and criminals are supplied and *protected.*   How invidious to treat them so generously, and leave honest, hard-working men exposed to destitution and abandonment !   They ought to be sent to the poor-house or penitentiary forthwith.

SECTION VII.

THE AMERICAN COLONIZATION SOCIETY AIMS AT THE UTTER EXPULSION OF THE BLACKS.

THE implacable spirit of this Society is most apparent in its determination not to cease from its labors, until our whole colored population be expelled from the country. The following is the evidence in confirmation of this charge :

' How came we by this population ? By the prevalence for a century of a guilty commerce. And will not the prevalence for a century of a restoring commerce, place them on their own shores ? Yes, surely ! '—[African Repository, vol. i. p. 347.]

' For several years the subject of abolition of slavery has been brought before you. I am decidedly opposed to the project recommended. NO SCHEME OF ABOLITION WILL MEET MY SUPPORT, THAT LEAVES THE EMANCIPATED BLACKS AMONG US. Experience has proved, that they become a corrupt and degraded class, as burthensome to themselves as they are hurtful to the rest of society. To permit the blacks to remain amongst us, after their emancipation, would be to aggravate and not to cure the evil.'—[Idem, vol ii. pp. 188, 189.]

' We would say, LIBERATE THEM ONLY ON CONDITION OF THEIR GOING TO AFRICA OR TO HAYTI.'—[Idem, vol. iii. p. 26.]

' *I am not complaining of the owners of slaves ;* IT WOULD BE AS HUMANE TO THROW THEM FROM THE DECKS IN THE MIDDLE PASSAGE, AS TO SET THEM FREE IN OUR COUNTRY.' *   *   *
' The Colonization Society, I undertake to show, presents such a scheme. Slaveholders have given it their approbation ; they will approve it, and they can approve of no other. *Any scheme of emancipation without colonization,* they know and see and feel to be productive of nothing but evil ; evil to all whom it affects : to the white population, to the slaves, to the *manumitted themselves.*'
*   *   * ' Throughout the slaveholding States there is a strong objection, even among the warmest friends of the African race, to slaves being liberated and allowed to remain among us ; and some States have enacted laws against it. *The objection is, in our individual opinion, well founded.*'—[Idem, vol. iv. pp. 226, 300, 340.]

' In connexion with this subject, your memorialists beg leave to mention, that by an act of the Virginia Legislature, passed in 1805, emancipated slaves forfeit their freedom by remaining for a longer period than twelve months, within the limits of the Commonwealth. This law, odious and unjust as it may at first view appear, and hard as it may seem to bear upon the liberated negro, was doubtless dictated by sound policy, and *its repeal would be regarded by none with more unfeigned regret, than by the friends of African Colonization.* It has restrained many masters from giving freedom to their slaves, and has thereby contributed to check the growth of an evil *already too great and formidable.*'
*   * ' Under the influence of a policy, already referred to, *and justified by the necessity from which it sprung*, the laws of Virginia have prohibited emancipa-

tion within the limits of the State, but on condition of the early removal of the individual emancipated.' * * ' While hundreds, perhaps we might say thousands, of the free colored people, are seeking a passage to Liberia ; hundreds who hold slaves, would willingly set them at liberty, were the means of their removal provided. And till those means *are* provided, the liberation of the slave would neither be a blessing to himself, nor the public. His liberty under any circumstances may be a debt due, in the abstract, to the claims of human nature ; but when applied to him individually, it would be a calamity. We cannot conceive of a more deplorable state of society, than what our slaveholding states would present, with their black population afloat, without a home, without the means of subsistence, and without those self-relying habits, which might lead them to obtain an independent livelihood. *It is not therefore incumbent upon those who hold slaves, to set them at liberty, till some means are provided for their removal, or at least for their subsistence.* They owe it neither to themselves, to their country, nor the unfortunate beings around them.' * * * ' Those slaves still in my possession, I cannot conscientiously emancipate, unless they shall be removed by the Society to Liberia.'—[Idem, vol. v. pp. 20, 53, 89, 177.]

' If the question were submitted, whether there should be either immediate or gradual emancipation of all the slaves in the United States, *without their removal or colonization*, painful as it is to express the opinion, I HAVE NO DOUBT THAT IT WOULD BE UNWISE TO EMANCIPATE THEM.' * * ' Is our posterity doomed to endure forever not only all the ills flowing from the state of slavery, but all which arise from incongruous elements of population, separated from each other by invincible prejudices, and by natural causes ? Whatever may be the character of the remedy proposed, we may confidently pronounce it inadequate, unless it provides efficaciously for the *total* and *absolute* separation, by an extensive space of water or of land, at least, of the white portion of our population from that, which is free, of the colored.' * * ' Who, if this promiscuous residence of whites and blacks, of freemen and slaves, is forever to continue, can imagine the servile wars, the carnage and the crimes which will be its probable consequences, without shuddering with horror ?' * * ' Gentlemen of the highest respectability from the South, assure us, that there is among the owners of slaves a very extensive and increasing desire to emancipate them. Their patriotism, their humanity, nay their self-interest, prompt to this ; but it is not expedient, it is not safe to do it, *without being able to remove them.*' * * ' How important it is, as it respects our character abroad, that we hasten to *clear our land of our black population!*'
' Some benevolent minds in the overflowings of their philanthropy, advocate amalgamation of the two classes, saying, let the colored class be freed, and remain among us as denizens of the Empire ; surely all classes of mankind are alike descended from the primitive parentage of Eden, then why not intermingle in one common society as friends and brothers. *No, Sir, no.* I hope to prove at no very distant day, that a Southron can make sacrifices for the cause of Colonization beyond seas ; but for a Home Department in those matters, I repeat, *no, Sir, no.* What right, I demand, have the children of Africa to an homestead in the white man's country ?'*
' Let the regenerated African rise to Empire ; nay, let Genius flourish, and Philosophy shed its mild beams to enlighten and instruct the posterity of Ham, returning " redeemed and disenthralled," from their long captivity in the New World. But, Sir, be all these benefits enjoyed by the African race under the shade of their native palms. *Let the Atlantic billow heave its high and*

---

* What right have we to an homestead in the red man's country ? Let us return to the land of our fathers, and leave this soil untarnished by the footprint of him who hath a white skin ! What right have the hosts of foreign emigrants, who are flocking to our shores, to an homestead among ourselves ?

everlasting barrier between their country and ours. Let this fair land, which the white man won by his chivalry, which he has adorned by the arts and elegancies of polished life, be kept sacred for his descendants, untarnished by the footprint of him who hath ever been a slave.'—[Idem, vol. vi. pp. 5, 12, 23, 110, 364, 371, 372.]

' The idea of emancipating our slaves, and *permitting them to remain within the limits of the U. S.* whether as a measure of humanity or of policy, is most decisively reprobated by universal public sentiment . . . Does any man in his senses desire this population to remain among us? If the whole community could reply, IT WOULD RESPOND IN ONE UNIVERSAL NEGATIVE.' —[Idem, vol. vii. pp. 230, 231.]

'In reflecting on the utility of a plan for colonizing the free people of color, with whom our country abounds, it is natural that we should be first struck by its tendency to confer a benefit on ourselves, by *ridding us of a population* for the most part idle and useless, and too often vicious and mischievous . . . All emancipation, to however small an extent, *which permits the persons emancipated to remain in this country,* is an evil, which must increase with the increase of the operation, and would become altogether intolerable, if extended to the whole, or even to a very large part, of the black population. I am therefore strongly opposed to emancipation, in every shape and degree, *unless accompanied by colonization.'*—[First Annual Report.]

' They will annex the condition that the emancipated SHALL LEAVE THE COUNTRY.'—[Second Annual Report.]

' They require that the *whole mass* of free persons of color, and those who may become such with the consent of their owners, *should be progressively removed* from among us, as fast as their own consent can be obtained, and as the means can be found for their removal and for their proper establishment in Africa. Nothing short of this progressive but complete removal can accomplish the great objects of this measure, in relation to the security, prosperity, and happiness of the United States.'—[Seventh Annual Report.]

' Is it either safe or prudent to retain amongst us a large population, on whom we can place no reliance, but from the control which the laws exercise over it? Can this class be animated by any feelings of patriotism towards a country by which they feel themselves oppressed? '—[Ninth Annual Report.]

' Colonization, to be correct, must be beyond seas—Emancipation, *with the liberty to remain on this side of the Atlantic,* IS BUT AN ACT OF DREAMY MADNESS ! '—[Thirteenth Annual Report.]

' Has our country the resources demanded for the accomplishment of an object of such magnitude? The transportation of more than two millions of souls to a remote country is indeed an object of formidable aspect. It obviously cannot be accomplished at once. But that the number can be gradually diminished, *till utterly extinguished,* may be made to appear, it is believed, from a little arithmetical calculation.' . . ' It has been said that the entire shipping of the country, both public and private, would hardly be competent for an object of this magnitude. But careful calculation has proved, that one eighteenth of the mercantile shipping alone, entirely devoted to the enterprise, is competent to carry it into complete consummation. And why might not our brilliant and growing *navy* aid to some extent the humane and patriotic cause? If necessary, why might not *the marine of other lands* be chartered? Strange indeed it is if shipping enough could be found half a century ago to reduce hundreds of thousands of this race in a single year to a wretched vassalage, and in this age of augmented light, and wealth, and improvement in every art, enough cannot be found for the single benevolent object before us !'—[Rev. Baxter Dickinson's Sermon delivered in Springfield in 1829.]

'How much soever we may regret that so little is done for the intellectual and moral improvement of the free colored population, as the surest preventive against crime, still we must acknowledge it is in vain to attempt raising their character to a level with that of the other inhabitants. They must find an asylum beyond the influence of the white population, or the majority of them will *ever be found unworthy of the boon of freedom.* There must be that asylum for them, or we despair of ever being able to improve materially their condition, or to eradicate slavery from our soil, and thus prevent the awful catas trophe which threatens our republic. They must be furnished with facilities to leave this country and establish themselves in a community of their own.'—
'I have alluded to the difficulties which are presented to the minds of benevolent and conscientious slaveholders, wishing to manumit their slaves. From what has been said, it is evident that unless some drain is opened to convey out of the country the emancipated, the laws which relate to emancipation, must continue in force with all their rigor. Without this drain, we can hope for no repeal, or relaxation of those laws where the slaves are very numerous. The mass of slaveholders can never let go their hold on their slaves, and suffer them, ignorant, vicious and treacherous, to roam at large. If no drain is opened, necessity will compel them, as their slaves increase, and consequently the danger, to add statute to statute in regard to their slaves, until it be found necessary to arm one part of the population to control the other. I may add, that as bitter an enemy as I am to slavery, I cannot greatly desire that these laws should be relaxed—that slavery should be abolished, *unless its unfortunate and degraded subjects can be removed from the country.* If this is not effected, whatever may be our views and wishes on this subject, I am confident that slaveholders will justify themselves in resorting to almost any measures to keep their slaves in entire subjection.'—[An advocate of the Society in the Middletown (Ct.) Gazette.]

'To talk of emancipating the slave population of these States without providing them with an asylum, is truly idle. The free blacks already scattered through the country, are a dangerously burthensome order of people. They cannot amalgamate with the population—the ordinances of nature are against it. They must, in the main, be a degraded order, hanging loosely upon society.'—[Idem.]

'The slaves *are* in their possession—they are entailed upon them by their ancestors. And can they set them free, *and still suffer them to remain in the country?* Would this be policy?—Would it be safe? NO. When they can be transported to the soil from whence they were derived—by the aid of the Colonization Society, by government, by individuals, or by any other means—then let them be emancipated, and not before.'—[Lowell (Mass.) Telegraph.]

'Avarice and iniquity have torn from that injured continent, within thirty years, no less than 1,500,000 slaves ; and cannot humanity, religion, and justice, restore an equal number in the same time? If we desire to accomplish this work, it is plain that we can do it, and that too with a sum contemptible when compared with the magnitude of the evil.'—[Address of Gabriel P. Disosway.]

'We thank God that the ultimate accomplishment of the great scheme of colonization is now placed beyond a doubt, in Maryland ; and that the day is not even distant when *the whole of our colored population* will have transferred themselves, by our assistance, from slavery or degradation here, to peace, and plenty, and power, and prosperity, and liberty, and independence, in a land which Providence originally gave them.'—[Baltimore Gazette.]

' It tends, and may powerfully tend, to rid us gradually and entirely, in the United States, of slaves and slavery : a great moral and political evil, of increasing virulence and extent, from which much mischief is now felt, and very great calamity in future is justly apprehended.'—[First Annual Report.]

' What can be done to mitigate or prevent the existing and apprehended evils, resulting from our black population ? EMANCIPATION, WITHOUT REMOVAL FROM THE COUNTRY, IS OUT OF THE QUESTION.' * * ' As long as our present feelings and prejudices exist, the abolition of slavery cannot be accomplished without the removal of the blacks—THEY CANNOT BE EMANCIPATED AS A PEOPLE, AND REMAIN AMONG US.'— [Second Annual Report of the New-York State Col. Soc.]

' It would gladly, however, grasp at a still grander object—that of restoring to the land of their fathers the whole colored race within our borders. Nor probably will it be satisfied to rest from its labors, till this object, in all its magnitude, is accomplished.'—[Rev. Baxter Dickinson's Sermon.]

' It must appear evident to all, that every endeavor to divert the attention of the community, or even a portion of the means, which the present crisis so imperatively calls for, from the Colonization Society, to measures calculated to bind the colored population to this country and seeking to raise them (*an impossibility*) to a level with the whites, whether by founding colleges or in any other way, tends directly in the proportion that it succeeds, to counteract and thwart the whole plan of colonization. Although none would rejoice more than myself to see this unhappy race elevated to the highest scale of human being, it has always seemed to me that this country was not the theatre for such a change. Far happier they, far happier we, had they never touched our soil, or breathed our air. As it is, to attain solid happiness and permanent respectability, they should now remove to a more congenial clime.'—[New Haven Religious Intelligencer for July, 1831.]

' The recent murderous movements of the people of color in some of the southern States, evinces the dreadful consequences of slavery, and the absolute necessity of colonizing all free blacks immediately, and of manumitting and colonizing slaves as fast as circumstances will justify the measure. We believe, and have for many years, that this is the only course, which will ensure prosperity and safety to our southern brethren.'—[New-Hampshire Observer.]

' The removal annually of one hundred thousand, it may be safely calculated, would sink the parent stock forty thousand in each year, and this in thirty years would reduce the blacks of the Union to a very small number—perhaps not one would remain.'--[National (Ohio) Historian.]

' We will demonstrate, that the conveyance of the present annual increase would, in less than thirty years, remove the whole to Africa. Let all, for instance, born in any single year, say of the age of twenty, be removed to Africa ; and in each succeeding year, let all of that age be removed in the same manner.—Then, admitting, what is far too much to admit, that a generation lasts fifty years, on an average, the generation on the stage when the process commenced, would have become extinct at the end of thirty years, and all their increase or offspring would have been removed to Africa. Thirty years would, even in this way, clear them entirely from this country.—But there are two circumstances which would, in fact, make the time much shorter.
' 1. It is known that a generation lasts but a little more than thirty years. The generation, then, on the stage at the commencement of the process, would virtually be extinct in a little more than ten years. 2. By the removal of the most prolific part, the annual increase would itself be diminished more than a thirtieth part, in each successive year ; that is, it would be diminished in an arithmetical

ratio, so that it would be reduced to nothing before the arrival of the thirtieth year.'—[American Spectator.]

'It is " a consummation devoutly to be wished," that we should get clear of the free people of color now, and as they are successively liberated, as well on their own account as ours ; and I trust and hope, we shall both have the pleasure to see a moral certainty of the removal of all these poor people back to the same country from which their ancestors were taken.'—[African Repository, vol. iii. p. 311.]

' Neither do we consider liberty worth their acceptance, *unless they can be sent out of the country.* There is no doubt that a large proportion of the slaves enjoy life quite as well as those who are free.'—[Oxford (Me.) Observer.]

' It is estimated that there are 2,350,680 blacks in the United States, 339,360 of whom are free denizens of this republic. The object of this Society is THE REMOVAL OF THESE TO AFRICA.'—[New-York Standard.]

' We hope to make it for the interest of the owners, in some way, to part with their slaves ;—not to be let loose among our white population, but to be carried back to the land of their fathers.'—[N. Y. Journal of Commerce.]

' If they are to be placed above their present degraded condition, they must be removed to a country where they can rise as high as any man—be eligible to any office—then you will see them rise with the rapidity of the tide.'—[Southern Religious Telegraph.]

' God has put a mark upon the black man.' . . ' The God of Nature intended they should be a *distinct,* free and independent community.'—[New-Haven Palladium.]

'We do not ask that the provisions of our Constitution and statute book should be so modified as to relieve and exalt the condition of the colored people, *whilst they remain with us.* LET THESE PROVISIONS STAND IN ALL THEIR RIGOR, to work out the ultimate and unbounded good of this people. Persuaded that their condition here is not susceptible of a radical and permanent improvement, WE WOULD DEPRECATE ANY LEGISLATION THAT SHOULD ENCOURAGE THE VAIN AND INJURIOUS HOPE OF IT.'—[Memorial of the New-York State Colonization Society.]

' Let the wise and good among us unite in removing the blacks from the country. Would it not be expedient for the properly constituted authorities to prevent the manumission of slaves in every case, unless provision is made, at the same time, to secure their removal from the country ?'—[Alexandria Gazette.]

' We should be in favor of the abolition of slavery, if its abolishment could be effected with safety, and the colored population sent back to Africa ; but merely to have them obtain freedom and let loose upon society, would be the greatest *curse* that could befal *them* or *community.*'—[Essex Chronicle and County Republican.]

' THE ABOLITION OF SLAVERY WAS NO OBJECT OF DESIRE TO HIM, UNLESS ACCOMPANIED BY COLONIZATION. So far was he from desiring it, unaccompanied by this condition, that HE WOULD NOT LIVE IN A COUNTRY WHERE THE ONE TOOK PLACE WITHOUT THE OTHER ' ! ! !—[Mr Mercer's Speech in Congress.]

In order to wipe off the reproach due to this violent expulsion, it was necessary, on the part of the Society, to find some

pretext that would not only seem to justify but confer credit on
the measure. Accordingly, it agreed to represent the colored
inhabitants of the United States as aliens and foreigners, who,
cast upon our shores by a cruel fatality, were sighing to return
to their native land. ' Poor unfortunate exiles !'—how touching the appeal, how powerful the motive to assist, how likely to
excite the compassion of the nation ! Ah ! what an air of disinterested benevolence, of generous compassion, of national
attachment, must such an enterprise wear in the eyes of the
world ! Who that loved his own country, and deprecated an
eternal absence from it, could refuse to help in restoring the
unfortunate Africans to their long-estranged home ? Such was,
and is, and is likely to be, the artifice resorted to, in order to
cover a base conspiracy, and give popularity to one of the wildest and most disgraceful crusades the world has ever witnessed.
Let the following evidence suffice :

' At no very distant period, we should see all the free colored people in our
land transferred to *their own country.*' * * ' Let us send them back to
their native land.' * * ' By returning them to *their own ancient land*
of Africa, improved in knowledge and in civilization, we repay the debt which
has so long been due them.'—[African Repository, vol. i. pp. 65, 146, 176.]

' And though we may not live to see the day when the sons of Africa shall
have returned to *their native soil*,' &c. * * ' To found in Africa an empire
of christians and republicans ; to reconduct the blacks to *their native land*,'
&c.—[Idem, pp. 13, 375.]

' Who would not rejoice to see our country liberated from her black population ? Who would not participate in any efforts to restore those children of misfortune to *their native shores* ?' * * ' The colored population of this country can never rise to respectability here ; in *their native soil* they can.' * *
' The only remedy afforded is, to colonize them in *their mother country.*' * *
' They would go to that *home* from which they have been long absent.' * *
' Shall we . . retain and foster the *alien enemies* ?'—[Idem, 88, 179, 185,
237.]

' Be all these benefits enjoyed by the African race under the shade of their
native palms.'—[Idem, vol. vi. p. 372.]

' We have a numerous people, who, though they are among us, *are not of
us.*'—[Second Annual Report of the N. Y. State Col. Soc.]

' Among us is a growing population of *strangers.*' * * ' It will furnish
the means of granting to *every African exile* among us a happy home in the
land of his fathers.'—[Rev. Baxter Dickinson's Sermon.]

' Africa is indeed inviting her long exiled children to return to her bosom.'—
[Circular of Rev. Mr Gurley.]

Nothing could be more invidious or absurd than the foregoing representation. The great mass of our colored popula-

tion were born in this country. This is their native soil ; here they first saw the light of heaven, and inhaled the breath of life ; here they have grown from infancy to manhood and old age ; from these shores they have never wandered ; they are the descendants of those who were forcibly torn from Africa two centuries ago ; their fathers assisted in breaking the yoke of British oppression, and achieving that liberty which we prize above all price ; and they cherish the strongest attachment to the land of their birth. Now, as they could not have been born in *two* countries, and as they were certainly born here, it follows that Africa is not their native home, and, consequently, that the Society has dealt in romance, or something more culpable, in representing them as strangers and aliens. It might as rationally charge them with being natives of Asia or Europe, or with having descended from the regions of the moon. To see ourselves gravely represented in a British periodical as natives of Great Britain, I doubt not would create great merriment ; and a scheme for our transportation would add vastly to our sport.

' But,' we are told, ' God has put a mark upon the black man.' True ; and he has also put a mark upon every man, woman and child, in the world ; so that every one differs in appearance from another—is easily identified—and, to make the objection valid, should occupy a *distinct* portion of territory, be himself a nation, enact his own laws, and live in perpetual solitude ! The difference between a black and a white skin is not greater than that between a white and a black one. In either case, the mark is distinctive ; and the blacks may as reasonably expel the whites, as the whites the blacks. To make such a separation we have no authority ; to attempt it, would end only in disappointment ; and, if it were carried into effect, those who are clamorous for the measure would be among the first to be cast out. The all-wise Creator, having ' made of *one blood* all nations of men to dwell on all the face of the earth,' it is proper for them to associate freely together ; and he is a proud worm of the dust who is ashamed to acknowledge this common relationship.

Again we are told : ' The God of Nature intended the blacks should be a *distinct* community.' But has he been frustrated in his intentions ? Where is the proof of such purpose ? Let us have something more than the *ipse dixit* of the Society. Yes, we are seriously assured that Nature has played falsely ! Colored persons were born by mistake in this country : they should have been born in Africa ! We must therefore rectify the error, with all despatch, by transporting them to their *native soil !* Truly, a most formidable enterprise ! There occur at least sixty thousand of such *mistakes,* annually ; while the Society has corrected only about two thousand in fourteen years ! But—courage ! men engaged in a laudable enterprise should never despair !

There are some difficulties, however, in the accomplishment of this mighty task, which cannot be easily overcome. Granting the position assumed by colonizationists, that the *blacks* and the *whites* should occupy different countries, how do they intend to dispose of that numerous and rapidly increasing class who are neither white nor black, called mulattoes ? We have not been informed to what country they belong ; but the point ought to be settled before any classification be made. Colonizationists must define, moreover, the exact shade of color which is to retain or banish individuals ; for every candid mind will admit, that it would be as unnatural to send *white* blood to Africa, as to keep *black* blood in America. ' If the color of the skin is to give construction to our constitution and laws, let us, at once, begin the work of excision. Let us raise an army of pure whites, if such an army can be found ; and let us drive out and transport to foreign climes, men, women and children, who cannot bring the most satisfactory vouchers, that their veins are flowing with the purest English blood. Indeed, let us shut up our ports against our own mariners, who are returning from an India voyage, and whose cheeks and muscles could not wholly withstand the influence of the breezes and tropics to which they were exposed. Let us make every shade of complexion, every difference of stature, and every contraction of a muscle, a Shibboleth, to detect and cut off a brother Ephraimite, at the fords of Jordan. Though such a crusade would turn every man's sword against his fellow ; yet, it might establish the right of precedence to different features, statures and colors, and oblige some friends of colonization to test the feasibility and equity of their own scheme.'

If I must become a colonizationist, I insist upon being consistent : there must be no disagreement between my creed and practice.   I must be able to give a reason why all our tall citizens should not conspire to remove their more diminutive brethren, and all the corpulent to remove the lean and lank, and all the strong to remove the weak, and all the educated to remove the ignorant, and all the rich to remove the poor, as readily as for the removal of those whose skin is ' not colored like my own ;' for Nature has sinned as culpably in diversifying the size as the complexion of her progeny, and Fortune in the distribution of her gifts has been equally fickle. I cannot perceive that I am more excusable in desiring the banishment of my neighbor because his skin is darker than mine, than I should be in desiring his banishment because he is a smaller or feebler man than myself. Surely it would be sinful for a black man to repine and murmur, and impeach the wisdom and goodness of God, because he was made with a sable complexion ; and dare I be guilty of such an impeachment, by persecuting him on account of his color ? I dare not : I would as soon deny the existence of my Creator, as quarrel with the workmanship of his hands. I rejoice that he has made one star to differ from another star in glory ; that he has not given to the sun the softness and gentleness of the moon, nor to the moon the intensity and magnificence of the sun ; that he presents to the eye every conceivable shape, and aspect, and color, in the gorgeous and multifarious productions of Nature ; and I do not rejoice less, but admire and exalt him more, that, notwithstanding he has made of one blood the whole family of man, he has made the whole family of man to differ in personal appearance, habits and pursuits.

I protest against sending any to Africa, in whose blood there is any mixture of our own ; for, I repeat it, white blood in Africa would be as repugnant to Nature, as black blood is in this country. Now, most unfortunately for colonizationists, the spirit of amalgamation has been so active for a long series of years,— especially in the slave States,—that there are comparatively few, besides those who are annually smuggled into the south from Africa, whose blood is not tainted with a foreign ingredient. Here, then, is a difficulty ! What shall be done ? All black blood *must* be sent to Africa ; but how to collect it is the question. What shall be done ! Why, we must resort to *phlebotomy !*

> ' Therefore, prepare thee to cut off the flesh.
> —————————— nor cut thou less nor more,
> But just a pound of flesh : if thou tak'st more,
> Or less, than just a pound,—be it but so much
> As makes it light, or heavy, in the substance,
> Or the division of the twentieth part
> Of one poor scruple ; nay, if the scale do turn
> But in the estimation of a hair,
> Thou diest, and all thy goods are confiscate !'

The colonization crusade cannot now fail of being popular. Phlebotomy being agreed to as a *dernier resort*, I shall briefly enumerate some of the various professions and classes which may expect to derive no inconsiderable gain from its execution ; for as our government, in conjunction with benevolent associations, is to appropriate millions of dollars to accomplish this object, the pay will be sure and liberal.

In the first place, there will be more than a million patients, for whose accommodation hospitals must be erected. These hospitals will employ brick-makers, masons, carpenters, painters, glaziers, &c. &c. &c. ; of course, the approval of a large body of mechanics is readily secured.

Physicians will next obtain an extensive practice. Their patients, in consequence of a free application of the lancet, must necessarily be debilitated, and can be kept ' quite low ' until a long score of charges be run up against the government.

Among so many patients and so much unavoidable sickness, druggists and apothecaries will obtain a profitable sale for their medicines. Nurses will be next in demand, who may expect high wages. Even the lowly washers of soiled clothes will find the life-blood of the victims ' coined into drachms ' for their reward. It is highly probable that many of the patients may die under the expurgatory process, and hence sextons and coffin-makers may calculate upon good times. With death come mourning and lamentation, and ' weeds of wo.' Dealers in crape will doubtless secure a handsome patronage. Lawyers may hope to profit by the demise of those who possess property. Indeed, almost every class in community must, to a greater or less extent, feel the beneficial effects of this philanthropic but novel experiment. The blood, taken from the veins of the blacks, may be transfused into our own, and the.general pulse acquire new vigor.

Supposing a majority of the patients should recover, three other classes will thrive by their expulsion—namely, ship-builders, merchants and seamen. As our vessels are all occupied in profitable pursuits, new ones must be built—freights will rise—and the wages of seamen be proportionably enhanced.—But a truce to irony.

The American Colonization Society, in making the banishment of the slaves the condition of their emancipation, inflicts upon them an aggravated wrong, perpetuates their thraldom, and disregards the claims of everlasting and immutable justice. The language of its most distinguished supporters is, ' Emancipation, with the liberty to remain on this side of the Atlantic, is but an act of dreamy madness'—' Emancipation, without removal from the country, is out of the question '—' All emancipation, to however small an extent, which permits the person emancipated to remain in this country, is an evil '—' They cannot be emancipated as a people, and remain among us.' Thus the restoration of an inalienable right, and an abandonment of robbery and oppression, are made to depend upon the practicability of transporting more than one sixth portion of our whole population to a far distant and barbarous land ! It is impossible to imagine a more cruel, heaven-daring and God-dishonoring scheme. It exhibits a deliberate and perverse disregard of every moral obligation, and bids defiance to the requisitions of the gospel.

Listen to the avowal of Mr Mercer of Virginia, one of the main pillars and most highly extolled supporters of the Society : ' The abolition of slavery was no object of desire to him, unless accompanied by colonization. So far was he from desiring it, unaccompanied by this condition, that *he would not live in a country where the one took place without the other '!* This language may be correctly rendered thus : ' I desire to see two millions of human beings plundered of their rights, and subjected to every species of wrong and outrage, *ad infinitum,* if they cannot be driven out of the country. I am perfectly willing to live with them while they are treated worse than cattle,—ignorant, vicious, and wretched,—and while they are held under laws which forbid their instruction ; and not only am I willing thus to live, but I am determined to practise the same oppression. But, if they should be emancipated with liberty to remain here, and placed in a situation favorable to their moral and intellectual improvement—a situation in which they could be no longer bought and sold, lacerated and manacled, defrauded and oppressed—I would abandon my native land, and never return to her shores.' And this is the language of a *philanthropist!* and this the moral principle of the boasted champion of the American Colonization Society ! Whose indignation does not kindle, whose astonishment is not profound, whose disgust is not excited, in view of these sentiments ?

But this is not the acme of colonization insanity. The assertion is made by a highly respectable partisan, and endorsed by the organ of the Society, that ' *it would be as humane to throw the slaves from the decks in the middle passage,* [i. e. into the ocean,] *as to set them free in our country'!!!* And even Henry Clay, who is an oracle in the cause, has had the boldness to declare, that the slaves should be held in everlasting servitude if they cannot be colonized in Africa ! ! And this sentiment is echoed by another, who says, ' Liberate them only on condition of their going to Africa or Hayti ' !

I will not even seem to undervalue the good sense and quick perception of the candid and intelligent reader, by any farther endeavors to illustrate the sacrifice of principle and inhumanity of purpose which are contained in the extracts under the present section. With so strong an array of evidence before him, no one, who is not mentally blind or governed by prejudice, can fail to rise from its perusal with amazement and abhorrence, and a determination to assist in overthrowing a combination which is

based upon the rotten foundation of expediency and violence.

The Colonization Society expressly denies the right of the
slaves to enjoy freedom and happiness in this country ; and this
denial incontestibly tends to rivet their fetters more firmly, or
make them the victims of a relentless persecution.

SECTION VIII.

THE AMERICAN COLONIZATION SOCIETY IS THE DISPAR-
AGER OF THE FREE BLACKS.

The leaders in the African colonization crusade seem to
dwell with a malignant satisfaction upon the poverty and degradation of the free people of color, and are careful never to let
an opportunity pass without heaping their abuse and contempt
upon them.   It is a common device of theirs to contrast the
condition of the slaves with that of this class, and invariably
to strike the balance heavily in favor of the former ! In this
manner, thousands are led to look upon slavery as a benevolent
system, and to deprecate the manumission of its victims. Nothing but a love of falsehood, or an utter disregard of facts, could
embolden these calumniators to deal so extensively in fiction.
What ! the slaves more happy, more moral, more industrious,
more orderly, more comfortable, more exalted, than the free
blacks ! A more enormous exaggeration, a more heinous libel,
a wider departure from truth, was never fabricated, or uttered,
or known.   The slaves, as a body, are in the lowest state of
degradation ; they possess no property; they cannot read ; they
are as ignorant, as their masters are reckless, of moral obligation ; they have no motive for exertion ; they are thieves from
necessity and usage ; their bodies are cruelly lacerated by the
cart-whip ; and they are disposable property.   And yet these
poor miserable, perishing, mutilated creatures are placed above
our free colored population in dignity, in enjoyment, in privilege, in usefulness, in respectability ! !

'There is a class, however, more numerous than all these, introduced amongst us by violence, notoriously ignorant, degraded and miserable, mentally diseased, broken-spirited, *acted upon by no motives to honorable exertions,* SCARCELY REACHED IN THEIR DEBASEMENT BY THE HEAVENLY LIGHT ; yet where is the sympathy and effort which a view of their condition ought to excite ? They wander unsettled and unbefriended through our land, or sit indolent, abject and sorrowful, by the " streams which witness their captivity." Their freedom is *licentiousness,* and to many RESTRAINT WOULD PROVE A BLESSING. To this remark there are exceptions ; exceptions proving that to change their state would be to elevate their character ; that virtue and enterprise are absent, only, because absent are the causes which create the one, and the motives which produce the other.'—[African Repository, vol. i. p. 68.]

'Free blacks are a greater nuisance than even slaves themselves.' * * *
'They knew that where slavery had been abolished it had operated to the advantage of the masters, not of the slaves : they saw this fact most strikingly illustrated in the case of the free negroes of Boston. If, on the anniversary celebrated by the free people of color, of the day on which slavery was abolished, they looked abroad, what did they see ? Not freemen, in the enjoyment of every attribute of freedom, with the stamp of liberty upon their brows ! No, Sir ; they saw a ragged set, crying out liberty ! for whom liberty had nothing to bestow, and whose enjoyment of it was but in name. He spoke of the great body of the blacks ; there were some few honorable exceptions, he knew, which only proved what might be done for all.'—[African Repository, vol. ii. p. 328.]

'Although there are individual exceptions distinguished by high moral and intellectual worth, yet the free blacks in our country are, as a body, more vicious and degraded than any other which our population embraces.' * * *
'If, then, they are a useless and dangerous species of population, we would ask, is it generous in our southern friends to burthen us with them? Knowing themselves the evils of slavery, can they wish to impose upon us an evil scarcely less tolerable? We think it a mistaken philanthropy, which would liberate the slave, unfitted by education and habit for freedom, and cast him upon a merciless and despising world, where his only fortune must be poverty, his only distinction degradation, and his only comfort insensibility.' * * * 'I will look no farther when I seek for the *most degraded, the most abandoned race on the earth,* but rest my eyes on this people. What but sorrow can we feel at the *misguided piety* which has set free so many of them by death-bed devise or sudden conviction of injustice ? Better, far better, for us, had they been kept in bondage, where the opportunity, the inducements, the necessity of vice would not have been so great. Deplorable necessity, indeed, to one borne down with the consciousness of the violence we have done. Yet I am clear that, whether we consider it with reference to the welfare of the State, or the happiness of the blacks, it were better to have left them in chains, than to have liberated them to receive such freedom as they enjoy, and greater freedom *we cannot, must not* allow them.' * * 'There is not a State in the Union not at this moment groaning under the evil of this class of persons, a curse and a contagion wherever they reside.' * * 'The increase of a free black population among us has been regarded as a greater evil than the increase of slaves.'—[African Repository, vol. iii. pp. 24, 25, 197, 203, 374.]

'Mr. Mercer adverted to the situation of his native State, and the condition of the free black population existing there, whom he described as a horde of miserable people—the objects of universal suspicion ; *subsisting by plunder.*'—[Idem, vol. iv. p. 363.]

'They leave a country in which though born and reared, they are strangers and aliens ; where *severe necessity* places them in a class of degraded beings ; where they are free without the blessings and privileges of liberty ; where in ceasing to be slaves of one, they have become subservient to many ; where, neither freemen nor slaves, but placed in an anomalous grade which they do not understand and others disregard ; where no kind instructer, no hope of preferment, no honorable emulation prompts them to virtue or deters from vice ; their industry waste, not accumulation ; their regular vocation, any thing or nothing as it may happen ; their greater security, sufferance ; their highest reward, forgiveness ; vicious themselves and the cause of vice in others ; discontented and *exciting discontent ;* scorned by one class and *foolishly envied by another ;* thus, and WORSE CIRCUMSTANCED, they, cannot but choose to move.'— [Idem, vol. v. p. 238.]

' Of all the descriptions of our population, *and of either portion of the African race,* the free people of color are, by far, as a class, the MOST CORRUPT, DEPRAVED, AND ABANDONED. The laws, it is true, proclaim them free ; but prejudices, more powerful than any laws, deny them the privileges of freemen. They occupy a middle station between the free white population and the slaves of the United States, and the tendency of their habits is to corrupt both.' * * * ' That the free colored population of our country is a great and constantly increasing evil must be readily acknowledged. Averse to labor, with no incentives to industry or motives to self-respect, they maintain a precarious existence by petty thefts and plunder, themselves, or by inciting their domestics, not free, to rob their owners to supply their wants.' * * * ' If there is in the whole world, a more wretched class of human beings than the free people of color in this country, I do not know where they are to be found. They have no home, no country, no kindred, no friends. They are lazy and indolent, because they have no motives to prompt them to be industrious. They are in general destitute of principle, because they have nothing to stimulate them to honorable and praise-worthy conduct. Let them be maltreated ever so much, the law gives them no redress unless some white person happens to be present, to be a witness in the case. If they acquire property, they hold it by the courtesy of every vagabond in the country ; and sooner or later, are sure to have it filched from them.'—[Idem, vol. vi. pp. 12, 135, 228.]

' The existence, within the very bosom of our country, of an amomalous race of beings, THE MOST DEBASED UPON EARTH, who neither enjoy the blessings of freedom, nor are yet in the bonds of slavery, is a great national evil, which every friend of his country most deeply deplores. . . . Tax your utmost powers of imagination, and you cannot conceive one motive to honorable effort, which can animate the bosom, or give impulse to the conduct of a free black in this country. Let him toil from youth to age in the honorable pursuit of wisdom—let him store his mind with the most valuable researches of science and literature—and let him add to a highly gifted and cultivated intellect, a piety pure, undefiled, and " unspotted from the world "—it is all nothing : he would not be received into the very lowest walks of society. If we were constrained to admire so uncommon a being, our very admiration would mingle with disgust, because, in the physical organization of his frame, we meet an insurmountable barrier, even to an approach to social intercourse, and in the Egyptian color, which nature has stamped upon his features, a principle of repulsion so strong as to forbid the idea of a communion either of interest or of feeling, as utterly abhorrent. Whether these feelings are founded in reason or not, we will not now inquire—perhaps they are not. But education and habit, and prejudice have so firmly riveted them upon us, that they have become as strong as nature itself— and to expect their removal, or even their slightest modification, would be as idle and preposterous as to expect that we could reach forth our hands, and remove the mountains from their foundations into the vallies, which are beneath them.'—[African Repository, vol. vii. pp. 230, 331.]

' We have been charged with wishing only to remove our free blacks, that we may the more effectually rivet the chains of the slave. But the class we first seek to remove, are neither freemen nor slaves ; *but between both,* AND MORE MISERABLE THAN EITHER.' * * * ' Who is there, that does not know something of the condition of the blacks in the northern and middle States? They may be seen in our cities and larger towns, wandering like foreigners and outcasts, in the land which gave them birth. They may be seen in our penitentiaries, and jails, and poor-houses. They may be found inhabiting the abodes of poverty, and the haunts of vice. But if we look for them in the society of the honest and respectable—if we visit the schools in which it is our boast that the meanest citizen can enjoy the benefits of instruction—we might also add, if we visit the sanctuaries which are open for all to worship,* and to hear the word of God ; we shall not find them there.' * * ' Leaving slavery and its subjects for the moment entirely out of view, there are in the United States 238,000 blacks denominated free, but whose freedom confers on them, we might say, no privilege but the *privilege of being more vicious and miserable than slaves can be.*'—[Seventh Annual Report, pp. 12, 87, 99.]

' Placed midway between freedom and slavery,-they know neither the incentives of the one, nor the restraints of the other ; but are alike injurious by their conduct and example, to all other classes of society.'—[Eight Annual Report.]

' Of all classes of our population, the most vicious is that of the free colored. It is the inevitable result of their moral, political, and civil degradation. Contaminated themselves, they extend their vices to all around them, to the slaves and to the whites.'—[Tenth Annual Report.]

' The question arises, where shall these outcasts go ? Ohio, and the free States of the West, which formerly invited them into their bosom, no longer offer them a welcome home. Disgusted with their laziness and vice, the inevitable concomitants of the anomalous relation in which they stand to society, the authorities of those States are seeking to get rid of what they find, too late, to be a curse to any settlement of whites—a thriftless race of vagabonds, whose footsteps are the sure precursors of indigence and crime. One of the most intelligent gentlemen of Ohio, (Mr Charles Hammond,) in a recent notice of this subject, says, " This dangerous class of population has increased considerably within a few years past, and the slaves States cannot too soon adopt efficient measures to get rid of it. Emigrations to Liberia ought to be provided for, and insisted upon, and the legislatures should pass laws to prevent emancipation, without adequate provision for the transportion of the manumitted." '—[Lynchburg Virginian.]

---

* A cruel taunt. The wonder is not that colored persons do not more generally visit our sanctuaries, but that they *ever* should attend. If they go, they are thrust into obscure, remote and unseemly pens or boxes, as if they were not embraced in the offers of redeeming love, and were indeed a part of the brute creation. It is an awful commentary upon the pride of human nature. I never can look up to these scandalous retreats for my colored brethren, without having my soul overwhelmed with emotions of shame, indignation and sorrow. No black man, however virtuous, respectable or pious he may be, can own or occupy a pew in a central part of any of our houses of worship. And yet it is reproachfully alleged—by a clergyman, too !—that ' if we visit the sanctuaries which are *open to all* (!) to worship, and to hear the word of God, we shall not find them there ' ! No—I hope they will respect themselves and the religion of Jesus more, than to occupy the places alluded to.

' As it is now, they are for the most part in a debased and wretched condition. They have the vices of our community without its virtues. And what is worse, I speak of the majority, they have no desire to rise from their state of abject depression—no wish to gain a respectable elevation of character. Consequently it is difficult, if not impossible, to present them motives which shall incite them to enter on a course of industry and virtue.' * * * ' Bound by no political ties to the community in which they dwell, and excluded for the most part from exercising the rights and privileges of freemen, on the ground of their alleged inferiority and worthlessness, they have no inducements to abandon lives of indolence, sensuality and recklessness, or to support the laws and institutions of the government placed over them. Nothing but the fear of suffering the penalty of violated law, can prevent them from preying on those among whom they live.'—[Middletown (Ct.) Gazette.]

' They have taken the free black that, as a class, dwells among us a living nuisance, nominally free, but bowed to the ground by public opinion— IN ONE PART OF THE COUNTRY DULL AS A BRUTISH BEAST, IN ANOTHER THE WILD STIRRER UP OF SEDITION AND INSURRECTION —they have shewn him to be capable of quiet and judicious self-government.— · . . We cannot shut our eyes any longer upon the disadvantages of our black population, whether in slavery or freedom. It is a sword perpetually suspended over our heads by a single hair ; it is the fountain of bitter waters that poisons all our enjoyments.'—[Speeches of J. R. Townsend, Esq. and W. W. Campbell, Esq. New-York city.]

' The fact was most glaring, without an inquiry, that the same shackles which bound them, fastened them also to the resources of the soil, and the interests of the community ; and when these were broken, and the incentives of authority removed, the weight of ignorance, the want of better incentives, and the fatal and untried power of grateful but ruinous idleness, sunk them to a state, which, however elevated in theory, was in fact more degraded and more miserable than that of bondage. In addition to all this, pauperism, with the numerous evils of corrupt and corrupting indolence, threatened to impose its sluggish weight upon a groaning community. Hence, the progress of emancipation was, for the time, most righteously arrested.'—[Address of the Board of Managers of the African Education Society.]

' Who are the free people of color in the United States ? In what circumstances does philanthropy find them ? There are indeed individuals and families, who are sober, industrious, pious. But what are the remainder, the mass ? Every one knows that their condition is deep and wretched degradation ; but, only a few have ever formed any accurate conception of the reality. The fact is, that as a class they are branded. They have no home, no country, no such personal interest in the welfare of the community, as gives a certain degree of manliness to almost every white man. . . . Three hundred thousand freemen in this country, are freemen only in name, forming only little else than a mass of pauperism and crime. . . . Here the black man is paralysed and crushed by the constant sense of inferiority. He has no effectual incentives to manly enterprise. He stands in a degraded class of society ; and out of that class he never dreams of rising.'—[Christian Spectator.]

' This is the true condition of the free colored population of our land. They are placed mid way between freedom and slavery ; they feel neither the moral stimulants of the one, nor the restraints of the other, and are alike injurious to every other class of the community.'—[Southern Religious Telegraph.]

I repel these charges against the free people of color, as unmerited, wanton and untrue. It would be absurd to pretend, that, as a class, they maintain a high character : it would be equally foolish to deny, that intemperance, indolence and crime prevail among them to a mournful extent. But I do not hesitate to assert, from an intimate acquaintance with their condition, that they are more temperate and more industrious than that class of whites who are in as indigent circumstances, but who have certainly far greater incentives to labor and excel ; that they are superior in their habits to the hosts of foreign emigrants who are crowding to our shores, and poisoning our moral atmosphere ; and that their advancement in intelligence, in wealth, and in morality, considering the numberless and almost insurmountable difficulties under which they have labored, has been remarkable. I am informed that twenty-five or thirty years ago, the colored inhabitants of Philadelphia scarcely owned a dollar's worth of real estate, whereas they now own enough to amount to hundreds of thousands of dollars. This fact speaks volumes in praise of their industry and economy ; for, be it remembered, they have had to accumulate this property in small sums, by shaving the beards, cleaning the boots and clothes, and being the servants of their white contemners, and in other menial employments. In Baltimore, Philadelphia, New-York, and other places, there are several colored persons whose individual property is worth from ten thousand to one hundred thousand dollars ;* and in all those cities, there are primary and high schools for the education of the colored population —flourishing churches of various denominations—and numerous societies for mutual assistance and improvement, &c. In Philadelphia alone, I believe, there are nearly fifty colored

---

* Francis Devany, the colored sheriff of Liberia, is reputed by colonizationists to be worth property to the value of twenty-five thousand dollars ; and they have trumpeted the fact all over the country, and so repeatedly as almost to lead one to imagine that he is the greatest and wealthiest man in all the world ! James Forten, the reputable colored sail-maker of Philadelphia,—a ·gentleman of highly polished manners and superior intelligence,—with whom Devany worked as a journeyman, can *buy him out* three or four times over. Joseph Cassey, another estimable and intelligent man of color, or the widow of Bishop Allen, both of Philadelphia, can purchase him. I mention their names, not to extol them, but simply to show, that what begets fame in Liberia is unproductive here.

associations for benevolent, literary, scientific and moral purposes.* Yet these are the people of whom it is said, ' they
are acted upon by no motives to honorable exertions ;' that they
are ' scarcely reached in their debasement by the heavenly light '
(almost a denial of the power of the Holy Ghost) ; that ' their
freedom is licentiousness ;' that ' they are a greater nuisance
than even the slaves themselves ;' that they are ' the most degraded, the most abandoned race on the earth ;' that they are

---

* The following statement, recently published in the Philadelphia ' Friend and
Advocate of Truth,' is very creditable to the colored inhabitants of that city :

' Many erroneous opinions have prevailed, with regard to the true character
and condition of the free colored people of Pennsylvania. They have been represented as an idle and worthless class, furnishing inmates for our poor-houses
and penitentiaries. A few plain facts are sufficient to refute these gratuitous allegations. In the city and suburbs of Philadelphia, by the census of 1830, they
constituted about eleven per cent., or one ninth of the whole population. From
the account of the guardians of the poor, printed by order of the board, it appears that of the out-door poor receiving regular weekly supplies, in the first
month, 1830, the time of the greatest need, the people of color were about one
to twenty-three whites ; or not quite four per cent., a disproportion of whites to
colored, of more than two to one in favor of the latter. When it is considered
that they perform the lowest offices in the community—that the avenues to what
are esteemed the most honorable and profitable professions in society, are in a
great measure, if not wholly closed against them, these facts are the more creditable to them. One cause of this disproportion, which we presume is but little
known, but which is worthy of special notice, will be found in the numerous
societies among themselves for mutual aid. These societies expended, in one
year, about six thousand dollars for the relief of the sick and the indigent of their
own color, from funds raised among themselves. Besides, the taxes paid by the
colored people of Philadelphia, exceed in amount the sums expended out of the
funds of the city for the relief of their poor.'

It is also a fact that the proportion of whites in the alms-house in New-York
is greater than that of the blacks. I am aware that other evidence, of a different kind, may be adduced in other places ; but it is in the highest degree unfair
to measure the whole body of blacks by the whole body of whites—for the privileges and advantages of the whites are as ten thousand to one : they monopo-
lise almost every branch of business and every pursuit of life—they have all the
means necessary to make men virtuous, intelligent, active, and opulent. Far
different is the situation of the free blacks. How slender are their means !
how mean and limited their occupations ! how inferior their advantages ! Almost
every avenue to wealth, preferment and usefulness, is closed against them.
How are they persecuted ! how avoided in the streets ! how excluded from the
benefits of society ! To point at them the finger of scorn, to taunt them for their
inferiority or helplessness, is like putting out the eyes and clipping the wings of
the eagle, and then reproaching him because he can neither see nor fly. To
boast of our superior refinement, intelligence and virtue, is the extreme of vain-
glory, and adding insult to injury. Shame ! shame !

' worse circumstanced than the slave population ;' that they have ' no privilege but the privilege of being more vicious and miserable than slaves can be ;' and that they are ' a thriftless race of vagabonds, whose footsteps are the sure precursors of indigence and crime.' And these false and infamous charges are brought against them by a Society which professes to cherish for them the highest regard, and to be anxious to give them respectability in the eyes of the world !

The truth is, the traducers of the free blacks have no adequate conception of the amount of good sense, sterling piety, moral honesty, virtuous pride of character, and domestic enjoyment, which exists among this class. The spirited remarks of the colored citizens of New-York, in their address to the public, (*vide* PART II. p. 16,) in reference to their calumniators, are exceedingly apposite : ' Their patrician principles prevent an intercourse with men in the middle walks of life, among whom a large portion of our people may be classed. We ask them to visit the dwellings of the respectable part of our people, and we are satisfied that they will discover more civilization and refinement, than will be found among the same number of white families of an equal standing.' A personal examination enables me to say that this challenge is neither presumptuous nor boastful. I confess, I have been most agreeably, nay, wonderfully disappointed, in my intercourse with them, which is daily elevating them in my estimation. Many of their number I proudly rank among my most familiar friends and correspondents.

With regard to the ' ragged set in Boston, crying out liberty !' every candid resident will testify that this is a libellous representation ; that our free blacks are a quiet, orderly, well-dressed, and (as far as they can obtain employment) industrious class of citizens ; and that their improvement is rapid and constant. Every curious observer who visits their houses of worship, will be surprised at the general neatness of attire and propriety of manners of the worshippers. ' A ragged set,' forsooth ! The slander may be uttered in the city of Washington, at an anniversary of the American Colonization Society ; but no man, who regards his character for veracity and intelligence, *dare* publish it in Boston.

The effects of this reiterated abuse are eminently mischievous. It serves to kindle the fires of persecution, to strengthen prejudice, to drive its victims to despair, and to increase the desire for their banishment. 'Tax your utmost powers of imagination,' says one of the colonization advocates, 'and you cannot conceive *one motive* to honorable effort, which can animate the bosom, or give impulse to the conduct of the free black in this country'! Is this language calculated to allay animosity, or beget confidence, or suppress contempt, or heal division, or excite sympathy? Far otherwise. Are there not thousands of living witnesses to prove the falsity of this assertion; thousands who adorn the doctrine of God their Saviour, and whose 'motives to honorable effort' are higher than heaven and vast as eternity; thousands, who, though their enemies spare no efforts to crush them in the dust, and in despite of mountains of difficulties, rise up with a giant's strength to respectability and usefulness? 'No motive to honorable effort'! Perish the calumny!

Again, they are stigmatized as the 'wild stirrers up of sedition and insurrection.' This charge is even more malignant than the other, and utterly groundless. Its propagation, however, tends directly to excite a persecution which may drive the accused to sedition, in self-defence. There is no evidence that any free man of color was enlisted in the late bloody struggle in Virginia, or in any manner accessary thereto. On the contrary, it was deprecated by our colored citizens generally, not only on account of its sanguinary acts, but because they knew it would operate to their own disadvantage by being placed to their account. The following honorable expression of feeling was made at a public meeting of the people of color in Wilmington, Delaware, about that period:

'The subscribers, having a knowledge of the alarm which prevails in the minds of some of the citizens of this place, on account of various reports which some mischievous person or persons have circulated, in regard to the colored population, beg leave to represent, on behalf of themselves and brethren, that having made inquiry into the subject, they have found said reports to be without the least foundation; and they owe it to themselves further to declare, that, so far from any disposition on the part of the colored people to disturb the peace and good order of the community, they are, on the contrary, fully aware that it consists not less with their interests than their duty to refrain from every act that would excite commotion or disorder, in which the colored people would have every thing to lose and nothing to gain. We have been treated by the citizens of Wilmington and its vicinity with kindness, for which we ought to be grateful, and it is our solemn purpose to pursue such a course of conduct as may merit a continuance of their favor and confidence. Should any among us be found so wicked and blinded as to enter into plots and contrivances, inimical to the present harmony, we thus solemnly pledge ourselves to our white friends and neighbors, that we will be among the first to sound the alarm, and unite in effecting their apprehension and suppression.'

The free colored citizens of Baltimore, Maryland, also came out unitedly in the following pacific and truly exemplary spirit :

'Whereas, there has prevailed in this city, during the past week, a very unpleasant excitement, originating from suspicions and reports totally without foundation, and highly derogatory to our good sense ; and whereas this excitement, though unnecessarily created, may, in its ultimate tendency, prove prejudicial to the interests of the free colored population of this State. Therefore,

Resolved, That we challenge the most rigid investigation as to the truth of those evil reports, which have recently been so industriously propagated in this city by the credulous, and those who are totally unacquainted with the character of colored Baltimoreans.

Resolved, That we are not so reckless of our true interest, so blind to utter helplessness—not to say so devoid of humanity, as to entertain the hostile designs, or to cherish the fiendish passions, which it seems have been, by the unthinking, so unjustly attributed to us.

Resolved, That we have been too long in the land of bibles, and temples, and ministers, to look upon blood and carnage with complacency—that we have been too long in this enlightened metropolis, to think of the amelioration of our condition, in any other way than that sanctioned by the Gospel of Peace.

Resolved, That we rely upon a peaceable and upright conduct, for a continuance of that favor and protection which we have hitherto enjoyed, and which, the liberal, the wise, and the good, are ever ready to accord.'

How impolitic, then, as well as unjust, to brand this meek and magnanimous class as ' the wild stirrers up of sedition and insurrection ' !

This treatment, I repeat, is impolitic—nay, suicidal. To abuse, proscribe and exasperate them, to trample them under our feet, to goad them on the right hand and on the left, is not the way to secure their loyalty, but rather to make them revengeful, desperate and seditious. Our true policy is, to meliorate their condition, invigorate their hopes, instruct their ignorant minds, admit them to an equality of privileges with ourselves, nourish and patronise their genius, and, by giving them mechanical trades and mercantile advantages, open to them the avenue to competence and wealth. We shall thus make them contented and happy, and place them in a situation which will lead them still more heartily to deprecate any insurrectionary movements among our slave population. The following is the

conciliatory and generous language of a man, who has been
denounced as a blood-hound and a monster.   It will be well for
us if we profit by it.

'Americans ! notwithstanding you have and do continue to treat us more
cruel than any heathen nation ever did a people it had subjected to the same condition that you have us, let us reason. Had you not better take our body, while
you have it in your power, and while we are yet ignorant and wretched, not
knowing but little, give us education, and teach us the pure religion of our Lord
and Master, which is calculated to make the lion lie down in peace with the
lamb, and which millions of you have beaten us nearly to death for trying to
obtain since we have been among you, and thus at once gain our affection while
we are ignorant ?   Throw away your fears and prejudices then, and enlighten us
and treat us like men, and we will like you more than we do now hate you.
And tell us now no more about colonization ; for America is as much our country as it is yours.   Treat us like men, and there is no danger but we will all
live in peace and happiness together ; for we are not, like you, hard-hearted, unmerciful, and unforgiving.   What a happy country this will be, if the whites
will listen !   What nation under heaven, will be able to do any thing with us,
unless God gives us up into its hand ?   But, Americans, I declare to you, while
you keep us and our children in bondage, and treat us like brutes, to make us
support you and your families, we cannot be your friends.   You do not look for
it, do you ?   Treat us then like men, and we will be your friends.   And there is
not a doubt in my mind, but that the whole of the past will be sunk into ob-
livion, and we yet, under God, will become a united and happy people.'*

SECTION   IX.

THE AMERICAN COLONIZATION SOCIETY DENIES THE POSSI-
BILITY OF ELEVATING THE BLACKS IN THIS COUNTRY.

THE detestation of feeling, the fire of moral indignation, and
the agony of soul which I have felt kindling and swelling within
me, in the progress of this review, under this section reach the
acme of intensity.   It is impossible for the mind to conceive,
or the tongue to utter, or the pen to record, sentiments more
derogatory to the character of a republican and christian people than the following :

'Introduced as this class has been, in a way which cannot be justified, injurious in its influence to the community, degraded in character and miserable in
condition, *forever excluded*, by public sentiment, by law and by a physical distinction, from the most powerful motives to exertion,' &c.   *   *   'In
addition to all the causes which tend to pollute, to degrade and render them miserable, there are principles of *repulsion* between them and us, which can *never*

---

* Walker's Appeal.

be overcome.'   *   *   'Their bodies are free, their minds enslaved. They can neither bless their brethren in servitude, nor rise from their own obscurity, nor add to the purity of our morals, nor to our wealth, nor to our political strength.'   *   *   'Let us recollect that our fathers have placed them here ; and that our prejudices, prejudices *too deep to be eradicated* while they remain among us, have produced the standard of their morals.'   *   *   'Nor will it be questioned that their establishment on the African coast . . . will confer on them invaluable blessings which *in this country* they can *never* enjoy.'   *   *   'They *must be* hewers of wood and drawers of water. Do what they will, there is but this one prospect before them.'—[African Repository, vol. 1, pp. 34, 144, 162, 176, 226, 317.]

'Shut out from the privileges of citizens, separated from us by the *insurmountable* barrier of color, they can *never* amalgamate with us, but must remain *for ever* a distinct and inferior race, repugnant to our republican feelings, and dangerous to our republican institutions.'   *   *   'It is not that there are some, but that there are so many among us of a different physical, if not moral, constitution, who *never* can amalgamate with the great body of our population.'—[African Repository, vol. ii. pp. 188, 189, 338.]

'In consequence of his own inveterate habits, and the no less inveterate prejudices of the whites, it is a sadly demonstrated truth, that the negro *cannot, in this country*, become an enlightened and useful citizen. Driven to the lowest stratum of society, and enthralled there for melancholy ages, his mind becomes proportionably grovelling, and to gratify his animal desires is his most exalted aspiration.'   *   *   'The negro, *while in this country*, will be treated as an inferior being.'   *   *   'Our slavery is such, as that no device of our philanthropy for elevating the wretched subjects of its debasement to the ordinary privileges of men, can descry one cheering glimpse of hope that our object can *ever* be accomplished. The very commencing act of freedom to the slave, is to place him in a condition still worse, if possible, both for his moral habits, his outward provision, and for the community that embosoms him, than even that, deplorable as it was, from which he has been removed. He is now a freeman ; but his complexion, his features, every peculiarity of his person, pronounce to him another doom,—that every wish he may conceive, every effort he can make, shall be *little better than vain*. Even to every talent and virtuous impulse which he may feel working in his bosom, obstacles stand in impracticable array ; not from a defect of essential title to success, but from *a positive external law, unreasoning and irreversible*.'   *   *   'The elevation of a degraded class of beings to the privileges of freemen, which, though free, they can *never* enjoy, and to the prospects of a happy immortality.'   *   *   'They again most solemnly repeat to the free colored people of Virginia their belief, that *in Africa alone* can they enjoy that complete emancipation from a degrading inequality, which in a greater or less degree pervades the United States, if not in the laws, in the whole frame and structure of society, and which in its effects on their moral and social state is scarcely less degrading than slavery itself.'—African Repository, vol. iii. pp. 25, 26, 66, 68, 345.]

'But there is one large class among the inhabitants of this country—degraded and miserable—whom none of the efforts in which you are accustomed to engage, can materially benefit. Among the twelve millions who make up our census, two millions are Africans—separated from the possessors of the soil by birth, *by the brand of indelible ignominy*, by prejudices, mutual, deep, *incurable*, by an *irreconcileable diversity of interests* They are aliens and outcasts ;— they are, as a body, degraded beneath the influence of nearly all the motives which prompt other men to enterprise, and almost below the sphere of virtuous affections. Whatever may be attempted for the general improvement of society, their wants are untouched.—Whatever may be effected for elevating the mass of the nation in the scale of happiness or of intellectual and moral character, their degradation is the same—dark, and deep, and *hopeless.* Benevolence seems to overlook them, or struggles for their benefit in vain. Patriotism forgets them, or remembers them only with shame for what has been, and with dire forebodings, of what is yet to come.'   *   *   'It is taken *for granted* that in present circumstances, any effort to produce a general and thorough amelioration in the character and condition of the free people of color must be to a great extent fruitless. In every part of the United States there is a broad and *impassible* line of demarcation between every man who has *one drop* of African blood in his veins and every other class in the community. The habits, the feelings, all the prejudices of society—prejudices which neither *refinement,* nor *argument,* nor *education,* nor *religion* itself can subdue—mark the people of color, whether bond or free, as the subjects of a degradation *inevitable* and *incurable.* The African in this country belongs by birth to the very lowest station in society ; and from that station *he can never rise,* BE HIS TALENTS, HIS ENTERPRISE, HIS VIRTUES WHAT THEY MAY. . . They constitute a class by themselves—a class out of which *no individual can be elevated,* and below which, none can be depressed. And this is the difficulty, the invariable and insuperable difficulty in the way of every scheme for their benefit. Much can be done for them—much has been done ; but still they are, and, *in this country,* ALWAYS MUST BE a depressed and abject race.'—[African Repository, vol. iv. pp. 117, 118, 119.]

'The distinctive complexion by which it is marked, *necessarily* debars it from all familiar intercourse with the more favored society that surrounds it, and of course denies to it *all hope* of either social or political elevation, by means of individual merit, however great, or individual exertions, however unremitted.'   *   *   'It is deemed unnecessary to repeat what has already been said, of the character of the population in question, of its *hopeless degradation,* and its baneful influence, in the situation in which it is now placed.'   *   *   * 'The colored population of this country can *never* rise to respectability and happiness here.'   *   *   'It was at an early period seen and acknowledged, that neither the objects of benevolence nor the interests of the nation could be materially benefitted by any plan or measures that permitted them to remain within the United States.'   *   *   'They leave a country in which though born and reared, they are strangers and aliens ; where severe necessity places them in a class of degraded beings.'   *   *   'With us they have been degraded by slavery, and STILL FURTHER DEGRADED *by the mockery of nominal freedom.* We have endeavored, but endeavored in vain, to restore them either to self-respect, or to the respect of others. *It is not our fault that we have failed ;* it is not theirs. It has resulted from a cause over which neither they, nor we, can ever have control. *Here,* therefore, they must be *for ever debased :* more than this, they must be *for ever useless ;* more even than this, they must be FOR EVER A NUISANCE, from which it were a blessing for society to be rid. And yet they, and they only, are qualified for colonizing Africa.'   *   *   * 'Whether bond or free, their presence will be *for ever a calamity.* Why then, in the name of God, should we hesitate to encourage their departure ? The existence of this race among us ; a race that can neither share our blessings nor incorporate in our Society, is already felt to be a curse.'—[African Repository, vol. v. pp. 51, 53, 179, 234, 238, 276, 278.]

'Is our posterity doomed to endure for ever not only all the ills flowing from the state of slavery, but all which arise from incongruous elements of population, separated from each other by *invincible prejudices,* and by natural causes?'   *   *   'Here *invincible prejudices* exclude them from the enjoyment of the society of the whites, and deny them all the advantages of freemen. The bar, the pulpit, and our legislative halls are shut to them by the irresistible force of public sentiment. No talents however great, no piety however pure and devoted, no patriotism however ardent, can secure their admission. They constantly hear the accents, and behold the triumphs, of a liberty *which here they* *can never enjoy.'* * * ' It is against this increase of colored persons, who take but a nominal freedom here, and *cannot rise* from their degraded condition, that this Society attempts to provide.' * * 'They may be emancipated ; but emancipation *cannot elevate their condition* or augment their capacity for self-preservation.—Want and suffering will gradually diminish their numbers, and they will disappear, as the inferior has always disappeared, before the superior race.' * * ' Our great and good men purposed it primarily as a system of relief for two millions of fellow men in our own county—a population dangerous to ourselves and *necessarily degraded here.'* * * 'The free blacks, by the moral necessity of their civil disabilities, are and *must for ever be a nuisance*—equally, and more to the owner of slaves, than to other members of the community.'--[African Repository, vol. vi. pp. 12, 17, 82, 168, 295, 368.]

' Incorporated into our country as freemen, yet separated from it by odious and degrading distinctions, they feel themselves condemned to a hopeless and debasing inferiority. They know that their very complexion will *for ever* exclude them from the rank, the privileges, the honors, of freemen. No matter how great their industry, or how abundant their wealth—no matter what their attainments in literature, science or the arts—no matter how correct their deportment or what respect their characters may inspire, they can never, NO, NEVER be raised to a footing of equality, not even to a familiar intercourse with the surrounding society.' * * ' To us it seems evident that the man of color may as soon *change his complexion*, as rise above all sense of past inferiority and debasement in a community, from the social intercourse of which, he must expect to be in a great measure excluded, not only until prejudice shall have no existence therein, but until the freedom of man in regulating his social relations is proved to be abridged by some law of morality or the gospel. . . . Is it not *wise*, then, for the free people of color and their friends to .*admit*, what cannot reasonably be doubted, that the people of color must, in this country, remain for ages, *probably for ever*, a separate and inferior caste, weighed down by causes, powerful, universal, inevitable ; *which neither legislation nor christianity can remove ?* '
' Let the free black in this country toil from youth to age in the honorable pursuit of wisdom—let him store his mind with the most valuable researches of science and literature—and let him add to a highly gifted and cultivated intellect, a piety pure, undefiled, and " unspotted from the world "—it is all nothing : he would not be received into the very lowest walks of society. If we were constrained to admire so uncommon a being, our very admiration would mingle with disgust, because, in the physical organization of his frame, we meet an insurmountable barrier, even to an approach to social intercourse, and in the Egyptian color, which nature has stamped upon his features, a principle of repulsion so strong as to forbid the idea of a communion either of interest or of feeling, as utterly abhorrent. Whether these feelings are founded in reason or not, we will not now inquire—perhaps they are not. But education and habit and prejudice have so firmly riveted them upon us, that they have become as strong as nature itself—and to expect their removal, or even their slightest modification, would be as idle and preposterous as to expect that we could reach forth our hands, and remove the mountains from their foundations into the vallies, which are beneath them.'—[African Repository, vol. vii. pp. 100, 195, 196, 231.]

' And can we not find some spot on this large globe which will receive them kindly, and where they may escape those prejudices which, in this country, must *ever* keep them *inferior* and *degraded* members of society ?'—[Third Annual Report.]

' A population which, even if it were not literally enslaved, *must for ever remain* in a state of degradation no better than bondage.' * * ' Here the thing is impossible ; a slave cannot be really emancipated. You may call him free, you may enact a statute book of laws to make him free, but you cannot bleach him into the enjoyment of freedom.' * * ' The Soodra is not farther separated from the Brahmin in regard to all his privileges, civil, intellectual, and moral, than the negro is from the white man by the prejudices which result from the difference made between them by the God of nature. A barrier more difficult to be surmounted than the institution of the caste, cuts off, and while the present state of society continues *must always* cut off, the negro from all that is valuable in citizenship.'—[Seventh Annual Report.]

' Let the arm of our government be stretched out for the defence of our African colony, and this objection will no longer exist. There, *and there alone*, the colored man can enjoy the motives for honorable exertion.'—[Ninth Annual Report.]

' In the distinctive and indelible marks of their color, and the prejudices of the people, an *insuperable* obstacle has been placed to the execution of any plan for elevating their character, and placing them on a footing with their brethren of the same common family.'—[Tenth Annual Report.]

' Far from shuddering at the thought of leaving the comfortable fireside among us, for a distant and unknown shore yet covered by the wilderness, they have preferred real liberty there, to a mockery of freedom here, and have turned their eyes to Africa, as the only resting place and refuge of the colored man, in the deluge of oppression that surrounds him.'—[Eleventh Annual Report.]

' The race in question were known, as a class, to be destitute, depraved—the victims of all forms of social misery. The peculiarity of their fate was, that this was not their condition by accident or transiently, but *inevitably* and *immutably*, whilst they remained in their present place, by a law as infallible in its operation, as any of physical nature.' * * ' Their residence amongst us is attended by evil consequences to society—causes *beyond the control of the human will* must prevent their *ever* rising to equality with the whites.' * * ' The Managers consider it clear that causes exist, and are operating to prevent their improvement and elevation to any considerable extent as a class, in this country, which are fixed, not only beyond the control of the friends of humanity, BUT OF ANY HUMAN POWER. *Christianity cannot do for them here, what it will do for them in Africa.* This is not the fault of the colored man, *nor of the white man, nor of Christianity; but an ordination of Providence, and no more to be changed than the laws of nature.* Yet, were it otherwise, did no cause exist but prejudice, to prevent the elevation, in this country, of our free colored population, still, were this prejudice so strong (which is indeed the fact) as to forbid the hope of any great favorable change in their condition, what folly for them to reject blessings in another land, because it is prejudice which debars them from such blessings in this ! But in truth no legislation, no humanity, no benevolence can make them insensible to their past condition, can unfetter their minds, can relieve them from the disadvantages resulting from inferior means and attainments, can abridge the right of freemen to regulate their social intercourse and relations, which will leave them *for ever a separate and depressed class* in the community ; in fine, nothing can in any way do much here to raise them from their miseries to respectability, honor and usefulness.'—[Fifteenth Annual Report.]

' That no adequate means of attaining this great end existed, short of the segregation of the black population from the white—that an IMPASSABLE BARRIER existed in the state of society in this country, between these classes—that whatever might be the liberal sentiments of some good men among us, the blacks were marked with an *indelible note of inferiority*—they saw placed high before them a station which here they *could never reach*, and by a natural reaction they fell back into a position where self-respect lent them no stimulus, and virtuous principles and actions lost more than half their motive—that in fact they were a branded and degraded caste—the Pariahs of the United States, and destined *as long as they remained with us* to be hewers of wood and drawers of water—that the increase of this population in a greater ratio than the whites, was calculated to excite just apprehension—that no one could say that when a few more millions should be added to their numbers, the example of Hayti might not rouse them to an effort to break their chains ; and he would ask what man could contemplate, without shuddering, all the complicated atrocity and bloody revenge of such a revolt ?'   *   *   ' Those persons of color who have been emancipated, are only nominally free, and the whole race, so long as they remain among us, and whether they be slaves or free, must *necessarily* be kept in a condition full of wretchedness to them and full of danger to the whites.'—[Second Annual Report of New-York State Colonization Society.]

' Many of those citizens who ardently wish for the removal of such of the free colored population, as are willing to go, to any place where they could enjoy, *what they can never enjoy here*, that is, all the advantages of society,' &c.   *   *   ' That the free colored population in this country labor under the most oppressive disadvantages, which their freedom can by no means counterbalance, is too obvious to admit of doubt. I waive all inquiry whether this is right or wrong. I speak of things as they are—not as they might, or as they ought to be. They are cut off from the most remote chance of amalgamation with the white population, by feelings or prejudices, call them what you will, that are ineradicable. Their situation is more unfavorable than that of many slaves. '' With all the burdens, cares and responsibilities of freedom, they have few or none of its substantial benefits. Their associations are, and must be, chiefly with slaves. Their right of suffrage gives them little, if any, political influence, and they are practically, if not theoretically excluded from representation and weight in our public councils.'' *No merit, no services, no talents can elevate them to a level with the whites.* Occasionally, an exception may arise. A colored individual, of great talents, merits, and wealth, may emerge from the crowd. Cases of this kind are to the last degree rare. The colored people are subject to legal disabilities, more or less galling and severe, in almost every state of the Union. Who has not deeply regretted their late harsh expulsion from the State of Ohio, and their being forced to abandon the country of their birth, which had profited by their labors, and to take refuge in a foreign land ? Severe regulations have been recently passed in Louisiana, to prevent the introduction of free people of color into the State. Whenever they appear, they are to be banished in sixty days. The strong opposition to a negro college in New-Haven, speaks in a language not to be mistaken, the jealousy with which they are regarded. And there is no reason to expect, that the lapse of centuries will make any change in this respect. THEY WILL ALWAYS UNHAPPILY BE REGARDED AS AN INFERIOR RACE.'—[Mathew Carey's ' Reflections.']

' Instances of emancipation have not essentially benefitted the African, and *probably never will*, while he remains among us. In this country, public opinion does, *and will*, consign him to an inferiority, *above which he can never rise*. Emancipation can NEVER make the African, while he remains in this country, a real free man. Degradation MUST and WILL press him to the earth ; no cheering, stimulating influence will he here feel, *in any of the walks of life*.'—[Circular of the Massachusetts Colonization Society for 1832.]

' With us color is the bar. Nature has raised up barriers between the races, *which no man with a proper sense of the dignity of his species desires to see surmounted*.'   *   *   ' What effects does emancipation produce without removal ? A discontented and useless population ; having no sympathies with the rest of the community, *doomed by immoveable barriers to eternal degradation*. I know that there are among us, those of warm and generous hearts, who believe that we may retain the black man here, and raise him up to the full and perfect stature of human nature. That degree of improvement can never take place except the races be amalgamated ; and amalgamation is a day-dream. It may seem strong, but it is true that " a skin not colored like our own " will separate them from us, *as long as our feelings continue a part of our nature.*'—[Speeches delivered at the formation of the Young Men's Auxiliary Colonization Society in New-York city.]

' These [subsistence, political and social considerations] they can *never* enjoy here.' * * ' You may manumit the slave, but you cannot make him a white man. He still remains a negro or a mulatto. The mark and the recollection of his origin and former state still adhere to him ; the feelings produced by that condition, in his own mind and in the minds of the whites, still exist ; he is associated by his color, and by these recollections and feelings, with the class of slaves ; and a barrier is thus raised between him and the whites, that is between him and the free class, which he can never hope to transcend.' * * ' A vast majority of the free blacks, as we have seen, are and *must be*, an idle, worthless and thievish race.'—[First Annual Report.]

' Here they are condemned to a state of *hopeless* inferiority, and consequent degradation. As they *cannot* emerge from this state, they lose, by degrees, the hope, at last the desire of emerging.'—[Second Annual Report.]

' The existence in any community of a people forming a distinct and degraded caste, *who are forever excluded by the fiat of society and the laws of the land*, from all hopes of equality in social intercourse and political privileges, must, from the nature of things, be fraught with unmixed evil. Did this committee believe it possible, by any acts of legislation, to remove this blotch upon the body politic, by so elevating the social and moral condition of the blacks in Ohio, that they would be received into society on terms of equality, and would by common consent be admitted to a participation of political privileges—WERE SUCH A THING POSSIBLE, even after a lapse of time and by pecuniary sacrifice, most gladly would they recommend such measures as would subserve the cause of humanity, by producing such a result. For the purposes of legislation, it is sufficient to know, that the blacks in Ohio *must always exist as a separate and degraded race*, that when the leopard shall change his spots and the Ethiopian his skin, then, BUT NOT TILL THEN, may we expect that the descendants of Africans will be admitted into society, on terms of social and political equality.'—[Report of a Select Committee of the Legislature of Ohio.]

' No possible contingency can ever break down or weaken the impassable barrier which at present separates the whites from social communion with the blacks. Neither education, nor wealth, nor any other means of distinction known to our communities, can elevate blacks to a level with whites, in the United States.'—[American Spectator.]

' However unjust may be the prejudices which exist in the whites against the blacks, and which operate so injuriously to the latter—*they are probably too deep to be obliterated ;* and true philanthropy would dictate the separation of two races of men, so different, WHOM NATURE HERSELF HAS FORBIDDEN TO MINGLE INTO ONE ; but of whom, while they remain associated, *one or the other must of necessity have the superiority.* For the future welfare of both, we trust that the project of colonizing the Africans, as they shall gradually be emancipated, although a work of time, may not be altogether hopeless.'—[Brandon (Vt.) Telegraph.]

' The character and circumstances of this portion of the community fall under every man's notice, and the least observation shows that they *cannot* be useful or happy among us.'—[Oration by Gabriel P. Disosway, Esq.]

' It is of vast importance to these people, as a class, that their hopes and expectations of temporal prosperity *should be turned to Africa*, and that they should *not* regard our country as their permanent residence, or as that country in which they will *ever*, as a people, enjoy equal privileges and blessings with the whites.'—[Rev. Mr Gurley's Letter to the Rev. S. S. Jocelyn.]

' To attain solid happiness and permanent respectability, they should now remove to a more congenial clime. . . . To raise them to a level with the whites is AN IMPOSSIBILITY.'—[New-Haven Religious Intelligencer.]

' In Liberia—the land of their forefathers, they will be restored to real freedom, which they have never yet enjoyed, and which it is folly for them to expect they can ever enjoy among the whites.'—[Norfolk Herald.]

' My bowels, my bowels! I am pained at my very heart; my heart maketh a noise in me.' Are we pagans, are we savages, are we devils? Can pagans, or savages, or devils, exhibit a more implacable spirit, than is seen in the foregoing extracts? It is enough to cause the very stones to cry out, and the beasts of the field to rebuke us.

Of this I am sure : no man, who is truly willing to admit the people of color to an equality with himself, can see any insuperable difficulty in effecting their elevation. When, therefore, I hear an individual—especially a professor of christianity— strenuously contending that there can be no fellowship with them, I cannot help suspecting the sincerity of his own republicanism or piety, or thinking that the beam is in his own eye. My bible assures me that the day is coming when even the ' wolf shall dwell with the lamb, and the leopard shall lie down with the kid, and the wolf and the young lion and the fatling together ;' and, if this be possible, I see no cause why those of the same species—God's rational creatures—fellow countrymen, in truth, cannot dwell in harmony together.

How abominably hypocritical, how consummately despicable, how incorrigibly tyrannical must this whole nation appear in the eyes of the people of Europe !—professing to be the *friends* of the free blacks, actuated by the purest motives of benevolence toward them, desirous to make atonement for past wrongs, challenging the admiration of the world for their patriotism, philanthropy and piety—and yet (hear, O heaven ! and be astonished, O earth !) shamelessly proclaiming, with a voice louder than thunder, and an aspect malignant as sin, that while their colored countrymen remain among them, they must be trampled beneath their feet, treated as inferior beings, deprived of all the invaluable privileges of freemen, separated by the brand of indelible ignominy, and debased to a level with the beasts that perish ! Yea, that they may as soon change their complexion as rise from their degradation ! that no device of philanthropy can benefit them here ! that they constitute a class out of which *no individual can be elevated*, and below which, *none can be depressed !* that no talents however great, no piety however pure and devoted, no patriotism however ardent, no industry however great, no wealth however abundant, can raise them to a footing of equality with the whites ! that ' let them toil from youth to old age in the honorable pursuit of wisdom—let them store their minds with the most valuable researches of science and literature—and let them add to a highly gifted and cultivated intellect, a piety pure, undefiled, and unspotted from the world, *it is all nothing*—they would not be received into the *very lowest walks of society*—admiration of such uncommon beings would mingle with *disgust !*' Yea, that ' there is a broad and impassible line of demarcation between every man who has *one drop* of African blood in his veins and every other class in the community ' ! Yea, that ' the habits, the feelings, all the prejudices of society—prejudices which neither *refinement*, nor *argument*, nor *education*, nor RELIGION itself can subdue— mark the people of color, whether bond or free, as the subjects of a degradation *inevitable* and *incurable* ' ! Yea, that ' *Christianity* cannot do for them here, what it will do for them in Africa ' ! Yea, that ' this is not the fault of the colored man, NOR OF THE WHITE MAN, nor of Christianity; but AN ORDINATION OF PROVIDENCE, *and no more to be changed than the* LAWS OF NATURE '!!!

Again I ask, are we pagans, are we savages, are we devils ? Search the records of heathenism, and sentiments more hostile to the spirit of the gospel, or of a more black and blasphemous complexion than these, cannot be found. I believe that they are libels upon the character of my countrymen, which time will wipe off. I call upon the spirits of the just made perfect in heaven, upon all who have experienced the love of God in their souls here below, upon the christian converts in India and the islands of the sea, to sustain me in the assertion that there *is* power enough in the religion of Jesus Christ to melt down the most stubborn prejudices, to overthrow the highest walls of partition, to break the strongest caste, to improve and elevate the most degraded, to unite in fellowship the most hostile, and to equalize and bless all its recipients. Make me *sure* that there is not, and I will give it up, now and for ever. ' In Christ Jesus, all are one : there is neither Jew nor Greek, there is neither bond nor free, there is neither male nor female.'

These sentiments were not uttered by infidels, nor by worthless wretches, but in many instances by professors of religion and *ministers of the gospel !* and in almost every instance by reputedly the most enlightened, patriotic and benevolent men in the land ! Tell it not abroad ! publish it not in the streets of Calcutta ! Even the eminent President of Union College, (Rev. Dr. Nott,) could so far depart, unguardedly I hope, from christian love and integrity, as to utter this language in an address in behalf of the Colonization Society :—' With us they [the free people of color] have been degraded by slavery, and *still further degraded by the mockery of nominal freedom.'* Were this true, it would imply that we of the free States are more barbarous and neglectful than even the traffickers in souls and men-stealers at the south. We have not, it is certain, treated our colored brethren as the law of kindness and the ties of brotherhood demand ; but have we outdone slaveholders in cruelty ? Were it true, to forge new fetters for the limbs of these degraded beings would be an act of benevolence. But their condition is as much superior to that of the slaves, as happiness is to misery. The second portion of this work, containing their proceedings in a collective capacity, shows whether they have made any progress in intelligence, in virtue, in piety, and in happiness, since their liberation. Again he says : ' *We have endeavored*, but endeavored in vain, *to restore them either to self-respect, or to the respect of others.'* It is painful to contradict so worthy an individual ; but nothing is more certain than that this statement is altogether erroneous. We have derided, we have shunned, we have neglected them, in every possible manner. They have had to rise not only under the mountainous weight of their own ignorance and vice, but with the additional and constant pressure of our contempt and injustice. In despite of us, they have done well. Again : '*It is not our fault that we have failed*; it is not theirs.' We *are* wholly and exclusively in fault. What have we done to raise them up from the earth ? What have we *not* done to keep them down ? Once more : ' It has resulted from a cause over which neither they, nor we, can ever have control.' In other words, they have been made with skins ' not colored like our own,' and *therefore* we cannot recognise them as fellow-countrymen, or treat them like rational beings ! One sixth of our whole population *must*, FOR EVER, in this land, remain a wretched, ignorant and degraded race,—and yet nobody be culpable—*none but the Creator* who has made us *incapable* of doing unto others as we would have them do unto us ! Horrible—horrible ! If this be not an impeachment of Infinite Goodness,—I do not say intentionally but *really*,—I cannot define it. The same sentiment is reiterated by a writer in the Southern Religious Telegraph, who says—' The exclusion of the free black from the civil and literary privileges of our country, depends on another circumstance than that of character—a circumstance, which, as it was entirely beyond his control, so it is unchangeable, and will for ever operate. This circumstance is—*he is a black man*' ! ! And the Board of Managers of the Parent Society, in their Fifteenth Annual Report, declare that ' *an ordination of Providence* ' prevents the general improvement of the people of color in this land ! How are God and our country dishonored, and the requirements of the gospel contemned, by this ungodly plea ! Having satisfied himself that the Creator is alone blameable for the past and present degradation of the free blacks, Dr. Nott draws the natural and unavoidable inference that ' here, therefore, they must be *for ever debased, for ever useless, for ever a nuisance, for ever a calamity*,' and then gravely declares (mark the climax !) ' and yet THEY, [these ignorant, helpless, miserable creatures !] AND THEY ONLY, are qualified for colonizing Africa ' ! ! ' Why then,' he asks, ' *in the name of God*,'—(the abrupt appeal, in this connexion, seems almost profane,)—' should we hesitate to encourage their departure ? '

Nature, we are positively assured, has raised up impassable barriers between the races. I understand by this expression, that the blacks are of a different species from ourselves, so that all attempts to generate offspring between us and them must prove as abortive, as between a man and a beast. It is a law of Nature that the lion shall not beget the lamb, or the leopard the bear. Now the planters at the south have clearly demonstrated, that an amalgamation with their slaves is not only possible, but a matter of course, and eminently productive. It neither ends in abortion nor produces monsters. In truth, it is often so difficult in the slave States to distinguish between the fruits of this intercourse and the children of white parents, that witnesses are summoned at court to solve the problem! Talk of the barriers of Nature, when the land swarms with living refutations of the statement! Happy indeed would it be for many a female slave, if such a barrier could exist during the period of her servitude to protect her from the lust of her master!

In France,* England,† Spain, and other countries, persons of color maintain as high a rank and are treated as honorably as

---

* Why is it that the free people of color are now, in almost every part of our country, threatened with banishment from State to State, and with hunting from city to city, until there shall be no place for the soles of their feet in this their native land? Is it because they are in reality, as slaveholders tell us, an inferior race of beings? No, my friends : their consistent conduct, their polished manners, and their great respectability, wherever they have enjoyed the advantages of equality of education and equality of motives, proclaim the contrary. The true cause of this almost universal prescription is to be found in the melancholy fact that we have been guilty of the most atrocious injustice to their forefathers and to themselves. We would therefore now banish the evidence of our guilt from before our eyes : for whom a man has injured, he is almost sure to hate. Some of the finest men I met with, during a residence of three years in London and Paris, were the offspring of African mothers. There no distinction is made in any grade of society, on account of color. I have repeatedly seen black gentlemen sitting on the sofas, conversing with the ladies, at the hospitable mansion of that universal philanthropist, LAFAYETTE ; and there were no persons present who appeared more respectable, or who were more respected.—[Address of Arnold Buffum, President of the New-England Anti-Slavery Society, delivered in Boston, Feb. 16, 1832.]

† In England, it is common to see respectable and genteel people open their pews when a black stranger enters the church ; and at hotels, nobody thinks it a degradation to have a colored traveller sit at the same table. We have heard a well authenticated anecdote, which illustrates the different state of feeling in the two countries on this subject. A wealthy American citizen was residing at London for a season, which time the famous Mr Prince Saunders was there. The London breakfast hour is very late ; and Prince Saunders happened to call upon the American while his family were taking their morning repast. Politeness and native good feelings prompted the lady to ask her guest to take a cup of coffee

any other class of the inhabitants, in despite of the ' impassable barriers of Nature.' Yet it is proclaimed to the world by the Colonization Society, that the American people can never be as republican in their feelings and practices as Frenchmen, Spaniards or Englishmen ! Nay, that *religion* itself cannot subdue their malignant prejudices, or induce them to treat their dark-skinned brethren in accordance with their professions of republicanism ! My countrymen ! is it so ? Are you willing thus to be held up as tyrants and hypocrites for ever ? as less magnanimous and just than the populace of Europe ? No—no ! I cannot give you up as incorrigibly wicked, nor my country as sealed over to destruction. My confidence remains, like the oak—like the Alps—unshaken, storm-proof. I am not discouraged—I am not distrustful. I still place an unwavering reliance upon the omnipotence of truth. I still believe that the demands of justice will be satisfied ; that the voice of bleeding humanity will melt the most obdurate hearts ; and that the land will be redeemed and regenerated by an enlightened and energetic public opinion. As long as there remains among us a single copy of the Declaration of Independence, or of the New Testament, I will not despair of the social and political elevation of my sable countrymen. Already a rallying-cry is heard from the East and the West, from the North and the South ; towns and cities and states are in commotion ; volunteers are trooping to the field ; the spirit of freedom and the fiend of oppression are in mortal

---

—but then *the prejudices of society*—how could she overcome *them* ? True, he was a gentleman in character, manners and dress ; but he had a black skin ; and how could white skins sit at the same table with him ? If his *character* had been as black as perdition, the difficulty might have been overcome, however reluctantly ; but his *skin* being black, it was altogether out of the question. So the lady sipped her coffee, and Prince Saunders sat at the window, occasionally speaking in reply to conversation addressed to him. At last all retired from the breakfast table—and then the lady, with an air of sudden recollection, said, ' I forgot to ask if you had breakfasted, Mr Saunders ! Won't you let me give you a cup of coffee ? ' ' I thank you, madam,' he replied, with a dignified bow, ' I am engaged to breakfast with the PRINCE REGENT this morning !'

We laugh at the narrow bigotry of the Mahometan, who feels contaminated if a Christian shares his dinner, and who will not give his vile carcass burial, for fear of pollution. Is our prejudice against persons of color more rational or more just ? The plain fact is, our prejudice has the same foundation as that of the Mahometan—both are grounded in pride and selfishness. A law has lately passed in Turkey, imposing a fine upon whoever shall call a Christian a dog. *Let us try to keep pace with the Turks in candor and benevolence.*—[Massachusetts Journal and Tribune.]

conflict, and all neutrality is at an end. Already the line of division is drawn : on one side are the friends of truth and liberty, with their banner floating high in the air, on which are inscribed in letters of light, ' IMMEDIATE ABOLITION '—' NO COMPROMISE WITH OPPRESSORS '—' EQUAL RIGHTS '—' NO EXPATRIATION '—' DUTY, AND NOT CONSEQUENCES '—' LET JUSTICE BE DONE, THOUGH THE HEAVENS SHOULD FALL ! '— On the opposite side stand the supporters and apologists of slavery in mighty array, with a black flag on which are seen in bloody characters, ' AFRICAN COLONIZATION '—' GRADUAL ABOLITION '—' RIGHTS OF PROPERTY '—' POLITICAL EXPE- DIENCY '—' NO EQUALITY '—' NO REPENTANCE '—' EXPUL- SION OF THE BLACKS '—' PROTECTION TO TYRANTS ! '— Who can doubt the issue of this controversy, or which side has the approbation of the Lord of Hosts ?

In the African Repository for September, 1831, there is an elaborate defence of the Colonization Society, in which occurs the following passage :—' It has been said that the Society is unfriendly to the improvement of the free people of color while they remain in the United States. *The charge is not true.*' I reiterate the charge ; and the evidence of its correctness is be- fore the reader. The Society prevents the education of this class in the most insidious and effectual manner, by constantly asserting that they must always be a degraded people in this country, and that the cultivation of their minds will avail them nothing. Who does not readily perceive that the prevalence of this opinion must at once paralyze every effort for their im- provement ? For it would be a waste of time and means, and unpardonable folly, for us to attempt the accomplishment of an impossible work—of that which we know will result in disap- pointment. Every discriminating and candid mind must see and acknowledge, that, to perpetuate their ignorance, it is only necessary to make the belief prevalent that they ' must be for ever debased, for ever useless, for ever an inferior race,' and their thraldom is sure.

I am aware that a school has been established for the educa- tion of colored youth, under the auspices of the Society ; but it is sufficient to state that none but those who consent to emi- grate to Liberia are embraced in its provisions.

In the Appendix to the Seventh Annual Report, p. 94, the position is assumed that ' it is a well established point, that the public safety forbids either the emancipation or *general instruction* of the slaves.' The recent enactment of laws in some of the slave States, prohibiting the instruction of free colored persons as well as slaves, has received something more than a tacit approval from the organ of the Society. A prominent advocate of the Society, (G. P. Disosway, Esq.,) in an oration on the fourth of July, 1831, alluding to these laws, says,—' The public safety of our brethren at the South requires them [the slaves] to be kept ignorant and uninstructed.' The Editor of the Southern Religious Telegraph, who is a clergyman and a warm friend of the colonization scheme, remarking upon the instruction of the colored population of Virginia, says :

' Teaching a servant to read, is not teaching him the religion of Christ. The great majority of the white people of our country are taught to read ; but probably not one in five, of those who have the Bible, is *a christian*, in the legitimate sense of the term. If black people are as depraved and as averse to true religion as the white people are—and we know of no difference between them in this respect—teaching them to read the Bible will make christians of *very* few of them. [What a plea !] . . If christian masters were to teach their servants to read, we apprehend that they would not feel the obligation as they ought to feel it, of giving them oral instruction, and often impressing divine truth on their minds. [! !] . . If the free colored people were generally taught to read, *it might be an inducement to them to remain in this country.* WE WOULD OFFER THEM NO SUCH INDUCEMENT. [! !] . . A knowledge of letters and of all the arts and sciences, cannot counteract the influences under which the character of the negro *must* be formed in this country. . . It appears to us that a greater benefit may may be conferred on the free colored people, by planting good schools for them in Africa, and encouraging them to remove there, than by giving them the knowledge of letters to make them contented in their present condition.'—[Telegraph of Feb. 19, 1831.]

Jesuitism was never more subtle—Papal domination never more exclusive. The gospel of peace and mercy preached by him who holds that ignorance is the mother of devotion ! who would sequestrate the bible from the eyes of his fellow men ! who contends that knowledge is the enemy of religion ! who denies the efficacy of education in elevating a degraded population ! who would make men brutes in order to make them better christians ! who desires to make the clergy infallible guides to heaven ! Now what folly and impiety is all this ! Besides, is it not mockery to preach repentance, and faith in the Lord Jesus Christ, to the benighted blacks, and at the same time deny them the right and ability to ' search the scriptures' for themselves ?

The proposition which was made last year to erect a College for the education of colored youth in New-Haven, it is well known, created an extraordinary and most disgraceful tumult in that place, (the hot-bed of African colonization,) and was generally scouted by the friends of the Society in other places. The American Spectator at Washington, (next to the African Repository, the mouth-piece of the Society,) used the following language, in relation to the violent proceedings of the citizens of New-Haven : ' We not only *approve the course,* which they have pursued, but we *admire the moral courage,* which induced them, *for the love of right,* (*!*) to incur the censure of both sections of the country.'

As a farther illustration of the complacency with which colonizationists regard the laws prohibiting the instruction of the blacks, I extract the following paragraph from the ' Proceedings of the New-York State Colonization Society, on its second anniversary :'

' It is the business of the free—*their safety requires it*—to keep the slaves in ignorance. Their education is utterly prohibited. Educate them, and they break their fetters. Suppose the slaves of the south to have the knowledge of freemen, they would be free, or be exterminated by the whites. This renders it necessary to prevent their instruction—to keep them from Sunday Schools, and other means of gaining knowledge. But a few days ago, a proposition was made in the legislature of Georgia, to allow them so much instruction as to enable them to read the bible ; which was promptly rejected by a large majority. I do not mention this for the purpose of *condemning the policy* of the slaveholding States, but to lament its *necessity.*'

Elias B. Caldwell, one of the founders, and the first Secretary of the Parent Society, in a speech delivered at its formation, advanced the following monstrous sentiments :

' The more you improve the condition of these people, the more you cultivate their minds, the more *miserable* you make them in their present state. You give them a higher relish for those privileges *which they can never attain,* and turn what you intend for a blessing into *a curse.* No, if they must remain in their present situation, *keep them in the lowest state of ignorance and degradation.* The nearer you bring them to the condition of *brutes,* the better chance do you give them of possessing their apathy.'

So, then, the American Colonization Society advocates, and to a great extent perpetuates, the ignorance and degradation of the colored population of the United States !

In a critical examination of the pages of the African Repository, and of the reports and addresses of the Parent Society and its auxiliaries, I cannot find in a single instance any impeachment of the conduct and feelings of society toward the

people of color, or any hint that the prejudice which is so prevalent against them is unmanly and sinful, or any evidence of
contrition for past injustice, or any remonstrance or entreaty
with a view to a change of public sentiment, or any symptoms
of moral indignation at such unchristian and anti-republican
treatment.   On the contrary, I find the doctrine every where
inculcated that this hatred and contempt, this abuse and proscription, are not only excusable, but the natural, inevitable and
incurable effects of constitutional dissimilitude, growing out of
an ordination of Providence, for which there is no remedy but
a separation between the two races.   If the free blacks, then,
have been ' still further degraded by the mockery of nominal
freedom,' if they ' must always be a separate and degraded
race,' if ' degradation must and will press them to the earth,'
if from their present station ' they can never rise, be their talents, their enterprise, their virtues what they may,' if ' in Africa
alone, they can enjoy the motives for honorable ambition,' the
American Colonization Society is responsible for their debasement and misery ; for as it numbers among its supporters the
most influential men in our country, and boasts of having the
approbation of an overwhelming majority of the wise and good
whose examples are laws, it is able, were it willing, to effect a
radical change in public sentiment—nay, it is at the present
time public sentiment itself.   But though it has done much, and
may do more, (all that it can it will do,) to depress, impoverish and dispirit the free people of color, and to strengthen and
influence mutual antipathies, it is the purpose of God, I am
fully persuaded, to humble the pride of the American people
by rendering the expulsion of our colored countrymen utterly
impracticable, and the necessity for their admission to equal
rights imperative.   As neither mountains of prejudice, nor the
massy shackles of law and of public opinion, have been able to
keep them down to a level with slaves, I confidently anticipate
their exaltation among ourselves.   Through the vista of time,
—a short distance only,—I see them here, not in Africa, not
bowed to the earth, or derided and persecuted as at present,
not with a downcast air or an irresolute step, but standing erect
as men destined heavenward, unembarrassed, untrammelled,
with none to molest or make them afraid.

SECTION X.

THE AMERICAN COLONIZATION SOCIETY DECEIVES AND MISLEADS THE NATION.

IT is now about fifteen years since the American Colonization Society sprang into existence—a space of time amply sufficient to test its ability. In its behalf the pulpit and the press (two formidable engines) have been exerted to an extraordinary degree ; statesmen, and orators, and judges, and lawyers, and philanthropists, have eloquently advocated its claims to public patronage. During this protracted period, and with such powerful auxiliaries, a careless observer might naturally suppose that much must have been accomplished towards abolishing slavery. But what is the fact ? Less than one hundred and fifty souls have been removed annually to Africa—in all, about two thousand souls in fifteen years ! !—a drop from the Atlantic ocean—a grain of earth from the American continent ! In the mean time, the increase of the slaves has amounted to upwards of *half a million !* and every week more than *one thousand* new-born victims are added to their number. Before a vessel, with one hundred and fifty passengers, can go to and return from Africa, more than ten thousand slave infants will have been added to our population : while she is preparing to depart, or waiting for a fair wind, the increase will freight her many times.

The following eloquent and comprehensive Circular (published last year in London by Capt. Charles Stuart, in consequence of the visit of Elliott Cresson, an agent who was sent out to dupe the philanthropists of England) exhibits the inefficiency and criminality of the Society in a striking light :

'AMERICAN COLONIZATION SOCIETY. LIBERIA.—This Society was formed in the United States, in 1817.

Its Thirteenth Annual Report has just reached this country.

Its object, as expressed by itself, (see the Thirteenth Report, page 41, app. 9, art. 2,) " Is to promote and execute a plan for colonizing the free people of color, residing in ' the United States ' in Africa, or such other place as Congress shall deem most expedient.''

The facts of the case are these :

1. That the United States have about 2,000,000 enslaved blacks.
2. That they have about 500,000 free blacks.
3. That both these classes are rapidly increasing.
4. That both are exceedingly depressed and degraded.

The duty of the United States to them, is the same exactly as we owe to our colored fellow-subjects in our slave colonies, viz. to obey God, by letting them go free, by placing them beneath wise and equitable laws, and by loving them all, and treating them like brethren ; that is to say, the unquestionable duty of the people of the United States is to emancipate their 2,000,000 slaves, and to raise the 500,000 free colored people to that estimation in their native country which is due to them.

But the American Colonization Society deliberately rejects both of these first great duties, and confines itself to the colonization in Africa of the free colored people. They say, in page 5, of their Thirteenth Report, " To abolition she could not look—and need not look." It " could do nothing in the slave States for the cause of humanity ;" and in page 8, " Emancipation, with the liberty to remain on this side of the Atlantic, is but an act of dreamy madness."

Now in thus deliberately letting the great crime of negro slavery alone ; and in thus substituting a little restricted act of very dubious benevolence to a few, for the great and sacred duty of right which they owe to all,—they hurt the great cause of everlasting truth and love, in the following particulars :

1. By offering to the nation a hope, at which many of their best men seem eagerly grasping, of getting rid of the colored people abroad—they conduce more and more, as this hope prevails, to keep out of mind the superior, unalterable, and immediate duty of righting them at home.

2. By removing whatever number it be, from their native country, the number which remains must be diminished,—and the more the number which remains is diminished, the more helpless will they become—the less will be the hope of their ever recovering their own liberty—and the more and longer will they be trampled upon.

3. The more the people of the United States (and this is equally true of Great Britain) substitute a *half-way* duty, difficult, expensive, and partial as it must be, and criminal as it unquestionably is—for the *whole* duty which they owe their negro fellow-subjects, of putting them, before the law, upon a par with themselves—the less will they be likely to feel their sin in continuing to wrong them ; and the less they feel their sin, the less likely will they be to repent of it, and to do their duty.

4. The greater the number of slaves transported, the greater will be the value of the labor of those who remain ; the more valuable their labor is, the greater will be the temptation to over-labor them, and the more, of course, they will be oppressed.

5. The American Colonization Society directly supports the false and cruel idea that the native country of the colored people of the United States, is not their native country, and that they never can be happy until they either exile themselves, or are exiled ; and thus powerfully conduces to extinguish in them all those delightful hopes, and to prevent all that glorious exertion, which would make them a blessing to their country. In this particular, the American Colonization Society takes up a falsehood, as cruel to the colored people, as it is disgraceful to themselves ; dwells upon it, as if it were an irrefragable truth ; urges it, as such, upon others ; and thus endeavors with all its force, to make *that practically true*, which is one of the greatest stains in the American character ; which is one of the greatest scourges that could possibly afflict the free colored people ; and which, in itself, is essentially and unalterably false. For be the pertinacity of prejudice what it may, in asserting that the blacks of America never can be amalgamated in all respects, in equal brotherhood with the whites, it will not the less remain an everlasting truth, that the wickedness which produced and perpetuates the assertion, is the only ground of the difficulty, and that all that is requisite to remove the whole evil, is the relenting in love of the proud and cruel spirit which produced it. Could the American Colonization Society succeed in establishing their views on this subject, as being really true of the people of the United States, it would only prove that the people of the United States were past repentance ; that they were given over, through their obstinacy in sin, finally to believe a lie ; to harden themselves, and to perish in their iniquity. But they

have not succeeded in establishing this fearful fact against themselves ; and as long as they continue capable of repentance, it *never* can be true, that the proud and baneful prejudices which now so cruelly alienate them from their colored brethren, may not, will not, must not, yield to the sword of the Spirit, to the Word of God, to the blessed weapons of truth and love.

The American Colonization Society is beautiful and beneficial as far as it supports the cause commenced at Sierra Leone, by introducing into Africa, civilization, commerce, and genuine Christianity—by checking the African slave trade —and by serving in love the emigrants who choose to pass to Liberia.

But it powerfully tends to veil the existing and outrageous atrocity of negro slavery ; and it corroborates against the people of color, whether enslaved or free, one of the most base, groundless, and cruel prejudices, that has ever disgraced the powerful, or afflicted the weak.

The following calculations may throw further light upon the subject.

The United States have about 2,000,000 slaves, and about 500,000 free colored people.

The American Colonization Society has existed for thirteen years, and has exported yearly, upon an average, about 150 persons.

Meanwhile the natural yearly increase has been 56,000 souls ; and nearly a million have died in slavery ! !

But it may be said, this is only the beginning—more may be expected hereafter.—Let us see.

The average price of transporting each individual is calculated at 30 dollars : suppose it to be reduced to 20, and then, as 56,000 must be exported yearly, in order merely to prevent increase, 1,120,000 dollars would be yearly requisite simply for transportation. Where is this vast sum to come from ? Or suppose it supplied, still, in the mass of crime and wretchedness, as it now exists, there would be *no decrease!* Two millions of human beings every 30 years would still be *born* and *die* in slavery ! !

But perhaps you wish to extinguish the crime in thirty years.

Then you must begin by transporting at least 100,000 yearly. In order to do this, you must have an annual income of upwards of 2,000,000 dollars ; and if you have not only to transport, but also to purchase, you would probably want yearly, *twenty millions* more ! !

Where are you to get this ?—

Or suppose it got, and still one generation would perish in their wretchedness ; 2,000,000 of immortal souls—plundered by you of the most sacred rights of human nature ; of rights *always the same,* and everlastingly *inalienable,* however plundered—would have perished *unredressed,* and gone to confront you at the bar of God.

And will He not make inquisition for blood ? And what will it avail you to say, " Oh, we satisfied ourselves, and traversed land and sea, and spent thousands to satisfy others, that if we transported a few hundreds or thousands of our oppressed fellow-subjects to a distant country, yearly, with care, we might guiltlessly leave the remaining hundreds of thousands, or the millions, in slavery, and harmlessly indulge the invincible repugnance which we felt to a colored skin. We really thought it better, to exile our colored brethren from their native country, or to render their lives in it, intolerable by scorn, should they obstinately persist in remaining in it ;—we really thought this better, than humbling ourselves before our brother and our God, and returning to both with repenting and undissembling love."

Is not such language similar to the swearer's prayer ! !

Great Britain and the United States, the two most favored, and the two most guilty nations upon earth, both need rebuke. They ought to be brethren, mutually dear and honorable to each other, in all that is true and kind. But never, never, let them support one another in guilt.

People of Great Britain, it is your business—it is *your duty,*—to give to negro slavery no rest, but to put it down—not by letting the trunk alone, while you idly busy yourselves in lopping off, or in aiding others to lop off, a few of the straggling branches—but by laying the axe at once to its roots, and by putting your united nerve into the steel, till this great poison-tree of lust and blood, and of all abominable and heartless iniquity, fall before you ; and law, and love, and God and man, shout victory over its ruin.

Hearken—thus saith the Lord, " Rob not the poor, because he is poor ; neither oppress the afflicted in the gate. For the Lord will plead their cause, and spoil the soul of those that spoiled them." Prov. xxii. 22, 23.

LONDON, July 15, 1831.   C. STUART.' *

Sometimes the Society professes to be able to remove the whole colored population in less than thirty years ! and the belief is prevalent that the project is feasible.   Again it tells us—

' Admitting that the colonization scheme contemplates the ultimate abolition of slavery, yet that result could only be produced *by the gradual and slow operation of* CENTURIES.'   *   *   ' How came we by this population ? By the prevalence for a century of a guilty commerce. And will not the prevalence *for a century* of a restoring commerce, place them on their own shores ? Yes, surely !'   *   *   ' There are those, Sir, who ask—and could not a quarter century cease and determine the two great evils ? You and I, my dear Sir, on whom the frost of time has fallen rather perceptibly, would say a century. And now, let me ask, could ever a century, in the whole course of human affairs, be better employed ?'—[African Repository, vol. i. pp. 217, 347 ; vol. v. p. 366.]

' It is not the work of a day nor a year, it is not a work of one time, nor of two, nor of three, but it is one which will now commence, *and may continue for ages.*'—[A new and interesting View of Slavery. By Humanitas, a colonization advocate. Baltimore, 1820.]

Wild enthusiasts in the cause may respond—' The Society never expected to accomplish much single-handed : it is about to enlist the energies of the General Government—and doubtless Congress will appropriate several millions of dollars annually for the purchase and colonization of the slaves.'

But are they sure, or is it probable, that Congress will make this appropriation ? And if it should, what can they do without the consent of the people of color to remove ? That con-

---

* ' We think the annual increase, as computed by Capt. Stuart, too low by 10 or 15,000. The estimate also of the expense of transportation is much below the actual cost. Besides, there is no provision made for the support of these helpless beings after their arrival in Africa, until they could provide for their own wants. Double the cost of transportation would be required for their subsistence till they could maintain themselves, without making any provision for implements of husbandry, mechanics' tools, &c. &c. without which they would all perish, even without the help of a pestiferous climate. But yet the table shows at one view the utter futility of the whole scheme of African Colonization. Slavery can no more be removed by these means than the waters of the Mississippi can be exhausted by steam engines. And the removal of slavery is the great consummation to which all benevolent efforts for benefitting the African race in this country, should ultimately tend. All schemes that do not promote this end will prove futile, and will end in disappointment. The axe must be laid to the root of the corrupt tree. It is a system that admits of no palliation, no compromise.' —[' Herald of Truth,' Philadelphia.]

sent can never be obtained. Is it, then, proposed to buy the slaves of their masters, as if the claim of property were valid ? It were better that the money should rust at the bottom of the deep !—better to buy bank-notes, and convert them to ashes ! To purchase slaves would only serve to make brisk the slave-market. Their value would immediately rise in all the slave States ; especially in Delaware, Maryland, Virginia, Kentucky, and North Carolina, where they are now comparatively worth-less—*and there would be an end to voluntary emancipation :* for who would sacrifice his ' property,' when he might obtain an equivalent for it ? Slave traders and slave owners would be zeal-ous to prevent any lack of miserable objects for the bounty offered by government : if the natural increase were not suffi-cient, they would be careful to make the importation from Africa exceed the exportation to that ill-fated continent. Such a pur-chase would be directly patronising the slave trade, at home and abroad, and bribing masters to keep their slaves for the highest bidder. Besides, it would be a gross violation of the great fun-damental principle, that ' man cannot hold property in man.'

I know it is easy to make calculations. I know it is an old maxim, that ' figures cannot lie :' and I very well know, too, that our philanthropic arithmeticians are prodigiously fond of FIG-URING, but of doing nothing else. Give them a slate and pencil, and in fifteen minutes they will clear the continent of every black skin ; and, if desired, throw in the Indians to boot. While they depopulate America, they find not the least difficulty in providing for the wants of the emigrating myriads to the coast of Africa : we have ships enough, and, notwithstanding the hardness of the times, money enough. O, the surpassing utility of the arithmetic ! it is more potent than the stone of the phi-losopher, which, *when discovered*, is to transmute, at a touch, base metal into pure gold !

In one breath, colonization orators tell us that the free blacks are pests in the community ; that they are an intemperate, ig-norant, lazy, thievish class ; that their condition is worse than that of the slaves ; and that no efforts to improve them in this country can be successful, owing to the prejudices of society. In the next breath we are told what mighty works these miserable outcasts are to achieve—that they are the missionaries of salvation,* who are to illumine all Africa—that they will build up a second American republic—and that our conceptions cannot grasp the result of their labors.   Now I, for one, have no faith in this instantaneous metamorphosis.†   I believe that neither a sea voyage nor an African climate has any miraculous influence upon the brain.   I believe that ignorant and depraved black men, who are transported across the ocean, will be ignorant and depraved black men on reaching the coast of Africa.   I believe, also, that they who are capable of doing well, surrounded by barbarians, may do better among a civilized and christian people.

It is stated in a Circular put forth by the Society last year, that ' from the *actual experience* of the Society, it has been found that $20, *or less*, will defray the whole expense of transporting an individual to the Colony.'   This is a very deceptive statement.   The receipts of the Society from 1820 to 1830, amounted to $112,841 89 ; the expenses during the same period were $106,457 72 ; balance on hand, $6,384 17.   Nine-

---

* ' Every emigrant to Africa is a *missionary* carrying with him credentials in the holy cause of civilization, religion, and free institutions' ! !—[Speech of H. Clay---Tenth Annual Report.]—Why does not Mr Clay increase this band of *missionaries*, by sending out some of his own slaves ?   Is he consistent ?

†' As to the morals of the colonists, I consider them *much better than those of the people of the United States.*   That is, you may take an equal number of inhabitants from any section of the Union, and you will find more drunkards, more profane swearers and Sabbath breakers, &c., than in Liberia.   Indeed I know of no country where things are conducted more quietly and orderly than in this colony ; you rarely hear an oath, and as to riots or breaches of the peace, I recollect of but one instance, and that of a trifling nature, that has come under my notice since I assumed the government of the colony.   The Sabbath is more strictly observed than I ever saw it in the United States.'—[Letter from J. Mechlin, Jr. Governor of the Colony of Liberia.]

' I saw no intemperance, nor did I hear a profane word uttered by any one.' [Letter of Capt. William Abels.]

If these statements be a true representation of the moral condition of the colonists ; if ' their morals are much better than those of the people of the United States ;' let us immediately bring back these expatriated *missionaries* to civilize and reform ourselves ; for, according to our own confession, we need their instruction and example as much as any heathen nation.   If these ' missionaries,' who, in this country, could ' scarcely be reached in their debasement by the heavenly light ;' if these ' most degraded, most abandoned beings on the earth,' have actually risen up to this exalted height of intelligence and purity, in so brief a period after a separation from ourselves, how desperately wicked and corrupt does the fact make our own conduct appear !

teen expeditions had been fitted out, and 1,857 emigrants,* *including re-captured Africans,* landing on the shores of Africa —averaging annually, for the ten years, about 186 persons, or since the organization of the Society, about 124 persons. ' The emigrants,' the Board of Managers inform us, in a recent address to Auxiliary Societies, ' for the last three years, average about 227, while the expenses, *exclusive of transportation, and temporary subsistence of the new colonists,* exceed TEN THOUSAND DOLLARS ' ! ! In the very last number of the African Repository, (for April, 1832,) the Vice-Agent at Liberia, A. D. Williams, writes to the Rev. R. R. Gurley as follows :— ' I think the price, say $35, fixed by the Board for the transportation of each emigrant, *is entirely too low :* it should be at least $40, if not $45.' Why, then, does the Society attempt to impose upon public credulity, by stating that only $20 are requisite for every individual transportation, when the actual cost has been more than thrice, and is likely to be more than double that amount ? †

---

* Of this number, nearly three-fourths were free persons of color. If the Society is anxious to emancipate the slaves, why does it not confine its efforts exclusively to their transportation, seeing so many are offered for that purpose ? Doubtless the reply will be—' O, it is important, in the incipient state of the colony, to send free persons of color, because they are more intelligent and virtuous.' Ah ! is it so ? What ! give the preference to those whom it elsewhere brands as ' more corrupt, depraved and abandoned than the slaves can be,' and who ' contribute greatly to the *corruption of the slaves ?* ' ' O !' it may reply, ' a careful selection is made between the virtuous and vicious—none are sent whose character is not reputable.' But what is to become of this choice selection, when it is able (as it hopes to be) to send off even as many as seventy thousand annually ?

† The expense of transporting such persons from the United States to the coast of Africa, has been variously estimated. By those who compute it at the lowest rate, the mere expense of this transportation has been estimated at $20 per head. In this estimate, however, is not comprehended the expense of transporting the persons destined for Africa, to the port of their departure from the United States, or the necessary expense of sustaining them, either there or in Africa, for a reasonable time after their first arrival. All these expenses combined, the Committee think they estimate very low, when they compute the amount at $100 per head. It has been estimated by some at double this amount ; and if past experience may be relied upon as proving any thing, the official documents formerly furnished to the Senate by the Department of the Navy, show that the expenses attending the transportation of the few captured slaves who have been returned to Africa by the United States, at the expense of this government, *far exceeds even the largest estimate.* But taking the expense to be only what the Committee have estimated it : Then the sum requisite to transport the whole number of the free colored population of the United States, would exceed twenty-eight millions of dollars ; and the expense of transporting a number, equal only to the mere annual increase of this population, would exceed seven hundred thousand

The Society has succeeded in making the people believe that the establishment of a colony or colonies on the coast of Africa is the only way to abolish the foreign slave trade : on this account it has secured an extensive patronage. Here is another fatal delusion. I shall show not only that it has not injured this trade in the least, but that the trade *continues to increase in activity and cruelty.* Let us look at its own admissions.

' We regret to say, that the slave trade appears to be carried on to a great extent, and with circumstances of the most revolting cruelty.' * * * The French slave trade, notwithstanding the efforts of the government, appears to be undiminished. The number of Spanish vessels employed in the trade is immense, and as the treaty between England and Spain only permits the seizure of vessels having slaves actually on board, many of these watch their opportunity on the coast, run in, and receive all their slaves on board in a single day.' * * ' By an official document from Rio de Janeiro, it appears that the following importations of slaves were made into that port in 1826 and 1827.

  1826, landed alive, 35,966....died on the passage 1,905
  1827, landed alive, 41,384....died on the passage 1,643

Thus it would seem, (says the Boston Gazette,) that to only one port in the Brazils, and in the course of two years, *seventy-seven thousand three hundred and fifty* human beings were transported from their own country, and placed in a state of slavery.'—[African Repository, vol. i. v. pp. 179, 181.]

' It is not by legal arguments, or penal statutes, or armed ships, that the slave trade can be prevented. Almost every power in christendom has denounced it. It has been declared felony—it has been declared piracy ; and the fleets of Britain and America have been commissioned to drive it from the ocean. Still, in defiance of all this array of legislation and of armament, slave ships ride triumphant on the ocean ; and in these floating caverns, less terrible only than the caverns which demons occupy, from sixty to eighty thousand wretches, received pinioned from the coast of Africa, are borne annually away to slavery or death. Of these wretches a frightful number are, with an audacity that amazes, landed and disposed of within the jurisdiction of this republic.'—[Idem, vol. v. 274.]

' Notwithstanding all the efforts that have been made to suppress the slave trade, by means of solemn treaties and laws declaring it to be piracy ; and not-

dollars per annum. Sums which would impose upon the people of this country, an additional burthen of taxation, greater than this Committee believe they could easily bear ; and much greater than ought to be imposed upon them for any such purpose.' * * ' The annual increase of the slave population, at present, is at least 57,000. Now allow the same sum per head for the transportation of these persons, that has been estimated for the transportation in the other similar case ; and the sum requisite to defray the expense of the transportation of all the slaves in the United States, would be one hundred and ninety millions of dollars ; and that requisite to defray the expense of the transportation of a number only equal to their mere annual increase, would be five millions seven hundred thousand dollars per annum. But to either of these sums must be added the reasonable equivalent, or necessary aid, to be paid by the United States to humane individuals, in order to induce them voluntarily to part with their property. The Committee have no ' data ' by which they can measure what this might be. But any sum, however small, will make so great an augmentation of the amount, as almost to baffle calculation, and to exhibit this project at once, as one exceeding, very far, indeed, any revenue which the United States could ever draw from their citizens, even if the object was to increase and multiply, instead of reducing the numbers of the class of productive labor.'—[Mr Tazewell's Report—U. S. Senate, 1828.]

withstanding the attempts to exterminate it by the naval forces of the United States and Great Britain, the inhuman traffic is still pursued to as great an extent as at any former period, and with greater cruelty than ever.'—[African Repository, vol. vi. p. 345.]

' The slave trade, which many suppose has been every where abolished for years, there is reason to believe is still carried on to almost as great an extent as ever. It has been recently stated in the papers, that an association of merchants at Nantz, in France, had undertaken to supply the island of Cuba with thirty thousand fresh negro slaves annually ! And in Brazil, it is well known, that for several years past, the importations have even exceeded this number.'—[Idem, vol. vii. p. 248.]

' Africa, for three long centuries, has been ravaged by the slave trade. Notwithstanding all that has been done to suppress that traffic, notwithstanding its formal abolition by all civilized nations, it is carried on at the present hour, *with all its atrocities unmitigated.* The flags of France, Portugal, Brazil, and Spain, with the connivance of those governments, afford to the slave trader, in spite of laws and treaties and armed cruisers, a partial protection, of which he avails himself to the utmost. And with what cruelty he carries on his war against human nature, every year affords us illustrations sufficiently horrible.'—[Christian Spectator for September, 1830.]

' This horrible traffic, notwithstanding its abolition by every civilized nation in the world, except Portugal and Brazil, and notwithstanding the decided measures of the British and American governments, is still carried on to almost as great an extent as ever. Not less than 60,000 slaves, according to the most moderate computation, are carried from Africa annually. This trade is carried on by Americans to the American states. And the cruelties of this trade, which always surpassed the powers of the human mind to conceive, *are greater now than they ever were before.* We might, but we will not, refer to stories, recent stories, of which the very recital would be torment.'—[Seventh Annual Report.]

' Notwithstanding the vigilance of the powers now engaged to suppress the slave trade, I have received information, that in a single year, in the single island of Cuba, slaves equal in amount to one half of the above number of fifty-two thousand have been illicitly introduced.'   *   *   ' Mr Mercer submitted the following preamble and resolutions :—Whereas, to the affliction of the Christian world, the African slave trade, notwithstanding all the efforts, past and present, for its suppression, still exists and is conducted *with aggravated cruelty,* by the resources of one continent, to the dishonor of another, and to an extent little short of the desolation of a third,' &c.—[Tenth Annual Report.]

' It is painful to state, that the Managers have reason to believe that the slave trade is still prosecuted, to a great extent, and with circumstances of undiminished atrocity. The fact, that much was done by Mr Ashmun to banish it from the territory, under the colonial jurisdiction, is unquestionable ; but, *it now exists, even on this territory ;* and a little to the north and south of Liberia, it is seen in its true characters—of fraud, rapine, and blood ! In the opinion of the late Agent, the present efforts to suppress this trade must prove abortive.'—[Thirteenth Annual Report.]

' Some appalling facts in regard to the slave trade have come to the knowledge of the Board of Managers during the last year. *With undiminished atrocity and activity* is this odious traffic now carried on *all along the African coast.* Slave factories are established *in the immediate vicinity of the Colony,* and at the Gallinas (between Liberia and Sierra Leone) not less than nine hundred slaves were shipped during the last summer, in the space of three weeks.'—[Fourteenth Annual Report, 1831.]

' In defiance of all laws enacted, it is estimated that no less than *fifty thousand* Africans were, during the last year, (1831,) carried into foreign slavery. During the months of February and March of the same year, two thousand were landed on the island of Cuba.'—[Circular published by the Massachusetts Colonization Society for 1832.]

Here, then, is the acknowledgment of the Society, that it has accomplished *nothing* toward the suppression of the slave trade in fifteen years ! Nor has the settlement at Sierra Leone effected aught in thirty years ! Nor have the untiring labors of Wilberforce and Clarkson, for a longer period, produced any visible effect ! The accursed traffic still continues to increase—and why ? Simply *because the market for slaves is not destroyed.* Break up this market, and you annihilate the slave trade. Keep it open, and you may line the shores of Africa and America with naval ships and armed troops, and the trade will continue. No proposition in Euclid is plainer. So long as there is a brisk market for goods, that market will be supplied. The assertion has been made in Congress by Mr Mercer of Virginia, (one of the Vice-Presidents of the Society,) that these horrible cargoes are smuggled into our southern states to a deplorable extent. In 1819, Mr Middleton, of South Carolina, declared it to be his belief ' that 13,000 Africans were annually smuggled into our southern states.' Mr Wright of Virginia estimated the number at 15,000 !!!—[*Vide* Seventh Annual Report—app.] —This number is seven times as great as that which the Colonization Society has transported in fifteen years ! * By letting the system of slavery alone, then, and striving to protect it, *the Society is encouraging and perpetuating the foreign slave trade !*

---

* The following amusing anecdote is a capital illustration of the folly of those colonizationists, who are endeavoring to suppress the rising tide of our colored population by extracting a few drops annually with their ' mop and pattens.' Dame Partington is clearly outdone by them, in regard to pertinacity of purpose and feebleness of execution. Rev. Sidney Smith, in his speech at the Taunton meeting, (England,) said :

' The attempt of the House of Lords to stop the progress of Reform, reminded him of the conduct of the excellent Mrs. Partington, during the great storm at Sidmouth, in 1824. The tide rose to an incredible height ; the waves rushed in upon the houses, and every thing was threatened with destruction. In the midst of the fearful commotion of the elements, Dame Partington, who lived upon the sea beach, was seen at the door of her house, with mop and pattens, trundling her mop and sweeping out the sea water, and vigorously pushing back the Atlantic. The Atlantic was roused, and so was Mrs. Partington ; but the contest was unequal. The Atlantic beat Mrs. Partington. She was excellent at a slop or a puddle, but she could do nothing with a tempest.'

END· OF PART I.

THOUGHTS

ON

AFRICAN COLONIZATION.

PART II.

SENTIMENTS OF THE PEOPLE OF COLOR.

IF the American Colonization Society were indeed actuated
by the purest motives and the best feelings toward the objects
of its supervision ; if it were not based upon injustice, fraud,
persecution and incorrigible prejudice ; still if its purposes be
contrary to the wishes and injurious to the interests of the free
people of color, it ought not to receive the countenance of the
public. Even the trees of the forest are keenly susceptible to
every touch of violence, and seem to deprecate transplantation
to a foreign soil. Even birds and animals pine in exile from
their native haunts ; their local attachments are wonderful ; they
migrate only to return again at the earliest opportunity. Perhaps there is not a living thing, from the hugest animal down to
the minutest animalcule, whose pleasant associations are not cir-
cumscribed, or that has not some favorite retreats. This universal preference, this love of *home*, seems to be the element of
being,—a constitutional attribute given by the all-wise Creator
to bind each separate tribe or community within intelligent and
well-defined limits : for, in its absence, order would be banished

[PART II.]   1

from the world, collision between the countless orders of creation would be perpetual, and violence would depopulate the world with more than pestilential rapidity.

Shall it be said that beings endowed with high intellectual powers, sustaining the most important relations, created for social enjoyments, and made but a little lower than the angels—shall it be said that their local attachments are less tenacious than those of trees, and birds, and beasts, and insects? I know that the blacks are classed, by some, who scarcely give any evidence of their own humanity but their shape, among the brute creation : but are they *below* the brutes ? or are they more insensible to rude assaults than forest-trees ?

' Men,' says an erratic but powerful writer*—' men are like trees : they delight in a rude [and native] soil—they strike their roots downward with a perpetual effort, and heave their proud branches upward in perpetual strife. Are they to be removed ?—you must tear up the very earth with their roots, rock and ore and impurity, or they perish. They cannot be translated with safety. Something of their home—a little of their native soil, must cling to them forever, or they die.'

This love of home, of neighborhood, of country, is inherent in the human breast. It accompanies the child from its earliest reminiscence up to old age : it is written upon every tangible and permanent object within the habitual cognizance of the eye—upon stone, and tree, and rivulet—upon the green hill, and the verdant plain, and the opulent valley—upon house, and garden, and steeple-spire—upon the soil, whether it be rough or smooth, sandy or hard, barren or luxuriant.

> ' Like ivy, where it grows, 't is seen
> To wear an everlasting green.'

The man who does not cherish it is regarded as destitute of sensibility ; and to him is applied by common consent the burning rebuke of Sir Walter Scott :

> ' Breathes there the man, with soul so dead,
> Who never to himself hath said,

---

* John Neal.

> This is my own, my native land !
> Whose heart hath ne'er within him burned,
> As home his footsteps he hath turned,
>   From wandering on a foreign strand !
> If such there breathe, go, mark him well ;
> For him no Minstrel raptures swell ;
> High though his titles, proud his name,
> Boundless his wealth as wish can claim ;
> Despite those titles, power, and pelf,
> The wretch, concentred all in self,
> Living, shall forfeit fair renown,
> And, doubly dying, shall go down
> To the vile dust, from whence he sprung,
> Unwept, unhonored, and unsung.'

Whose bosom does not thrill with pleasurable emotion whenever he listens to that truest, sweetest, tenderest effusion,— ' Home, sweet home ?'

> ' 'Mid pleasures and palaces though we may roam,
> Be it ever so humble, there 's no place like home ;
> A charm from the skies seems to hallow us there,
> Which, seek thro' the world, is ne'er met with elsewhere.
>   Home—home !
>   Sweet, sweet home !
> *There 's no place like home !'*

> An exile from home, splendor dazzles in vain—
> O give me my lowly thatched cottage again ;
> The birds singing gaily that came at my call—
> Give me them, with the peace of mind dearer than all !
>   ' Home—home !
>   Sweet, sweet home !
> *There 's no place like home !'*

No one will understand me to maintain that population should never be thinned by foreign emigration ; but only that such an emigration is unnatural. The great mass of a neighborhood or country must necessarily be stable : only fractions are cast off and float away on the tide of adventure. Individual enterprise or estrangement is one thing : the translation of an entire people to an unknown clime, another. The former may be moved by a single impulse—by a love of novelty, or a desire of gain, or a hope of preferment : he leaves no perceptible void in society. The latter can never be expatriated but by some extraordinary calamity, or by the application of intolerable restraints. They must first be rendered broken-hearted or loaded with chains—hope must not merely sicken but die—cord after cord must be sundered—ere they will seek another home. Our pilgrim-fathers were driven out from the mother country by ecclesiastical domination : to worship God according to the dictates of their own consciences, was the only cause of their exile. Had they been permitted to enjoy this sacred right,—no matter how great were their temporal privations, or their hopes of physical enjoyments,—they would not have perilled their lives on the stormy deep, to obtain an asylum in this western hemisphere.

It may be said, in reply to the foregoing remarks upon the love of home and of country, that the people of color cannot cherish this abhorrence of migration, because here they have no ' continuing city,' and are not recognised as fellow-countrymen. In PART I., I have shown, by copious extracts, that colonizationists artfully represent them as aliens and foreigners, wanderers from Africa—destitute of that *amor patriæ*, which is the bond of union—seditious—without alliances—irresponsible—unambitious—cherishing no attachment to the soil—feeling no interest in our national prosperity—ready for any adventure—eager to absent themselves from the land—malignant in their feelings towards society—incapable of local preference—content to remain in ignorance and degradation—&c. &c. &c.

Every such representation is a libel, as I shall show in subsequent pages. The language of the people of color is,—' This is our country : here were we born—here will we live and die—we know of no other place that we can call our true and appropriate home—here are our earliest and most pleasant associations—we are freemen, we are brethren, we are countrymen and fellow-citizens—we are not for insurrection, but for peace and equality.' This is not the language of sedition or alienated affection. Their *amor patriæ* is robust and deathless : like the oak, tempests do but strengthen its roots and confer victory upon it. Even the soil on which the unhappy slave toils and bleeds, is to him consecrated earth.

African colonization is directly and irreconcileably opposed to the wishes of our colored population as a body. Their desires ought to be tenderly regarded. In all my intercourse with them in various towns and cities, I have never seen one of their number who was friendly to this scheme—and I have not been backward in canvassing their opinions on this subject. They are as unanimously opposed to a removal to Africa, as the Cherokees from the council-fires and graves of their fathers. It is remarkable, too, that they are as united in their respect and esteem for the republic of Hayti. But *this is their country* —they are resolute against every migratory plot, and willing to rely on the justice of the nation for an ultimate restoration to all their lost rights and privileges. What is the fact ? Through the instrumentality of BENJAMIN LUNDY,* the distinguished and veteran champion of emancipation, a great highway has been opened to the Haytien republic, over which our colored population may travel *toll free*, and at the end of their brief journey be the free occupants of the soil, and meet such a reception as was never yet given to any sojourners in any country, since the departure of Israel into Egypt. One would think, that, with such inducements and under such circumstances, this broad thoroughfare would present a most animating spectacle ; that the bustle and roar of a journeying multitude would fall upon the ear like the strife of the ocean, or the distant thunder of the retiring storm ; and that the song of the oppressor and the oppressed, a song of deliverance to each, would go up to heaven, till its echoes were seemingly the responses of angels and justified spirits. But it is not so. Only here and there a traveller is seen to enter upon the road—there is no noise of preparation or departure ; but a silence, deeper than the breathlessness of midnight, rests upon our land—not a shout of joy is heard throughout our borders !

---

* *Vide* the Fourth Volume of the Genius of Universal Emancipation for 1829.

How shall we account for this amazing apathy but on the ground that our colored population are unwilling to leave their native homes, no matter how strong soever are the inducements held out to them abroad ?

If it be said that they are not compelled to emigrate against their wishes—I answer, it is true that direct *physical force* is not applied ; but why are they induced to remove ? Is it because they instinctively prefer Africa to their native country ? Do they actually *court* the perils of the sea,—the hostilities of a savage tribe,—the sickening influences of an African climate ? Or are they not peremptorily assured that they never can, *and never shall,* enjoy their rights and privileges at home—and thus absolutely compelled to leave all that is dear behind, and to seek a shelter in a strange land—a land of darkness and cruelty, of barbarism and wo ?

The free people of color, and even the slaves, have on numerous occasions given ocular demonstration of their attachment to this country.   Large numbers of them were distinguished for their patient endurance, their ardent devotion, and their valorous conduct during our revolutionary struggle.   In the last war, they signalized themselves in a manner which extorted the applause even of their calumniators—of many who are doubtless at the present day representing them as seditious and inimical to the prosperity of the country.   I have before me a Proclamation in the French language, issued by General Andrew Jackson, of which the following is a translation ;

' Proclamation to the Free People of Color.

' Soldiers !—When on the banks of the Mobile, I called you to take up arms, inviting you to partake the perils and glory of your white fellow citizens, *I expected much from you ;* for I was not ignorant that you possessed qualities most formidable to an invading enemy.   I knew with what fortitude you could endure hunger and thirst, and all the fatigues of a campaign.   *I knew well how you loved your* native *country,* and that you had, as well as ourselves, to defend what man holds most dear —his parents, relations, wife, children and property.   You have done more than I expected.   In addition to the previous qualities I before knew you to possess, I found, moreover, among you *a noble enthusiasm* which leads to the performance of great things.

Soldiers !—The President of the United States shall hear how praiseworthy was your conduct in the hour of danger, and the Representatives of the American people will, I doubt not, give you the praise your exploits entitle you to. *Your General anticipates them in applauding your noble ardor.*

The enemy approaches ; his vessels cover our lakes ; our brave citizens are united, and all contention has ceased among them. Their only dispute is, who shall win the prize of valor, or who the most glory, its noblest reward.

By order.

THOMAS BUTLER, *Aid de Camp.*'

In commenting upon the above Proclamation, an intelligent writer in the New-Orleans ' LIBERALIST' of March 15, 1830, very expressively remarks :—' Those who served in the memorable campaign of 1814 will know if the hero of the west was guilty of exaggeration. Just as fatal as was every glance of his keen eye to the English lines, so is every word of this Proclamation a killing thunderbolt to the detractors of this portion of our fellow beings, now so inhumanly persecuted.' Yes—when peril rears its crest, and invasion threatens our shores, then prejudice is forgotten and the tongue of detraction is still—then the people of color are no longer brutes or a race between men and monkeys, no longer turbulent or useless, no longer aliens and wanderers from Africa—but they are complimented as intelligent, patriotic citizens from whom much is expected, and who have property, home and country at stake ! Ay, and richly do they merit this compliment.

A respectable colored gentleman in the city of New-York, referring to this famous Proclamation, makes the following brief comment : ' When we could be of any use to the army, we possessed all the cardinal virtues ; but now that time has passed, we forsooth are the most miserable, worthless beings the Lord in his wise judgment ever sent to curse the rulers of this troublesome world ! I feel an anathema rising from my heart, but I have suppressed it.'

How black is the ingratitude, how pitiful the hypocrisy, manifested in our conduct as a people, toward our colored popula-

tion ! Every cheek should wear the blush of shame—every
head be bowed in self-abasement !

From the organization of the American Colonization Society,
down to the present time, the free people of color have publicly and repeatedly expressed their opposition to it. They
indignantly reject every overture for their expatriation. It has
been industriously circulated by the advocates of colonization,
that I have caused this hostility to the African scheme in the
bosoms of the blacks ; and that, until the Liberator was established, they were friendly to it. This story is founded upon
sheer ignorance. It is my solemn conviction that I have not
proselyted a dozen individuals ; for the very conclusive reason
that no conversions were necessary. Their sentiments were
familiar to me long before they knew my own. My opponents
abundantly overrate my influence, in acknowledging that I have
overthrown, in a single year, the concentrated energies of the
mightiest men in the land, and the perpetual labors of fifteen
years. They shall not make me vain. Such a concession
affords substantial evidence of perverted strength and misap-
plied exertion.

If the people of color were instantly to signify their willingness
to emigrate, my hostility to the American Colonization Society
would scarcely abate one jot : for their assent could never justify the principles and doctrines propagated by the Society.
Those principles and doctrines have been shown, I trust, to be
corrupt, selfish, proscriptive, opposed to the genius of republicanism and to the spirit of christianity.

The first public demonstration of hostility to the colonization
scheme was made in 1817, by the free colored inhabitants of
Richmond, Virginia. The proceedings of their meeting, copies
of which were printed for distribution, I have accidentally mislaid. To the sentiments of the people of color, as expressed
in the following pages, I cannot too earnestly solicit the serious
attention of every good man and true philanthropist. After
such an exhibition, persistance in expelling this portion of our
population from our shores must be productive of aggravated
guilt and the most dreadful collisions.

A VOICE FROM PHILADELPHIA.

PHILADELPHIA, January, 1817.

AT a numerous meeting of the people of color, convened at Bethel church, to take into consideration the propriety of re-monstrating against the contemplated measure, that is to exile us from the land of our nativity ; James Forten was called to the chair, and Russell Parrott appointed secretary. The intent of the meeting having been stated by the chairman, the follow-ing resolutions were adopted, without one dissenting voice.

Whereas our ancestors (not of choice) were the first suc-cessful cultivators of the wilds of America, we their descend-ants feel ourselves entitled to participate in the blessings of her luxuriant soil, which their blood and sweat manured ; and that any measure or system of measures, having a tendency to ban-ish us from her bosom, would not only be cruel, but in direct violation of those principles, which have been the boast of this republic.

Resolved, That we view with deep abhorrence the unmerited stigma attempted to be cast upon the reputation of the free peo-ple of color, by the promoters of this measure, ' that they are a dangerous and useless part of the community,' when in the state of disfranchisement in which they live, in the hour of dan-ger they ceased to remember their wrongs, and rallied around the standard of their country.

Resolved, That we never will separate ourselves voluntarily from the slave population in this country ; they are our brethren by the ties of consanguinity, of suffering, and of wrong ; and we feel that there is more virtue in suffering privations with them, than fancied advantages for a season.

Resolved, That without arts, without science, without a proper knowledge of government, to cast into the savage wilds of Africa the free people of color, seems to us the circuitous route through which they must return to perpetual bondage.

Resolved, That having the strongest confidence in the justice of God, and philanthropy of the free states, we cheerfully sub-mit our destinies to the guidance of Him who suffers not a sparrow to fall, without his special providence.

Resolved, That a committee of eleven persons be appointed to open a correspondence with the honorable Joseph Hopkin-son, member of Congress from this city, and likewise to inform him of the sentiments of this meeting, and that the following named persons constitute the committee, and that they have power to call a general meeting, when they in their judgment may deem it proper.

[PART II.]　　2

Rev. Absalom Jones, Rev. Richard Allen, James Forten, Robert Douglass, Francis Perkins, Rev. John Gloucester, Robert Gorden, James Johnson, Quamoney Clarkson, John Summersett, Randall Shepherd.

JAMES FORTEN, Chairman.

RUSSELL PARROTT, Secretary.

At a numerous meeting of the free people of color of the city and county of Philadelphia, held in pursuance of public notice, at the school house in Green's court, on the evening of August 10th, for the purpose of taking into consideration the plan of colonizing the free people of color of the United States, on the coast of Africa, James Forten was appointed chairman, and Russell Parrott, secretary.

Resolved unanimously, That the following address, signed on behalf of the meeting, by the Chairman and Secretary, be published and circulated.

To the humane and benevolent Inhabitants of the city and county of Philadelphia.

The free people of color, assembled together, under circumstances of deep interest to their happiness and welfare, humbly and respectfully lay before you this expression of their feelings and apprehensions.

Relieved from the miseries of slavery, many of us by your aid, possessing the benefits which industry and integrity in this prosperous country assure to all its inhabitants, enjoying the rich blessings of religion, by opportunities of worshipping the only true God, under the light of Christianity, each of us according to his understanding; and having afforded to us and to our children the means of education and improvement; we have no wish to separate from our present homes, for any purpose whatever. Contented with our present situation and condition, we are not desirous of increasing their prosperity but by honest efforts, and by the use of those opportunities for their improvement, which the constitution and laws allow to all. It is therefore with painful solicitude, and sorrowing regret, we have seen a plan for colonizing the free people of color of the United States on the coast of Africa, brought forward under the auspices and sanction of gentlemen whose names give value to all they recommend, and who certainly are among the wisest, the best, and the most benevolent of men, in this great nation.

If the plan of colonizing is intended for our benefit; and those who now promote it, will never seek our injury; we humbly and respectfully urge, that it is not asked for by us;

nor will it be required by any circumstances, in our present or future condition ; as long as we shall be permitted to share the protection of the excellent laws and just government which we now enjoy, in common with every individual of the community.

We, therefore, a portion of those who are the objects of this plan, and among those whose happiness, with that of others of our color, it is intended to promote ; with humble and grateful acknowledgments to those who have devised it, renounce and disclaim every connexion with it ; and respectfully but firmly declare our determination not to participate in any part of it.

If this plan of colonization now proposed, is intended to provide a refuge and a dwelling for a portion of our brethren, who are now held in slavery in the south, we have other and stronger objections to it, and we entreat your consideration of them.

The ultimate and final abolition of slavery in the United States, by the operation of various causes, is, under the guidance and protection of a just God, progressing. Every year witnesses the release of numbers of the victims of oppression, and affords new and safe assurances that the freedom of all will be in the end accomplished. As they are thus by degrees relieved from bondage, our brothers have opportunities for instruction and improvement ; and thus they become in some measure fitted for their liberty. Every year, many of us have restored to us by the gradual, but certain march of the cause of abolition—parents, from whom we have been long separated—wives and children whom we had left in servitude—and brothers, in blood as well as in early sufferings, from whom we had been long parted.

But if the emancipation of our kindred shall, when the plan of colonization shall go into effect, be attended with transportation to a distant land, and shall be granted on no other condition; the consolation for our past sufferings and of those of our color who are in slavery, which have hitherto been, and under the present situation of things would continue to be, afforded to us and to them, will cease for ever. The cords, which now connect them with us, will be stretched by the distance to which their ends will be carried, until they break ; and all the sources of happiness, which affection and connexion and blood bestow, will be ours and theirs no more.

Nor do we view the colonization of those who may become emancipated by its operation among our southern brethren, as capable of producing their happiness. Unprepared by education, and a knowledge of the truths of our blessed religion, for their new situation, those who will thus become colonists will themselves be surrounded by every suffering which can afflict the members of the human family.

Without arts, without habits of industry, and unaccustomed to provide by their own exertions and foresight for their wants, the colony will soon become the abode of every vice, and the home of every misery. Soon will the light of Christianity, which now dawns among that portion of our species, be shut out by the clouds of ignorance, and their day of life be closed, without the illuminations of the gospel.

To those of our brothers, who shall be left behind, there will be assured perpetual slavery and augmented sufferings. Diminished in numbers, the slave population of the southern states, which by its magnitude alarms its proprietors, will be easily secured. Those among their bondmen, who feel that they should be free, by rights which all mankind have from God and from nature, and who thus may become dangerous to the quiet of their masters, will be sent to the colony ; and the tame and submissive will be retained, and subjected to increased rigor. Year after year will witness these means to assure safety and submission among their slaves, and the southern masters will colonize only those whom it may be dangerous to keep among them. The bondage of a large portion of our brothers will thus be rendered perpetual.

Should the anticipations of misery and want among the colonists, which with great deference we have submitted to your better judgment, be realized ; to emancipate and transport to Africa will be held forth by slaveholders as the worst and heaviest of punishments ; and they will be threatened and successfully used to enforce increased submission to their wishes, and subjection to their commands.

Nor ought the sufferings and sorrows, which must be produced by an exercise of the right to transport and colonize such only of their slaves as may be selected by the slaveholders, escape the attention and consideration of those whom with all humility we now address. Parents will be torn from their children—husbands from their wives—brothers from brothers—and all the heart-rending agonies which were endured by our forefathers when they were dragged into bondage from Africa, will be again renewed, and with increased anguish. The shores of America will, like the sands of Africa, be watered by the tears of those who will be left behind. Those who shall be carried. away will roam childless, widowed, and alone, over the burning plains of Guinea.

Disclaiming, as we emphatically do, a wish or desire to interpose our opinions and feelings between all plans of colonization, and the judgment of those whose wisdom as far exceeds ours as their situations are exalted above ours ; *we humbly*, respectfully, and fervently intreat and beseech your disapprobation of the plan of colonization now offered by ' the American Society for colonizing the free people of color of the United States.'— Here, in the city of Philadelphia, where the voice of the suffering sons of Africa was first heard ; where was first commenced the work of abolition, on which heaven has smiled, for it could have had success only from the Great Maker ; let not a purpose be assisted which will stay the cause of the entire abolition of slavery in the United States, and which may defeat it altogether ; which proffers to those who do not ask for them what it calls benefits, but which they consider injuries ; and which must insure to the multitudes whose prayers can only reach you through us, MISERY, *sufferings, and perpetual slavery.*

> JAMES FORTEN, Chairman.
> RUSSELL PARROTT, Secretary.

A VOICE FROM NEW-YORK.

NEW-YORK, January, 1831.

At a public meeting of the colored citizens of New-York, held at Boyer Lodge Room, on Tuesday evening, the 25th ult. Mr Samuel Ennals was called to the chair, and Mr Philip Bell appointed secretary. The chairman stated that the object of the meeting was to take into consideration the proceedings of an association, under the title of the ' New-York Colonization Society.' An address to the ' Citizens of New-York ' relative to that Society, was read from the Commercial Advertiser of the 8th ult. ; whereupon the following resolutions were unanimously adopted.

Whereas a number of gentlemen in this city, of mistaken views with respect to the wishes and welfare of the people of this state, on the subject of African colonization, and in pursuance of such mistaken views are using every exertion to form ' African Colonization Societies ;' and whereas a public document, purporting to be an address to the people of the ' city of New-York ' on this subject, contains opinions and assertions regarding the people of color as unfounded as they are unjust and derogatory to them—Therefore

Resolved, That this meeting do most solemnly protest against the said address, as containing sentiments with respect to the people of color, unjust, illiberal and unfounded ; tending to excite the prejudice of the community.

Resolved, That in our opinion the sentiments put forth in the

resolution at the formation of the ' Colonization Society of the
city of New-York,' are such as to impress this community with
the belief that the colored population are a growing evil, im-
moral, and destitute of religious principles.

Resolved, That we view the resolution calling on the worshippers of Christ to assist in the unholy crusade against the
colored population of this country, as totally at variance with
true Christian principles.

Resolved, That we claim *this country, the place of our birth,
and not Africa,* as our mother country, and all attempts to send
us to Africa we consider as gratuitous and uncalled for.

Resolved, That a committee of three persons be appointed
to draft an address to the people of New-York, and to be published, together with these resolutions, and the same be signed
by the Chairman and Secretary.

SAMUEL ENNALS, Chairman.

Philip Bell, Secretary.

An Address to the Citizens of New-York.

In protesting against the sentiments and declarations to our
prejudice with which the above noticed ' address ' and ' resolutions ' abound, we are well aware of the power and influence
we have attempted to resist. The gentlemen named as officers
of the ' Colonization Society ' are men of high standing, their
dictum is law in morals with our community; but we who feel
the effect of their proscription, indulge the hope of an impartial
hearing.

We believe many of those gentlemen are our friends, and we
hope they all mean well; we care not how many Colonization
Societies they form to send slaves from the south to a place
where they may enjoy freedom; and if they can ' drain the
ocean with a bucket,' may send ' *with their own consent,*' the
increasing free colored population : but we solemnly protest
against that Christian philanthropy which in acknowledging our
wrongs commits a greater by vilifying us. The conscientious
man would not kill the animal, but cried ' mad dog,' and the
rabble despatched him. These gentlemen acknowledge the
anomaly of those political ethics which make a distinction between man and man, when their foundation is, ' that all men are
born equal,' and possess in common ' unalienable rights ;' and
to justify the withholding of these ' rights ' would proclaim to
foreigners that we are ' a distinct and inferior race,' without
religion or morals, and implying that our condition cannot be
improved here because there exists an unconquerable prejudice
in the whites towards us. We absolutely deny these positions,

and we call upon the learned author of the 'address' for the indications of distinction between us and other men. There are different *colors* among all species of animated creation. A difference of color is not a difference of species. Our structure and organization are the same, and not distinct from other men ; and in what respects are we inferior ? Our political condition we admit renders us less respectable, but does it prove us an inferior part of the human family ? Inferior indeed we are as to the means which we possess of becoming wealthy and learned men ; and it would argue well for the cause of justice, humanity and true religion, if the reverend gentlemen whose names are found at the bottom of President Duer's address, instead of showing their benevolence by laboring to move us some four thousand miles off, were to engage actively in the furtherance of plans for the improvement of our moral and political condition in the country of our birth. It is too late now to brand with inferiority any one of the races of mankind. We ask for proof. Time was when it was thought impossible to civilize the red man. Yet our own country presents a practical refutation of the vain assertion in the flourishing condition of the Cherokees, among whom intelligençe and refinement are seen in somewhat fairer proportions than are exhibited by some of their white neighbors. In the language of a writer of expanded views and truly noble sentiments, ' the blacks must be regarded as the real authors of most of the arts and sciences which give the whites at present the advantage over them. While Greece and Rome were yet barbarous, we find the light of learning and improvement emanating from this, by supposition, degraded and accursed continent of Africa, out of the midst of this very woolly-haired, flat-nosed, thick lipped, and coal black race, which some persons are tempted to station at a pretty low intermediate point between men and monkeys.'* It is needless to dwell on this topic ; and we say with the same writer, the blacks had a long and glorious day : and after what they have been and done, it argues not so much a mistaken theory, as sheer ignorance of the most notorious historical facts, to pretend that they are naturally inferior to the whites.

We earnestly desire that this address may not be misunderstood. We have no objection in the abstract to the Colonization Society ; but we do protest against the means which that Society uses to effect its purposes. It is evident, to any impartial observer, that the natural tendency of all their speeches, reports, sermons, &c. is to widen the breach between us and

* Alexander H. Everett, Esq. vide his work entitled 'America, or a General Survey,' &c. &c. pp. 212, 225.

the whites, and give to prejudice a tenfold vigor. It has produced a mistaken sentiment toward us. Africa is considered
the home of those who have never seen its shores. The poor
ignorant slave, who, in all probability, has never heard the name
of Christ, by the colonization process is suddenly transformed
into a ' missionary,' to instruct in the principles of Christianity
and the arts of civilized life. The Friends have been the last
to aid the system pursued by the Society's advocates. And
we say (for we feel it) that in proportion as they become colonizationists, they become less active and less friendly to our
welfare as citizens of the United States.

There does exist in the United States a prejudice against us ;
but is it unconquerable ? Is it not in the power of these gentlemen to subdue it ? If their object is to benefit us, why not
better our condition here ? What keeps us down but the want
of wealth ? Why do we not accumulate wealth? Simply because we are not encouraged. If we wish to give our boys a
classical education, they are refused admission into your colleges. If we consume our means in giving them a mercantile
education, you will not employ them as clerks ; if they are
taught navigation, you will not employ them as captains. If we
make them mechanics, you will not encourage them, nor will
white mechanics work in the same shop with them. And with
all these disabilities, like a mill-stone about us, because we cannot point to our statesmen, bankers and lawyers, we are called
an inferior race. Look at the glaring injustice towards us. (A
foreigner, before he knows one of our streets from another,
mounts a cart under the license of another man, or is a public
porter, a lamp-lighter, a watchman, &c.)

These gentlemen know but little of a large portion of the
colored population of this city. Their opinions are formed
from the unfortunate portion of our people whose characters
are scrutinized by them as judges of courts. Their patrician
principles prevent an intercourse with men in the middle walks
of life, among whom a large portion of our people may be classed. We ask them to visit the dwellings of the respectable part
of our people, and we are satisfied that they will discover more
civilization and refinement than will be found among the same
number of white families of an equal standing.

Finally, we hope that those who have so eloquently pleaded
the cause of the Indian, will at least endeavor to preserve consistency in their conduct. They put no faith in Georgia, although she declares that the Indians shall not be removed but
' *with their own consent.*' Can they blame us if we attach the
same credit to the declaration that they mean to colonize us

' only with our consent ?' They cannot indeed use force ; that is out of the question. But they harp so much on ' inferiority,' ' prejudice,' ' distinction,' and what not, that there will no alternative be left us but to fall in with their plans. We are content to abide where we are. We do not believe that things will always continue the same. The time must come when the declaration of independence will be felt in the heart as well as uttered from the mouth, and when the rights of all shall be properly acknowledged and appreciated. God hasten that time. This is our home, and this our country. Beneath its sod lie the bones of our fathers : for it some of them fought, bled, and died. Here we were born, and here we will die.

A VOICE FROM BOSTON.

Boston, March 12, 1831.

Pursuant to public notice, a meeting was held by the colored citizens of Boston, February 15th, at their school-house, for the purpose of expressing their sentiments in a remonstrance against the doings of the State Colonization Society, Feb. 10th. It was called to order by Mr J. G. Barbadoes. Mr Robert Roberts was elected chairman, and Mr James G. Barbadoes secretary. A prayer was then offered up to the throne of grace, by the Rev. Mr Snowden. The chairman having explained the object of the meeting, sundry resolutions were offered by Mr Barbadoes, and fairly discussed. On motion, a committee of five was chosen to amend the resolutions, and to draft an address to certain white citizens who had formed a State Society auxiliary to the American Colonization Society, and to the enlightened public. John T. Hilton, James G. Barbadoes, Rev. Hosea Easton, Thomas Dalton and Thomas Cole were placed on the committee.

The committee, to whom was referred the subject of an attempt, by certain white citizens, to establish in this State a Society auxiliary to the American Colonization Society, whose supposed object was the removal of the free colored population to western Africa, have with diligence sought for and obtained every fact within their reach, relative to what was enjoined upon them by the respectable body by whom they were delegated ; and now respectfully

REPORT :

That they have attended to the duty with which they were charged, with all the wisdom, prudence and fidelity which they possessed, and which the merits of the case required. They therefore submit to the consideration of the meeting their several conclusions on the subject.

The duty of your committee seemed to be divided into three general inquiries :—1st. To ascertain whether the Society above named was truly established in this metropolis. 2d. By whom it was established, and for what purpose. 3d. If established for the purpose entertained by the free colored population, what method should be adopted in regard to expressing their disapprobation thereto.

As to the first inquiry, your committee can state, that every doubt is now removed respecting the formation of such a Society, the proceedings of the meeting being published, together with the names of the officers.

On the second inquiry, your committee refer you to the 2d Article of the Constitution of said Society, (published in the Boston Courier of Feb. 16, 1831,) which reads thus :

' The object to which this Society shall be exclusively devoted, shall be to aid the parent institution at Washington, in the colonization of the free people of color of the United States on the coast of Africa ; and to do this not only by the contribution of money, but by the exertion of its influence to promote the formation of other societies.'

We deem any explanation here unnecessary.

In regard to the third and most essential inquiry, your committee report, that they know of no better way of expressing their disapprobation of such measures, than to use every exertion to persuade their brethren not to leave the United States upon any consideration whatever ; but if there are or should be any exasperated in consequence of abuse from their white countrymen, and who are determined to leave the country, we think it desirable to recommend them to Hayti or Upper Canada, where they will find the laws equal. Your committee deem it expedient also to urge this duty upon the several ministers of color throughout the United States, and all other persons of color whose influence may have any bearing in preventing their brethren from yielding to a request so unjust and cruel.

And if your respectable body should not think your committee were going beyond the bounds of their duty, they would recommend the clerical order throughout the United States, who have had or who are having any thing to do with the deceptive scheme above alluded to, to read the 13th chapter of Ezekiel. Read it—read it—and understand it. Your committee would recommend those clergymen, who have not defiled their garment with the blood of the innocent, to read the 1st, 2nd, 11th and 12th verses of the 24th chapter of Proverbs.

In support of the sentiments thus expressed, it becomes

necessary that our reasons should accompany them, why we object to the plan of dragging us to Africa—a country to us unknown, except by geography. In the first place, we are told that Africa is our native country; consequently the climate will be more congenial to our health. We readily deny the assertion. How can a man be born in two countries at the same time? Is not the position superficial to suppose that American born citizens are Africans? In regard to the climate, what better proof do we want of its salubrity, than to know that of the numerous bodies who have embarked, a large portion of them have immediately fallen victims, on their arrival, to the pestilence usual to that place?

It is again said, that the establishment of a colony on the coast of Africa will prevent the slave trade. We might as well argue, that a watchman in the city of Boston would prevent thievery in New-York, or any other place; or that the customhouse officers there would prevent goods being smuggled into any other port of the United States.

We are aware, that such an unnecessary expense devoted to the application of a remedy so far from the disease, is absolutely contrary to common sense. We are sensible that the moral disease, *slavery*, is in America, and not in Africa. If there was no market for the vending of slaves, there would be no inducement for the thief to steal them. The remedy for this evil, we humbly conceive, consists of three general prescriptions, viz. 1st. Let him who stealeth obey the word of God, and steal no more. 2d. Let him who hath encouraged the thief by purchase, (and consequently is a partaker with him,) do so no more. 3rd. Let the clerical physicians, who have encouraged, and are encouraging, both the thief and the receiver, by urging their influence to the removal of the means of their detection, desist therefrom, and with their mighty weight of influence step into the scale of justice: then will be done away this horrible traffic in blood.

From the above considerations, we sincerely recommend to our white countrymen honor and humanity, which will render useless the transportation of the colored population to the coast of Africa, it being altogether gratuitous and uncalled for.

We proceed to offer several objections to the operation alluded to—one is, the circumstance of the project originating with those who were deeply interested in slavery, and who hold slaves as their property. We consider the fact no evidence of the innocence of its design. We further object, because its members admit slavery to be an evil, and use no means to destroy it; but are exerting all their influence to urge every free person of color to Africa, (whose right to this soil holds good with any other citizen,) thereby rivetting the chains of slavery stronger than ever upon their oppressed brethren.

Again we object, because the whole spring of action seems to originate in the fear lest the free colored people may whisper liberty in the ears of the oppressed. We would suggest, however, that they who are fond of liberty should not be annoyed at its sound, from whatever source it may come.

Again we object, on the ground of there being sufficient land in the United States, on which a colony might be established that would better meet the wishes of the colored people, and at a much cheaper rate than could possibly be done by sending them to a howling wilderness far away, and to them unknown.

One of the leaders of the newly formed Society argued that in case a colony was formed for the blacks in the United States, they would in a short time be removed, as has been the case with the poor Indians. To obviate this objection, we here inform him that Hayti will hold all the slaves he will send her ; and as for the free people, we expect they can go where they please, either to Africa, Hayti or Upper Canada, or remain at home, without asking the consent of a slaveholding party. Nor can we conceive why free citizens, acting this liberty, should interfere with them, if they are—as they have represented themselves to be—honest and benevolent men. We conceive that the question in view stands in two distinct points—the removal of the free colored population from this country, or the acknowledgment of them as citizens. The former position must be acknowledged, on all sides, a means of perpetuating slavery in our land ; the latter, of abolishing it ; consequently it may be seen who are for the well-being of their country.

We regret that our interest has thus drawn us before the public, on account of the regard we entertain towards many of our warmest friends who have been deceived by a cloak of philanthropy, smooth words, and a sanctified appearance. We remind them, however, that the blood of Abel is beginning to be heard by many who are willing to acknowledge that they hear it.

We cannot close our duty without gratefully acknowledging the respect we entertain for those who have defended our cause with more than Spartan courage. It is the opinion of your committee, that they are to be respected as our countrymen, our brethren, and our fellow citizens—not to say they are to be applauded as men, whose great acts are based upon the acclamation of their fellow men ; but rather let us hold up their hands, and let their works praise them. We shall only add an expression of our hopes, that the Spirit of Liberty, recently awakened in the old world, may redouble its thundering voice, until every tyrant is seized with a Belshazzar tremble at the hand-writing upon the wall of his corrupt palace.

In addition to the above, your committee submit the following resolutions for your acceptance.

Resolved, That this meeting contemplate, with lively interest, the rapid progress of the sentiments of liberty among our degraded brethren, and that we will legally oppose every operation that may have a tendency to perpetuate our present political condition.

Resolved, That this meeting look upon the American Colonization Society as a clamorous, abusive and peace-disturbing combination.

Resolved, That this meeting look upon the conduct of those clergymen, who have filled the ears of their respective congregations with the absurd idea of the necessity of removing the free colored people from the United States, as highly deserving the just reprehension directed to the false prophets and priests, by Jeremiah the true prophet, as recorded in the 23d chapter of his prophecy.

Resolved, That this meeting appeal to a generous and enlightened public for an impartial hearing relative to the subject of our present political condition.

Resolved, That the gratitude of this meeting, which is so sensibly felt, be fully expressed to those editors whose independence of mind and correct views of the rights of man have led them so fearlessly to speak in favor of our cause ; that we rejoice to behold in them such a strong desire to extend towards us the inestimable blessing in the gift of a wise Providence which is demanded by all nature, and for which their veteran fathers struggled in the revolution.

ROBERT ROBERTS, Chairman.

JAMES G. BARBADOES, Secretary.

___

A VOICE FROM BALTIMORE.

BALTIMORE, March 21, 1831.

At a respectable meeting of persons of color, convened, pursuant to public notice, for the purpose of expressing their sentiments in regard to the pretensions of the American Colonization Society, William Douglass was called to the chair, and William Watkins appointed secretary. The object of the call having been explicitly stated, the meeting immediately proceeded to the consideration of the following resolutions, which were unanimously adopted :—On motion,

Resolved, That it is the belief of this meeting, that the American Colonization Society is founded more in a selfish policy, than in the true principles of benevolence ;—and, therefore, so far as it regards the life-giving spring of its operations, is not entitled to our confidence, but should be viewed by us with all that caution and distrust which our happiness demands.

Resolved, That we are not insensible to the means usually employed by that Society, and its auxiliaries, to effectuate our removal—that we sincerely deprecate their gratuitous and illiberal attacks upon, and their too frequently exaggerated statements of our moral standing in the community—that such means are unworthy of a magnanimous people, and of a virtuous and noble cause.

Resolved, That we consider the land in which we were born, and in which we have been bred, our only ' *true and appropriate home*,'—and that when *we* desire to remove, we will apprise the public of the same, in due season.

Resolved, That we are deeply sensible that many of our warm and sincere friends have espoused the colonization system, from the purest motives,—and that we sincerely regret their efforts to ameliorate our condition are not more in accordance with our wishes.

Resolved, That the proceedings of this meeting be published in the daily papers of this city, signed by the Chairman and Secretary.

WILLIAM DOUGLASS, Chairman.

WILLIAM WATKINS, Secretary.

A VOICE FROM WASHINGTON.

WASHINGTON, May 4, 1831.

Pursuant to previous notice, a large and very respectable meeting of the colored citizens of Washington, D. C., convened at the African Methodist Episcopal church on Wednesday evening last, for the purpose of expressing their views upon the subject of African colonization. Mr John W. Prout was called to the chair, and Arthur Waring was appointed secretary.

The chairman briefly explained the object of the meeting, in a short speech well adapted to the occasion, which was followed by several neat and very appropriate addresses delivered by sundry gentlemen present.

The following preamble and resolutions were offered and adopted, nearly unanimously.

Whereas we consider that the period has arrived for the colored citizens of this place to express their opinion upon the subject of colonization in Liberia ; a subject of great importance to themselves, as well as to the colored citizens of the United States generally ; and whereas our brethren at a distance are desirous of obtaining information relative to the object and policy pursued by the American Colonization Society : Therefore, be it

Resolved, That this meeting view with distrust the efforts made by the Colonization Society to cause the free people of color of these United States to emigrate to Liberia on the coast of Africa, or elsewhere.

Resolved, That it is the declared opinion of the members of this meeting, that the soil which gave them birth is their only *true and veritable home*, and that it would be impolitic, unwise and improper for them to leave their home without the benefits of education.

Resolved, That this meeting conceive that among the advocates of the colonization system, they have many true and sincere friends ; and do regret that their actions, although prompted no doubt by the purest motives, do not meet our approbation.

Resolved, That we believe the PRESS to be the most efficient means of disseminating light and knowledge among our brethren ; and that this meeting do acknowledge with gratitude the efforts made in our behalf, by the editors of the Genius of Universal Emancipation, and the Liberator ;—and do most earnestly recommend their respective papers to our brethren generally, for their approval and support.

Resolved, That the foregoing resolutions be signed by the Chairman and Secretary, and published.

JOHN W. PROUT, Chairman.
ARTHUR WARING, Secretary.

A VOICE FROM BROOKLYN.

BROOKLYN, (N. Y.) June 3, 1831.

At a numerous and respectable meeting of the colored inhabitants of the village and township of Brooklyn, convened in the African Hall, Nassau-street, for the purpose of taking into consideration our views in relation to the Colonization Society—

The throne of grace was addressed by the Rev. Mr Hogarth, after which Henry C. Thompson was called to the chair, and George Hogarth appointed secretary.

Appropriate addresses were delivered by Messrs George Hogarth, James Pennington, and George Woods. The following resolutions were then adopted :—

Resolved, unanimously, That the call of this meeting be approved of; and that the colored citizens of this village have, with friendly feelings, taken into consideration the objects of the American Colonization Society, together with all its auxiliary movements, preparatory for our removal to the coast of Africa; and we view them as wholly gratuitous, not called for by us, and not essential to the real welfare of our race: That we know of no other country in which we can justly claim or demand our rights as citizens, whether civil or political, but in these United States of America, our native soil: And, that we shall be active in our endeavors to convince the members of the Colonization Society, and the public generally, that we are *men,* that we are *brethren,* that we are *countrymen* and *fellow-citizens,* and demand an equal share of protection from our federal government with any other class of citizens in the community.

It was also Resolved, That the following persons, viz.: James Pennington, Henry C. Thompson, and George Woods, be appointed a committee to draft an address to the public, expressing our views more fully in relation to the Colonization Society; and that a delegate be appointed to proceed to the city of Philadelphia, to represent us in the ensuing convention, (which will commence its sitting the 6th inst.) to co-operate with the measures that may then be adopted for the general welfare of our race.

        HENRY C. THOMPSON, Chairman.
    GEORGE HOGARTH, Secretary.

Address to the Colored Citizens of Brooklyn, (N. Y.) and its Vicinity.

Respected brethren, and fellow-citizens:—As men and as christians, whose secular and eternal interests are the same, we are seriously called upon by truth and reason, and every thing of which human action is composed, to take into consideration the objects of the American Colonization Society; which aims to remove us, the free people of color, from this, our beloved and native land, to the coast of Africa; a country unknown to us in every respect.

As they propose to remove us with our own free will and consent, we do not contradict the assertion, that their objects, in the abstract, are salutary and benevolent; but when we hear those influential gentlemen, who are advocating this cause, generalize by language directly calculated to increase that prejudice, which is already one grand reason of our wretchedness, we are moved by a spirit of reliance upon justice and humanity, to lift our positive and decided voice against their proceedings.; and consider them as a stigma upon our morals as a people, as natives and citizens of this country, to whom equal rights are guaranteed by the Declaration of Independence.

When we consider that by abridging men in their moral liberty, we touch their responsibility to the highest authority in the universe, we should shudder at the thought of retaining such feelings as would lead to any irreligious or impolitic acts ; nor should we be willing to yield one particle of ours to others, unless it be on the ground of expediency, and in some way conducive to the glory of God.

We are sorry to say that those gentlemen have injured their cause, and perhaps caused much good to be evil spoken of, by making use of improper language, in their discussions upon our character and condition in this country ; without using one effort to improve or prepare us for the posts of honor and distinction which they hold forth to us, whenever we set foot on this much talked of, and long expected promised land. We would ask the Colonization Society, what are they doing at home to improve our condition ? It is a true proverb, that ' charity begins at home.' How can they extend their charities with christian sympathies and feeling some thousand miles across the Atlantic ocean, when they are not willing, with a few exceptions, to give us even a christian instruction while among them ? To prove the assertion, we would inquire, how many of our sable brethren have been elevated to any post of distinction in this country ? Even in states, where our numbers have almost doubled, have we seen one statesman, one officer, or one juror ? No ! in our village and its vicinity, how many of us have been educated in colleges, and advanced into different branches of business ; or taken into mercantile houses, manufacturing establishments, &c. ? Are we not even prohibited from some of the common labor and drudgery of the streets, such as cartmen, porters, &c. ? It is a strange theory to us, how these gentlemen can promise to honor and respect us in Africa, when they are using every effort to exclude us from all rights and privileges at home.

They say, ' that those of our friends, who look for the day when we shall have equal rights in this country, are mistaken.' May we not accept it as an assurance, that they will do all they can to prevent us from arriving to any degree of respectability at home, in our own land ? Away then with such false sympathies and friendships ! they are as foreign to us as the coast of Africa !

We truly believe, that many gentlemen who are engaged in the Colonization Society are our sincere friends and well-wishers ; they wish to do something for us, consequently they have subscribed largely to it, because there was no other plan on foot.   Some of them have been deluded into its schemes, with a view of thoroughly civilizing and christianizing Africa, by our free people of color and emancipated slaves, who may, from time to time, be colonized on its coasts, with their consent.   We conceive that such measures are fraught with inconsistency, and in no way calculated to have such an effect.   To send a parcel of uninstructed, uncivilized, and unchristianized people, to the western coast of Africa, with bibles in their hands to teach the natives the truths of the gospel, social happiness, and moral virtue, is mockery and ridicule in the extreme.

Missionary families should be well instructed in the rudiments of our holy religion, that their example may shine forth as lights in that much neglected and benighted land.   We are much in favor of christianizing Africa ; but not according to the plans of the Colonization Society, to purchase their lands of them, with a few paltry guns, beads, &c., and then establish forts and garrisons, to protect traders and traffickers, without, perhaps, once naming the religion of Jesus to them.   We well know that the examples of traders and traffickers are in no way calculated to induce heathens to embrace our religion.   For example, we will refer to the early settlements of our American colonies, and inquire what religious impressions did the settlers make (who were wise and learned from Europe) upon the aborigines of our country ?   We believe that a few men, well instructed and possessing a true missionary spirit, are calculated to do more good in that country, than a thousand on the colonization plan.

Many wish us to go to Africa, because they say that our constitutions are better adapted to that climate than this.   If so, we would ask why so many of our hearty, hale and healthy brethren, on arriving in that country, fall victims to the malignant fevers and disorders, prevalent in those regions ?   We would observe, that none are exempt from being touched with the contagion.   It operates more severely upon those from the higher latitudes.

Some of our brethren have come to the conclusion to leave this country, with all its prejudices, and seek an asylum in foreign climes.   We would recommend to your serious consideration, the location in Upper Canada ; a place far better adapted to our constitutions, our habits, and our morals ; where prejudice has not such an unlimited sway ; where you will be surrounded by christians, and have an opportunity to become civilized and christianized.

Brethren, it is time for us to awake to our interests ; for the

Colonization Society is straining every nerve for the accomplishment of its objects. By their last publications we see, that they have invoked all christian assemblies and churches throughout the Union, to exert their influence, by raising subscriptions to send us (the strangers within their gates, as they call us) to the coast of Africa. They have got the consent of eleven states, who have instructed their senators to do something in the next Congress for our removal. Maryland calls imperatively on the general government to send us away, or else they will colonize their own free blacks. They have, by their influence, stopped the emancipation of slaves in a measure, except for colonization purposes.

We owe a tribute of respect to the state of New-York, for her not having entered into the confederacy. Though she is the last in proclaiming general emancipation to the slave, yet we find her slow in adopting any such unchristian measures. We may well say, she is deliberate in her councils, and determinate in her resolutions.

Finally, brethren, we are not strangers ; neither do we come under the alien law. Our constitution does not call upon us to become naturalized ; we are already American citizens ; our fathers were among the first that peopled this country ; their sweat and their tears have been the means, in a measure, of raising our country to its present standing. Many of them fought, and bled, and died for the gaining of her liberties ; and shall we forsake their tombs, and flee to an unknown land ? No ! let us remain over them and weep, until the day arrive when Ethiopia shall stretch forth her hands to God. We were born and nurtured in this christian land ; and are surrounded by christians, whose sacred creed is, to do unto all men as ye would they should do unto you—to love our neighbors as ourselves ; and which expressly declares, if we have respect to persons, we commit sin. Let us, brethren, invoke the christian's God, in our behalf, to do away the prejudices of our brethren, that they may adopt the solemn truths of the gospel, and acknowledge that God is no respecter of persons—that he has made of one blood all the nations that dwell on the face of the earth—that they may no longer bring their reasonings in contact with the omniscience of Deity ; and insinuate to the public, that our intellect and faculties are measurably inferior to those of our fairer brethren. Because adversity has thrown a veil over us, and we, whom God has created to worship, admire and adore his divine attributes, shall we be held in a state of wretchedness and degradation, with monkeys, baboons, slaves, and cattle, because we possess a darker hue ?

We feel it our duty ever to remain true to the constitution of our country, and to protect it, as we have always done, from foreign aggressions. Although more than three hundred thousand of us are virtually deprived of the rights and immunities of citizens, and more than two millions held in abject slavery, yet we know that God is just, and ever true to his purpose. Before him the whole world stands in awe, and at his command nations must obey. He who has lately pleaded the Indian's cause in our land, and who has brought about many signal events, to the astonishment of our generation, we believe is in the whirlwind, and will soon bring about the time when the sable sons of America will join with their fairer brethren, and re-echo liberty and equal rights in all parts of Columbia's soil.

We pray the Lord to hasten the day, when prejudice, inferiority, degradation and oppression shall be done away, and the kingdoms of this world become the kingdoms of our God and his Christ.

Signed in behalf of a public meeting in Brooklyn.

H. C. THOMPSON, Chairman.

George Hogarth, Secretary.

A VOICE FROM HARTFORD.

Hartford, Ct., July 14, 1831.

At a large and respectable meeting of the colored inhabitants of the city of Hartford and its vicinity, convened at the vestry room of the African church, on the 13th inst. for the purpose of expressing their views in relation to the American Colonization Society, Mr Henry Foster was called to the chair, and Mr Paul Drayton appointed secretary. The object of the meeting was then stated in a brief and pertinent manner, after which extracts from several speeches delivered by the founders of the colonization scheme, together with the general sentiments of colonizationists extracted from the African Repository, were laid before the meeting, and the following resolutions were unanimously adopted :

Resolved, That it is the opinion of this meeting, that the American Colonization Society is actuated by the same motives which influenced the mind of Pharaoh, when he ordered the male children of the Israelites to be destroyed.

Resolved, That it is the belief of this meeting, that the Society is the greatest foe to the free colored and slave population with whom liberty and equality have to contend.

Resolved, That we look upon the man of color that would be influenced by the Society to emigrate to Liberia, as an enemy to the cause and a traitor to his brethren.

Resolved, That it is the opinion of this meeting, that many of those who are engaged in this unjust scheme would be willing, if it were in their power, to place us before the point of the bayonet, and drive us out of existence—so that they may get rid of that dark cloud, as we are termed, which hangs over these United States.

Resolved, That, in our belief, we have committed no crime worthy of banishment, and that we will resist all the attempts of the Colonization Society to banish us from this our native land.

Resolved, That we consider ourselves the legitimate sons of these United States, from whence we will never consent to be transported.

Resolved, That we will resist, even unto death, all the attempts of this Society to transport us to the pestilential shores of Liberia.

Resolved, That we will not countenance the doctrine of any pretended minister of the gospel, who is in league with those conspirators against our rights. We would, therefore, warn them to beware of following the footsteps of Balaam, who taught Balak to cast a stumbling block in the way of the children of Israel ; for we verily believe, that if God almighty have to deliver his people by his mighty arm of power, they will share the fate of that false prophet.

Resolved, That, though we be last in calling a meeting, we feel no less the pernicious influence of this Society than the rest of our brethren ; and that we consider all their pretexts, whether under the cloak of religion or philanthropy, gratuitous and uncalled for. We would, therefore, advise the Society, that as we have learned that there are one hundred and fifty thousand dollars in its funds, it had better appropriate this sum in meliorating the condition of our brethren the slaves, in this their native land, and raising them from that degradation into which they are plunged.

Resolved, That the thanks of the meeting be returned to Messrs William Lloyd Garrison, Isaac Knapp, and every friend of emancipation, for their benevolent exertions in our behalf.

Resolved, That the proceedings of this meeting be signed by the Chairman and Secretary, and sent to the Liberator for publication.

HENRY FOSTER, Chairman.

PAUL DRAYTON, Secretary.

A VOICE FROM MIDDLETOWN.

MIDDLETOWN, Ct., July 15, 1831.

At a meeting of the colored citizens of Middletown, pursuant to public notice, held in the Lecture Room in the African church—Mr Joseph Gilbert was called to the chair, and Amos L. Beman appointed secretary. The meeting being thus opened, it was warmly and freely addressed by Messrs Jeffrey, Condoll and Gilbert, when, on motion, it was

Resolved, That the proceedings of our brethren in Brooklyn, N. Y., meet our entire approbation : they breathe our sentiments in full, and may our voices cheerfully accord with them in protesting against leaving this our native soil. Why should we leave this land, so dearly bought by the blood, groans and tears of our fathers ? Truly this is our home : here let us live, and here let us die. What! emigrate to Liberia, a land so detrimental to our health ! We have now before us a letter written by a friend who emigrated from this place to the burning shores of Africa, in hopes of splendor, wealth and ease ; and he says that ' sickness and distress prevail to a great extent— and it is a clear case that those who come from the United States must undergo a long and protracted sickness with this country's fever, and I would not advise my friends to emigrate.'

JOSEPH GILBERT, Chairman.

AMOS G. BEMAN, Secretary

A VOICE FROM NEW-HAVEN.

NEW-HAVEN, August 8, 1831.

At a meeting of the Peace and Benevolent Society of Afric-Americans, held on the 7th inst., Mr Henry Berrian was called to the chair, and Mr Henry N. Merriman was appointed secretary. The following resolutions were then unanimously adopted.

Resolved, That we consider those christians and philanthropists, who are boasting of their liberty and equality, saying, that all men are born free and equal, and yet are endeavoring to remove us from our native land, to be inhuman in their proceedings, defective in their principles, and unworthy of our confidence.

Resolved, That we consider those colonizationists and ministers of the gospel, who are advocating our transportation to an unknown clime, because our skin is a little darker than theirs, (notwithstanding God has made of one blood all nations of men,

and has no respect of persons,) as violaters of the command-
ments of God and the laws of the bible, and as trying to blind
our eyes by their vain movements—their mouths being smooth
as oil, and their words sharper than any two-edged sword.

Resolved, That, while we have no doubt of the sinister motives of the great body of colonizationists, we believe some of
them are our friends and well-wishers, who have not looked
deeply into the subject ; but when they make a careful examination, we think they will find themselves in error.

Resolved, That it is our earnest desire that Africa may speedily become civilized, and receive religious instruction ; but not
by the absurd and invidious plan of the Colonization Society—
namely, to send a nation of ignorant men to teach a nation of
ignorant men. We think it most wise for them to send missionaries.

Resolved, That we will resist all attempts made for our removal to the torrid shores of Africa, and will sooner suffer
every drop of blood to be taken from our veins than submit to
such unrighteous treatment.

Resolved, That we know of no other place that we can call
our true and appropriate home, excepting these United States,
into which our fathers were brought, who enriched the country
by their toils, and fought, bled and died in its defence, and left
us in its possession—and here we will live and die.

Resolved, That we consider the American Colonization Society founded on principles that no Afric-American, unless very
weak in mind, will follow ; and any man who will be persuaded
to leave his own country and go to Africa, as an enemy to his
country and a traitor to his brethren.

Resolved, That we have heard with pleasure of the proceedings of our brethren in neighboring cities ; and that a number
of this Society will willingly become auxiliary to the parent Society of Philadelphia, for the mutual benefit of the Afric-Americans throughout the United States.

Resolved, That the proceedings of this meeting be signed by
the Chairman and Secretary, and sent to the Liberator for publication.

HENRY BERRIAN, Chairman.

Henry N. Merriman, Secretary.

A VOICE FROM COLUMBIA.

Columbia, Pa., August 5, 1831.

At a respectable meeting of Afric-Americans convened pursuant to public notice, at their school-house, with a view of

taking into consideration the novel scheme of the American Colonization Society, Mr Stephen Smith was called to the chair, and Mr James Richards appointed secretary. A prayer was then offered to the throne of grace, by Mr Smith. The chairman called the house to order, and explained the object of the meeting in a few preliminary remarks ; after which, the meeting proceeded to business, and adopted the subsequent resolutions.

Resolved, That we view the country in which we live as our only true and appropriate home ; and let colonizationists pour contempt upon our race, and slaveholders look on our brethren as a nuisance to the country, yet here will we live, here were we born, this is the country for which some of our ancestors fought and bled and conquered, nor shall a conspiring world be able to drive us hence.

Resolved, That it is our firm belief, that the Colonization Society is replete with infinite mischief, and that we view all the arguments of its advocates as mere sophistry, not worthy our notice as freemen. Being citizens of these United States, we could call upon our brethren to awake from their slumber of ignorance, break the chain of prejudice that has so long bound them, and in the strength of the omnipotent Spirit give their hearts to God.

Resolved, That we will resist all attempts to send us to the burning shores of Africa. Beware of Alexander, the coppersmith, for he hath done us much harm. May the Lord reward him ! We verily believe that if by an extraordinary perversion of nature, every man and woman, in one night, should become white, the Colonization Society would fall like lightning to the earth.

Resolved, That we will not be duped out of our rights as freemen, by colonizationists, nor by any other combination of men. All the encomiums pronounced upon Liberia can never form the least temptation to induce us to leave our native soil, to emigrate to a strange land.

Resolved, That we readily coalesce with our brethren in the different towns and cities, and take the liberty to say, that we as a little flock feel a fixed resolution to maintain our ground, till the great Author of our being shall say to those who deprive us of our rights, —Thus saith the Lord, because ye have not hearkened to me in proclaiming liberty, every one to his brother, and every man to his neighbor, behold I will proclaim liberty for you, saith the Lord, to the sword, to the pestilence, and to the famine.

Resolved, That it is the decided opinion of this meeting, that

African colonization is a scheme of southern policy, a wicked device of slaveholders who are desirous of riveting more firmly, and perpetuating more certainly, the fetters of slavery ; who are only anxious to rid themselves of a population whose presence, influence and example have a tendency (as they suppose) to produce discontent among the slaves, and to furnish them with incitements to rebellion.

Resolved, That this meeting will not encourage a scheme, which has for its basis prejudice and hatred. Though there may be some good wheat, yet it is to be feared the enemy has sown tares among it.

Resolved, That we will support the colony at Canada, the climate being healthier, better adapted to our constitutions, and far more consonant with our views than that of Africa.

Resolved, That we unanimously agree to patronize the Liberator, and use our best endeavors to get subscribers for the same ; and that we are under renewed obligations to God, that he ever raised up such honest hearted men as Messrs Garrison and Knapp.

Resolved, That this meeting cause its proceedings to be sent to the Liberator for publication ; praying that the Lord will succeed all the lawful efforts of its conductor to meliorate the condition of our brethren in these United States, trusting his weapons are not carnal, but mighty through God to pull down the strong holds of the devil.

Signed by the Chairman and Secretary.

STEPHEN SMITH, Chairman.
JAMES RICHARDS, Secretary.

A VOICE FROM NANTUCKET.

NANTUCKET, August 5, 1831.

At a respectable meeting of the colored inhabitants of the town of Nantucket, convened for the purpose of taking into consideration our views in relation to the American Colonization Society, Mr Arthur Cooper was called to the chair, and Edward J. Pompey appointed secretary.

Addresses were delivered by Messrs William Harris and Edward J. Pompey, in which they took a general view of the Colonization Society, of its leading members, and some of the speeches and remarks made by gentlemen at the meetings of said Society. The following resolves were then adopted :

Resolved, That the call of this meeting be approved of, and that the colored citizens of this town have with friendly feel-

[PART II.]   5

ings taken into consideration the objects of the Colonization Society, together with its movements preparatory for our removal to the coast of Africa ; and we view them as wholly gratuitous, not called for by us, and in no way essential to the welfare of our race ; and we believe that our condition can be best improved in this our own country and native soil, the United States of America.

Resolved, That we hold this truth to be self-evident, that all men are born free and equal ; and we are men, and therefore ought to share as much protection and enjoy as many privileges under our federal government as any other class of the community.

Resolved, That we will be zealous in doing all that lies in our power to improve the condition of ourselves and brethren in this our native land.

Resolved, That there is no philanthropy towards the people of color in the colonization plan, but that it is got up to delude us away from our country and home into a country of sickness and death.

Resolved, That the thanks of this meeting be returned to every friend who vindicates our rights and interests.

Resolved, That the proceedings of this meeting be signed by the Chairman and Secretary, and sent to Boston, to be published in the Liberator.

ARTHUR COOPER, Chairman.

EDWARD J. POMPEY, Secretary.

A VOICE FROM PITTSBURGH.

PITTSBURGH, (Pa.,) Sept. 1, 1831.

At a large and respectable meeting of the colored citizens of Pittsburgh, convened at the African Methodist Episcopal church, for the purpose of expressing their views in relation to the American Colonization Society, Mr J. B. Vashon was called to the chair, and Mr R. Bryan appointed secretary. The object of the meeting was then stated at considerable length, and in an appropriate manner, by the chairman. The following resolutions were then unanimously adopted :

Resolved, That ' we hold these truths to be self-evident : that all men are created equal, and endowed by their Creator with certain inalienable rights ; that among these are life, liberty, and the pursuit of happiness '—Liberty and Equality now, Liberty and Equality forever !

Resolved, That it is the decided opinion of this meeting, that African colonization is a scheme to drain the better informed part of the colored people out of these United States, so that the chain of slavery may be rivetted more tightly ; but we are determined not to be cheated out of our rights by the colonization men, or any other set of intriguers. We believe there is no philanthropy in the colonization plan towards the people of color, but that it is got up to delude us away from our country and home to the burning shores of Africa.

Resolved, That we, the colored people of Pittsburgh and citizens of these United States, view the country in which we live as our only true and proper home. We are just as much natives here as the members of the Colonization Society. Here we were born—here bred—here are our earliest and most pleasant associations—here is all that binds man to earth, and makes life valuable. And we do consider every colored man who allows himself to be colonized in Africa, or elsewhere, a traitor to our cause.

Resolved, That we are freemen, that we are brethren, that we are countrymen and fellow-citizens, and as fully entitled to the free exercise of the elective franchise as any men who breathe ; and that we demand an equal share of protection from our federal government with any class of citizens in the community. We now inform the Colonization Society, that should our reason forsake us, then we may desire to remove. We will apprise them of this change in due season.

Resolved, That we, as citizens of these United States, and for the support of these resolutions, with a firm reliance on the protection of divine providence, do mutually pledge to each other our lives, our fortunes, and our sacred honor, not to support a colony in Africa nor in Upper Canada, not yet emigrate to Hayti. Here we were born—here will we live by the help of the Almighty—and here we will die, and let our bones lie with our fathers.

Resolved, That we return our grateful thanks to Messrs Garrison and Knapp, publishers of the Liberator, and Mr Lundy, editor of the Genius of Universal Emancipation, for their untiring exertions in the cause of philanthropy.

Resolved, That the proceedings of this meeting be signed by the Chairman and Secretary, and published in the Liberator.

J. B. VASHON, Chairman.

R. Bryan, Secretary.

A VOICE FROM WILMINGTON.

WILMINGTON, July 12, 1831.

At a large and respectable meeting of the people of color of the borough of Wilmington, convened in the African Union Church, July 12th, 1831, for the purpose of considering the subject of colonization on the coast of Africa :

On motion, the Rev. Peter Spencer was called to the chair, and Thomas Dorsey appointed secretary.

The meeting was addressed by Abraham D. Shad, Junius C. Morell, Benjamin Pascal and John P. Thompson, after which the following resolutions were unanimously adopted.

Resolved, That this meeting view with deep regret the attempt now making to colonize the free people of color on the western coast of Africa ; believing as we do that it is inimical to the best interests of the people of color, and at variance with the principles of civil and religious liberty, and wholly incompatible with the spirit of the Constitution and Declaration of Independence of these United States.

Resolved, That we disclaim all connexion with Africa ; and although the descendants of that much afflicted country, we cannot consent to remove to any tropical climate, and thus aid in a design having for its object the total extirpation of our race from this country, professions to the contrary notwithstanding.

Resolved, That a committee of three persons be appointed to prepare as soon as practicable an address to the public, setting forth more fully our views on the subject of colonization. The following persons were appointed : Abraham D. Shad, Rev. Peter Spencer and W. S. Thomas.

Signed on behalf of the meeting.

PETER SPENCER, Chairman.
THOMAS DORSEY, Secretary.

Address of the Free People of Color of the Borough of Wilmington, Delaware.

We the undersigned, in conformity to the wishes of our brethren, beg leave to present to the public in a calm and unprejudiced manner, our decided and unequivocal disapprobation of the American Colonization Society, and its auxiliaries, in relation to the free people of color in the United States. Convinced as we are, that the operations of this Society have been unchristian and anti-republican in principle, and at variance with our best interests as a people, we had reason to believe that the precepts of religion, the dictates of justice and humanity, would have prevented any considerable portion of the community from lending their aid to a plan which we fear was designed to deprive us of rights that the Declaration of Independence declares are the 'unalienable rights' of all men. We were content to remain silent, believing that the justice and patriotism of a magnanimous people would prevent the annals of our native and beloved country from receiving so deep a stain. But observing the growing strength and influence of that institution, and being well aware that the generality of the public are unacquainted with our views on this important subject, we feel it a duty we owe to ourselves, our children and posterity, to enter our protest against a device so fraught with evil to us. That many sincere friends to our race are engaged in what they conceive to be a philanthropic and benevolent enterprise, we do not hesitate to admit ; but that they are deceived, and are acting in a manner calculated most seriously to injure the free people of color, we are equally sensible.

We are natives of the United States ; our ancestors were brought to this country by means over which they had no control ; we have our attachments to the soil, and we feel that we have rights in common with other Americans ; and although deprived through prejudice from entering into the full enjoyment of those rights, we anticipate a period, when in despite of the more than ordinary prejudice which has been the result of this unchristian scheme, 'Ethiopia shall stretch forth her hands to God.' But that this formidable Society has become a barrier to our improvement, must be apparent to every individual who will but reflect on the course to be pursued by the emissaries of this unhallowed project, many of whom, under the name of ministers of the gospel, use their influence to turn public sentiment to our disadvantage by stigmatizing our morals, misrepresenting our characters, and endeavoring to show what they are pleased to call the sound policy of perpetuating our civil and political disabilities for the avowed purpose of indirectly forcing us to emigrate to the western coast of Africa. That Africa is neither our nation nor home, a due respect to the good sense of the community forbids us to attempt to prove ; that our language, habits, manners, morals and religion are all different from those of Africans, is a fact too notorious to admit of controversy. Why then are we called upon to go and settle in a country where we must necessarily be and remain a distinct people, having no common interest with the numerous inhabitants of that vast and extensive country ? Experience has proved beyond a doubt, that the climate is such as not to suit the constitutions of the inhabitants of this country ; the fevers and various diseases incident to that tropical clime, are such as in most cases to bid defiance to the force of medicine.

The very numerous instances of mortality amongst the emigrants who have been induced to leave this their native, for their adopted country, clearly demonstrate the fallacy of those statements so frequently made by the advocates of colonization in regard to the healthiness of Liberia.

With the deepest regret we have witnessed such an immense sacrifice of life, in advancing a cause which cannot promise the least advantage to the free people of color, who, it was said, were the primary objects to be benefitted by this ' heaven-born enterprise.' But we beg leave most respectfully to ask the friends of African colonization, whether their christian benevolence cannot in this country be equally as advantageously applied, if they are actuated by that disinterested spirit of love and friendship for us, which they profess ? Have not they in the United States a field sufficiently extensive to show it in ? There is embosomed within this republic, rising one million free people of color, the greater part of whom are unable to read even the sacred scriptures. Is not their ignorant and degraded situation worthy of the consideration of those enlightened and christian individuals, whose zeal for the cause of the African race has induced them to attempt the establishment of a republican form of government amid the burning sands of Liberia, and the evangelizing of the millions of the Mahometans and pagans that inhabit the interior of that extensive country ?

We are constrained to believe that the welfare of the people of color, to say the least, is but a secondary consideration with those engaged in the colonization project. Or why should we be requested to move to Africa, and thus separated from all we hold dear in a moral point of view, before their christian benevolence can be exercised in our behalf ? Surely there is no country of which we have any knowledge, that offers greater facilities for the improvement of the unlearned ; or where benevolent and philanthropic individuals can find a people, whose situation has greater claims on their christian· sympathies, than the people of color. But whilst we behold a settled determination on the part of the American Colonization Society to remove us to Liberia, without using any means to better our condition at home, we are compelled to look with fearful diffidence on every measure of that institution. At a meeting held on the 7th inst. in this borough, the people of color were politely invited to attend, the object of which was to induce the most respectable part of them to emigrate. The meeting was addressed by several reverend gentlemen, and very flattering accounts given on the authority of letters and statements said to have been received from individuals of unquestionable veracity. But we beg leave to say, that those statements differ so widely from letters that we have seen of recent date from the colony, in regard to the condition and circumstances of the colonists, that we are compelled in truth to say that we cannot reconcile such contradictory statements, and are therefore inclined to doubt the former, as they appear to have been prepared to present to the public, for the purpose of enlisting the feelings of our white friends into the measure, and of inducing the enterprising part of the colored community to emigrate at their own expense. That we are in this country a degraded people, we are truly sensible ; that our forlorn situation is not attributable to ourselves is admitted by the most ardent friends of colonization ; and that our condition cannot be bettered by removing the most exemplary individuals of color from amongst us, we are well convinced, from the consideration that in the same ratio that the industrious part would emigrate, in the same proportion those who would remain would become more degraded, wretched and miserable, and consequently less capable of appreciating the many opportunities which are now offering for the moral and intellectual improvement of our brethren. We, therefore, a portion of those who are the objects of this plan, and amongst those whose happiness, with that of others of our color, it is intended to promote, respectfully but firmly disclaim every connexion with it, and declare our settled determination not to participate in any part of it.

But if this plan is intended to facilitate the emancipation of those who are held in slavery in the South, and the melioration of their condition, by sending them to Liberia ; we question very much whether it is calculated to do either. That the emancipation of slaves has been measurably impeded through its influence, except where they have been given up to the Board of Managers, to be colonized in Africa, to us is manifest. And when we contemplate their uneducated and vitiated state, destitute of the arts and unaccustomed to provide even for themselves, we are inevitably led to the conclusion that their situation in that pestilential country will be miserable in the extreme.

The present period is one of deep and increasing interest to the free people of color, relieved from the miseries of slavery and its concomitant evils, with the vast and (to us) unexplored field of literature and science before us, surrounded by many friends whose sympathies and charities need not the Atlantic between us and them, before they can consent to assist in elevating our brethren to the standing of men. We therefore particularly invite their attention to the subject of education and improvement ; sensible that it is much better calculated to remove prejudice, and exalt our moral character, than any system of colonization that 'has been or can be introduced ; and in which we believe we shall have the co-operation of the wisest and most philanthropic individuals of which the nation can boast.   The utility of learning and its salutary effects on the minds and morals of a people, cannot have escaped the notice of any rational individual situated in a country like this, where in order successfully to prosecute any mechanical or other business, education is indispensable.   Our highest moral ambition, at present, should be to acquire for our children a liberal education, give them mechanical trades, and thus fit and prepare them for useful and respectable citizens ; and leave the evangelizing of Africa, and the establishing of a republic at Liberia, to those who conceive themselves able to demonstrate the practicability of its accomplishment by means of a people, numbers of whom are more ignorant than even the natives of that country themselves.

In conclusion, we feel it a pleasing duty ever to cherish a grateful respect for those benevolent and truly philanthropic individuals, who have advocated, and still are advocating our rights in our native country.   Their indefatigable zeal in the cause of the oppressed will never be forgotten by us, and unborn millions will bless their names in the day when the all-wise Creator, in whom we trust, shall have bidden oppression to cease.

> ABRAHAM D. SHAD, ⎫ Committee to pre-
> PETER SPENCER, ⎬ pare an Address.
> WM. S. THOMAS, ⎭

A VOICE FROM HARRISBURG.

HARRISBURG, Pa., October, 1831.

At a large, well informed and respectable meeting of the citizens of Harrisburg, convened at the African Wesleyan Methodist church, for the purpose of expressing their sentiments in a remonstrance against the proceedings of the American Colonization Society, Rev. Jacob D. Richardson was called to the chair, and Jacob G. Williams appointed secretary.   After singing and prayer, Rev. Mr Richardson in some concise remarks,—equalled by few, and exceeded by none,—expressed the object of the meeting.   The chairman called the house to order, and the following resolutions were unanimously acceded to :

Resolved, That we hold these truths to be self-evident, (and it is the boasted declaration of our independence,) that all men (black and white, poor and rich) are born free and equal ; that they are endowed by their Creator with certain inalienable rights ; that among these are life, liberty, and the pursuit of happiness. This is the language of America, of reason, and of eternal truth.

Resolved, That we feel it to be our duty to be true to the constitution of our country, and are satisfied with the form of government under which we now live ; and, moreover, that we are bound in duty and reason to protect it against foreign invasion. We always have done so, and will do so still.

Resolved, That we view the efforts of the Colonization Society as officious and uncalled for by us. We have never done any thing worthy of banishment from our friends and home : but this we would say—if the Colonization Society will use their best endeavors to get our slave brethren transported to Liberia, when we as a free body of people wish to go, we will give the colonizationists timely notice.

Resolved, That it is the firm and decided opinion of this meeting, that were there no free people of color among us, or if those who are free had remained in the degraded character of slaves, (or, as they sometimes call us, monkeys, apes and' baboons,) they would never have got up the chimerical scheme for our transportation to the burning shores of Africa, with the fancied vision of elevating us, as they say, to dignity and affluence.

Resolved, That we cannot remain inactive while colonizationists are straining every nerve and racking their inventions to find out arguments to persuade our free colored brethren to migrate to an unknown land, which we can no more lay claim to than our white brethren can to England or any other foreign country.

Resolved, That we reject the inhuman and unchristian measures taken by the Colonization Society, for the illumination of the colored citizens of the United States, their appropriate home, in a land of sickness, affliction and death, when they are not willing, with few exceptions, to give us a christian education while among them. We would wish to know of the colonizationists, how, in the name of common sense and reason, do they expect to do any thing for us thousands of miles across the Atlantic, when they oppose almost every measure taken by our white friends and brethren to improve our condition here ?

Resolved, That it is the united opinion of this meeting, that the enemies of our race, who are members of the Colonization

Society, see that the great Author of universal existence, who ' is no respecter of persons,' who taught Balaam's ass to speak, and taught Solomon wisdom, is now enlightening the sable sons of America : hence their object to drain the country of the most enlightened part of our colored brethren, so that they may be more able to hold their slaves in bondage and ignorance.

Resolved, That we object to leaving the land of our birth, as there is sufficient land in these United States, on which a colony can be established that would be far more consonant to the wishes of the colored population generally, and would be more adapted to their constitution : neither would it involve the country in such expense as would be incurred by sending them to a howling wilderness, far away from the graves of their forefathers, unknown to us in every respect, unless by geography, which few of us understand.

Resolved, That this meeting look upon the Colonization Society as a vicious, nefarious and peace-disturbing combination, and that its leaders might as well essay to cure a wound with an argument, or set a dislocated bone by a lecture on logic, as to tell us their object is to better our condition ; because its members acknowledge slavery to be a national evil, and use no means to annihilate it, but are exerting all their energies and influence to persuade the free people of color to remove to Africa, whose rights to Columbia's happy soil holds good with any other citizen in America.

Resolved, That we look upon the conduct of those clergymen who have misled their respective congregations with the preposterous idea of the necessity of transporting the free people of color to Africa, as highly deserving the just reprehension directed to the false priests and prophets by the true prophets of the Most High ; yet we gratefully acknowledge the respect we entertain for those who have defended our cause—we mean our white friends.

Resolved, That this meeting appoint Mr George Chester of Harrisburg, as agent for the Liberator, and will use our utmost endeavors to get subscribers for the same.

Resolved, That we will support the Colony in Canada, the climate being healthy and the rights of our brethren secured.

Resolved, That the gratitude of this meeting, which is so sensibly felt, be fully expressed to the Editors of the Liberator and Genius of Universal Emancipation, Messrs Garrison and Lundy, whose independence of mind and correct views of the rights of man have led them so intrepidly to speak in favor of our cause.

Resolved, That the proceedings of this meeting be signed by the Chairman and Secretary, and sent to the Liberator for publication.

JACOB D. RICHARDSON, Chairman.
JACOB G. WILLIAMS, Secretary.

A VOICE FROM ROCHESTER.

ROCHESTER, N. Y., October, 1831.

A large number of the colored citizens of Rochester having convened themselves together, for the important object of taking into consideration the anti-republican principles of the American Colonization Society, the Rev. Mr Johnson was called to the chair, and Mr A. Lawrence was appointed secretary.

The meeting was then briefly addressed by the secretary as follows :

Countrymen and Brothers—When viewing the inhumanity and anti-christian principles of the American Colonization Society, in plotting our removal to Africa, (which is unknown to us as our native country,) it seems as though we were called upon publicly to express our feelings on the subject. We do not consider Africa to be our home, any more than the present whites do England, Scotland, or Ireland. This is the land our fathers have tilled before us ; this is the land that gave us our birthright.—The meeting then

Resolved, That we never will remove to Africa ; but should any of our brethren wish to emigrate, we would recommend Canada as a country far more congenial to our constitutions ;— that we give our most sincere thanks to our friendly advocates Messrs Garrison and Knapp, and Mr Benjamin Lundy, who are crying unto their fellow men, night and day, to let their countrymen go free : they will be called blessed by many generations yet to come. The Colonization Society say that they cannot treat us as men while we are with them ; but if we will go out of their reach, they will begin their charity. What should we think of such religion as this ? Because our skin is a little darker than theirs, they say they cannot think of treating us as men. The scripture says, ' Beware of wolves in sheep's clothing '—and such they seem to be. We earnestly believe, with our generous friend Garrison, that it would not be a hard matter to exceed them in doing right. Our blessed Lord said, that we should do to all men as we would have them do to us. Now what would they think, if we should tell them that they would be better off in New Holland or in Tartary ?

Resolved, That we will do all in our power to support the Liberator, printed by Mr Garrison, and all other works in our behalf.

Resolved, That the foregoing proceedings be published in the Liberator.

HENRY JOHNSON, Chairman.

A. LAWRENCE, Secretary.

A VOICE FROM PROVIDENCE.

PROVIDENCE, November 1, 1831.

At a respectable meeting of the colored people of Providence, R. I., duly appointed and publicly holden at the African church, on the 31st of October, 1831, to take into consideration the objects and motives of the American Colonization Society, Mr George C. Willis was called to the chair, and Mr Alfred Niger appointed secretary. The meeting was then addressed at some length by the chairman, stating their object in assembling together, and exposing the injustice and prejudice by which he believed the friends of African colonization were actuated. The following preamble and resolutions were read by the secretary, and unanimously adopted :

Whereas our brethren, in different parts of the United States, have thought proper to call meetings to express their disapprobation of the American Colonization Society ; we, concurring fully with them in opinion, have assembled ourselves together for the purpose of uniting with them, in declaring that we believe the operations of the Society have been unchristian and anti-republican, and at variance with our best interests as a people. Therefore,

Resolved, That we will use every fair and honorable means in our power, to oppose the operations of the above mentioned Society.

Resolved, That we are truly sensible that we are in this country a degraded and ignorant people ; but that our ignorance and degradation are not to be attributed to the inferiority of our natural abilities, but to the oppressive treatment we have experienced from the whites in general, and to the prejudice excited against us by the members of the Colonization Society, their aiders and abettors.

Resolved, That we view, with unfeigned astonishment, the anti-christian and inconsistent conduct of those who so strenuously advocate our removal from this our native country to the burning shores of Liberia, and who with the same breath contend against the cruelty and injustice of Georgia in her attempt to remove the Cherokee Indians west of the Mississippi.

Resolved, That we firmly believe, from the recent measures adopted by the freemen of the city of New Haven, in regard to the establishment of a College for our education in that place, that the principal object of the friends of African colonization is to oppose our education and consequent elevation here, as it will deprive them of one of their principal arguments for our removal.

Resolved, That as our fathers participated with the whites in their struggle for liberty and independence, and believing with the Declaration of that Independence, ' that all men are created free and equal ; that they are endowed by their Creator with certain unalienable rights, among which are life, liberty, and the pursuit of happiness ;' and as we have committed no crime worthy of banishment—Therefore

Resolved, That we will not leave our homes, nor the graves of our fathers, and this boasted land of liberty and christian philanthropy.

Resolved, That, our unfeigned and sincere thanks be tendered to Messrs Garrison and Knapp, and to every true friend to our cause, for their unwearied and truly benevolent exertions in our behalf.

Resolved, That we will earnestly recommend the Liberator, published in Boston by the above mentioned gentlemen, to the patronage of our friends throughout the country.

Resolved, That the proceedings of this meeting be signed by the Chairman and Secretary, and sent to Boston, with the request that they may be published in the Liberator.

GEORGE C. WILLIS, Chairman,

ALFRED NIGER, Secretary.

A VOICE FROM TRENTON.

TRENTON, November 30, 1831.

At a respectable meeting of the free people of color in Trenton, convened in the Mount Zion church, November 30, 1831, for the purpose of considering the subject of colonization on the coast of Africa—On motion, the Rev. Lewis Cork was called to the chair, and Abner H. Francis appointed secretary. The meeting was addressed by Messrs Gardener and Thompson ; after which, the following resolutions were unanimously adopted.

Resolved, Inasmuch as we, free people of color, have done all that is in our power to convince the white inhabitants of these United States, that it is our wish to live peaceably with all men; and inasmuch as our general demeanor has been that of industry and sobriety, notwithstanding there are some among us to the contrary, as well as among the whites ; therefore we do most solemnly declare, that the statements made to the contrary by the Rev. Mr Crosby, in his late addresses in this city, and all statements by petitioners to legislative bodies, and by the Colonization Society, or any thing of the same nature, are a positive libel on our general character.

Resolved, Whereas we have lived peaceably and quietly in these United States, of which we are natives, and have never been the cause of any insurrectionary or tumultuous movements as a body, that we do view every measure taken by any associated bodies to remove us to other climes, anti-christian and hostile to our peace, and a violation of the laws of humanity.

Resolved, That if, in the opinion of government, our stay or liberty can no longer be granted in the States in which we live, we see nothing contrary to the constitution of these United States, or to christianity, justice, reason or humanity, in granting us a portion of the Western territory, as a state, with the same franchise as that of Pennsylvania, New Jersey, or any other free State ; for we challenge the Union to prove that, as free men, we have ever given the least ground for the uncharitable censures that have been cast upon us.

Resolved, That we view the American Colonization Society as the most inveterate foe both to the free and slave man of color ; forasmuch as the agents thereof, and its members who have petitioned the several legislatures, have unequivocally declared its object, to wit, the extermination of the free people of color from the Union ; and to effect this they have not failed to slander our character, by representing us as a vagrant race ; and we do therefore disclaim all union with the said Society, and, once for all, declare that we never will remove under their patronage ; neither do we consider it expedient to emigrate any where, but to remain in the land and see the salvation of God. Nevertheless, if any of our brethren should be compelled or see proper to emigrate, we would recommend to them Upper Canada or Mexico.

Resolved, That we view with the highest emotion of gratitude, the benevolence of Great Britain and that of the Canada Company, in affording an asylum in the Wilberforce settlement, in Upper Canada, for our oppressed brethren of the South, who have been or may be forced, by unconstitutional laws, to leave their rightful home and place of nativity, without any cause except that of having a dark skin.

Resolved, That this meeting approve the establishment of a college, as recommended by the Annual Convention held in Philadelphia last June, and that we give all possible aid to that institution.

Resolved, That we view the Liberator, edited by William Lloyd Garrison, as a great herald in the cause of liberty, and that we recommend to the colored citizens of Trenton the utility of subscribing to the above named paper.

Resolved, That there be a committee of three appointed to draft an address more expressive of our views on the above subject.

Resolved, That the following persons compose that committee—Sampson Peters, Robert Thomas, George Cole.

LEWIS CORK, Chairman.

ABNER H. FRANCIS, Secretary.

ADDRESS.

We, the undersigned, in conformity to the above appointment, beg leave to present to the public, in a calm, unprejudiced manner, our decided disapprobation of the American Colonization Society and its auxiliaries, in relation to the people of color in the United States. We are well convinced, from the mass that has been written on the above subject by those who have preceded us, that it will be difficult to avoid repetition ; nevertheless; we hope to touch some points which have not been fairly understood by that Society. They have supposed that our objections are to civilizing and evangelizing Africa ; but we beg leave to say, that it is an error. We are well aware, that there is no surer way to effect this great object than to plant among the heathen, colonies of christian missionaries. We wish, therefore, to be understood, that we highly approve of the evangelizing of Africa, but disapprove of the present measures of the American Colonization Society, if their motives have not been misrepresented by their agents and others, in some previous addresses in this city and elsewhere. But viewing them as we now do, we must say that, in our opinion, their false representations of our general character—their recommending our removal from our native land—their opposition to our having a part of the West appointed to us—their objections to our proposed college, and of our march to science— their false statements in relation to the health of the colony at Liberia, with a·variety of other subjects of the same nature— all lead to a conclusion, that it is our greatest foe.

We would here ask the public a few questions. First—Is the gospel of Jesus Christ calculated to lead to insurrectionary measures ? If so, why then send it to the heathen ? Second—What gentleman, who has set his slaves free, has been murdered by them for so doing ? Third—What have those States, who have washed their hands clean of the cursed stain of slavery, lost by it ? Fourth—What neighborhood, where education and general information have been disseminated among the people of color, is the worse for it ?

In closing our remarks, we would say, that we do think that the subjects looked to by the Colonization Society, to civilize Africa, are incompetent ; for we do suppose that men selected for such an important enterprise, should be men of deed and sound piety—men of regular and industrious habits, of scientific knowledge and general experience : that such men can be obtained, we have no doubt ; and if there cannot, let us first prepare some in this country.

SAMPSON PETERS,
ROBERT THOMAS, } Committee.
GEORGE COLE,

A VOICE FROM LYME.

LYME, Ct., January 9, 1832.

At a respectable meeting of the colored citizens of this place, held pursuant to public notice—Mr Luther Wright was called to the chair, and Mr Daniel R. Condol appointed secretary.

After some animated remarks by Messrs Wright and Condol, it was

Resolved, That it is the sincere opinion of this meeting, that the American Colonization Society is one of the wildest projects ever patronised by a body of enlightened men ; and further, that many of those who support it would be willing, if it were in their power, to drive us out of existence.

Resolved, That though we be last in calling a meeting, we feel no less the pernicious influence of this Society than the rest of our brethren ; and that we will resist every attempt to banish us from this our native land.

Resolved, That we place unshaken reliance upon the promises of Jehovah, and believe that he will take our reproach away, and give freedom to those who are held in captivity.

Resolved, That we are not for insurrection, but for peace, freedom and equality.

Resolved, That the thanks of this meeting be rendered to Messrs Garrison and Knapp, for their benevolent exertions in behalf of the oppressed descendants of Africa ; and that they be requested to insert these proceedings in the Liberator.

LUTHER WRIGHT, Chairman.

DANIEL R. CONDOL, Secretary.

A VOICE FROM LEWISTOWN.

LEWISTOWN, Pa., January 9, 1832.

At a numerous meeting held by the free people of color of the borough of Lewistown, in the African Methodist Episcopal church, Samuel Johnston was called to the chair, and Martin Johnston appointed secretary: The following resolutions were then read, and unanimously adopted :

Resolved, That we will not leave these United States, the land of our birth, for a home in Africa.

Resolved, That we will strenuously oppose the colonizing of the free people of color in Liberia.

Resolved, That we are willing to emigrate to any part of the United States which may be granted to us.

Resolved, That we will support the Liberator, a paper published in Boston, edited by William Lloyd Garrison ; and also the colony in Upper Canada as an asylum for our oppressed brethren.

Resolved, That a committee be appointed to prepare an address to be published in the Liberator.

Resolved, That the proceedings of this meeting be signed by the Chairman and Secretary, and forwarded to the editor of the Liberator for publication.

SAMUEL JOHNSTON, Chairman.

MARTIN JOHNSTON, Secretary.

ADDRESS.

We, the undersigned, in conformity to the above appointment, beg leave to present to the public, in a calm and unprejudiced manner, our reasons for opposing the scheme of African colonization. This is the land of our birth. The Declaration of Independence declares, that ' all men are born free and equal :' it does not say that the *white* man or the *black* man is free,—but all, without respect to color, tongues, or nation. We therefore consider all laws to enslave or degrade the people of color as contrary to the letter and spirit of this Declaration ;

[PART II.]   7

and that according to it we are freemen, and have as indisputable a right to enjoy our liberty as any white man. To deny it to us, because we differ in color, is oppression. To say that Africa is our native country is untrue. Here we were born, and here we mean to die ; for all men are born free.

We wish to return our grateful thanks to our friends, and to the friends of the abolition of slavery. We consider slavery a national sin, which, if not speedily overthrown, will cause this nation to mourn and weep ; for God has declared that Ethiopia shall stretch forth her hands unto him, and he will hear her cry.

We would say to colonizationists that we consider them our foes instead of our friends. It is vain for them to say that we would do better in Liberia ; for we do not believe it. There is room enough in this country for us ; and if they be our friends, let them meliorate our condition here. Let them join in the work of immediate abolition of slavery. Let them wash out the stains which disfigure the national character. And then let them tell us about Liberia.

One reason why we are opposed to leaving these United States is this : you have so long denied us the enjoyment and protection of the laws of God and man in this country, that you wish now to oppress us still more. But thanks be to Him who holds all things in his hand, we believe He will plead our cause. Your skirts are already dyed with the blood of millions of souls. ' Vengeance is mine—I will repay,' saith the Lord.

Awake, ye wolves in sheep's clothing. Your cup is now full. You are daily causing innocent blood to be shed. How long, ye slavites, ye kidnappers, ye that traffic in human flesh, will you sleep ? When will you awake to your best interests ? For remember that you will not always be able to hold your victims in servile chains.

J. G. SMITH,
M. WALKER, } Committee.
M. JOHNSTON,

A VOICE FROM NEW-BEDFORD.

NEW-BEDFORD, January 23, 1832.

At a meeting of the people of color in New-Bedford, January 23d, for the purpose of considering and giving their opinion of the American Colonization Society, and the actual evil or benefit of that Society to the objects of its supervision, the free people of color, Mr Richard Johnson was called to the chair, and Richard G. Overing appointed secretary. After an address from the chair, it was moved that resolutions expressive of the views of the meeting, respecting the Colonization Society, be drawn up, and published in some newspaper not adverse to the rights and well being of all men, be their color what it may. The following are the resolves of the meeting :

Resolved, That in whatever light we view the Colonization Society, we discover nothing in it but terror, prejudice and oppression ; that the warm and beneficent hand of philanthropy is not apparent in the system, but the influence of the Society on public opinion is more prejudicial to the interest and welfare of the people of color in the United States, than slavery itself.

Resolved, That the Society, to effect its purpose, the removal of the free people of color, (not the slaves) through its agents, teaches the public to believe that it is patriotic and benevolent to withhold from us knowledge and the means of acquiring subsistence, and to look upon us as unnatural and illegal residents in this country ; and thus by force of prejudice, if not by law, endeavor to compel us to embark for Africa, and that too, apparently, by our own free will and consent.

Resolved, That as great a nuisance as we may be in the estimation of that Society, we yet have a hope in Him who has seen fit to continue our existence through days worse than which we do not fear, and which emboldens us as peaceable citizens, to resolve to abide the issue of coming days in our native land, in which we ask no more than the age in which we live demands, and which this nation, as republicans and christians, should not refuse to grant.

Signed in behalf of the meeting.

RICHARD JOHNSON, Chairman.

R. G. Overing, Secretary.

———

The foregoing resolutions and addresses are given in plain, it may be occasionally in severe language ; and display an intensity of feeling, a depth of abhorrence, and a firmness of purpose, honorable to men who appreciate their rights and love their country. Before I proceed, however, to comment upon these important proceedings, I shall make some quotations from the essays and addresses of colored writers, in order to sustain my assertion that the American Colonization Society is directly opposed to the wishes of our free colored population.

' A Colored Baltimorean '* records his sentiments in
the following style :

' We believe, sirs, that the people of color in the United
States will never be prevailed over to abandon the land of their
birth, and every thing vernacular with them—to forego many
advantages which they now possess, and many more which they
have in prospect, for the imaginary, or if real, the fleeting and
short-lived honors held out to them by our " Americo-African
empire." Why should we exchange a temperate and salubrious
climate, adapted to our constitutions as Americans, for one, to
us, fraught with disease and death ? Why should we leave a
land in which the arts and sciences are flourishing, and which is
beginning to yield to our research, for one, where the irradiat-
ing beams of the sun of science have yet to be announced by
the bright star of hope ? Why should we leave a land illumin-
ated with the blaze of gospel light, for one enshrouded in pagan
gloom ? Why should we, who are in tolerable circumstances
in America, who enjoy many of the comforts of life, and are
evidently on the advanced march of mind, cast away these certain, real, and growing advantages, for those which are precarious and chimerical ? Why should we abandon our firesides,
and every thing associated with the dear name of *home*—undergo
the fatigues of a perilous voyage, and expose ourselves, our
wives, and our little ones, to the deleterious influences of an
uncongenial sun, for the enjoyment of a liberty divested of its
usual accompaniments, surrounded with circumstances which
diminish its intrinsic value, and render it indeed " a dear earned
morsel "?   *   *   *   *   *   *
' But " it is the hope of accomplishing the entire subversion
of the slave trade and Mahometan superstition, and all their sub-
sidiary concomitants, that has actuated the christian and stimu-
lated the philanthropist." Noble objects indeed ! And who are
those christians and philanthropists ? Our friend tells us, without distinction, that they are " those noble and heroic men who
have enlisted under the banner of colonization." But how happens it that some of the most distinguished of these *christians*
and *philanthropists* are themselves slaveholders, and so far
abettors of the *slave trade* as to be actually guilty of selling into
a cruel and interminable vassalage the hapless victims of their
tender mercies ? Again, how is it that none but the free people
of color have been chosen to evangelize Africa ? Is it because
they are under an exclusive moral obligation to dispel the " gloom

* Genius of Universal Emancipation for November 27, 1829.

of Mahometan superstition?" Is it because they are pre-eminently qualified in point of morals and information for the missionary enterprise ? None will say this. Perhaps we shall be told, that the identity of their color gives them a decided advantage over every other people. But how is it that those wicked white men, who are in the habit of resorting thither for the most nefarious purposes, have access to these people ? And we have not forgotten that during the visit of the Rev. G. R. McGill, in Baltimore, he informed us that colored men from the United States, being thought by the natives to be men of information, are received and treated as white men, and denominated by the same epithet. Since then it does not appear that we are pre-eminently qualified for this work, why should it be pressed upon us ?   *   *   *   *

' Tell us not that the Sovereign Ruler of the universe, who is not a respecter of persons, whose " tender mercies are over all his works," will *never* elevate us to the dignity of men and christians, unless we emigrate to Africa. Tell us not that in this *christian* country, this " land of the free and home of the brave," we must *for ever* remain a degraded and proscribed race—that we must *for ever* be treated as the outcasts of creation. We are aware that this doctrine has been asserted with all the confidence of inspiration by *some* of our gospel ministers. We have heard them proclaim it in a tone calculated to strengthen the prejudices existing against us. They seem to forget that there is a superintending providence—that He, who " sits upon the whirlwind and directs the storm," has ever manifested himself a friend to the oppressed of every clime. They seem to forget that the religion of Jesus, wherever it reigns with unrestrained sway, demolishes every partition wall, and exterminates out of the heart all those bitter prejudices which impede the march of the Messiah's kingdom. We should like to have these prophets give us their ideas in relation to the millennial reign of Christ. We should like to have them inform us whether or not the general prejudices and their inseparable accompaniments, which now lie upon, and operate against us, on account of our color, will be consistent with this glorious reign of *peace*, and *love*, and *joy*. Let these ministers consider that much of our degradation is chargeable to the indifference (to say the least) that they manifest in regard to our situation—that if they as patterns of piety hold us at a distance, it is but natural for the inconsiderate to follow their example. Let them recollect that while they are making powerful and irresistible appeals to the humanity of the American people in behalf of the oppressed of other climes, they have a people among them whose claims

upon their liberality are paramount to those of any other.   Let
these ministers tell us how often they make it their business to
visit those portions of their flocks whose crime is, their color.
Nay, one of them said not long since, to be familiar with the
people of color would destroy his *usefulness* among the whites.
But whether they do their duty in relation to us or not, we indulge in no fears in regard to our future condition.   We are not
distrustful of the goodness and power of Him who has over-
ruled the evil designs of those men that first tore our ancestors
from their native shores, who is still overruling, and who will
continue to overrule the designs of all who would treat us as
the offscouring of the earth, because our Creator has not given us
a color as white as their own.   If ever there was a people who
could look up to Heaven with unshaken confidence for protection, it is that people whose sufferings are not the consequences
of their crimes ; it is that people whose misfortunes work in
them the graces of faith, patience and hope.   And why should
we not cherish these invaluable graces ?   We are told by high
authority, that " *all things* shall work together *for good* to them
that love God "—that " He will give grace and glory, and *no
good thing* will He *withhold* from them that walk uprightly."
You see, sirs, we have one straight forward course to pursue—
one marked out by the hand of unerring wisdom.   This course
we intend to pursue, without giving ourselves any uneasiness as
to the issue ; this we leave to Him who has the administration
of the universe in his hands, and who has declared for our encouragement, " even the very hairs of your head are all num-
bered." Tell us not of the wisdom, and power, and number
of our enemies ; He who has given us a hope, which at least
makes our condition tolerable, will say to them, as He did to
the tempestuous billows, " Hitherto shalt thou come, but no
further ; and here shall thy proud waves be stayed." '

*   *   *   *   *   *   *   *   *

' What effect have the evils of slavery in this *happy* land
upon the mind of the liberal, the unprejudiced, and philanthropic Lafayette ?

' Hear him, he will speak for himself : " When I am indulg-
ing in my views of American prospects and American liberty,
it is mortifying to be told that in that very country a large portion of the people are slaves.   It is a dark spot on the face of
the nation.   *Such a state of things cannot always exist.*" It was
a sight of the evils alluded to, and their inseparable concomitants, that extorted from the pen of Mr Jefferson that comprehensive and soul-thrilling sentence—" I tremble for my country
when I reflect that God is just, and that his justice cannot sleep

for ever." But may we not indulge the hope that the evils spoken of will yet awaken the sympathies of the American people—soften their cruel prejudices—arouse their slumbering energies—and produce in them an unconquerable determination to wash from their " stars and stripes " one of the blackest spots that ever cursed the globe, or stained the historic page ? Shall we be told that *invincible* prejudices render this great desideratum impracticable ? And what is this but a libel upon the American people ? What is it but to say, there is in them a moral incapacity to do justice, love mercy, and walk uprightly ? Colonization orators, designing politicians, ministers of Jesus, tell me, how can you thus libel your countrymen ? Surely, there is a regenerating, a redeeming spirit in the land—a spirit transforming misanthropes into philanthropists—bondmen into freemen—abettors of slavery into champions of liberty—a spirit that will yet drive from America the demon of slavery, and render it indeed " the land of the free and the home of the brave." ' *

*   *   *   *   *   *   *   *

' I have just found time to notice a few very exceptionable features of a communication over the signature of " A Marylander," published, a few days ago, in the American of our city. The writer is unquestionably entitled to the credit of being a thorough-going colonizationist. He writes in the *true spirit* of the cause. He seems to be under an excitement produced by the publication of our anti-colonization resolutions. This being the case, it is not to be expected that he would, throughout his communication, avail himself of the guarded, accommodating, and conciliating language usual with colonization writers and declaimers. After being convinced that the people of color are not to be persuaded to leave the land of their birth, and every thing vernacular with them, for " regions " which he tells us are " now dark as the valley of the shadow of death," he says, " I would propose then that Maryland should colonize her own free blacks." He does not add the usual qualification, " *with their own consent :*" he knows this will never be obtained. He therefore says : " I earnestly *hope* that the time *is now* come when our state will wake up to all the importance of this subject, and will instantly commence *a system of measures* imperatively demanded by the *sternest* principles [colonization principles ?] of *sound* policy." We would tell this precocious statesman that we are not to be intimidated into colonization " *measures* " by the angry effusions of his illiberal soul ; that we had rather die in Maryland under the pressure of unrighteous and

---

* Genius of Universal Emancipation, January 29, 1830.

cruel laws than be driven, like cattle, to the pestilential clime
of Liberia, where grievous privation, inevitable disease, and
premature death, await us in all their horrors.   We are embold-
ened thus to speak, not from a reliance on the mere arm of
flesh ; no—it is the righteousness of our cause, a knowledge of
the attributes of Deity, combined with a consciousness of innocence under suffering, that have inspired us with a moral cour-·
age which no oppression shall shake, no fulminations overawe.
Our limits will not permit us to expatiate, at this time, on the
import of the terms, " *a system of measures—the sternest prin-*
ciples," &c.   We would barely remark that the climax of injustice and cruelty, here suggested, nay, recommended, is the
legitimate fruit of the operations of the American colonization
societies relative to the free people of color.   We have always
believed that the " *system of measures* " here recommended,
would be the dernier resort of these *christian* associations. The
unmerited abuse, that has been so unsparingly heaped upon us
by colonizationists for expressing our opinions of their project
as connected with our happiness, their manifest determination
to effectuate their object regardless of our consent, abundantly
corroborate the opinion we have long since entertained.   We
turn, however, from the contemplation of the persecution and
oppression, which, it seems, are in reserve for us, to notice,
briefly, the moving cause of this virulent and relentless attack
upon our rights and happiness.   " The *census just taken,*" says
A Marylander, " *admonishes* us in the strongest manner, of the
necessity of prompt and efficient measures to drain off this description of our population."   Here then is the *patriotic,* the
benevolent, the *christian* principle, by which the colonization
societies, throughout our land, are actuated.   This is the selfish
policy of which we complain, and which should be execrated
by all *true* patriots, philanthropists, and christians.   Our increase is represented as an " *alarming evil—an evil,*" said one
of our colonization orators in the pulpit, not long since, " which
threatens our very *existence.*"   Now, if all this be true, how
can they, on their own principles, say we can *never* be a people
in this country ?   Surely, they are taking effectual steps to convince us, that the enjoyment of our rights in this, our native
land, is not only possible, but highly probable.   This we have
always believed.   And we hope and pray, that it may be accomplished in a way sanctioned by the gospel of peace : " without confused noise, or garments rolled in blood."   But this
glorious victory over pride and prejudice, by gospel weapons,
will never be accomplished by colonization principles.   Nor
will those ministers of the gospel have any part or lot in this

matter, who solemnly declare, in the face of heaven and earth, that we can *never enjoy, in this country,* those inalienable rights of man, whose inviolable preservation promotes the welfare of the whole human family. Such ministers virtually declare that they do not believe the doctrines they are bound to preach ; that He, from whom they profess to have received their commission, is, indeed, " a hard man, reaping where he has not sown, and gathering where he has not strawed ;" that He requires of them and their flocks, that which they are morally incapable of performing ; that they *cannot* love their neighbor as themselves, or do unto others what they wish done unto themselves, because their Lord, in his wisdom, has given some of their fellow creatures a different color from their own. These temporising, retrograde reformers are doing a serious injury to the people of color. They heed not the warning of Heaven : " Do my people no harm." They are doing more to strengthen the cruel and unchristian prejudices, already too powerful against us, than all the slaveholders in the Union. They hesitate not to declare, that, in America, we are out of the reach of humanity. They seem to think that the religion of the benevolent Saviour which enjoins, "*honor all men,*" and which explicitly says, "*if* ye have *respect to persons,* ye *commit sin,*" is nothing more than a dead letter, or must *for ever* remain powerless, 'in the United States 'of America. And have these men the face to contend with the infidels of our land ? Why, one infidel, with the bible in his hands, would " chase a thousand, and two put ten thousand to flight." But notwithstanding these discouraging circumstances, our cause will yet triumph. He who is for us, is stronger than all that are against us. " The rulers " of the land may " take counsel together," and some of the professed ministers of Jesus may "come into their secret," but "He that sitteth in the heavens shall laugh : the Lord shall have them in derision." Fear not then, my colored countrymen, but press forward, with a laudable ambition, for all that heaven has intended for you and your children, remembering that the path of duty is the path of safety, and that " righteousness " alone " exalteth a nation." '

If excellence of style, a dignified carriage, sound logic, a high and abiding faith, and fervent piety, confer credit upon a writer, few have ever better illustrated these traits than ' A COLORED BALTIMOREAN,' or deserved a nobler tribute of praise. He who would be ashamed to acknowledge such a man as his countryman and brother, has yet to learn his own insignificance and what constitutes the majesty of human nature.

[PART II.]   8

The following is an extract of a letter from a colored gentleman of wealth and respectability in Philadelphia, whose friendship is courted by honorable men, and whose usefulness is scarcely exceeded by any other citizen :

' Is it not preposterous to one, like myself, whose family has resided in the state of Pennsylvania ever since the great lawgiver, William Penn, came last to this state from England ; and who fought for the independence of my country, whose Declaration asserts, that all men are born with free and equal rights—is it not preposterous to be told that this is not my country ? I was seven months on board of the old Jersey Prison ship in the year 1780, " the times that tried men's souls ;" and am I now to be told that Africa is my country, by some of those whose birth-place is unknown ? Is it not a contradiction to say that a man is an alien to the country in which he was born ? To separate the blacks from the whites is as impossible, as to bale out the Delaware with a bucket. I have always been decidedly of opinion, that if the Colonization Society would take but half the pains to improve the children of color in their own country, and expend but half the money that they are devoting to accomplish their visionary scheme of christianizing Africa, by offering premiums to master mechanics to take them as apprentices, they would do more to destroy prejudice than any thing else. When I look at this globe, containing eight or nine hundred millions of inhabitants, and see that they differ in color from the frozen to the temperate and torrid zones, and that every thing is variegated, I am astonished that any man should be so prejudiced against his fellow-man ; but we pray for the aid of the Almighty to take the scales from their eyes ; and that the Liberator may be one of the instruments in commencing the work.' *

' I would ask some of our pretended white friends, and the members of the American Colonization Society, why they are so interested in our behalf as to want us to go to Africa ? They tell us that it is our home ; that they desire to make a people of us, which we can never be here ; that they want Africa civilized ; and that we are the very persons to do it, as it is almost impossible for any white person to exist there. I deny it. Will some of those guardian angels of the people of color tell me how it is that we, who were born in the same city or state with themselves, can live any longer in Africa than they ? I consider

---

* ' The Liberator ' for January 22, 1832.

it the most absurd assertion that any man of common sense could make, unless it is supposed, as some have already said, that we are void of understanding. If we had been born on that continent, the transportation would be another matter ; but as the fact is the reverse, we consider the United States our home, and not Africa as they wish to make us believe ;—and if we do emigrate, it will be to a place of our own choice.

I would also mention to the supporters of the Colonization Society, that if they would spend half the time and money that they do, in educating the colored population and giving them lands to cultivate here, and secure to them all the rights and immunities of freemen, instead of sending them to Africa, it would be found, in a short time, that they made as good citizens as the whites. Their traducers would hear of fewer murders, highway robberies, forgeries, &c. &c. being committed, than they do at present among some of the white inhabitants of this country.' *

' Colonization principles, abstractly considered, are unobjectionable ; but the means employed for their propagation, we think, are altogether objectionable. We are deprived of our birthright, and pointed by the colonization partisans to another country as a home. They speak of the prejudices which exist against us, as an insuperable hindrance to the improvement of our situation here. We are sickened by the constant reiteration of " *extraneous mass,*" " *African inferiority,*" &c. which tends immediately to justify the slaveholder in his crime, and increase already existing prejudice. The Colonization Society never will effect the removal of slavery. The God of justice will never, in my opinion, let this nation off so easily. It is in vain to hold back. The eyes of all will ultimately be opened to see that nothing but universal emancipation can possibly avert impending wrath.'†

' How long, oh ! ye boasters of freedom, will ye endeavor to persuade us, your derided, degraded fellow countrymen, to the belief that our interest and happiness are prized in high estimation among you ? Be it known, that we are not all such misguided, deluded mortals as to be duped by your plans ; that we will not suffer ourselves to become so infatuated as to " hurl reason from her throne," and succumb to your glittering, showy, *dissimulating* path to eminence. We spurn with contempt your

---

* ' A Colored Philadelphian '—vide ' The Liberator ' for Feb. 12, 1831.
† Correspondent of ' The Liberator,' Feb. 26, 1831.

unrighteous schemes, and point the finger of derision at your fruitless attempts. You have commenced them in a day, when liberty, justice and equality are claimed by almost all, as nature's rights ; for behold ! a beam of science, lucid as the sun, has divinely fallen upon the lightless intellects of a portion of that ignoble part of your fellow creatures, who have been so long the victims of your fell injustice and inhumanity. Would to God that conscience might subdue your malignant prejudices. Tell us not that our condition can never be bettered in the land of our birth : you know it not. Make but the attempt in consecrating a portion of your time, talents and money upon us here, and you would soon find the cause of Afric's injured race vindicated by her descendants ; and the day which now dawns would be speedily ushered into blazing light, declaring in its effulgence the joyful sound of Liberty—Justice—Equality, to all mankind.'*

' There is much to be surprised at, little to admire, and nothing worthy of imitation, in the "bubbles" of our friends, the colonizationists. They have enlisted the prejudices and the support of the wealthy and influential in their favor ; they have succeeded in sending some two or three thousand to Liberia ; and they are flattered with their partial success, and no doubt look forward to the time when they will behold the whole of the colored inhabitants of America, in the far distant land of Africa. But let them not anticipate too much ; they have yet one obstacle to overcome which threatens to overthrow their "baseless fabric ;" or at any rate impede their progress. Their proceedings have not obtained the approbation of those, whose approbation is most needed, *the colored people themselves.* They are most strangely mistaken if they suppose that it is an easy matter to win them, either by *sophistry* or *force.* The press has begun its revolutionizing work, overturning in its progress every thing calculated to suppress inquiry or to blind the understanding. Already have the intrigues of the designing been exposed, and already have the colored people set their faces against oppression.

The Colonization Society has erred in matters of *policy ;* for instead of exerting themselves to gain the confidence of the colored people, and thus by persuasion to have rid the country of them, they have acted in a manner calculated to disgust every humane mind, and have rendered it an utter *impossibility* to remove them ; and it is most fortunate for the unfortunate, that

---

* Correspondent of ' The Liberator,' March 12, 1831.

they have detected those intriguing spirits in their *humane* and *charitable* undertaking.

How many hours of anguish, how much incalculable misery has been prevented ; in short, how many human beings have been saved from an untimely grave, by the timely interposition of the PRESS ! It has said, let it be so, and it *was* so ; its thunders have been heard, and the oppressor trembles like the earthquake : it has overthrown, yea, totally demolished the sharp-edged sword of the Colonization Society.

Support the PRESS then, ye people of color, and the result will be a total overthrow of all the darling schemes of the aforesaid darling Society ; it has accomplished wonders, yea, wonders already ; much more can, nay, will be done ; again I say, support the PRESS.' *

' The African Colonization Society declares that we the people of color shall have no part nor lot in the free institutions of this country. Why ? Because the Creator of all—the sovereign Ruler of the universe, who holds in his hands the destiny of nations, thought fit and proper, in his infinite wisdom, to tincture us with a darker hue than the paler part of community ! or, if I may say, because the lot of our predecessors happened to be cast in the torrid zone, beneath the scorching beams of a vertical sun ! These are the objections the African Colonization Society offer to this community to our remaining in this country—in the land of freemen ! These are the considerations that prompt them to tell us that we the descendants of Africa can never be men unless we abandon the land of our birth, our homes and people, and submit to that uncongenial clime, the barbarous regions of Africa, amidst unyielding contagion and mortality ! O, that man would remember, that knowledge and virtue, not complexion, are the emblems that constitute the value of human dignity ! With these, we are worthy —without them, we are unworthy. By the acts and operations of wicked men, shielded under a cloak of religion, we the people of color are doomed to all the miseries that the human body is able to sustain—deprived of light, knowledge and social intercourse, by the colonization gentlemen. With all their pretended zeal and love of liberty, manifested towards the African race, I count them as enemies, not friends. I do not solicit their love, nor regard their friendship. I speak for one : I never did, and never will court an enemy as a friend, knowingly, let him be whom he may—let him belong to church or state, I feel

---

* ' African Sentinel,' Oct. 8, 1831, printed at Albany.

the weight of their predominant power, and the finishing blow they are about to strike. Thus we move by them, poor and pennyless, despised and forsaken by all ; creeping through your streets, submissively bowed down to every foot whose skin is tinctured with a lighter hue than ours—thus we sojourn in solitude, not for our crimes but color.

' I came here for the purpose of showing to this community, that the people of color of the United States disapprove of the African Colonization plan. They do not wish to emigrate to Africa. These six hundred or more, that the gentleman tells you are now waiting for a passage to Liberia, are not the free people of color of the United States ; they are, if any, the poor, old, worn-out southern slaves, freed on the condition to go to Africa, or die in the tracks of slavery, no more fit for their cotton and rice fields—for the laws of those states forbid the master, let him be possessed of all the fine feelings that the human mind is able to contain'; unless he banishes them to some distant region, across that " mighty ocean " they speak of, they cannot be free. According to the laws of those states, and the basis on which the Society is built, the emancipated slaves are not free until they stand upon the shores of Liberia. Thus the Northern and Middle States are called upon for donations to enable the monarch of the south to bury his slaves in the sands of Africa ; thus far, northern capital is instrumental in parting asunder parents and children—no more to meet, until Jehovah will stand upon the four corners of the earth, and proclaim deliverance to the captive !—when the arm of tyrants shall cease to sway the rod of tyranny over the heads of their helpless children—until all creation shall vanish and crumble into nothing.

' About the time of the formation of this Society, the people of color, in different sections of the Union, took the alarm— they thought there was something wrong in the views of that combined body. So, the free people of color of Richmond, convened themselves together in the state of Virginia, where the gentleman says the African Colonization Society first originated. They assembled themselves together for the purpose of ascertaining each other's feelings with regard to that combined body, and after mature reflection, they petitioned Congress—I will give you the words of their memorial, which are sufficient evidence to substantiate in the mind of every rational person, that the people of color wish to remain in this country.

' " At a meeting of a respectable portion of the free people of color of the city of Richmond, on Friday, January 24, 1817,

William Bowler was appointed chairman, and Lentey Craw, secretary. The following preamble and resolution were read, unanimously adopted, and ordered to be printed.

' " Whereas a Society has been formed at the seat of government, for the purpose of colonizing, with their own consent, the free people of color of the United States ; therefore we, the free people of color of the city of Richmond, have thought it advisable to assemble together under the sanction of authority, for the purpose of making a public expression of our sentiments on a question in which we are so deeply interested. We perfectly agree with the Society, that it is not only proper, but would ultimately tend to the benefit and advantage of a great portion of our suffering fellow creatures, to be colonized ; but while we thus express our approbation of a measure laudable in its purposes, and beneficial in its designs, it may not be improper in us to say, that we prefer being colonized in the most remote corner of the land of our nativity, to being exiled to a foreign country—and whereas the president and board of managers of the said Society have been pleased to leave it to the entire discretion of Congress to provide a suitable place for carrying these laudable intentions into effect—Be it therefore

' " Resolved, That we respectfully submit to the wisdom of Congress whether it would not be an act of charity to grant us a small portion of their territory, either on the Missouri river, or any place that may seem to them most conducive to the public good and our future welfare, subject, however, to such rules and regulations as the government of the United States may think proper to adopt."

WM. BOWLER, Chairman.

LENTEY CRAW, Secretary." ' *

' The *colonization craft* is a diabolical pursuit, which a great part of our christian community are engaged in. Now, brethren, I need not enlarge on this point. You that have been observing, have already seen the trap under the bait ; and although some of our population have been foolish enough to sell their birthright for a mess of pottage, yet I doubt whether the Colonization Society will entrap many more. It is too barefaced, and contrary to all reason, to suppose, that there is any

---

* Extracts from ' An Address to the Gentlemen and Ladies of the County of Otsego, N. Y., delivered on the 30th September, 1830, by Hayden Waters, a man of color.' The proceedings of the colored inhabitants of Virginia, incorporated into this Address, are those referred to on page 8 as having been accidentally mislaid.

good design in this project. If they are willing to restore four-fold for what they have taken by false accusation, they can do it to better advantage in the bosom of our country, than at several thousand miles off. How would you do, brethren, if your object was really to benefit the poor ? Would you send them into a neighboring forest, and there deal out that food which they were famishing for ? Now we stand different from beggars. Our ancestors were stolen property, and ' property which belonged to God. This is well known by our religious community ; and they find that the owner is about to detect them. Now if they can slip away the stolen goods, by smug-gling all those out of the country, whîch God would be likely to make an instrument of, in bringing them to justice, and keep the rest in ignorance ; by such means, things would go on well with them, and they would appease their consciences by telling what great things they are doing for the colored population and God's cause. But we understand better how it is. The de-ception is not so well practised, but that we can discover the mark of the beast. They will steal the sons of Africa, bring them to America, keep them and their posterity in bondage for centuries, letting them have what education they can pick up of themselves ; then transport them back to Africa ; by whioh means America gets all her drudgery done at little expense, and endeavors to flatter the Deity, by making him a sacrifice of good works of this kind. But to the awful disappointment of all such blasphemers, they will meet the justice of God, which will be to them a devouring sword.'*

' Though delivered from the fetters of slavery, we are op-pressed by an unreasonable, unrighteous, and cruel prejudice, which aims at nothing less, than the forcing away of all the free colored population of the United States to the distant shores of Africa. Far be it from me to impeach the motives of every member of the American Colonization Society. The civilizing and christianizing of that vast continent, and the extirpation of the abominable traffic in slaves, (which, notwithstanding all the laws passed for its suppression, is still carried on in all its hor-rors,) are no doubt the principal motives, which induce many to give it their support.

But there are those, and those who are most active and influ-ential in this cause, who hesitate not to say, that they wish to rid the country of the free colored population ; and there is suf-

---

* ' Address delivered before the colored population of Providence, R. I., No-vember 27, 1828, by Rev. Hosea Easton.'

ficient reason to believe that with many, this is the principal motive for supporting that Society ; and that whether Africa is civilized or not, and whether the slave-trade be suppressed or not, they would wish to see the free colored people removed from this country to Africa.

'Africa could certainly be brought into a state of civil and religious improvement, without sending all the free people of color in the United States there.

'A few well-qualified missionaries, properly fitted out and supported, would do more for the instruction and improvement of the natives of that country, than a host of colonists, the greater part of whom would need to be instructed themselves, and all of whom for a long period would find enough to do to provide for themselves, instead of instructing the natives.

'How inconsistent are those who say, that Africa will be benefitted by the removal of the free people of color of the United States there, while they say, they are the *most vile and degraded* people in the world!—If we are as vile and degraded as they represent us, and they wish the Africans to be rendered a virtuous, enlightened and happy people, they should not *think* of sending *us* among them, lest we should make them worse instead of better.

'The colonies planted by white men on the shores of America, so far from benefitting the aborigines, corrupted their morals, and caused their ruin ; and yet those who say *we* are the most vile people in the world, would send us to Africa, to improve the character and condition of the natives ! Such arguments would not be listened to for a moment, were not the minds of the community strangely warped by prejudice.

'Those who wish that that vast continent should be *compensated* for the injuries done it, by sending thither the light of the gospel and the arts of civilized life, should aid in sending and supporting well qualified missionaries, who should be wholly devoted to the work of instruction, instead of sending colonists, who would be apt to turn the ignorance of the natives to their own advantage, and do them more harm than good.

'Much has also been said by colonizationists, about improving the character and condition of the people of color of this country, by sending them to Africa. This is more inconsistent still. We are to be improved by being sent far from civilized society. This is a novel mode of improvement. What is there in the burning sun, the arid plains, and barbarous customs of Africa, that is so peculiarly favorable to our improvement? What hinders our improving here, where schools and colleges abound, where the gospel is preached at every corner, and where all the arts and sciences are verging fast to perfection ? Nothing, nothing but prejudice. It requires no large expenditures, no hazardous enterprises, to raise the people of color in the United States to as highly improved a state, as any class of the community. All that is necessary is, that those who profess to be anxious for it, should lay aside their prejudices, and act towards them as they do by others.

'We are NATIVES of this country; we ask only to be treated as well as FOREIGNERS. Not a few of our fathers suffered and bled to purchase its independence ; we ask only to be treated as well as those who fought against it. We have toiled to cultivate it, and to raise it to its present prosperous condition ; we ask only to share equal privileges with those who come from distant lands to enjoy the fruits of our labor. Let these moderate requests be granted, and we need not go to Africa nor any where else, to be improved and happy. We cannot but doubt the purity of the motives of those persons who deny us these requests, and would send us to Africa, to gain what they might give us at home.

'But they say, the prejudices of the country against us are invincible ; and as they cannot be conquered, it is better that we should be removed beyond their influence. This plea should never proceed from the lips of any man, who professes to believe that a just God rules in the heavens.

'The American Colonization Society is a numerous and influential body. Would they lay aside their *own* prejudices, much of the burden would be at once removed ; and their example (especially if they were as anxious to have *justice done us here,* as to send us to Africa,) would have such an influence upon the community at large, as would soon cause prejudice to hide its deformed head.

'But alas ! the course which they have pursued, has an opposite tendency. By the *scandalous misrepresentations,* which they are continually giving of our character and conduct, we have sustained much injury, and have reason to apprehend much more.

'Without any charge of crime, we have been denied all access to places, to which we formerly had the most free intercourse ; the colored citizens of other places, on leaving their homes, have been denied the privilege of returning ; and others have been absolutely driven out.

'Has the Colonization Society had no effect in producing these barbarous measures ?

'They profess to have no other object in view, than the colonizing of the free people of color on the coast of Africa, with their *own consent ;* but if our homes are made so uncom-

fortable that we cannot continue in them ; or if, like our brethren of Ohio and New Orleans, we are driven from them, and
no other door is open to receive us but Africa, our removal
there will be any thing but voluntary.

' It is very certain, that very few free people of color *wish*
to go to that *land*. The Colonization Society *know* this, and
yet they do certainly calculate, that in time they will have us
all removed there.

' How can this be effected, but by making our situation worse
here, and closing every other door against us ?' *

' My attention was forcibly attracted by a communication in
Mr Poulson's Daily Advertiser of the 16th inst. which states,
that Mrs Stansbury of Trenton, N. J. has presented *one thousand dollars* to the Colonization Society. Now I think it is
greatly to be regretted, that this highly generous and benevolent
lady has been induced to make this donation for the purpose of
conveying some of the superannuated slaves to Africa, when
objects of much greater importance could be attained by offering a premium to master mechanics to take colored children as
apprentices, so that they would become useful to themselves
and others. It is an inquiry becoming of the utmost importance,
what is to become of those children who are arriving at the age
of manhood ?

' I am greatly astonished that the ministers of the gospel
should take so active a part, in endeavoring to convey the freemen of color to Africa. Even in Boston and New-York, they
have taken the lead in support of this object. They cannot be
aware of the great injury they will be the means of inflicting
on us : instead of doing this, they should endeavor to remove
prejudice, to ameliorate and improve the condition of the colored people by education, and by having their children placed in
a situation to learn a trade. I hope, through the assistance of
Divine Providence, that the Liberator may be the means (especially in Boston, the Cradle of Liberty and Independence)
of guiding the people of this country in the path, which equal
justice and the public good so evidently indicate.

' I have never conversed with an intelligent man of color,
(not swayed by interested and sinister motives,) who was not
decidedly opposed to leaving his home for the fatal clime of

---

* ' A Discourse delivered in St. Philip's Church, for the benefit of the colored
community of Wilberforce, in Upper Canada, on the Fourth of July, 1830.
By Rev. Peter Williams, Rector of St. Philip's Church, New-York.' Mr Williams is a clergyman of superior talents and great moral worth, and beloved by
an extensive circle of acquaintance.

Africa.   I am well acquainted with all the masters of vessels,
belonging to this port, who have been to the coast of Africa ;
and they all agree in representing it as one of the most unhealthy
countries in the latitude of 40.   In the months of June and July,
the thermometer is at from 88 to 90 degrees.   What must it be,
then, in the latitude of 6 or 7, under a vertical sun, and where,
after the rainy season, the effluvium which arises from the putre-
faction of vegetables is productive of the most fatal effects ?
Sir James L. Yeo agrees with their account, in his statement
laid before the Admiralty of Great Britain.

    ' Has any one, in either of our southern States, given any
thing like a thousand dollars to promote emigration to Africa ?
Not one has shown so much compassion for the oppressed slave.
General Mercer,—who is, I believe, the President of the Colonization Society,—promised to emancipate his slaves, and to
sell his large possessions in Virginia, and to remove with them
to Africa—(my friends inform me, and I believe him to be one
of the most humane and best of masters.)   Mr Key, the great
advocate, and the late Judge Washington, promised to liberate
their slaves : I believe that neither of them has performed his
promise.

    ' According to a statement made by Mr Key, they have re-
moved in fourteen years about as many hundred emigrants.   I
will venture to say, that at least a half million have been born
during the same period.   We ask not their compassion and aid,
in assisting us to emigrate to Africa : we are contented in the
land that gave us birth, and for which many of our fathers
fought and died, during the war which established our independence.   I well remember that when the New England regi-
ment marched through this city on their way to attack the English army under the command of Lord Cornwallis, there were
several companies of colored people, as brave men as ever
fought ; and I saw those brave soldiers who fought at the battle
of Red Bank, under Col. Green, where Count Donop the commander was killed, and the Hessians defeated.   All this appears
to be forgotten now ; and the descendants of these men, to
whom we are indebted for the part they took in the struggle for
independence, are intended to be removed to a distant and in-
hospitable country, while the emigrants from every other country are permitted to seek an asylum here from oppression, and
to enjoy the blessings of both civil and religious liberty, equally
with those who are entitled to it by birthright.

    ' I think the ministers of the gospel might do much towards
destroying the domestic slave trade, which breaks asunder the
sacred ties of husband, wife and children.   Not a voice is

raised by them against this most cruel injustice. In the British colonies, this is not permitted ; yet it exists in the only true republic on earth.' *

' *My Friends and Countrymen :*—I trust, by this time, you have known well my sentiments in relation to the American Colonization Society ; and the great objects, which have been set forth, of a general union of interest, in funds and education, for the permanent establishment and furtherance of our prosperity, in this our native country.

' In addition to what has been already said on the subject, I shall briefly set forth some of the leading causes of our wretchedness and misery ; and the prominent motives of the Colonization Society in sending us away. Much, theory has been used, in the discussions upon our civil and political situation, in this country. We have been branded, in many instances,— may I not say, in the highest courts of the nation, courts of justice and equity, in public and family circles ?—as being an inferior race of beings, not possessing like intellect and faculty with the whites. We are represented as being incapable of acting for ourselves ; consequently not educated and qualified to be admitted into public places, to vindicate the integrity of our race, and the qualifications we are capable of acquiring. Many of our noble statesmen, orators and lawyers, have made our capital ring with the empty sound of inferiority,—degradation, —the impossibility of tolerating equality with the blacks. Sacred writ has been carefully examined by these gentlemen of science, and construed to suit their narrow consciences. Prophets have arisen among them, who hold forth to the people the continuation of our political thraldom, unless there be a general removal of all the free among us to the coast of Africa. Others argue, that, although they have good feelings towards us, and would do any thing for us, if we were out of their sight and out of the hearing of their slaves, yet to admit us into their circles would be to pervert the present order of society, and the happiness of the good white citizens of the country. These are generally bible men, such as hold forth the true oracles of God ; yet deny him, in their actions and words, the supreme control over all his creatures. There is hardly ever an action performed, whether good or bad, but there is generally a reason given for so doing ; and he is a wicked, daring character, who cannot find a cloak, at any time, to cover his

---

* From the pen of the Colored Gentleman in Philadelphia, referred to on page 58—vide ' The Liberator,' March 12, 1831.

hideous crimes. The men who have been foremost, in with-holding from us our dearest and most sacred rights, have always held out false colors to the community at large, (such as, infe-riority, degradation, nuisance, pest, slaves, species of monkey, apes, &c.) to justify their inhuman and unchristian acts towards us, and to deaden the severe pangs of conscience that harass them. They would wish to appear innocent before the world ; as doing unto all men as they would they should do unto them. Do they base their objects, in full, upon such frivolous excuses as these ? No. The truth is, actions speak louder than words. It is my candid opinion, there would have been no Coloniza-tion Society formed for our transportation to the western coast of Africa, had there been no free colored people, and did not our numbers increase daily. If we, as a free body of people, had remained in the same character with slaves, monkeys and baboons, there would not have been so much excitement in the community about us ; but as they see by our improvement, (a great improvement, indeed, within forty years,) that the period is hastening on, when there will be no other alternative but we must rank among them in civilization, science and politics, they have got up this colonization scheme to persuade us to leave our slave brethren, and flee to the pestilential shores of Africa, where we shall be in danger of being forced to hang our harps upon the willows, and our song of liberty and civilization will be hushed by the impelling force of barbarian despots.' *

' And in pursuit of this great object [the elevation of the peo-ple of color] various ways and means have been resorted to ; among others, the American Colonization Society is the most prominent. Not doubting the sincerity of many friends who are engaged in that cause ; yet we beg leave to say, that it does not meet with our approbation. However great the debt which these United States may owe to injured Africa, and however unjustly her sons have been made to bleed, and her daughters to drink of the cup of affliction, still we who have been born and nurtured on this soil, we, whose habits, manners and cus-toms are the same in common with other Americans, can never consent to take our lives in our hands, and be the bearers of the redress offered by that Society to that much afflicted country.

' Tell it not to barbarians, lest they refuse to be civilized, and eject our christian missionaries from among them, that in

---

* ' Address delivered before a Colored Association in Brooklyn, N. Y., Au-gust 5, 1831,' by George Hogarth. Vide 'The Liberator' for August 27, 1831.

the nineteenth century of the christian era, laws have been enacted in some of the States of this great republic, to compel an unprotected and harmless portion of our brethren to leave their homes and seek an asylum in foreign climes : and in taking a view of the unhappy situation of many of these, whom the oppressive laws alluded to, continually crowd into the Atlantic cities, dependent for their support upon their daily labor, and who often suffer for want of employment, we have had to lament that no means have yet been devised for their relief.' *

' The Convention has not been unmindful of the operations of the American Colonization Society ; and it would respectfully suggest to that august body of learning, talent and worth, that, in our humble opinion, strengthened, too, by the opinions of eminent men in this country, as well as in Europe, that they are pursuing the direct road to perpetuate slavery, with all its unchristianlike concomitants, in this boasted land of freedom ; and, as citizens and men whose best blood is sapped to gain popularity for that Institution, we would, in the most feeling manner, beg of them to desist : or, if we must be sacrificed to their philanthropy, we would rather die at home. Many of our fathers, and some of us, have fought and bled for the liberty, independence and peace which you now enjoy ; and, surely, it would be ungenerous and unfeeling in you to deny us a humble and quiet grave in that country which gave us birth !' †

' Sir, upon the whole, my view of the operations of the Colonization Society, in relieving the slave States of the evil which weighs them down more than a hundred tariffs, is illustrated by an old fable, in which it is stated, that a man was seen at the foot of a mountain, scraping away the dust with his foot. One passing by, asked him what he was doing ? I wish to remove this mountain, said he. You fool, replied the other, you can never do it in that way. Well, said he, I can raise a dust, can't I ?

' Sir, I do not wish to censure the motives of this Society, but surely they are visionary. Its supporters are bewildered in their own dust, which is well calculated to injure the vision of good men. The Commercial Advertiser says they do indeed wish to wipe away from the national records the stain of slavery, " but hope it may be accomplished (as the Virginia Enquirer has it) surely but quietly." Yes, Sir, and quietly enough !

---

* Conventional Address of the People of Color in Philadelphia, in 1830.

† ' Minutes and Proceedings of the First Annual Convention of the People of Color, held by adjournment in the city of Philadelphia, in June, 1831.'

' Our ambition leads not to superiority, but to our *freedom* and *political rights. Grant this !* we ask no more ! If the places in which we dwell are too straight for us and the white population, place us in a state far to far the West—take us into the Union—give us our *rights* as *freemen.* Let the southern states make all born after a date not two years distant, free ! and let the Colonization Society turn its attention and energies to the removing of liberated slaves there : the free people will go without their aid. But if the Government is fearful of retaliation, it may allay its fears by a consideration of the fact of there not being one freeman engaged in the late insurrections—of freemen informing against slaves—the peaceable manner in which we live in the neighborhoods of the south, and throughout the whole Union. The meetings that have lately been held, and resolutions passed expressive of our disapprobation of such measures, may all show that such fears are groundless. I repeat again— *Give us our rights—we ask no more !*

' Yes, Sir, if I possessed the Indies, I would pledge the whole that if such measures were taken, and such grants made, no retaliation would be made by us as a body for former evils.' *

' In no age of our existence have there been more pains taken by priests and people, in public and private, in church and state, to give them currency, than at present. The whole theme of that wicked, persecuting combination—the Colonization Society—is calulated to impress upon the mind of the public these atrocious maxims which every day strengthen a prejudice not only cherished by the whites against the blacks, but by the blacks against the whites. That foul fiend of hell, that destroying angel who hath power to take peace from the earth, and to kill with the sword, is gaining a commanding influence very fast over both parties. And who, but the advocates of the Colonization Society, receive him as a welcome guest ? Who but they have built him a temple, and cried, " Long live Prejudice against free born Americans of sable hue !" Who but they are continually crying, " The free blacks are dangerous ! the free blacks are dangerous ! Away with them—away with them to Africa !" Who but they are the apologists for murder, theft, and all the horrid concomitants of slavery ? Who but they have defiled our temples of worship dedicated to God for his service, making merchandise of the souls of men by transferring them over to the keeping of prejudice ?' †

---

* ' Philadelphia Evangelist '—vide ' The Liberator ' for November 26, 1831.

† Correspondent of ' The Liberator,' December 17, 1831.

Other extracts might be recorded, but these must suffice. I have given the sentiments of the people of color as expressed individually, in public orations, in conventions of delegates, and in popular assemblies. Their proceedings evince a keen discrimination between true and false philanthropy, and an intellectual ability successfully to defend their cause. Their instincts are more than a match for the specious sophistry and learned sense of colonizationists : they meet them on every point, and on every point achieve a victory. Conscious of the fact that in their complexion is found the only motive for their banishment, they clearly illustrate the hypocrisy and injustice of the African crusade. Their union of purpose is such as cannot be broken. How intense is their love of country ! how remarkable their patient endurance of wrongs ! how strong their abhorrence of expatriation ! how auspicious the talents which they display !

Every humane and honorable man will assent to the proposition, that no scheme for the removal of a numerous people from one continent to another, ought to be prosecuted contrary to their desires. A scheme cannot be benevolent which thrives upon persecution. Benevolent oppression is a solecism.

Another self-evident truth is, that no such removal can be effected merely by the presentation of selfish inducements, or without resorting to coercive measures. To show that coercion is openly advocated by some of the prominent supporters of the Colonization Society, I make the following extracts from the speeches of Messrs Broadnax and Fisher, delivered during the ' Great Debate ' in the Virginia House of Delegates a short time since. Mr Broadnax said :

'IT IS IDLE TO TALK ABOUT NOT RESORTING TO FORCE. Every body must look to the introduction of force of some kind or other—and it is in truth a question of expediency ; of moral justice ; of political good faith —whether we shall fairly delineate our whole system on the face of the bill, or leave the acquisition of extorted consent to other processes. The real question —the only question of magnitude to be settled, is the great preliminary question —Do you intend to send the free persons of color out of Virginia, or not ?'
' If the free negroes are willing to go, they will go—if not willing, they must be compelled to go. Some gentlemen think it politic not now to insert this feature in the bill, though they proclaim their readiness to resort to it when it becomes necessary ; they think that for a year or two a sufficient number will consent to go, and then the rest can be compelled. For my part, I deem it better to approach the question and settle it at once, and avow it openly. The intelligent portion of the free negroes know very well what is going on.—Will they not see your debates ? *Will they not see that coercion is ultimately to be*

resorted to ? They will perceive that the edict has gone forth, and that it
MUST FALL, if not now, in a short time upon them.'

'I have already expressed it as my opinion that few, very few, will *voluntarily* consent to emigrate, if no COMPULSORY MEASURE be adopted.—
With it—many, in anticipation of its sure and certain arrival, will, in the
mean time, go away—they will be sensible that the time would come when they
would be forced to leave the State. Without it—you will still, no doubt, have
applicants for removal equal to your means. Yes, Sir, people who will not only
consent, but beg you to deport them. But what sort of *consent*—a consent
extorted by a series of oppression calculated to render their situation among us
insupportable. Many of those who have already been sent off, went with *their
avowed consent*, but under the influence of a more decided compulsion than
any which this bill holds out. I will not express, in its full extent, the idea I
entertain of what has been done, or what enormities will be perpetrated to induce this class of persons to leave the State. Who does not know that when a
free negro, by crime or otherwise, has rendered himself obnoxious to a neighborhood, how easy it is for a party to visit him one night, take him from his bed
and family, and apply to him the gentle admonition of a severe flagellation, to
induce him to *consent* to go away ? In a few nights the dose can be repeated,
perhaps increased, until, in the language of the physicians, *quantum suff.* has
been administered to produce the desired operation ; and the fellow then becomes *perfectly willing* to move away. I have certainly heard, if incorrectly,
the gentleman from Southampton will put me right, that of the large cargo of
emigrants lately transported from that country to Liberia, all of whom *professed*
to be *willing* to go, were rendered so by some such severe ministrations as those
I have described. A lynch club—a committee of vigilance—could easily exercise a kind of inquisitorial *surveillance* over any neighborhood, and convert any
desired number, I have no doubt, at any time, into a willingness to be removed.
But who really prefers such means as these to the course proposed in this bill ?
And one or the other is inevitable. For no matter how you change this bill—
sooner or later the free negroes will be *forced* to leave the State. Indeed, Sir,
ALL OF US LOOK TO FORCE of some kind or other, direct or indirect, moral
or physical, legal or illegal. Many who are opposed, they say, to any compulsory feature in the bill, desire to introduce such severe regulations into our police
laws—such restrictions of their existing privileges—such inability to hold property—obtain employment—rent residences, &c., as to make it impossible for
them to remain amongst us. *Is not this force ?* '

Mr Fisher said :

'If we wait until the free negroes consent to leave the State, we shall wait
until " time is no more." *They never will give their consent ;* and if the
House amend the bill as proposed, their consent is in a manner pointed out by the
gentleman from Dinwiddie—and it is a great question whether we shall force the
people to extort their consent from them in this way.—He believed if the compulsory principle were stricken out, this class of people would be forced to leave
by the harsh treatment of the whites. The people in those parts of the State
where they most abound, were determined,—as far as they could learn through
the newspapers and other sources,—to get rid of the blacks.'

What a revelation, what a confession, is here ! The free
blacks taken from their beds, and severely flagellated, to make
them willing to emigrate ! And legislative compulsion openly
advocated to accomplish this nefarious project ! Yes, the gentlemen say truly, ' few, very few will *voluntarily* consent to
emigrate '—' they never will give their consent '—and therefore they must be expelled by force ! It is true, the bill pro

posed by Mr Broadnax was rejected by a small majority ; but it serves to illustrate the spirit of the colonization leaders.

The editor of the Lynchburg Virginian, an advocate of the Society, uses the following language :

'But, if they will not consider for themselves, WE *must consider for them.* The safety of the people is the supreme law ; and to that law all minor considerations must bend. If the free negroes will not emigrate, *they must be contented to endure those privations which the public interest and safety call for.*—In the last Richmond Enquirer we notice an advertisement, setting forth, that "a petition will be presented to the next legislature of Virginia, from the county of Westmoreland, praying the passage of some law to *compel* the free negroes in this commonwealth to emigrate therefrom, under a penalty which will effectually promote this object." So, too, at a meeting of the citizens of Prince George county, in Maryland, it was resolved to " petition the next legislature to remove all the free negroes out of that State, and to prohibit all persons from manumitting slaves without making provision for their removal." '

I close this work with a specimen of the sophistry which is used to give *eclat* to the American Colonization Society.

In the month of June, 1830, I happened to peruse a number of the Southern Religious Telegraph, in which I found an essay, enforcing the duty of clergymen to take up collections in aid of the funds of the Colonization Society on the then approaching fourth of July. After an appropriate introductory paragraph, the writer proceeds in the following remarkable strain :

'But—we have a plea like a peace offering to man and to God. We answer poor blinded Africa in her complaint—that we have her children, and that they have served on our plantations. And we tell her, look at their returning ! We took them barbarous, though measurably free,—untaught—rude—without science—without the true religion—without philosophy—and strangers to the best civil governments. And now we return them to her bosom, *with the mechanical arts....with science....with philosophy.....*with civilization....with republican feelings....and above all, with the true knowledge of the true God, and the way of salvation through the Redeemer.'

' The mechanical arts ! '—with whom did they serve an apprenticeship ? ' With philosophy ! '—in what colleges were they taught ? It is strange that we should be so anxious to get rid of these scientific men of color—these philosophers—these republicans —these christians, and that we should shun their company as if they were afflicted with the hydrophobia, or carried a deadly pestilence in their train ! Certainly, they *must* have singular notions of the christian religion which tolerates—or, rather, which is so perverted as to tolerate—the oppression of God's rational creatures by its professors! They must feel a peculiar kind of brotherly love for those *good men* who banded together to remove them to Africa, because they were too proud to associate familiarly with men of a sable complexion ! But the writer proceeds :

'We tell her, look at the little colony on her shores. We tell her, look to the consequences that must flow to all her borders from religion, and science, and knowledge, and civilization, and republican government ! And then we ask her —*is not one ship load of emigrants returning with these multiplied blessings, worth more to her than a million of her barbarous sons ?*'

So ! every ship load of ignorant and helpless emigrants is to more than compensate Africa for every million of her children who have been kidnapped, buried in the ocean and on the land, tortured with savage cruelty, and held in perpetual servitude ! Truly, this is a compendious method of balancing accounts. In the sight of God, of Africa, and of the world, we are consequently blameless—and rather praiseworthy—for our past transgressions. It is such sophistry as is contained in the foregoing extract, that kindles my indignation into a blaze. I abhor cant —I abhor hypocrisy—and if some of the advocates of the Colonization Society do not deal largely in both, I am unable to comprehend the meaning of these terms.

Of the whole number of individuals constituting the officers of the Society, nearly three-fourths, I believe, *are the owners of slaves*, or interested in slave property ; not one of whom, to my knowledge, has emancipated any of his slaves to be sent to Liberia ! ! The President of the Society, (CHARLES CARROLL,) owns, I have understood, nearly *one thousand slaves !* And yet he is lauded, beyond measure, as a patriot, a philanthropist, and a christian ! The former President, (Judge BUSHROD WASHINGTON,) so far from breaking the fetters of his slaves, actually while holding his office offered a large reward for a runaway female slave, to any person who would secure her by putting her into any jail within the United States ! What a mockery it is for such persons to profess to deplore the existence of slavery, or to denounce the foreign slave trade ! for they neither cease from their own oppressive acts, nor act much more honestly than the slave dealers—the latter stealing those who are born on the coast of Africa, and the former those who are born in this country !

END OF PART II.

AMERICAN COLONIZATION SOCIETY,

AND THE

COLONY AT LIBERIA.

PUBLISHED BY THE MASSACHUSETTS COLONIZATION SOCIETY.

BOSTON:

PRINTED BY PERKINS & MARVIN.

....

1832.

MASSACHUSETTS COLONIZATION SOCIETY.

THE first Annual Meeting of this Society, was held in the Hall of the House of Representatives, on Thursday evening, the 26th of January, 1832. In the absence of the President, the chair was taken by the Hon. WILLIAM B. CALHOUN, Speaker of the House of Representatives. The meeting was opened with prayer by the Rev. Howard Malcom, one of the chaplains of the House. The report of the Managers was read by the Rev. E. S. Gannett, of Boston. The receipts of the Society, during the year, amounted to nearly $2,000. The meeting was addressed by William Ladd, Esq. of Minot, Maine, Thomas A. Greene, Esq. of New Bedford, George S. Bulfinch, and Rev. E. S. Gannett, of Boston.

The following officers were elected.

OFFICERS OF THE MASS. COLONIZATION SOCIETY, FOR 1832.

HON. SAMUEL LATHROP, PRESIDENT.

VICE PRESIDENTS.

Rt. Rev. ALEXANDER V. GRISWOLD,
Hon. HENRY A. S. DEARBORN,
Hon. WILLIAM B. CALHOUN,
Hon. ISAAC C. BATES,
Hon. ALEXANDER H. EVERETT,
Rev. SAMUEL OSGOOD,

THEODORE SEDGWICK, Esq.
Hon. BENJAMIN F. VARNUM,
Hon. JOHN A. PARKER,
Hon. STEPHEN C. PHILLIPS,
Hon. JAMES H. DUNCAN.

JEROME V. C. SMITH, M. D. Secretary, Boston.

ISAAC MANSFIELD, Esq. Treasurer, Boston.

BOARD OF MANAGERS.

Rev. EBENEZER BURGESS, Dedham.
JOSIAH ROBBINS, Esq. Plymouth.
SAM'L. T. ARMSTRONG, Esq. Boston.
Hon. JOHN W. LINCOLN, Worcester.
Rev. HOWARD MALCOM, Boston.
Rev. E. S. GANNETT, Boston.
ELIPHALET WILLIAMS, Esq. Northampton.
Dea. MOSES GRANT, Boston.
Rev. CHARLES TRAIN, Framingham.
CHARLES TAPPAN, Esq. Boston.
Hon. GEORGE HULL, Sandisfield.

Prof SAM'L. M. WORCESTER, Amherst Coll.
GEORGE A. TUFTS, Esq. Dudley.
Dr. JOHN S. BUTLER, Worcester.
THOMAS A. GREENE, Esq. New Bedford.
PATRICK BOIES, Esq. Granville.
IRA BARTON, Esq. Oxford.
BELA B. EDWARDS, Boston.
WM. B. REYNOLDS, Esq. Boston.
CHARLES STODDARD, Boston.
Rev. WILLIAM HAGUE, Boston.

The resolution which follows, was unanimously adopted.

Resolved, That the clergymen in this commonwealth, of all denominations, be requested to present the claims of the Society to their respective congregations, and take up collections for its funds, on the Fourth of July, or the Sabbath next preceding or succeeding that day.

AFRICAN REPOSITORY.

THIS work is published in Washington, monthly. Each number contains 32 octavo pages—Price, two dollars a year, payable in advance. Any person, who obtains five subscribers and remits $10, receives a copy gratis. Every clergyman, who takes up a collection for the Society, will receive a copy gratis.

STATEMENT OF FACTS.

Organization of the Society.

THE Society was organized at the city of Washington, in the winter of 1816. Previously to this period, nothing of importance had been done to colonize people of color.

Its object.

"The object to which its attention is to be exclusively directed, is to promote and execute a plan of colonizing (with their own consent) the free people of color residing in our country, in Africa, or such other place as Congress shall deem expedient."

Funds.

The income of the Society has been gradually increasing since its formation, though it never has received assistance from the treasury of the general government. The amount of donations from 1821 to to 1828, inclusive, was between $82,000 and $83,000. In 1829, $20,295 61. In 1830, $27,209 39. In 1831, more than $32,000.

Resolutions of State Legislatures.

Resolutions, approving the object of the Society have been passed in the Legislatures of the following States, viz. ;—New Hampshire, Vermont, Massachusetts, Connecticut, New Jersey, Pennsylvania, Maryland, Virginia, Georgia, Tennessee, Kentucky, Ohio, and Indiana. And most of them have recommended the Society to the patronage of the National Government.

Views of distinguished men.

A large number of men, of distinguished eminence, in various parts of the Union, have warmly espoused the cause of the Society. Among whom are Hon. Charles Carroll, Hon. William H. Crawford, Hon. Henry Clay, Jeremiah Day, D. D., Chief Justice Marshall, Hon. Richard Rush, Rt. Rev. Bishop White, Hon. Theodore Frelinghuysen, Hon. John Cotton Smith, Hon. Edward Everett, Hon. David L. Morrill, and Hon. Elijah Paine, of Vermont. Gen. Lafayette is a warm friend, and is one of its Vice Presidents.

Auxiliary Societies.

Auxiliary Societies have been organized in the following States, viz. : —Maine, New Hampshire, Massachusetts, Connecticut, Vermont, New

York, New Jersey, Pennsylvania, Maryland, Virginia, North Carolina, Alabama, Tennessee, Kentucky, Ohio, and Indiana. There are numerous other societies, of less extent.

Establishment and progress of the Colony.

Soon after the formation of the American Colonization Society, two agents, Mr. Burgess and Samuel J. Mills, were sent to Africa to make provision for the settlement of a colony. The island of Sherbro, situated about 100 miles south of Sierra Leone, was selected as the place. President Monroe, being then Chief Magistrate of the United States, was favorably disposed towards the project, and lent his influence to advance its interests. Two agents were sent by the national government to co-operate with the agents of the Society. In February, 1820, the first colonists, eighty-eight in number, sailed for Africa. The expedition was an unfortunate one. In March, 1821, twenty-eight embarked for the same place. It was now decided that Sherbro was unfavorable, from its situation, to the prosperity of the colony, and Montserado, situated about 200 miles farther south, was purchased. In August, 1822, Mr. Ashmun arrived at the colony with 35 emigrants. There had been, several times, some little altercation between the colonists and the natives, though nothing that had demanded much attention. Mr. Ashmun thought he could discover signs of a plot to destroy the new settlers. He therefore considered it wise to make provision against an assault. Scarcely had the colonists put themselves in a defensive position, when they were attacked by about 800 natives, who were easily repulsed. Two weeks after, they were again attacked by double the former number. The colonists succeeded in maintaining their position and the natives were entirely defeated. Probably nothing has given the natives so favorable an impression in regard to their new neighbors, as this occurrence. Since that time, the colonists have been but little disturbed.

In 1824, the settlement was named Liberia, and the town at the cape, Monrovia; the latter as an acknowledgement of benefits received from the President of the United States. In 1825, several agriculturists arrived, who expressed a strong desire to settle upon plantations, rather than in the town. For this purpose, a fertile tract of land was purchased, about twenty miles in length and from three to six in breadth, lying on St. Paul's River. Several additions have since been made. Emigrants have from time to time been added to the colony, so that notwithstanding the numerous obstacles against which the Society has been obliged to contend, 2,000 have, by their own consent, been transported to Liberia.

Fertility of the Soil.

The country called Liberia, extends along the coast one hundred and fifty miles, and reaches twenty or thirty miles into the interior. It is watered by several rivers, some of which are of considerable size. The soil is *extremely fertile*, and abounds in all the productions of tropical climates.* Its hills and plains are covered with perpetual verdure. It would be difficult to find in any country, a region more pro-

---

* See an excellent article respecting Liberia in the Revue Encyclopedique, of Paris.

ductive, a soil more fertile. The natives, with very few of the implements of husbandry, without skill, and with but little labor, raise more
grain and vegetables than they can consume, and often more than they
can sell.

The land on the rivers is of the very best quality, being a rich, light
alluvion, equal, in every respect, to the best lands on the southern
rivers of the United States.

Captain Woodside, after his return from Africa, thus speaks of Caldwell, situated seven miles north of the outlet of Montserado; "The
beauty of its situation, *the fertility of its soil*, and the air of comfort
and happiness which reigns throughout, will remain, I hope, an everlasting evidence of the unceasing exertions of our departed friend,
Ashmun."

Agriculture of the Colony.

The colonists have not, as yet, paid much attention to agriculture.
Many of the emigrants cannot wait for the slow returns of agricultural
industry, but prefer mercantile speculations. The advantages, however, of the older merchants in trade, will diminish the chances of success to the new-comers, and thus they will be led to turn their attention
to agriculture. The settlement of Caldwell is more of an agricultural
establishment than the other towns, and is in a very flourishing condition. Its farmers hold agricultural meetings to discuss the best methods of tilling.

The colonists have all the domestic animals of this country, and raise,
in great abundance, many varieties of fruits and vegetables. They are
turning their attention to the cultivation of coffee. This article, it is
believed, will prove a great source of wealth to the colony. The labor
and expense of cultivation is small; they have only to clear away the
forest trees, and the plantations are ready to their hands. There are
two descriptions of this plant indigenous; one is a shrub, the same,
probably, as that of Mocha, but yielding a superior flavor. The other
is much larger, and often attains the height of forty feet.

Commercial advantages.

By the position of the colony great commercial advantages are enjoyed.
It is the central point in a long extent of sea-coast, and relations of
trade may be established between it and the interior. Millsburg, situated twenty-five miles north east of Monrovia, having several navigable
streams, may easily be made the medium of commerce between the
interior towns and the coast. The harbor of Monrovia is formed by the
mouth of the river Montserado, and is convenient for vessels of moderate size.

The commerce of the colony is increasing rapidly. The amount for
1831, greatly exceeded that of any previous year. During this year,
forty-six vessels entered the port of Monrovia, twenty-one of which were
from America. The articles of export are rice, palm oil, ivory, gold,
shells, dye-wood, &c. The amount of exports the last year was
$88,911. Some of the colonists own small vessels, which are employed
in the carrying trade between cape Montserado, and the factories
along the shore, under the direction of the government. Some individuals in the colony have already acquired property to the amount of

several thousand dollars. Francis Devany, an emancipated slave, who went out to the colony eight years ago, testified before a committee of Congress, in 1830, that in seven years he had accumulated property to the amount of $20,000.

Among the numerous arrivals at Monrovia, mentioned in the Liberia Herald for 1831, is a vessel from *France, consigned to Devany.* The trade with the nations of the interior is, of all others, the most profitable. The large profits, which it yields, may be seen by reference to the travels of Laing, Clapperton, and Bowditch. In the article of salt, for instance, which may be made in great abundance by evaporation all along the coast, the colonists enjoy a very profitable trade. Bartering in this article, they receive in exchange gold dust, ivory, dye-wood, &c. at the rate of two dollars per quart.

The nett profits on the two articles, wood and ivory, which passed through the hands of the colonists in the year 1826, was more than $30,000.

Climate.

The charge of unhealthiness, as it respects men of color, made against the climate of Liberia, cannot be sustained by facts. Reason and experience are both opposed to it. Africa is the birth place of the black man, and to which his constitution is suited. It is *physically* his home. There he is lord of the soil, and the white man becomes the "lusus naturæ."

The result of a most careful investigation, is, *that for people of color, the climate is decidedly salubrious.* The existence now of two thousand persons in the colony, is conclusive evidence on this point. To them the climate is as healthy as the southern portions of the United States. The western coast of Africa is not desolated by the plague as Turkey, nor by malaria as the Antilles.

"The natives on that part of the coast are remarkably healthy. *So are the acclimated emigrants.* Many of the deaths which have occurred in the colony are to be attributed, not so much to the influence of climate, as to irregularity in regard to diet and exposure, and the want of proper medical aid." Such were the causes for the great mortality among those who went out in the Carolina. But effective measures were taken to prevent the like occurrence; and of the eighty-five persons who went out soon afterwards, only two small children died. When once acclimated, Africa proves a more congenial climate to the man of color than any portion of the United States. There he enjoys a greater immunity from disease.

It was to be expected, that during the early years of the colony, many deaths would occur for want of suitable houses; on account of the fatigue and danger to which they were necessarily exposed; and more particularly in consequence of their irregular modes of life, which were at that time unavoidable. Those days, however, are past.

But the mortality at Liberia is small, when compared with the loss of life in the early settlement of this country. The colony which settled at Jamestown was, at one time, reduced from *five hundred,* to *sixty persons,* by disease, famine, and war. In twelve years, after £80,000 of the public stock had been expended, and the Virginia

Company were left £5,000 in debt, only six hundred souls remained in the colony. Out of the fifteen hundred persons, who came with John Winthrop to Boston in 1630, *two hundred died in six months.* In 1634, after £150,000 had been expended, and more than nine thousand persons had been sent out from England to the colony, only eighteen hundred remained.

No mortality like this can be shown in the history of Liberia. The blacks from the slave-holding States have nothing to fear in removing to Africa. Many who have gone out from the Carolinas and Georgia, have become acclimated without the slightest attack of fever.

To the white man the climate seems unhealthy. So is almost every tropical region. But what, if it be so? Thousands of lives are sacrificed at New Orleans, Havana, and Calcutta every year by men in pursuit of *gain;* and shall the philanthropist fear to encounter the inclemencies of a tropical climate in order to enlighten and save an ignorant, degraded brother of the human family? So thought not Mills and Ashmun.

Government.

A system of government, in which the colonists take part, as far as prudence will admit, has been established, and is now in full and successful operation. The supreme government is yet in the hands of the society. The colonial agent is recognized as governor. Great care is taken by the agent to habituate the colonists to republican forms, and to the real spirit of liberty. The election of their magistrates takes place annually. A court of justice has been established, composed of the agent, and two judges chosen from among the colonists. This court exercises jurisdiction over the whole colony. It assembles monthly at Monrovia. The crimes usually brought before it, are thefts committed most commonly by the natives admitted within the colonial jurisdiction. No *crime of a capital nature has as yet been committed in the colony.* The trials are by jury, and are decided with all possible formality. The political and civil legislation of Liberia is embraced in three documents.

1. The constitution. This grants them rights and privileges, as in the United States. The fifth article of which forbids all slavery in the colony. The sixth declares the common law of the United States to be that of the colony.

2. The forms of civil government. By the thirteenth article of which, censors are appointed to watch over the public morals, to report the idle and the vagabond, and to bring to legal investigation all that may tend to disturb the peace, or injure the prosperity of the colony.

3. A code of procedures and punishments. This has been extracted principally from American digests. Experience has fully shown, that these laws are sufficient to preserve the public order, and secure the prosperity of the colony.

Of this government, the colonists in an address to their brethren in America thus speak: "Our laws are altogether our own : they grow out of our circumstances, are formed for our exclusive benefit, and are administered either by officers of our own appointment, or by such as possess our confidence. We have all that is meant by liberty of conscience; the time and mode of worshipping God, as prescribed in his word, and dictated by our conscience, we are not only free to follow, but are protected in following. 'In Monrovia, you behold,' says the editor of the Liberia Herald, 'colored men exercising all the duties of officers; many fulfilling their important trusts with much dignity. We have a republic in miniature.' "

Literary advantages.

The subject of education has ever been one of primary importance with the Colonization Society, and its interests have been promoted as far as circumstances would permit. In 1827, there were six schools in the colony. The education of children has been considerably retarded for want of suitable teachers—a difficulty which has, in part, been removed. In 1830, the Board of Managers determined to establish permanent schools in the towns of Monrovia, Caldwell, and Millsburg. They adopted a thorough system of instruction, which is now in successful operation. There are also two female schools, one of which was established by the liberality of a lady of Philadelphia, who sent out the necessary books and a teacher. A law was passed the last year in the colony, taxing the real estate of the colonists one half per cent.; which tax, together with the proceeds of the sales of the public lands, and duties on spirituous liquors, is to be devoted to the interests of education.

A public library has been established at Monrovia, and a journal (the Liberia Herald) is published by Mr. Russwurm, one of the colonists, and a graduate of Bowdoin college. It has 800 subscribers. The commander of the United States' ship Java, thus speaks on the subject of education : "I was pleased to observe that the colonists were impressed with the vast importance of a proper education, not only of their own children, but of the children of the natives ; and that to this they looked confidently, as the means of accomplishing their high object, the civilization of their benighted brothers of Africa."

Religious state of the Colony.

Much is done to promote the cause of religion in the colony. There are three churches, a Methodist, Baptist, and Presbyterian. Divine service is regularly attended in them on the Sabbath, and on Tuesday and Thursday evenings. In these societies Sabbath schools have been established, to which all their most promising young men have attached themselves, either as teachers or scholars. Bibles and tracts have been sent to the colony for a Sabbath school library. A gentleman in Baltimore, the last year, gave $200 for this specific object. Several young men of color in the United States are preparing to go to Liberia as ministers of the gospel.

Captain Abels, who visited the colony in 1831, and who spent 13 days at Monrovia, says : " My expectations were more than realized. I saw no intemperance, nor did I hear a profane word uttered by any one. Being a minister of the gospel, I preached both in the Methodist and Baptist churches, to full and attentive congregations of from four to five hundred persons each. I know of no place where the Sabbath seems to me more respected than in Monrovia." The colonists are remarkable for their morality and religious feeling. One who had resided seven years in the colony, said, that during all that time he had seen but one fight, and that was provoked by a person from Sierra Leone. To prevent intemperance, they require $300 for a license to sell ardent spirits. Many of the settlers are engaged in acquiring religious instruction.

The little band at Liberia, who are spreading over the wilderness around them an aspect of beauty, are in every respect a missionary station. Many of the neighboring tribes have already put themselves under the protection of the colony, and are anxiously desirous to receive from them religious instruction. "We have here," says the colonial agent, "among our re-captured Africans many who, on their arrival here, were scarcely a remove from the native tribes around us, in point of civilization, but who are at present as pious and devoted servants of Christ as you will find in any community. Their walk and conversation afford an example worthy of imitation. They have a house for public worship, and Sabbath schools, which are well attended. Their church is regularly supplied every Sabbath by some one of our clergy. As to the morals of the colonists, I consider them much better than those of the people in the United States; that is, you may take an equal number of inhabitants from any section of the Union, and you will find more drunkards, more profane swearers and Sabbath breakers, than in Liberia. Indeed, I know of no place where things are conducted more quietly and orderly. The Sabbath is more strictly observed than I ever saw it in any part of the United States." The Rev. Mr. Skinner (the Baptist missionary, who went out to the colony a few years since, but who, like other devoted servants of Christ in the same field, has fallen) said, "I was surprised to find every thing conducted in so orderly a manner, and to see the Sabbath so strictly observed. Thus we see that light is breaking in upon benighted Africa. May it be like the morning light, which shineth brighter and brighter until the perfect day!"

Means of Defence.

The colonists have but little to fear from the native tribes around them. These they have completely intimidated, so that they have no fears of an incursion from any or all of them. The exposure of the colony is on the sea-shore. Their means of defence here are, a fortification, and several small vessels, six volunteer companies of 500 men, which compose the national militia, twenty field pieces, and 1,000 muskets. They have reason to fear an attack from the pirates, those enemies of human happiness, who frequent the western coast of Africa to kidnap the blacks. These freebooters have sworn eternal enmity against the colony. And it is feared, should two or three such vessels, well armed, attack Monrovia, they might do very great injury, notwithstanding all the means of defence which the colony could bring against them.

Progress of the Society and Colony during 1831.

In no one year has the society gained such important accessions of strength as during the past.. The insurrectionary movements among the slaves at the south, have opened the eyes of many on this subject. Men of influence and distinction have laid aside their opposition, and

2

warmly espoused the cause of the Colonization Society. The State of Maryland has set a most benevolent example to her sister States, in granting from her State treasury $200,000 to enable the free blacks of that State to remove to Africa. It is truly a noble, patriotic act!

Up to October, 1831, the society had fitted out nineteen expeditions, and landed upon the shores of Africa 1,831 persons, including re-captured Africans, to all of whom a farm or town lot had been granted. Four towns have been established—New Georgia, Millsburg, Caldwell, and Monrovia, which are all in a flourishing condition. The colonists have now good and substantial houses, some of them handsome and spacious. In view of the efforts of the society, and the flourishing state of the colony, the venerable Thomas Clarkson, not long since, remarked to the society's agent in England, "that for himself he was free to confess, that, of all things which had been going on in our favor since 1787, when the abolition of the slave trade was first seriously proposed, that which was going on in America was the most important." To the same individual, Wilberforce, no less benevolent, said, "you have gladdened my heart by convincing me, that sanguine as had been my hopes of the objects to be accomplished by your institution, all my anticipations have been scanty and cold compared with the reality."

The last accounts from the colony represent the aspect of things there, the health, harmony, order, industry, and general prosperity of the settlers, in a light peculiarly pleasing to every friend of the injured African. During the past year, several distinguished gentlemen have visited Liberia. Captain Kennedy thus speaks of the colony, "With impressions unfavorable to the scheme of the Colonization Society, I commenced my inquiries. I sought out the most shrewd and intelligent of the colonists, and by long and wary conversations, endeavored to elicit from them any dissatisfaction with their situation (if such existed), or any latent desire to return to America. Neither of these did I observe. But, on the contrary, I could perceive that they considered that they had *started into a new existence*—that disencumbered of the mortifying relations in which they formerly stood in society, they felt themselves proud in their attitude.

"Many of the settlers appear to be rapidly acquiring property; and I have no doubt they are doing better for themselves and for their children, in Liberia, than they could do in any other part of the world."

The colony now consists of 2,000 persons. It is provided with two able physicians and a full supply of medicine. A hospital has been erected during the past year, intended particularly for sick emigrants. The progress of improvement is rapid. The elements of wealth and greatness, namely, commerce, agriculture, and a Christian population, are fully enjoyed.

"Nothing strikes me," says Dr. Mechlin, "as more remarkable, than the great superiority in intelligence, manners, conversation, dress, and general appearance in every respect, of the people over their brethren in America. The prospects of the colony were never brighter than at present. (1831.) The improvements in agriculture, commerce, buildings, &c. during my short visit to the United States, have been astonishingly great. In Monrovia, upwards of twenty-five substantial stone and frame dwelling-houses have been erected within the short space of five months. Indeed, the spirit of improvement has gone abroad in the colony, and the people seem awake to the importance of more fully developing the resources of the country. Our influence over the native tribes in our vicinity is rapidly increasing. Several tribes at their urgent request have been admitted under our protection. This I find the most effectual way of civilizing them; associating with the colonists, they insensibly adopt our manners, and thus, from a state of paganism, they become enlightened Christians."

How forcibly do these facts teach us that there is nothing in the physical, or moral nature of the African, which condemns him to a state of ignorance and degradation. Extraneous causes press him to the earth. Light and liberty can, and do, under fair circumstances, raise him to the rank of a virtuous and intelligent being.

Extension of Civilization and Christianity into the Interior.

There is reason to believe, that nearly all the tribes in the neighborhood of the colony are disposed to place themselves under its protection. The natives esteem it no small privilege to be permitted to call themselves *Americans*. They frequently prefer to have their disputes settled by the civil courts of Monrovia, rather than by their own usages. Eight or ten of the chiefs of the towns on the north eastern branch of the Montserado river, lately united in a request that they might be received and treated as subjects of the colony, and that settlements might be made in their territory. It is the intention of the Board to comply with such requests wherever practicable. Thus the oppressed natives of Africa will find in the colony of Liberia, a power friendly and Christian, ready at all times to be exerted in defence of the helpless. Measures have been taken for exploring the interior, and also for ascertaining the comparative advantages of different points on the coast, for the founding of new settlements. The territory chosen as most favorable, and on which the Managers have directed that a settlement shall be forthwith commenced, is that of Grand Bassa, distant about 80 miles from Monrovia, intersected by the river St. Johns, of easy and safe access to vessels of 80 to 100 tons, fertile, salubrious, and abounding in camwood, rice, and cattle. The chiefs and head-men have recently sent a pressing invitation to the colonial agent to visit them, and to establish a settlement among them. The whole course of the Junk river has been examined, (this river is more than 50 miles long,) and it is found to afford many situations well suited for agriculturists. The whole region may soon be covered with cotton and coffee plantations. "The civilization of the interior of Africa," in the language of Mr. Edward Everett, "is a topic which has not received its share of consideration. Of this mighty continent, four times as large as Europe, one third part at least is within the direct reach of influences, from the west of Europe and America,—influences, which, for 300 years, have been employed through the agency of the slave-trade, to depress and barbarize it; to chain it down to the lowest point of social degradation. I trust these influences are now to be employed in repairing the wrongs, in healing the wounds, in gradually improving the condition of Africa. I trust that a great re-action is at hand. Can it be believed that this mighty region, most of it overflowing with tropical abundance, was created and destined for eternal barbarity?"

History of Slavery.

It is generally agreed that as early as 1442, the Portuguese accepted some negroes from the Moors, as a ransom for Moorish captives. These were reduced to servitude, and their value rose so rapidly that in a few years upwards of thirty ships were fitted out for importing negroes. In 1502, the Spaniards began to employ African slaves in the mines of Hispaniola, the island now called St. Domingo, or Hayti; and in 1517, Charles V. of Spain, at the solicitation of a Roman Cardinal, (Las Casas,) granted his patent for the importation of *four thousand* slaves *annually* into Cuba, Jamaica, Hispaniola and Porto Rico. The first enslaved Africans were introduced into this country by the Dutch in 1620, and were landed and disposed of, (20 in number,) at Jamestown, the first settlement in Virginia. They were subsequently introduced in great numbers by the English, but not without the *serious remonstrance* of the colonists. They even proceeded so far as to present, in 1772, to George III. a petition, praying that the introduction of slaves might be discontinued. They speak in strong and decisive language : " We are encouraged to look up to the throne, and implore your majesty's paternal assistance in averting a calamity of a most alarming nature. The importation of slaves into the colonies from the coast of Africa, *hath long been considered as a trade of great inhumanity*, and under its present encouragement, we have too much reason to fear, will endanger the existence of your majesty's American dominions." Mr. Burke, in a speech on American conciliation, says, " her refusal to deal any longer in the inhuman traffic of human slaves, was one of the causes of her quarrel with Great Britain." And it is much for the credit of the framers of our Declaration of Independence, that among other grievances set forth in that memorable manifesto, it is declared that the king had violated our rights by " prompting our negroes to rise in arms against us—those very negroes, whom, by an inhuman use of his negative, he has *refused us permission* to exclude by law." This generous feeling at length died away, and the ships of the north and south have vied together in the odious practice of importing slaves into the United States.

Abolition of the Slave Trade.

As early as 1792, Sweden passed laws prohibiting the importation of slaves into her borders after 1803. In 1807, the governments of Great Britain and the United States passed similar enactments, to take effect after March, 1808. But these were nearly a *dead letter*, until it was further declared, afterwards, that the Slave Trade is *piracy*, and that those proved to be engaged in it shall *suffer death*.

Slave Trade still carried on extensively and with great cruelty.

In defiance of all laws enacted, it is estimated that not less than 50,000 Africans were, during the last year, (1831,) carried into foreign slavery. During the months of February and March of the same year, 2,000 were landed on the island of Cuba. Two English vessels, the Fair Rosamond and Black Joke, tenders of the Dryad frigate, cruising off the coast of Africa, captured *three* slave ships which had originally *eighteen hundred slaves on board*. The Fair Rosamond first captured a vessel with 106 Africans, and shortly after saw the Black Joke in chase of two others: she joined the pursuit, but the vessels succeeding in getting into the Bonny river where they landed 600 slaves before the *pursuers* could take possession of them. They found on board only 200 Africans, but understood that the crew had thrown overboard 180, chained together, and four only out of the whole, were picked up and delivered from a watery grave.

"The slaves, male and female, are crowded into the *middle* passage," says Sir George Collier, who lately commanded a squadron on the coast of Africa, "so as not to give the power to move, and are linked one to another by the legs or neck, never to be unfettered while the voyage lasts, or till their iron shall have fretted the flesh almost to the bone; forced under a deck, as I have seen them, not *thirty inches in height*, breathing an atmosphere the most *putrid*, with little food and less water. In this *loathsome prison*, *thousands* die in the *ravings* of *despair*, and many when let out to breath the *balmy air*, rather than return to their dungeons, plunge themselves into the ocean to sleep among its pearls and corals."

African Colonization the best check on the Slave Trade.

The country now occupied by our colony on the coast of Africa, has been, until recently, a seat of this cursed traffic. At the present, no slave ships visit that coast, and the adjacent chiefs have given up the trade, some voluntarily, and others by compulsion. The colony at Sierra Leone has also put an end to the trade in that region, and cleared the coast for many miles of slave vessels. It is in a great measure owing to the co-operation of these colonies with our own government, and that of Great Britain, that the African slave trade has been so effectually checked. With all the former vigilance of the latter powers, without the *united efforts* of the former, little would have been accomplished, comparatively, in detecting the *robbers*, not only of *property*, but of *men*, women and helpless children.

Colored population in the United States.

According to the census of 1830, there were in

	Free blacks.	Slaves.		Free blacks.	Slaves.
Maine	1,207		Georgia	2,483	217,470
New Hampshire	623		Alabama	1,541	117,294
Vermont	885		Mississippi	529	65,659
Massachusetts	7,006		Louisiana	16,753	109,631
Connecticut	8,004	23	Tennessee	4,513	142,382
Rhode Island	3,565	14	Kentucky	4,816	165,350
New York	45,080	46	Ohio	9,586	
New Jersey	18,307	2,246	Indiana	3,565	
Pennsylvania	37,990	386	Missouri	546	24,990
Delaware	15,829	3,305	Arkansas	138	4,578
Maryland	52,942	102,878	Michigan	253	27
Virginia	47,102	469,724	Floridas	840	15,500
North Carolina	19,575	246,462	Dist. of Columbia	6,163	6,060
South Carolina	7,915	315,665			

	Free.	Slaves.
The whole number of colored people in 1830 were	319,476	2,010,572
The census of 1820 was	223,540	1,538,064
Making an increase in 10 years of	95,936	472,508

The increase of the colored population during the last year (1831) was nearly 52,000.

Condition of the free colored people in the United States.

We may form some opinion of the condition of the free colored people in this country, from the reports of our state prisons. In Liberia, since the establishment of the colony, there has scarcely been a crime committed by one of the colonists, which in this land would have subjected him to confinement in the penitentiary; while in this country during the same period our prisons have been full of these unfortunate people. In 1826, the free colored people in Massachusetts comprised one seventy-fourth part of the entire population, and yet one-sixth part of the convicts. In Connecticut they were one thirty-fourth of the population, and yet furnished one-third of the convicts. In Vermont there were but 918, of whom 24 were in the penitentiary. In New York they composed one thirty-fifth of the entire population, and yet had one-fourth of all the convicts. In Pennsylvania they were as in Connecticut, but more than one-third of the convicts were from their ranks. In the States of Massachusetts, Connecticut and New York, the entire colored population in 1823 was 54,000, and for the support of the convicts from this small population, these States, in ten years ending with 1823, have expended *eighty-two thousand nine hundred and thirty-four dollars.* In 1827, the returns from several prisons showed that while the number of white convicts was stationary, in some instances *decreasing,* that of the colored was *increasing.*

Throughout the non-slave-holding States, as a body, they are idle, ignorant and vicious. For this reason, Ohio, not long since, passed a law, compelling them to leave her territory, or to give security for their good behavior, which not one in fifty could do. These outcasts from human sympathy sought refuge in Canada, while that country in turn has petitioned Parliament to forbid their entering the British possessions.

In the non-slave-holding States, it is estimated that they do not compose more than *one-fortieth* of the entire population, and yet, it is said that about *one-sixth* of all their paupers and convicts are colored. The reason of all this is obvious. In these States there are from one to two hundred thousand persons, who are *nominally* free, but who have no interests in common with the community—at liberty to act, and yet have no motive for exertion. Instances of emancipation have not essentially benefitted the African, and probably never will, while he remains among us. In this country, public opinion does, and will, consign him to an inferiority, above which he can never rise.

Emancipation can never make the African, while he remains in this country, a *real free man.* Degradation must and will press him to the earth; no cheering, stimulating influence will he here feel, in any of the walks of life. If he go to Liberia, the scene will be changed: there he may rise—there he may and will, if he act correctly, feel the ennobling influence of public opinion urging him onward to high and manly exertion.

Slavery a great national evil.

Those who are conversant with the debates in the Virginia legislature on this subject the last winter, need no proof that slavery has been a curse, at least to the States tolerating it. In them the spirit of industry and enterprize has been checked. Many of the young and active citizens have sought a more happy and congenial home in the "distant west." The enterprising men of New England, and of other countries, aware of the discredit cast upon white labor in slave States, have mingled with the tide which so rapidly flows into, and nourishes non-slaveholding States. Facts speak louder than words. The white population

Of Pennsylvania, in 1820, was 1,018,000, in 1830, 1,309,296, increase in 10 years, 290,322
Of Virginia, in 1820, was 602,000, in 1830, 694,439, increase in 10 years, 92,138

making the ratio of increase *per cent.* in Pennsylvania to the same in Virginia, nearly as 9 to 5. To what, if not to slavery, shall we attribute this disproportionate increase of the white population in these two States? Something similar might be said of other slave States. These appalling facts have not escaped the vigilance of at least some of the guardians and legislators of our slave States. These and their kindred topics called forth, in the last Virginia legislature, efforts and feelings, which we believe will continue until the evil is wholly eradicated. The community in that State are awake on this momentous question. Among the memorials presented to the Legislature, we find one from the ladies of Fluvanna, which speaks in terms like these ; "We cannot conceal from ourselves that an evil is among us, which threatens to outgrow the growth, and eclipse the brightness of our national blessings. A shadow deepens over the land, and casts its thickest gloom upon the sacred shrine of our domestic bliss, darkening over us as time advances. We reflect with gratitude that no error in the framers of our constitution, entailed this evil upon us. We drew that taint from the bosom that fostered us, which is gradually mingling with the vital principles of our national existence. It can no longer remain dormant and inert in the social system, but calls loudly for redress from the sages of our land. To their honor be it said, these sentiments will find a response in the breasts of thousands of Virginia's fair daughters." The same may be said of her sons, who so recently boldly discussed and defended the rights of suffering humanity. In the language of one of the speakers ; "The spell has been broken, and the scales have fallen from our eyes. These open doors, those crowded galleries, and this attentive audience, prove to me that I am at liberty to speak any and every opinion which I entertain on this subject. For two hundred years the thoughts, words and actions of Virginians have been suppressed, and a solemn silence has closed the mouth and stifled investigation on this subject. The question of slavery is one which seems in all countries, and in all ages in which it has been tolerated, either directly or indirectly to have called to its aid a mystic sort of right, a superstitious veneration, that has deterred even the most intrepid mind from an investigation into the rights, and an exposure of the wrongs, on which it has been sustained."

Another speaker remarks ; "Has slavery interfered with our means of enjoying life, liberty, property, happiness and safety ? Look at Southampton. The answer is written in letters of blood, on the soil of that unhappy county." This is strong language, and especially in the ears of those who were acquainted with the insurrection alluded to. In that cool-blooded butchery, fifty-five whites fell victims to the incensed negroes. The ring-leader, before his execution, related the circumstances of an assault upon a family composed of a widow, a son, and several daughters. The rest of the party reached the house, entered it, and commenced the work of death before he arrived. As he approached, a lovely female rushed out of the house and took shelter under the covering of a cellar, but perceiving she was detected, fled from her retreat, pursued by the negro, who, by a few strokes with a broken sword across the head and neck, prostrated her at his feet, and then picked up a fence-rail, and despatched his victim.

These are a few of the calamities, attendant upon slavery, in our country. At the present time, the peaceful citizen, when he lays his head upon his pillow at night, places his pistols near his bed, ready to take alarm at the first idle noise ; and mothers, at the thought of Southampton, trembling for their own safety, press more closely to their bosoms, their helpless infants. Is it then surprising that emigrants should stand aloof from slave States, and that many of their own sons, foreseeing the gathering tempest, should flee from it ? In the language of one of the speakers, above alluded to, "If the slave population increase as it has for some years past, in the year 1880, less than fifty years hence, there will be in the seven States, Virginia, North Carolina, South Carolina, Georgia, Alabama, Louisiana, and Mississippi, more than *five millions* of slaves, an amount too appalling for a statesman not to apprehend some danger. I acknowledge I tremble for the fate of my country, at some future day, unless we do something." "What" says another, "will be the result, when every State, which has heretofore afforded the immense drain to your black population, amounting to 85,000 annually, shall have closed her market ; when every State south of us shall stand sword in hand, to guard their country against the importation of our slaves into their borders? When the great southwestern world refuses, [as it since then has,] to permit the sale of our slaves there ? When this whole redundant population shall be thrown back upon our State, I ask you what will be our fate ? Those mountains, amid which our security has been felt, will no longer be secure ; our tall forests will fall before the stroke of the slave ; our rich soil will be tilled by the hands of slaves, and our free and happy country, will become the home of the slave." Who that knows any thing of slavery in this and in other countries, does not have similar forebodings, and if so, does not feel it to be a national evil? The genius of our government is such, that the peace and prosperity of the whole is invested in a part. Our political interests are embarked together, and together must stand or fall. Like the human frame in its connection, where the decay of one limb, unless restored, endangers all, so the different States are bound together by indissoluble ties. It is in this symmetry and union, we behold so much to excite surprise and astonishment. In this lies the strength, prosperity, and perpetuity of our national glory. Who does not feel that slavery has already interrupted the peace and harmony of this union, and will continue to be a subject of contention, while a vestige remains? If then it be a national, as well as a moral disease, and if the ships of the north—of New England, (as we have seen,) have aided in producing it, why not unite, one and all, in applying the remedy ?

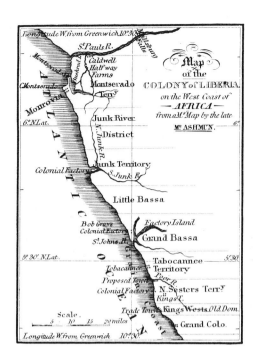

Map of the COLONY of LIBERIA, on the West Coast of AFRICA from a M⁵ Map by the late M⁵ ASHMUN.

Longitude W. from Greenwich 10°30'

St Pauls R.
Caldwell
Half way Farms
Montserado
Montserado Terr⁵
C. Montserado
Monrovia
6° N. Lat.   6°
Junk River
District
Junk Territory
Colonial Factory
S. Junk R.
Little Bassa
Bob Grays Colonial Factory
Factory Island
St Johns R.
Grand Bassa
5° 30' N. Lat.   5.30
Tabocannee Territory
Tobacannee
Proposed Town
Colonial Factory
Poor R.
N. Sesters Terr⁵
Kings T.
Trade Town Kings Wests Old. Dom.
Grand Colo.
Scale.
5   10   15   20 miles
Longitude W. from Greenwich 10°30'

ATLANTIC OCEAN

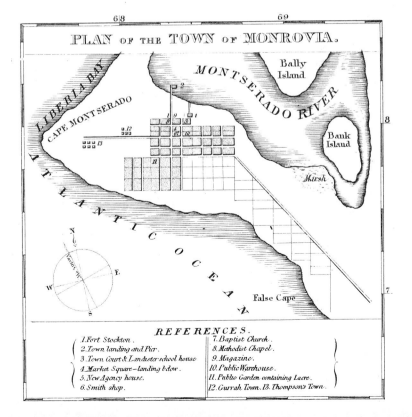

PLAN OF THE TOWN OF MONROVIA.

68   69

LIBERIA BAY
CAPE MONTSERADO
BALLY Island
MONTSERADO RIVER
Bank Island
Marsh
ATLANTIC OCEAN
False Cape

REFERENCES.

1. Fort Stockton.
2. Town landing and Pier.
3. Town Court & Lancaster school house
4. Market Square – landing below.
5. New Agency house.
6. Smith shop.
7. Baptist Church.
8. Methodist Chapel.
9. Magazine.
10. Public Warehouse.
11. Public Garden containing Lucre.
12. Gurrah Town. 13. Thompson's Town.

LETTERS

ON THE

COLONIZATION SOCIETY;

WITH A VIEW OF

ITS PROBABLE RESULTS,

UNDER THE FOLLOWING HEADS:

The Origin of the Society; *Increase of the Coloured Population*;
Manumission of Slaves in this country;

DECLARATIONS OF LEGISLATURES, AND OTHER ASSEMBLED BODIES, IN FAVOUR OF THE SOCIETY;

Situation of the Colonists at Monrovia and other towns; Moral and Religious Character of the Settlers; Soil, Climate, Productions, and Commerce of Liberia;

Advantages to the free coloured Population, by emigration to Liberia; Disadvantages of slavery to the white population; Character of the Natives of Africa, before the irruptions of the Barbarians; Effects of Colonization on the Slave Trade, with a slight sketch of that nefarious and accursed traffic.

ADDRESSED TO THE HON. C. F. MERCER, M. H. R. U. S.

BY M. CAREY.

SECOND EDITION, ENLARGED AND IMPROVED.

" Nearly **2,000** persons have kindled a beacon fire at Monrovia, to cast a broad blaze of light into the dark recesses of that benighted land ; and though much pains have been taken to overrate the cost, and undervalue the results, yet the annals of colonization may be triumphantly challenged for a parallel.

" Five years of preliminary operations were requisite for surveying the coast—propitiating the natives—and selecting the most eligible site. Numerous agents were subsequently employed—ships chartered—the coast cleared—schools, factories, hospitals, churches, government buildings and dwellings erected—and the many expenses requisite here were defrayed ;—and yet, for every fifty dollars expended by the society from its commencement, we have not only a settler to show, but an ample and fertile territory in reserve, where our future emigrants may ' sit down under their own vines and fig trees, with none to make them afraid.' During the last year, an amount, nearly equal to the united expenditures, has been exported by the colonists. *From Philadelphia alone, eleven vessels have sailed;* three of them chartered through the efforts of the Pennsylvania Society, and bearing to the land of their fathers a large number of slaves, manumitted by the benevolence of their late owners."—*Cresson.*

Philadelphia, April 26, 1832.

YOUNG, PRINTER.

" We may boldly challenge the annals of human nature for the record of any human plan, for the melioration of the condition or advancement of the happiness of our race, which promised more unmixed good, or more comprehensive benefi- cence than that of African colonization, if carried into full execution. Its benevo- lent purpose is not limited by the confines of one continent, nor to the prosperity of a solitary race ; but embraces two of the largest quarters of the earth, and the peace and the happiness of both of the descriptions of their present inhabitants, with the countless millions of their posterity who are to succeed. It appeals for aid and support to the friends of liberty, here and elsewhere. The colonists, reared in the bosom of this republic, with a perfect knowledge of all the blessings which freedom imparts, altho' they have not always been able themselves to share them, will carry a recollection of it to Africa, plant it there, and spread it over her boundless terri- tory. And may we not indulge the hope, that, in a period of time not surpassing in duration, that of our own colonial and national existence, we shall behold a con- federation of republican states, on the western shores of Africa, like our own, with their congress and annual legislatures, thundering forth in behalf of the rights of man, and making tyrants tremble on their thrones?"—*Mr. Clay.*

" It will enable them to become a free, independent, civilized and christian nation in the land of their forefathers. Elevated in character and in full enjoyment of the rights of man, they will not only assume a station in the great human family, which it is impossible for them to attain in this country ; but their example and influence will gradually extend over those numerous tribes, which, through all time have remained in a state of barbarism and degradation, and cruelly subjected to slavery by surrounding and distant nations."—*Dearborn.*

" They point to Africa, sitting beneath her own palm trees, "clothed in sack- cloth, and weeping for her children, and refusing to be comforted," because they have been murdered on her desolated shores, and buried beneath the billows of the ocean, and carried into hopeless and interminable slavery. Wretched Africa ! she has indeed fallen among thieves, who have robbed and wounded her, and she is now bleeding from a thousand wounds—*who will act to her the part of a good Samaritan?* Who will " bind up her wounds, and pour into them *wine and oil*," and protect her from her enemies, and chase away those human vultures, that are perpetually ho- vering on her coasts, and feeding on the flesh and blood of her children? Who will light for her the lamp of science, and publish the glad tidings of salvation to her sons and daughters? and raise her from that state of moral degradation, into which she has sunk in the lapse of ages ?"—*M'Kinney.*

" There is not, we believe, another benevolent enterprize on earth, so well cal- culated to secure the favourable opinion and enlist the hearty good will of ALL MEN, as this is, when its objects and bearings are fully understood. In relation to this society it is eminently the fact, that opposition and indifference have their origin in prejudice or want of information. Ignorance may raise an objection which it requires knowledge to remove ; and to rest one's refusal to co-operate in what he is told is a good work, on his own ignorance, is both weak and wicked. Especially in relation to a benevolent enterprize of such magnitude as this, and which has been some ten or fifteen years before the public, the plea of ignorance is made with a very ill grace."

"Is a nation like this to be embarrassed by an annual appropriation of little more than a million of dollars to the cause of humanity? a nation that can extinguish in a year twelve millions of national debt, and at the same time prosecute with vigour its majestic plans of defence and internal improvement? a nation, one of whose states can hazard six millions of dollars on the project of opening a canal—a nation, whose canvass whitens every sea, and proudly enters almost every harbour of the globe?—a nation, whose villages and cities are rising, as by magic, over a fertile territory of two millions of square miles:—a nation, destined within the compass of the passing century to embosom a white population of eighty millions? With the past smiles of Divine Providence, our national debt will be soon annihi- lated. And from that glad hour, let the government provide liberally for all its ne- cessary operations—let it push forward in its splendid machinery of political im- provement, and then give to our cause but the surplus of its revenue: and as regards the expense of transportation, *it will [at no distant day] furnish the means of granting to every African exile* among us, a happy home in the land of his fathers."—Rev. B. DICKINSON.

PREFACE.

From the ardent opposition made to the Colonization Society by some of our white citizens, and by a number of the free coloured population, it might be supposed, by those unacquainted with the nature of the case, that the emigrants were absolutely pressed, like British seamen, and hurried off against their inclinations— that they were here in the enjoyment of all the solid advantages of society, each man "sitting under his own vine and his fig tree, and none to make him afraid"—that in Liberia they were to be in some degree enslaved—and that the climate was pestilential and the soil sterile and ungrateful. Were this a true picture of the case, the opposition to the society could not be more ardent or zealous.

I have treated on the situation of the free coloured population of this country, (p. 27) and shall not therefore refer to it here: but so far as regards the colony at Liberia, it is proved, by evidence of the most undeniable character—of American Captains, Kennedy, Sherman, Nicholson, and Abels; by that of Mr. Devany, a coloured man, High Sheriff of Liberia, who had been in the colony for six years, made a handsome fortune, and returned to this country to visit his friends and relations;—and more especially by that of a committee of the colonists at Monrovia, appointed to draw up an address to their brethren in this country; that the project of colonization has fully realized, and not merely realized, but exceeded the most sanguine expectations formed of it by its ardent supporters ; that the contrast between the situation of the colonists and that of their brethren in this country is immensely in favour of the former; and that the condition of the most favoured of the free coloured population here, is inferior in many important particulars to that of the great mass of the colonists, any one of whom may, by good behaviour, aspire to the highest office in the colony, and not one of whom can be taxed but by his representatives, in whose election he has as free a voice as Mr. Madison or Mr. Adams has in the election of state and United States' officers.

It is, therefore, difficult to conceive what good purpose can be answered by the opposition to the plan of colonization, or by what motive its opposers can be influenced.

There are three strong points of view in which this subject may be considered, which must gain for colonization the zealous and efficient support of every man, white or coloured, who is not under the dominion of inveterate and incurable prejudice. I omit other important points which might be mooted.

I. The colony has arrested the progress of the nefarious and accursed slave trade in its neighbourhood ; destroyed some slave factories, and liberated a number of slaves who were on the point of being transported across the Atlantic, subject to all the horrors of the passage, and, if they escaped with life, to the horrors of perpetual slavery; and there cannot be a doubt that at no distant day the trade will be annihilated on the whole of the western coast of Africa.

II. It has been the means of securing the emancipation of hundreds of slaves, in various parts of the United States, who are now in a genial climate, enjoying the luxury of freedom with all its attendant blessings; and, from the present disposition of the citizens of some of the slave states, particularly Virginia, there is no doubt that thousands will be emancipated as fast as means of transportation can be procured.

III. It has commenced spreading the blessings of civilization, morals, and religion among the natives in the neighbourhood of the colony, whom it has taught to depend on honest industry in the cultivation of the soil, instead of the demoniac operation of setting fire to towns and villages, for the horrible purpose of seizing the wretched fugitives flying from the flames, which was their former occupation.

Now I freely appeal to Mr. Garrison, and Mr. Lundy, the most formidable opposers of colonization, and to their friends, and beg them to lay their hands on their hearts, and answer in the presence of their Maker, if any one of those objects does not repay tenfold the sacrifice which the whole have cost?

Among the objections—how easy to make plausible objections!—offered to the colonization plan, one is, that considering the immense number of the coloured people in this country, about 2,400,000, it is impossible to make any serious impression on them by emigration, especially as the colony at present, after twelve years existence, contains but 2,000 souls. Let us examine this objection.

The annual increase, as I have shown, is about 60,000. The expense to the government, or the society, will probably be $25 per head for all the emigrants large and small (taking into consideration those who pay, or whose masters will pay their passage), or about $1,500,000 per ann. for that number. This sum, provided the subject were cordially taken up by the state legislatures and congress, would not be attended with the slightest difficulty. Indeed, if encountered with the zeal which its importance demands, twice the sum could be easily raised. But then the objectors emphatically demand, how shall we provide for the transportation of such a number!

It appears from Walsh's Sketches of Brazil that in the year 1828, there were no less than 43,000 slaves received in the single port of Rio de Janeiro—and it is fairly presumable that an equal number were received at the Havanna and other ports—making, with those that died on board, at least 100,000 ravished from their native land in one year. If the wretches engaged in that nefarious traffic could find means of transporting 100,000 human beings in one year across the Atlantic, surely this powerful nation could, to accomplish the great objects in view, and to rescue itself by degrees from the odious stain of slavery, accomplish the conveyance of 60, or even 100,000 to a land where they will be "lords of the soil." 60 or 70,000 persons have emigrated in one year from Great Britain and Ireland.

It is asked how shall provision be made for such a number in Liberia? they will perish for want of sustenance.

Can there exist any fear on this subject, when the soil of Liberia produces two regular crops a year, with the most imperfect culture? Philad'a, April 26, 1832.

LETTERS, &c.

LETTER I.

The Southampton Massacre.—Difference between the State of Slavery in Greece and Rome, and in the United States.— Various Plans of Colonization.—Objects of the Colonization Society.

TO THE HON. CHARLES F. MERCER.

Dear Sir—

The tragical issue of the insurrection in Southampton, in which above sixty whites fell a sacrifice to the vengeance of their slaves, and subsequently to which a great number of slaves suffered the penalties of the violated laws of the state, has awakened the slave states out of their slumbers, and excited considerable attention towards our coloured population, and the awful consequences likely to ensue, sooner or later, from the admixture of two heterogeneous castes in the country, without the least probability, at any future period, however remote, of an amalgamation between them, in consequence of the diversity of colour.

In this respect our situation is widely different from that of Greece or Rome. The great mass of their slaves were of the same colour as their masters, and a complete amalgamation might take place in a generation or two. Against such a result there is in this country an insuperable barrier.

This subject had occupied the attention of some of the wisest and best men of the country for above half a century. Several attempts were made in different provinces to prevent the importation of slaves, and laws were passed for the purpose, but they were uniformly rejected by the governors, under instructions from the British privy council—or by that council when the acts were transmitted for royal approbation. So early as 1772, the house of burgesses of Virginia unanimously agreed upon an address to the king of Great Britain, praying him " to remove those restraints on the governors of the colony, which inhibited them from assenting to such laws as might check so very pernicious a commerce."

" The importation of slaves into the colonies, from the coasts of Africa, has long been considered as a trade of great inhumanity, and under its encouragement, we have too much reason to fear, WILL ENDANGER THE VERY EXISTENCE OF YOUR MAJESTY'S AMERICAN DOMINIONS.

" We are sensible that some of your majesty's subjects in Great Britain may reap emolument from this sort of traffic; but when we consider that *it greatly retards the settlement of the colonies with more white inhabitants, and may in time have the most destructive influence*, we presume to hope that the interests of a few will be

2

disregarded, when placed in competition with the security and happiness of such numbers of your majesty's dutiful and loyal subjects."

This and various other efforts were entirely fruitless—the trade remained unrestrained until the declaration of independence, when Virginia and some other states prohibited it altogether.

Unfortunately the sound sentiments displayed by the burgesses of Virginia in 1772, were forgotten, or had lost their influence in 1787, when the federal constitution was formed—for by that instrument congress was prohibited from passing laws to prevent the importation of slaves for twenty years. A courtly style was employed. It was not thought proper to introduce the word "slaves"—"A rose by any other name would smell as sweet."

" The migration or importation of such persons as any of the states now existing, shall think proper to admit, shall not be prohibited by the congress prior to the year 1808; but a tax or duty may be imposed on such importation, not exceeding ten dollars for each person."

In consequence of this unfortunate constitutional legitimation of the slave trade, it was carried on for twenty years on a large scale, and sowed a seed which has germinated with fatal fertility, and threatens a heavy retribution.

In the discussion of the best means of averting or at least of mitigating the evil to be dreaded from the existence among us of a class of people, who, although free, and therefore righteously entitled to all the advantages and privileges of freemen, were nevertheless, in a great degree, debarred from them by the inexorable force of public prejudice, and, in most of the states, were subject to rules and regulations and proscriptions, of the most oppressive and galling kind—in this discussion, I say, public opinion settled down in favour of an extensive system of colonization.

On the subject of the location, there was not the same degree of unanimity. Some of our citizens were in favour of selecting a portion of the vacant territory of the United States, and setting it apart for the purpose. Others were, and some still are, for making an arrangement with the government of Mexico, and sending the class in question to Texas. Others, again, advocated a settlement on the western coast of Africa, as the *natale solum* of their ancestors, and as the climate is better suited to the great majority of the coloured people of this country. The last plan was finally adopted.

The objects of the friends of colonization are—

I. To rescue the free coloured people from the disqualifications, the degradation, and the proscription to which they are exposed in the United States.

II. To place them in a country where they may enjoy the benefits of free government, with all the blessings which it brings in its train.

III. To avert the dangers of a dreadful collision at a future day of the two castes, which must inevitably be objects of mutual jealousy to each other.

IV. To spread civilization, sound morals and religion throughout the vast continent of Africa, at present sunk in the lowest and most hideous state of barbarism.

V. And though last, not least, to afford slave owners who are conscientiously scrupulous about holding human beings in bondage, an asylum to which they may send their manumitted slaves.

The last item has recently assumed a greatly increased importance. Manumissions are prohibited in some of the slave states, unless the parties remove beyond their boundaries; and the entrance of free negroes into others, is prohibited; so that manumissions, without deportation, appear to be almost wholly at an end. It remains to be seen, in the sequel, from the results that have already taken place, how far the benign purposes of the society are likely to be accomplished.

With such noble objects in view, it is truly wonderful, that although the society has been in existence for twelve years, the whole of the contributions public and private, (except the support by the government of the United States, of negroes captured from slave traders) received by the society for carrying them into effect, has been but about $125,000, not a cent a head for the entire population of the most prosperous nation in the world; a nation, moreover, in which other objects, some of them of inferior usefulness, are most liberally supported! This must have arisen from an impression entertained by many, that the scheme is absolutely impracticable. Hence many liberal individuals have wholly withheld their contributions. Of this opinion was the writer of these letters, at an early stage of the existence of the society. He regarded it as one of the wildest projects ever conceived by enlightened men; and therefore, in the language of Sterne respecting the Monk, he was "predetermined not to give them a single sous." Mature reflection has, however, convinced him of his error: he is now satisfied that the project is not more benignant and beneficent, than practicable, provided the general and state governments, and public spirited individuals yield it a support in any degree commensurate with its importance.

In the hope of converting others, as he himself has been converted, he believes he may render an acceptable service to his country, by placing before the public, in plain, unadorned language, the leading features of the case, under the following prominent heads.

1. The origin of the society.

2. The progress of the colony compared with that of Massachusetts, Virginia and North Carolina.

3. The increase of the coloured population, free and slaves.

4. The declarations of legislatures and other public bodies in favour of the society.

5. The manumission of slaves in this country.

6. The situation and future prospects of the colonists at Monrovia, Caldwell, &c.

7. Their moral and religious character.

8. The soil, climate, productions, and commerce of Liberia.

9. The disadvantages under which the free coloured population labour in this country, and those resulting to the white population from the existence of slavery.

10. The character of the natives of Africa before the irruption of the barbarians.

11. The salutary effects of the colony in repressing the slave trade, with a slight sketch of that nefarious traffic.

This, you will say, is a wide field. I agree with you. How far I shall have succeeded in my attempt, must be decided when I reach the close of my labours, the "Finis."

Yours, &c. M. C.

Philadelphia, April 8, 1832.

LETTER II.

Early plans of Colonization.—Mr. Jefferson's and Mr. Thornton's.—Resolve of the Legislature of Virginia.—Ineffectual Negotiations.—Formation of the Colonization Society.

DEAR SIR—

As early as the year 1777, Mr. Jefferson formed a plan for colonizing the free coloured population of the United States. The particulars I have not been able to obtain. There is reason to believe, that he proposed the settlement in some of the western vacant lands. Be that as it may, the project proved an abortion, owing partly to the distractions and difficulties of the war, and partly to the novelty and magnitude of the undertaking. How much to be deplored the result! Had he succeeded, what a source of danger and disaster would have been dried up for ever!

In the year 1787, Dr. Thornton, of Washington, formed a plan for establishing a colony of that population on the western coast of Africa, and published an address to those residing in Massachusetts and Rhode Island, inviting them to accompany him. A sufficient number of them agreed to go, and were prepared for the expedition. But this project likewise failed for want of funds. The public mind was not then prepared for affording pecuniary support. About the year 1800 or 1801, the legislature of Virginia, in secret session, instructed Mr. Monroe, then governor of the state, to apply to the president of the United States, and urge him to institute negotiations with some of the powers of Europe possessed of colonies on the coast of Africa, to grant an asylum to which our emancipated negroes might be sent. Mr. Jefferson opened a negotiation with the Sierra Leone Company, for the purpose, but without success. He subsequently applied to the government of Portugal, and equally failed. The project was then abandoned as hopeless.

In the session of the legislature of Virginia, in 1816, the subject was again brought forward, and the following resolution was adopted by a large majority.

"Whereas the General Assembly of Virginia have repeatedly sought to obtain an asylum, beyond the limits of the United States, for such persons of colour as had been or might be emancipated under the laws of this Commonwealth, but have hitherto found all their efforts frustrated, either by the disturbed state of other nations, or domestic causes equally unpropitious to its success:

"They now avail themselves of a period when peace has healed the wounds of humanity, and the principal nations of Europe have concurred with the government of the United States, in abolishing the African Slave Trade (a traffic which this Commonwealth, both before and since the revolution, zealously sought to exterminate,) to renew this effort, and do therefore,—

"*Resolve*, That the executive be requested to correspond with the President of the United States, for the purpose of obtaining a territory on the coast of Africa, or at some other place, not within any of the states or territorial governments of the United States, to serve as an asylum for such persons of colour as are now free, and may desire the same, and for those who may hereafter be emancipated within this Commonwealth; and that the Senators and Representatives of this state in the Congress of the United States, be requested to exert their best efforts to aid the President of the United States in the attainment of the above objects.

"*Provided*, That no contract or arrangement respecting such territory shall be obligatory on this Commonwealth, until ratified by the legislature."

It thus appears that the scheme of colonization which is now violently denounced in some of the southern papers, as a conspiracy against the rights and property of the slave holders, and forms one of the means whereby the dangerous effervescence in South Carolina has been excited, originated with the great leading slave state, which possesses more than a third of all the slaves in the five original slave states.

At length the time arrived when the country was ripe for the establishment of the society. In December, 1816, a considerable number of citizens, very nearly all slave holders, met at Washington, to take the subject into consideration. Bushrod Washington presided. Long debates ensued. Henry Clay, John Randolph, of Roanoke, and various other powerful orators, addressed the meeting in support of the plan. Mr. Randolph observed, that

"If a place could be provided for their reception, and a mode of sending them hence, there were hundreds, nay, thousands, who would, by manumitting their slaves, relieve themselves from the cares attendant on their possession!"

At this meeting, a letter from Mr. Jefferson, dated in 1811, was read, in which, having mentioned his negotiations with the Sierra Leone Company and Portugal, he adds—

"Indeed nothing is more to be wished, than that the United States would themselves undertake to make such an establishment on the coast of Africa."*

A constitution was formed; Bushrod Washington was appointed president, and Messrs. Crawford, Clay, Rutgers, Howard, &c., vice presidents. An eloquent memorial to Congress was drawn up, which Mr. Randolph undertook to present to that body.

Yours, &c. M. C.

Philadelphia, April 10, 1832.

---

* African Repository, vol. VI. page 199.

LETTER III.

Agents sent to Africa to explore the coast for a suitable situ-
ation.—Land purchased.—Conflict with the natives.—
Agent seized by them.—Monrovia besieged.—In imminent
danger.—Colonists triumph.—Peace.

DEAR SIR—

In November, 1819, the society appointed two agents, the Rev.
S. J. Mills and Mr. Ebenezer Burgess, to proceed to the coast of
Africa, via England, to make the necessary explorations and inquiries as to a suitable location for a settlement.   The object of
landing in England, was to procure letters to the leading men at
Sierra Leone, and also to gain such general information respecting
the coast of Africa as might be attainable.   They succeeded in both
objects, and procured, moreover, recommendations from the Court
of Copenhagen, to its colonial authorities on the coast.   They sailed
from the Downs on the 7th of February, 1820, and arrived at Sierra Leone early in March.   They visited all the ports from Sierra
Leone to Sherboro.   At this last place they found a small colony of coloured people settled by John Kizel, a South Carolina
slave, who had joined the British in the revolutionary war, and
at its close was taken to Nova Scotia, from whence he sailed
with a number of his countrymen to Africa, where he established
this small settlement, which was, at the arrival of the agents, in a
prosperous situation.   By Kizel and his people, the agents were
kindly and hospitably received.   After gaining all the information
necessary for their purpose, they sailed from the coast in May, and
arrived in the United States in the following month.   Mr. Mills
died on the passage.

The slave trade having been abolished by Congress, and the
American vessels of war being authorized to capture all vessels engaged in it, under the American flag, one of them was taken, and the
liberated Africans were brought to this country, landed in Georgia,
and were about to be sold by virtue of an act of that state.   A clause
in the act directed the constituted authorities to deliver such slaves
up to the Colonization Society, on payment of all expenses incurred
since their capture and condemnation.   With this condition the
society complied, and received the slaves, about thirty in number.

To guard against a recurrence of a similar state of things, Congress, on the 3d of March, 1819, passed an act authorising the
president " to make such rules and regulations as he might deem
expedient for the safe keeping, support, and removal of slaves captured in vessels engaged in the slave trade; and to appoint a proper
person or persons, as agent or agents on the coast of Africa for receiving them."

It was obvious that the objects of the government could be better accomplished in conjunction with the Colonization Society,

than separately. Accordingly, in the year 1820 the Elizabeth was chartered, and took out to the coast two agents of the government, one from the society, and about eighty emigrants. The latter were to be employed at the expense of the government, in preparing accommodations for the reception of recaptured negroes.

They were in the outset extremely unfortunate. They found it impossible to obtain a suitable place, and "were compelled, by a variety of untoward circumstances, to make a temporary establishment in the low, unhealthy island of Sherbro." Here they were detained some time endeavouring to purchase land—and were attacked by fatal diseases which carried off the three agents, and twenty of the colonists.

The colony was in a lamentable state in the spring of 1821. Great confusion and want of subordination prevailed, in consequence of the death of the agents. At that time four new ones arrived, Messrs. Andrews, Wiltberger, Winn, and Bacon; the two first on the part of the society, and the others on that of the United States. They brought out twenty-eight emigrants—and from the difficulties that had occurred in procuring land, they proceeded with the old and new hands to the neighbourhood of Freetown, in the colony of Sierra Leone. One of the agents, Mr. Bacon, being taken sick, returned to the United States. Mr. Andrews died in August, and Mr. Winn in September.

This was a most appalling state of things, and would have discouraged ordinary men from a prosecution of the scheme. Fortunately, such timid counsels did not prevail. The society determined to persevere, trusting that more experience, and the choice of a more salubrious situation would guard against a repetition of those disasters.

A new agent, Dr. Ayres, was appointed, who, with lieutenant Stockton, on the part of the United States, sailed in November, 1821, and arrived on the coast of Africa in December. On a careful examination of the coast, they purchased the country called Montserado, where the colony is now settled. The price agreed upon, was three hundred dollars, payable in powder and ball, fire arms, tobacco, clothing, &c.

The Africans who had been landed at Sierra Leone, were now sent for, and affairs wore a promising aspect, when an untoward circumstance occurred, which threatened a total failure of the scheme.

A small slave vessel, prize to an English schooner, with thirty recaptured slaves on board, and bound for Sierra Leone, put in for water at Perseverance Island, part of the purchased territory, where the colonists were stationed. Having unfortunately parted her cable, she drifted on shore, where she was wrecked. The custom of the coast appropriates to the petty chief on whose lands a wreck takes place, the vessel and her entire contents. King George, on whose territory the accident happened, sent his people to take possession. They were resisted by the captain and crew, and were discomfited. While the natives were preparing to renew the attack, the captain sent to the agent for assistance, which was readily granted. A boat was instantly manned, and sent to his relief, and a brass field piece on the island brought to bear on the assailants, who were accordingly put to the rout, with the loss of two killed and several wounded. The crew and slaves were brought in safety to land, but the vessel went to pieces, and most of the stores and property was lost.

This exasperated the natives, not merely by the loss of their prey and their men, but by the prospect it held out of similar interferences in future. They anticipated the total interruption of the slave trade, which was their principal dependence for procuring supplies of whatever they might want. They, therefore, determined to extirpate the colony, while in its feeble and defenceless state.

Only part of the goods had been delivered, and the natives refused to take the remainder, and insisted on returning what they had received. This, of course, the agent refused, and they had recourse to a stratagem to accomplish their purpose. They invited him to an amicable conference, and as soon as they had him in their power, made him a prisoner, and detained him until he consented to take the articles back. Then they insisted on the colonists withdrawing from the settlement altogether. Pleading the difficulty of removal, for want of a place to which to retire, he was permitted to remain till he could make a purchase of land. Meanwhile he made an appeal to Boatswain, one of the native kings, who enjoyed a sort of supremacy among them, and who, on hearing the respective allegations, gave an award in favour of the colonists, that the bargain had been fair on both sides; that there was no ground for rescinding it; and therefore, that the natives should receive the stipulated goods, and relinquish the purchased territory. With this judgment his perfidious regal brethren were forced to comply, as he threatened them with his vengeance if they proved refractory.

They brooded over the discomfiture in the field, and before the arbiter, and determined, on his departure to his own station, to make a decisive attempt to extirpate the colony. The colonists had information of their preparations, and made every exertion to be enabled to meet them. But their number was small, having but 35 effective men; their defences were incomplete; they had but few cannon; and the agent, the Rev. Mr. Ashmun, a man of extraordinary zeal, ardour, and energy, was dangerously ill; but had, nevertheless, to give all the necessary orders, some of them dictated from his bed, as he had no adequate substitute.

The enemy consisted of a body of eight hundred men, and made a most furious attack on the 8th of November, 1822. Unfortunately one pass was neglected to be properly defended, and there the enemy forced an entrance, and captured one of the guns, which happily they knew not how to manage. The colony was saved by their want of discipline. Had they pushed forward, their success was certain; the colonists could not have resisted; but the assailants betook themselves to plunder, in great confusion : this afforded the colonists time to rally; they recaptured the gun; and turned it on the enemy, who were wedged in a solid mass. Great destruction took place, and they fled in utter confusion; it was supposed they had 60 or 80 killed. The loss on the other side was considerable, three men and one woman killed, two men and two women severely wounded, and seven children captured.

The colonists, as soon as the enemy had disappeared, immediately began to complete their defences, and prepare for another attack, which they understood from their spies, was to be made with a greater force at the close of the month. The attack accordingly commenced on the 30th, with 1,500 assailants. The fortifications were in a far better state than before, but the number of effective men less, not quite 30. The besiegers were, after a long and ardent struggle, finally defeated, with severe loss. The garrison had one man killed, and two badly wounded. Mr. Ashmun's services were invaluable, and were the means of saving the place.

His Britannic Majesty's schooner, Driver, fortunately arrived in the harbour at this time, and the commander kindly offered his services as mediator, which were gladly accepted by both parties, as they were equally tired of " the unprofitable contest." The native princes signed an engagement "to observe an unlimited truce with the colony, and submit all their differences to the arbitration of the governor of Sierra Leone."

Since that period the colonists have not been molested. They are objects of respect and veneration, and their friendship is sought after by all the petty kings in their neighbourhood.

A regular form of government was adopted in 1824, which produced the happiest effects on the morals and manners of the Colonists. In truth, this period may be stated as almost the commencement of the establishment—the four preceding years having been the reign of anarchy and confusion.

Yours, &c., M. C.

Philadelphia, April 12, 1832.

LETTER IV.

Increase of the coloured Population.

DEAR SIR—

The dangers arising from the great increase of a caste in the nation, who are by custom cut off from all chance of amalgamation with their fellow beings of a different colour, are yearly augmenting by the natural horror of slavery, which is constantly gaining strength in the breasts of the slaves; by the unceasing discussions in our papers, especially by those that recently took place in the legislature of Virginia; and by the inflammatory publications, which are clandestinely spread among the slaves, in spite of the vigilance and denunciations of their masters. Circumstances, too, are occasionally occurring which tend to fan the flame; among which may be reckoned the general manumission of the slaves in the royal colonies of Great Britain, and the steady and persevering efforts making in and out of parliament in that kingdom, to procure a total emancipation in all the British colonies.

In the discussion of this subject, it is only necessary to cast a furtive glance at the scenes in St. Domingo, and the various insurrections planned and attempted in this country, to be satisfied that the subject has not hitherto attracted that consideration in general, to which it is entitled by its great magnitude and importance. Although there is, I hope and trust, no great danger of such insurrectionary attempts proving successful, yet they may, and in all probability will, produce repetitions of the horrible scenes which took place at Southampton, at which humanity shudders.

On this view of the subject, it could scarcely have been anticipated, that the scheme proposed by the Colonization Society, of removing such of the free people of colour as are disposed to emigrate to the land of their fathers, and such slaves as are emancipated, on condition of removal to that land, should have met with any opposition. It is, nevertheless certain, that it has been violently opposed in two quarters where it might have rationally been supposed likely to meet with most favour, in South Carolina, and among some of the free blacks.

We shall in the sequel consider the opposition of the free blacks. At present we shall confine ourselves to the case of South Carolina. That state is by far more particularly interested in the success of the scheme than any other, except perhaps Louisiana; as these are the only two states in which the slave population exceeds that of the whites.

Population of South Carolina.	Whites	Slaves.
In 1790	131,181	107,094
1830	257,878	315,565

Thus it appears that while the slaves very nearly trebled their numbers, the whites did not quite double theirs.

The relative situation of the white and coloured population east of the Blue Ridge, in Virginia, places this subject in a striking point of view. It appears that the latter have gained on the former in forty years, 106,176, being more than a fourth part of the number of whites at present in that part of the country. To render this case more remarkable, it is to be observed, that during this period, the shipment of slaves from that portion of Virginia to the more southern states, has been carried to an enormous extent.

Population east of the Blue Ridge.	Total. Whites.	Blacks.	Majority. Whites.	Blacks.
In 1790	314,523	289,425	25,098	
1800	336,289	339,293		3,004
1810	338,553	386,942		48,389
1820	348,873	413,928		65,055
1830	375,935	457,013		81,078

The following table exhibits the increase of the free coloured people in the United States from the year 1790 to the present time.

| In 1790 | 59,481 | | In 1810 | 186,446 | | In 1830 | 319,467 |
| 1800 | 110,073 | | 1820 | 233,530 | | | |

A multiplication nearly six fold in forty years, and above 33 per cent. in the last ten years.

The disparity of increase of the white and coloured population in the five original slave states, deserves attention.

	1790.		1830.	
	Whites.	Slaves.	Whites.	Slaves.
Maryland,	208,650	103,036	291,093	102,878
Virginia,	442,127	292,627	694,439	469,724
North Carolina,	288,204	100,572	472,433	246,462
South Carolina,	130,178	107,094	257,878	315,665
Georgia,	52,886	29,264	296,614	217,407
	1,122,045	632,593	2,012,457	1,352,136

It thus appears, that the whites, in forty years, increased only about eighty per cent.; while the slaves increased one hundred and twelve. In North Carolina, the whites increased but sixty-four per cent.; while the slaves increased one hundred and forty five. The number of slaves in Maryland has slightly decreased, partly by manumissions, and partly by the shipment of slaves to the more southern states, both of which have taken place in that state on a large scale. The free coloured population in 1790, was only 8,042, whereas, in 1830, it was 52,942.

Table of the number of coloured people, free and slaves, in the United States, at the various periods of taking the census, together with a statement of the numbers that will be in the country every decennial census, till 1880, at the rate of increase that took place between 1820 and 1830, viz., at 35 per cent.

1790	- - -	757,178		1840	- - -	3,145,552
1800	- - -	1,006,912		1850	- - -	4,246,495
1810	- - -	1,377,780		1860	- - -	5,732,768
1820	- - -	1,771,658		1870	- - -	7,739,236
1830	- - -	2,330,039		1880	- - -	10,447,968

Yours, &c., M. C.

Philadelphia, April 14, 1832.

LETTER V.

Expense of Passage—Manumissions.

Dear Sir—

It remains to ascertain as nearly as possible, the expense of emigration.

The passage is at present calculated at about twenty dollars, and the expense for the maintenance of each emigrant for six months at about 15 dollars; making all together, 35 dollars.

But children from two to twelve years of age are taken at half price, and below two years free of charge; allowing for a due proportion of children, thirty dollars will be a tolerably fair estimate for passage and support.

Moreover, when the situation of the colony becomes better known, and the prejudices which have been industriously created against it are done away, many emigrants will defray their own expenses, and many humane and charitable masters will, as has taken place already, pay the passage of their manumitted slaves.

Again. For a long time to come there will be, as there is at present, a great demand in the colony for labourers, and able-bodied men will, immediately on landing, be able to procure employment. In a late report it is stated, that of the whole number of emigrants that arrived in one vessel, only seven were unemployed in twenty days. Considering all these circumstances, we might be authorised to assume an average of twenty dollars for each; but if we err at all, it is better to err on the safe side, and assume twenty-five.

It appears that the annual increase is about 2½ per cent. In the former edition we erroneously assumed 3½.

Two and a half per cent. on the present number of coloured people in the United States, probably 2,400,000, amounts to 60,000 annually. Supposing the object to be to prevent any increase, and that therefore provision would have to be made for the conveyance of 60,000 annually, at 25 dollars each, the expense would be $1,500,000.

This sum is large, and would require considerable sacrifices. But was any grand object ever attained without great sacrifices? We were, when in a comparatively feeble state, able to raise $100,000,000 in a year and a half for the support of a war. Our revenue has been, for years, from 20 to $25,000,000, and the national debt is nearly paid off. The direct tax of the state of Pennsylvania in the year 1815 was $730,958, and that of Virginia $738,036, which were paid without any oppression of the citizens of either. And surely if reason and common sense have fair play, it will not be difficult to procure an amendment of the constitution (if such an amendment be necessary, which is doubted by many of our citizens) by three-fourths of the states, allowing the appropriation of a sum necessary for the purpose; and never did a nation make a more useful appropriation.

There are thirteen non-slaveholding States. There can be no doubt that these would ratify such an amendment; and from the prevalence of the conviction in Maryland, Virginia, and North Carolina, of the dangers that menace the country from this source, their immediate concurrence might be calculated on, and the consent of two more would probably be had in a year or two, as the subject came to be more fully discussed, and of consequence better understood.

Among the most promising and encouraging circumstances attending the career of this society, are the numerous manumissions that have taken place in almost all the slave states, on the express condition of the freed people being sent to Liberia.

These manumissions have occurred on a scale that the most sanguine friends of the scheme could not have anticipated. Entire families have been blest with their freedom, from the most pure motives, a conviction of the immorality and injustice of slavery—and in many cases ample provision has been made for the expense of their passage, and in some for their support in Liberia. They have been thus released from the debasement and degradation of slavery, and sent to the land of their fathers, to partake of all the happiness that freedom and the certainty of enjoying all the fruits of their labour, can inspire.

In this work of benevolence, the society of Friends, as in so many other cases, have nobly distinguished themselves, and assumed a prominent attitude. They have, in North Carolina, liberated no less than 652 slaves, whom they had under their care, besides, as says my authority, an unknown number of children, husbands and wives, connected with them by consanguinity. In the performance of these acts of benevolence, they expended $12,759. They had remaining under their care in Dec. 1830, 402 slaves, for whom the same arrangements were to be made.

It holds out every encouragement to the Colonization Society, that the applications for the transportation of free negroes, and slaves proposed to be emancipated on condition of removal to Liberia, far exceed its means. There are in North Carolina and the adjacent states, from three to four thousand of both descriptions, ready to embark, were the Society in a situation to send them away.

Yours, &c., M. C.

Philadelphia, April 14, 1832.

LETTER VI.

Progress of Liberia.—Inauspicious commencement in Massachusetts, Virginia, and North Carolina.

DEAR SIR—

A brief comparison of the progress made in Liberia, with the colonization of Massachusetts, Virginia and North Carolina, will place the first on high ground, and dispel the doubts of the most sceptical as to the ultimate success of this magnificent and benignant undertaking, if it receive a due degree of support. Let it be observed, that the society never made any calculation on being able to accomplish the mighty object of their enterprise by private resources alone. That would have been extravagant folly. The success must, they well knew, ultimately depend on the patronage of the general and state governments, united; the attainment of which they confidently hope for. The society has done its duty in proving the practicability of the scheme, and will steadily continue its exertions on a scale proportioned to the means placed at its disposal. Further than this it never promised.

The first expedition to Liberia took place in the year 1820, but met with so many difficulties and embarrassments at the commencement, that it was not until the year 1824, that any order or good government was established. All that has been accomplished worth notice has taken place within the last eight years. What, then, is the state of the case?

There are now above 2000 souls settled, contented, happy and prosperous; enjoying all the apparatus of a regular government; an improving agriculture; a prosperous and increasing commerce; settlements rapidly extending; a large territory, possessed of extraordinary advantages of soil, climate, and situation for commerce, fairly and honourably purchased, one hundred and fifty miles on the coast, and extending into the interior of the country thirty or forty miles; several slave factories destroyed and the slaves liberated; the slave trade abolished in the neighbourhood of the settlement; the circumjacent aboriginals tranquilized, regarding the settlers with reverence, and looking up to them for protection from the ferocious violence of those *hostes humani generis*, the slave traders; the attacks of some hostile petty kings repelled in 1822, in the very infancy of the colony, and in its most feeble state; education carefully attended to; the children of the natives sent in for instruction to the schools of the colonists; morals and religion flourishing. In a word, the most sanguine expectations of the founders of the colony more than realized, at this very early stage of its existence. It may be doubted whether any colony ever throve more completely in so short a space of time.

One feature in this colony most honourably distinguishes it from almost every other colony established in ancient or modern times. Of all other colonies the founders were impelled by a desire of conquest; a thirst of aggrandizement, or of the acquisition of wealth. With no such views were the founders of Liberia actuated. Pure benevolence alone inspired the illustrious men, the Finleys, the Thorntons, the Washingtons, the Mercers, the Ashmuns, the Caldwells, who projected or aided in the formation of the society. The benefit of the colonists and the peace and happiness of this country were the objects. For their attainment they devoted their time, and their substance, and endured the scoffs and ridicule and scorn to which their grand enterprise, in common with all great novel undertakings was subjected.

Let us now cast an eye on the early results of the attempts at the colonization of Massachusetts, Virginia and North Carolina.

The pilgrims who commenced the settlement of Massachusetts, landed in *December*, 1620, to the number of 120; and so ill were they provided with provisions and clothing, and so inclement was the season, that about fifty of them perished in the course of the winter and the ensuing spring. * And though they received fre-

* Marshall's Life of Washington, Vol. I. page 94.

quent reinforcements, one half of the whole number of the settlers perished in the severe winter of 1629, and there remained but three hundred in the year 1630. *

What a striking contrast Liberia exhibits! How exhilarating and encouraging to its friends, and how useful a lesson does it hold out to its enemies!

But inauspicious as the incipient operations were in Massachusetts, the result was far worse for 25 years in Virginia. The first attempt at a settlement took place in 1585, and was succeeded for years by several numerous reinforcements, which in a great measure fell victims to their own irregularities, or to the hostile attacks of the Indians, whom those irregularities provoked. In 1610, the heroic Smith, the father of the colony, brought out a strong reinforcement, and returned home for further supplies of men, provisions, arms and ammunition, leaving the colony, as he supposed, secure against any contingency, however adverse, whether from the severity of the weather, or the assaults of the Indians. But all his calculations were miserably defeated by the worthlessness, the insubordination, and the licentiousness of the colonists.

"Smith left the colony furnished with three ships, good fortifications, twenty-five pieces of cannon, arms, ammunition, apparel, commodities for trading, and tools for all kinds of labour. At James Town there were nearly sixty houses. The settlers had begun to plant and to fortify at five or six other places. The number of inhabitants was nearly five hundred.—They had just gathered in their Indian harvest, and besides, had considerable provision in their stores. They had between five and six hundred hogs, an equal number of fowls, some goats and some sheep. They had also boats, nets, and good accommodations for fishing. But such was the sedition, idleness, and dissipation of this mad people, that they were soon reduced to the most miserable circumstances. No sooner was Capt. Smith gone, than the savages, provoked by their dissolute practices, and encouraged by their want of government, revolted, hunted and slew them from place to place. Nansemond, the plantation at the falls, and all the out-settlements, were abandoned. In a short time, nearly forty of the company were cut off by the enemy. Their time and provisions were consumed in riot; their utensils were stolen or destroyed; their hogs, sheep, and fowls killed and carried off by the Indians. The sword without, famine and sickness within, soon made among them surprising destruction. Within the term of six months, of their whole number, sixty only survived. These were the most poor, famishing wretches, subsisting chiefly on herbs, acorns, and berries. Such was the famine, that they fed on the skins of their dead horses: nay, they boiled and ate the flesh of the dead. Indeed they were reduced to such extremity, that had they not been relieved, the whole colony in eight or ten days would have been extinct. Such are the dire effects of idleness, faction, and want of proper subordination."†

All the difficulties and disasters that have occurred in Liberia from the commencement of the settlement till the present time, fall far short of the tithe of the calamities in Virginia in six months.

We have not as many details of the disasters in North Carolina. Williamson, its historian, is very brief on the subject; but he tells enough to prove that similar disorders and similar disasters took place there. The colony was commenced in 1668, and in 1694, " the list of taxables was only 787, being little more than half the number that were there in 1677," seventeen years before. " Such," says the writer, " were the baneful effects of rapine, anarchy and idleness."*

Yours, &c., M. C.

Philadelphia, April 18, 1832.

LETTER VII.

Legislative proceedings in favour of the Society.—Connecticut, New-Jersey, Kentucky, Delaware, Massachusetts, Tennessee, Indiana, Pennsylvania and Maryland.—Synod of Utica.—General Assembly of the Presbyterian Church.—Methodist Episcopal Conference.

DEAR SIR—

The Colonization Society has, by perseverance and by the intrinsic merits of its views, at length " won golden opinions" from the greater part of the nation. The Legislatures of fourteen States, New-Hampshire, Vermont, Connecticut, New-York, New-Jersey, Pennsylvania, Delaware, Maryland, Virginia, Georgia, Tennessee, Kentucky, Ohio and Indiana, have passed resolutions distinctly recommending the scheme of colonizing the free coloured population, and most of them approving of the objects of the Society. Eleven of those states have instructed their senators, and requested their representatives in Congress to promote, in the general government, measures for removing such free persons of colour as are desirous of emigrating to Africa. And " nearly all the ecclesiastical bodies in the United States have, by resolutions, fully expressed their opinion, that the Society merits the consideration and favour of the whole Christian community, and earnestly recommend it to their patronage." I annex a few specimens:

Resolve of the Legislature of Connecticut, 1824.

" Resolved, That the existence of Slavery in the United States is a great national evil, and that the people and the States ought to participate in the burdens and duties of removing it by all just and prudent measures, which may be adopted *with a due regard to their internal peace and mutual harmony:* and that a system of colonization under the patronage of the General Government, may reasonably be deemed conducive to so desirable an object."

Resolve of the Legislature of New-Jersey, 1825.

" Resolved, That in the opinion of this Legislature, a system of Foreign Colonization, with correspondent measures, might be adopted, that would in due time, effect the entire emancipation of slaves in this country, and furnish an asylum for the free blacks, *without any violation of the National Compact, or infringement of the rights of individuals;* and that such a system should be predicated upon the principle, that the evil of slavery is a national one, and *that the People and the States of this union ought, mutually, to participate in the duties and burdens of removing it.*"

Resolve of the Legislature of Kentucky, 1827.

" Resolved by the General Assembly of the Commonwealth of Kentucky, That they view with deep and friendly interest, the exertions of the American Colonization Society, in establishing an asylum on the coast of Africa, for the free people of colour of the United States; and that the Senators and Representatives in Congress from this state, be and they are hereby requested, to use their efforts to facilitate

* Williamson's History of North Carolina, Vol. I. page 144.

the removal of such free persons of colour as may desire to emigrate from the United States to the colony in Africa, and to insure to them the protection and patronage of the General Government, so far as shall be deemed consistent with the safety and interest of the United States."

Of the Legislature of Delaware.

"Resolved, By the Senate and House of Representatives of the State of Delaware, in General Assembly met, That it is requisite for our prosperity, and, what is of more important concern, essential to our safety, that measures should be taken, for the removal from this country, of the free negroes and mulattoes.

" Resolved, That this General Assembly approve the objects of the American Colonization Society, and consider that those objects deserve public support, and that they ought to be fostered and encouraged by the National Government, and with the National funds."

Resolution of the Senate of Pennsylvania, 1829.

" Be it resolved by the Senate and House of Representatives of Pennsylvania, in General Assembly met, That in the opinion of this general assembly, the American Colonization Society eminently demands the support of the national government, and that our Senators be directed, and the Representatives in Congress be requested to aid the same by all proper and constitutional means."

Resolution of the Legislature of Maryland, 1829.

"Resolved unanimously, That the governor be requested to communicate to the President of the United States, and to our Senators and Representatives in Congress, the opinion of the general assembly, that a wise and provident policy suggests the expediency, on the part of our national government, of procuring through negociation, by cession or purchase, a tract of country on the western coast of Africa, for the colonization of the free people of colour of the United States."

Resolution of the State of Tennessee.

" Resolved, by the General Assembly of the State of Tennessee, That the Senators in Congress from this State, be, and they are hereby requested and instructed ; and that the Representatives be, and they are hereby requested, to give to the government of the United States any aid in their power, in devising and carrying into effect a plan which may have for its object the colonizing, in some distant country, the free people of colour who are within the limits of the United States, or within the limits of any of their Territories."

Resolution of the State of Indiana, 1829.

" Be it resolved by the General Assembly of the State of Indiana, That our Senators and Representatives in Congress be, and they are hereby requested, in the name of the State of Indiana, to solicit the assistance of the general government to aid the laudable designs of the Colonization Society, in such manner as Congress in its wisdom may deem expedient."

Resolution of the Senate of Massachusetts in 1830.

" Resolved, That our Senators and Representatives in Congress, be, and they are hereby requested, in the name of the State of Massachusetts, to solicit the assistance of the general government, to aid the laudable designs of the Colonization Society, in such manner as Congress in its wisdom may deem expedient."

Resolution of the Synod of Utica, N. Y. 1829.

" Resolved, That all clergymen within the bounds of this Synod, be, and they hereby are most earnestly requested to take up collections and subscriptions yearly, on or near the fourth of July, as a proper mode of aiding the funds of the Colonization Society ; and that as far as practicable, they enable their people to understand the history, design, progress and prospects of the Society."

Resolution of the General Assembly of the Presbyterian Church, 1830.

" Resolved, That it be recommended to all the churches under the care of the general assembly, to take up collections for the Colonization Society, on the next 4th of July."

Resolution of the Philadelphia Conference of the Methodist Episcopal Church, 1831.

" Resolved, That the Conference highly approving of the plan and purposes of the American Colonization Society, do recommend that collections be taken up throughout the churches within our bounds, so far as is practicable, on the 4th of July next, in aid of the funds of the above Society."

LETTER VIII.

Situation of the Colonists in Liberia.—Testimony of a Committee in Monrovia.—Of Captain Nicholson—Of Captain Kennedy—Of Captain Sherman—Of Captain Abels.—Morals and Manners.

DEAR SIR—

The subject discussed in this letter is of paramount importance. Whatever considerations of policy in regard to this country, might plead in favour of the scheme of colonization, it would not have the sanction of the friends of mankind, of those who commiserate the depressed situation of the coloured population of the United States, if the situation of the emigrants were not manifestly improved. To place this vital point on a basis as firm as the rock of Gibraltar, I have collected what may be regarded as a superfluity of testimony; as that of any one of the parties would be sufficient to remove all doubts from the minds of all persons open to conviction. But it seemed right in such a case, " to make assurance doubly sure."

In a Circular forwarded by a Committee of the inhabitants of Monrovia, to their brethren in the United States, they give the following description of their situation:

" The first consideration which caused our voluntary removal to this country, and the object we regard with the deepest concern, was liberty—liberty in the sober, simple, but complete sense of the word—not a licentious liberty—nor a liberty without government, or which should place us without the restraint of salutary laws —but that liberty of speech, action and conscience, which distinguishes the free enfranchised citizens of a free state. We did not enjoy that freedom in our native country; and from causes, which, as regards ourselves, we shall soon forget for ever, we were certain, it was not there attainable for our children or ourselves. * * We truly declare, that our expectations and hopes, in this respect, have been realized.

" Our constitution secures to us, so far as our condition allows, all the rights and privileges enjoyed by the citizens of the United States; and these rights and these privileges are ours: We are proprietors of the soil we live on, and possess the rights of freeholders. Our suffrages, and, what is of more importance, our sentiments and opinions, have their due weight in the government we live under. Our laws are altogether our own; they grow out of our circumstances, are framed for our exclusive benefit, and administered either by officers of our own appointment, or such as possess our confidence. We have a judiciary, chosen among ourselves: we serve as jurors on the trial of others, and are liable ourselves to be tried only by jurors of our fellow-citizens. We have all that is meant by *liberty of conscience.* The time and mode of worshipping God, as prescribed to us in his word, and dictated by our conscience, we are not only free to follow, but are protected in following.

" Forming a community of our own in the land of our forefathers, having the commerce, and soil, and resources of the country at our disposal; we know nothing of that debasing inferiority with which our very colour stamped us in America;

there is nothing here to create the feeling on our part—nothing to cherish the feeling of superiority in the minds of foreigners who visit us. It is this moral emancipation—this liberation of the mind from worse than iron fetters—that repays us ten thousand times over all that it has cost us, and makes us grateful to God and our American patrons, for the happy change which has taken place in our situations."

Extract of a letter from Captain Nicholson, of the United States Navy, who spent some time at Liberia.

"The appearance of all the colonists, those of Monrovia, as well as those of Caldwell, indicated more than contentment. Their manners were those of freemen, who experienced the blessings of liberty, and appreciated the boon. Many of them had by trade acquired a competency.   *   *   *   The children born in the country are fine looking, and I presume can be raised as easily as those of the natives. All the colonists with whom I had communication (and with nearly the whole of them did I communicate, in person, or by my officers) *expressed their decided wish to remain in their present situation, rather than return again to the United States.* I cannot give you better evidence of the prosperity of the colony, than by mentioning, that *eight of my crew (coloured mechanics,) after going ashore two several days, applied for and received their discharge, in order to remain as permanent settlers.* These men had been absent from their country upwards of three years, and had among them nearly two thousand dollars in clothes and money. Had they not been thoroughly convinced that their happiness and prosperity would be better promoted by remaining among their free brethren in Liberia, they would not have determined on so momentous a step as quitting the United States, perhaps forever, where they all had left friends and relatives."

Extract of a Letter from Captain Kennedy, of the Java, who left Monrovia, Dec. 27th, 1830.

Norfolk, June 22, 1831.

"It may not be improper to observe, that my inquiries were commenced under auspices very unfavourable to the practicability of the scheme of the society; for while I trust, I yielded unfeigned acknowledgments of the piety and purity of purpose which governed its worthy and disinterested projectors, yet the vast difficulties attending the prosecution of their labours, and the very problematical results in the want of success, left an impression on my mind altogether unfavourable to the institution. Under these impressions, therefore, I commenced my inquiries with great caution. I sought out the most shrewd and intelligent of the colonists, many of whom were personally known to me, and by long and wary conversations, endeavoured to elicit from them any dissatisfaction with their situation, if such existed, or any latent desire to return to their native country. Neither of these did I observe. On the contrary, I thought I could perceive that *they considered that they had started into a new existence;* that, disencumbered of the mortifying relations in which they formerly stood in society, they felt themselves proud in their attitude, and seemed conscious, that while they were the founders of a new empire, they were prosecuting the noble purpose of the regeneration of the land of their fathers."

Extract of a Letter from Captain Sherman, of the Liberia, dated Philadelphia, May 10, 1830.

"The agent is the chief magistrate of the colony, and the physician his assistant. No white people are allowed to reside in the colony, for the purpose of trade, or of pursuing any mechanical business, such being intended for the exclusive benefit of the coloured people. The coloured secretary, collector of customs, surveyor and constables are appointed by the agent. The port agent, sheriff, treasurer and other officers, are elective, and all the offices, except that of agent and physician, are filled by coloured people.

"Two native kings have put themselves and their subjects, supposed to amount to ten thousand, under the protection of the colony, and are ready, should it be thought necessary or expedient by the settlers to put arms in their hands, to make common cause with them in case of hostilities by any of the natives, which, however, is not anticipated, as the most friendly disposition is manifested by all the natives of the country from whom any danger might have been apprehended.

"The township of Caldwell is about seven miles from Monrovia, on St. Paul's river, and contains a population of five hundred and sixty agriculturists. The soil is exceedingly fertile and pleasant, and the people satisfied and happy. The emigrants carried out by me, and from whom I received a pleasing and satisfactory account of that part of the territory, are located there."

Letter from Captain Abels, of the Schooner Margaret Mercer, Washington, Feb. 10, 1832.

"Having just arrived in the United States from the colony of Liberia, to which place I went as master of the schooner Margaret Mercer, and where I remained thirteen days, during which time I was daily on shore, and carefully observed the state of affairs, and inquired into the condition of the people, I venture to state some facts in regard to the circumstances and prospects of the colony. On the 14th of December I arrived, and on the 15th went on shore, and was received in the most polite and friendly manner by the governor, Dr. Mechlin, who introduced me to the ministers and principal inhabitants. All the colonists appeared to be in good health. *All my expectations in regard to the aspect of things, the health, harmony, order, contentment, industry, and general prosperity of the settlers, were more than realized.* There are about two hundred buildings in the town of Monrovia, extending along the Cape Montserado, not far from a mile and a quarter.— Most of these are good substantial houses and stores, (the first story of many of them being of stone,) and some of them handsome, spacious, painted, and with Venitian blinds. Nothing struck me as more remarkable than the great superiority, in intelligence, manners, conversation, dress, and general appearance in every respect, of the people over their coloured brethren in America. So much was I pleased with what I saw, that I observed to the people, should I make a true report, it would hardly be credited in the United States. Among all that I conversed with, *I did not find a discontented person, or hear one express a desire to return to America.* I saw no intemperance, nor did I hear a profane word uttered by any one. Being a Minister of the Gospel, on Christmas day I preached both in the Methodist and Baptist Church, to full and attentive congregations of from three to four hundred persons in each. I know of no place where the Sabbath appears to be more respected than in Monrovia. I was glad to see that the Colonial Agent or Governor is a constant attendant on Divine service, and appears desirous of promoting the moral and religious welfare of the people. Most of the settlers appear to be rapidly acquiring property; and I have no doubt they are doing better for themselves and their children in Liberia, than they could do in any other part of the world. Could the free people of colour in this country but see the real condition of their brethren who have settled in Africa, I am persuaded they would require no other motive to induce them to emigrate. This is my decided and deliberate judgment.

"P. S. I have several times dined with the Colonists, and I think no better tables could be set in any part of the world. We had every thing that heart could desire, of meats, and fish, and fowls, and vegetables, and wines," &c. &c.

Extract of a letter from Mr. Mechlin, Colony Agent.

"As to the morals of the colonists, I consider them much better than the people of the United States; that is, *you may take an equal number of the inhabitants from any section of the Union, and you will find more drunkards, more profane swearers and sabbath-breakers, &c., than in Liberia.* Indeed, I know of no country where things are conducted more quietly and orderly than in this colony. You rarely hear an oath, and as to riots and breaches of the peace, I recollect of but one instance, and that of a trifling nature, that has come under my notice since I assumed the government of the colony. The sabbath is more strictly observed, than I ever saw it in the United States. Our Sunday schools are well attended, not only by the children of the colonists, but also by the native children who reside amongst us. The natives themselves are so well acquainted with our strict observance of this day, that you never find them offering any thing for sale, nor can you hire them to work for you; I mean those who have been amongst us, and at all acquainted with our customs."

Extract from the examination of Mr. Devany, High Sheriff of Liberia, before a Committee of the House of Representatives of the U. S., May 27–28, 1830.

"Some instances of intemperance have occurred—but the habit is confined to two persons only, and does not go to such an extent, as to be of serious injury to the families of the individuals, who are blacksmiths. There are three churches, frame buildings, one of them with a steeple. One belongs to the baptists, one to the methodists, and one, not yet finished,' to the presbyterians. *Divine service is attended three times on Sundays, and also on Thursday and Friday evenings.* The Sunday schools are attended by many of the native children. All who can be decently clad, are in the habit of attending."

*   *   *   *   *   "The court holds its sessions on the first Monday in every month. Juries are empanneled as with us. The jurisdiction of the court extends over the whole colony. The trials are principally for larceny, and *the criminals generally natives,* who commit thefts in the settlements. A few instances of kidnapping have occurred. These depredations were committed on the recaptured Africans. *To the honour of the emigrants be it mentioned, that but five of their number have been committed for stealing or misdemeanor since* 1827.

"There is much hospitality to be found in Monrovia; and among the inhabitants, *a greater proportion of moral and religious people, than in this city,* [*Philadelphia.*] *I never saw a man intoxicated, or heard any profane swearing during the three weeks I was there."*—Captain Sherman.

Yours, &c. M. C.

Philadelphia, April 22, 1832.

LETTER IX.

Soil and Climate of Liberia.—Commerce and Productions.— Disadvantages of Slavery to the White population.—Advantages of Colonization to our Free Coloured Population.

Dear Sir—

The colonists in their address to the coloured population of the United States, dated September 1827, observe that "The soil is not exceeded for fertility, or productiveness, when properly cultivated, by any soil in the world. The hills and plains are covered with perpetual verdure. *The productions of the soil go on through the year, without intermission.* Notwithstanding the imperfections of the farming tools used by the natives, they raise more than they can consume, and frequently more than they can sell. We have," they add, "no dreary winter here, for one-half the year, to consume the productions of the other half. *Nature is constantly renovating herself, and constantly pouring her treasures all the year round, into the lap of the industrious.*

"The true character of the African climate," continue the colonists, "is not understood in other countries. Its inhabitants are as robust, as healthy, and as long-lived, to say the least, as those of any other country. Nothing like an epidemic has ever appeared in the colony—nor can we learn from the natives, that the calamity of a sweeping sickness ever yet existed in that part of the continent. But the change from a temperate to a tropical country, is a great one—too great not to affect the health, more or less—and in the case of old people, and very young children, it often causes death. In the early years of the colony, want of good houses, the great fatigues and dangers of the settlers, their irregular mode of living, and the hardships and discouragements they met with, greatly helped the other causes of sickness, which prevailed to an alarming extent, and were attended with great mortality. But *we look back to these times as to a season of trial long past, and nearly forgotten. Our houses and circumstances are now comfortable; and for the last two or three years not one person in fifty, from the middle and southern states, has died from the change of climate."*

"For beauty and fertility, *the country is surpassed by none in the world; for salubrity of situation, excellent water, and facility of being brought under cultivation, by none equally unpeopled in Africa.* Imagine a fine river, half a mile wide, and affording across its channel from bank to bank from three to four fathoms of water—the country on either side champaign, and the level about twenty to thirty feet above that of the river—the banks every where perpendicular, exhibiting, in order, the different strata of which the general bed of the country is composed—the waters of the river to be sweet at a very small distance above the mouth, eight months in the year—at nine miles, the year round—and you have a correct, but still imperfect idea of this noble river, and the adjacent country. The original growth is exuberant, and the soil a rich, deep and loose loam, entirely destitute of stones, exhibiting in some places a prevalence of sand, and in others of a fat clay—but all about equally productive."—*Ashmun.*

"Not an hour have I spent here without feeling the refreshing and salutary influences of a fresh breeze from the ocean. The settlement can never be without it. * * No situation of Western Africa can be more salubrious. The sea air does all that can be done for it in this climate. One peculiarity is, that the night air is nearly as pure as any other. * * The rapidity and luxuriance of vegetation here, the natives of temperate latitudes can hardly imagine."—*Idem.*

Dr. Mechlin states in a recent communication, that "to those emigrants who have had the fever, and are in a great measure acclimated, Africa proves a more congenial clime than the United States. There they enjoy a greater immunity from disease: and pulmonary affections, so rife among the coloured population in the United States, are almost unknown in Liberia."

"It has been objected that the climate is very unhealthy—this is true as it respects the whites, but erroneous as respects the coloured people. Those from the middle and northern states have to undergo what is called a seasoning,—that is, they generally take the fever the first month of their residence; but it has rarely proved fatal since accommodations have been prepared for their reception: those from Georgia, the Carolinas, and the southern parts of Virginia, either escape the fever altogether, or have it very slightly. Deaths occur there indeed, as in other places: but Dr. Mechlin, the agent, assured me that the bills of mortality would show a less proportion of deaths, than those of Baltimore, Philadelphia, or New York."—Captain Sherman.

The uniform experience of the colonists has proved that emigrants from the Southern States become speedily acclimated. If they have the fever of the country, it affects them very lightly—and those who are prudent, and observe the advice of the settlers, are in no more danger than emigrants from Europe to this country.

Commerce and Productions—The commerce of Liberia, as yet in its infancy, is respectable, and increasing annually. The exports are rice, palm oil, ivory, tortoise shell, dye wood, gold, hides, wax, and coffee. Coffee and cotton grow spontaneously. Indigo and the sugar cane succeed, and will be cultivated to advantage. Camwood is abundant, and mahogany grows at the cape. The timber of Liberia is various and durable, and well adapted to building. The imports consist of an assortment of the productions of Europe, the West Indies and America. The port of Monrovia is seldom clear of European and American vessels, loading and unloading.

A trading company has been formed at Monrovia, with a capital of $1000; and an agreement entered into, that no dividend shall be made until the profits increase the capital to $20,000. The stock has risen from 50 to 75 on transfer shares.

A colonist, of the name of Waring, sold goods to the amount of $70,000, in the year 1830. The sales of Mr. Devany, the sheriff, amounted to between 24 and $25,000, and his property was worth about $20,000, made during the six years in which he has resided in Monrovia.

"The commerce of the colony, during the year 1831, has greatly exceeded that of any former year. Within that period 46 vessels visited the port, of which 21 were Americans, and a majority of the remainder English. The exports amounted to nearly 90,000 dollars, and the merchandize and produce on hand, at the close of the year, amounted to about 23,000 dollars."

Disadvantages to the Whites resulting from Slavery.

"To provide for the free negro a country, is alike the dictate of humanity towards him, and of policy towards ourselves. While he remains here, no white labourer will seek employment near him. Hence it is, that in some of the richest counties east of the Blue Ridge, the white population is stationary, and in many others it is retrograde. *Virginia, once the first state in numbers, as she is still in territory, has become the third, and will soon have to descend to the fourth rank. The valuation of the lands of New York, exceeds the estimate of all the lands and slaves in Virginia.*"—*Richmond and Manchester Colonization Society.*

"Experience has taught us, that slaves add nothing to our wealth. Where they exist, labour is not only high, but badly performed; and the communities growing up around us, which are clear of this evil, flourish over us, and by their cheapness of labour, nicer mechanism, and more abundant industry, are making us tributary. The progress of light—the conduct of other nations—and particularly that of our South American neighbours, in liberating their slaves—the growing belief of the disadvantages of slavery, with other causes, contribute to increase the conviction that *slavery is an evil, and that its consequences may one day or other become terrible.*"—*Kentucky Colonization Society.*

"Slavery is ruinous to the whites—retards improvement—roots out an industrious population, banishes the yeomanry of the country—deprives the spinner, the weaver, the smith, the shoemaker, the carpenter, of employment and support. This evil admits of no remedy—it is increasing, and will continue to increase, until the whole country will be inundated with one black wave covering its whole extent, with a few white faces here and there floating on the surface. The master has no capital but what is vested in human flesh—the father, instead of being richer for his sons, is at a loss to provide for them—there is no diversity of occupations, no incentive to enterprise. *Labour of every species is disreputable, because performed mostly by slaves. Our towns are stationary, our villages almost every where declining—and the general aspect of the country marks the curse of a wasteful idle, reckless population, who have no interest in the soil, and care not how much it is impoverished.* Public improvements are neglected, and the entire continent does not present a region for which nature has done so much, and art so little. If cultivated by free labour, the soil of Virginia is capable of sustaining a dense population, among whom labour would be honourable, and where 'the busy hum of men' would tell that all were happy, and that all were free."—*Speech of T. Marshal, of Fauquier Co. in the legislature of Virginia.*

The advantages of Colonization to our Free Coloured People.

That the free coloured population in this country labour under the most oppressive disadvantages, which their freedom can by no means counterbalance, is too obvious to admit of doubt. I waive all inquiry whether this be right or wrong. I speak of things as they are—not as they might, or ought to be. They are cut off from the most remote chance of amalgamation with the white population, by feelings or prejudices, call them what you will, that are ineradicable. Their situation is more unfavourable than that of many slaves. "With all the burdens, cares and responsibilities of freedom, they have few or none of its substantial benefits. Their associations are, and must be, chiefly with slaves. Their right of suffrage gives them little, if any, political influence, and they are practically, if not theoretically excluded from representation and weight in our public councils." No merit, no services, no talents can ever elevate many of them to a level with the whites. Occasionally, an exception may arise. A coloured individual, of great talents, merits, and wealth, may emerge from the crowd. Cases of this kind are to the last degree rare. The coloured people are subject to legal disabilities, more or less galling and severe, in almost every state in the Union. Who has not deeply regretted their late harsh expulsion from the state of Ohio, and their being forced to abandon the country of their birth, which had profited by their labours, and to take refuge in a foreign land? Severe regulations have been recently passed in Louisiana, and various other states, to prevent the introduction of free people of colour. Whenever they appear, they are to be banished in sixty days. The strong opposition to the establishment of a negro college in Newhaven, speaks in a language not to be mistaken, the jealousy with which they are regarded. And there is no reason to expect, that the lapse of centuries will make any change in this respect. They will always, unhappily, be regarded as an inferior race. In some of the states, they are actually doomed to idleness, because, however skilful they may be, in any branch of manufactures, white operatives cannot generally be induced to work with them. Such being their situation in this country, surely they ought to long as eagerly for a settlement in the land of their ancestors, as the captive tribes of Israel hungered for a return to the land of Canaan.

What a contrast to their situation in Liberia! There they will be lords of the soil, and have every inducement and every opportunity to cultivate their minds. They will not be borne down by that sense of inferiority, from whose goadings they cannot escape here, and which is enough to depress minds the most highly gifted. According to their respective merits, they may aspire to any of the offices of honour and profit and influence, in the colony. The bar, and the bench, and the medical profession, will be open to them, from which they are debarred here by an impassible barrier.

It is but fair and impartial to give the views of a portion of the coloured people, in regard to the plan of colonization. It remains for the reader to decide on their correctness, when he has duly weighed the contents of letter VIII.

The following resolutions were passed by a meeting of the people of Colour in New Bedford, January 22, 1832.

"*Resolved*, That in whatever light we view the Colonization Society, we discover nothing in it but terror, prejudice and oppression; that the warm and beneficent hand of philanthrophy is not apparent in the system, but the influence of the Society on public opinion is more prejudicial to the interest and welfare of the people of colour in the United States, than slavery itself.

"*Resolved*, That the Society, to effect its purpose, the removal of the free people of colour (not the slaves) through its agents, teaches the public to believe that it is patriotic and benevolent to withhold from us knowledge and the means of acquiring subsistence, and to look upon us as unnatural and illegal residents in this counry; and thus by force of prejudice, if not by law, endeavour to compel us to embark for Africa, and that too, apparently by our own free will and consent."

LETTER X.

Of Africa before the Irruptions of the Barbarians.—Effects of the Colonization on the slave trade.—Slight sketch of that nefarious traffic.

DEAR SIR,

Those who argue, from the present state of the coloured population of this country, against the prospect of a high degree of civilization in Africa, reason from very imperfect data. Here the coloured people have laboured, and still labour, under almost every possible disadvantage. In most of the southern states, slaves are debarred from the attainment of the slightest rudiments of knowledge. And even in states free from slavery, the coloured people have little opportunity of cultivation. Condemned by poverty, almost universally, to the lowest occupations, they have neither time nor means to improve themselves. But they will not suffer much, on a fair comparison with whites of the same grade. The best criterion, however, by which to judge, is the progress they have made in Liberia, where they escape the degradation to which they are exposed here. Of their improvement in morals, and manners, and habits, the testimony of Captains Sherman, Kennedy, Nicholson, and Abels, from which I have made large quotations in the preceding pages, precludes all doubt. It may be confidently stated, that few of the American colonies made greater advances in the same space of time than they have done in the eight years that have elapsed since the establishment of order and good government in 1824. The distance between the Colonists at Liberia and the people of the United States, is not so great as between the inhabitants of Great Britain at present, and those in olden times, when the latter painted their bodies, had no chimnies to their houses, lay upon straw on the ground, covered themselves with skins fastened with skewers, and were tenants in common with the pigs which partook of the hospitality of their houses.

Africa, though brutalized by wars, the invasions of barbarians, and the most grinding despotism, was once on as proud an eminence in point of civilization as any part of Europe. Carthage contended for the supremacy with Rome for one hundred and twenty years—and, but for domestic factions, the bane of republics, would probably have subjugated Italy. The destruction of the Carthaginian annals by the Romans renders it impossible to enumerate any of her great men, except her warriors. Rome never produced a greater general than Hannibal. Some of his relations were men of great talents in the same department. Jugurtha was superior to most of the Romans who were sent against him. Terence, the dramatist, was an African.

Christianity and civilization were early introduced into Africa. There were several provincial councils held there. At one of them, held in Carthage, in 397, the canon of the Roman Catholic

Bible was settled. Another was held in the same place in 410—and two others at Milevi. In the fifth century, the number of Catholic Bishops in Africa, was four hundred. Origen, Tertullian, Cyprian and Augustine, among the great lights of Christianity in their day, were Africans. And it is not too much to expect that future Hannibals and Terences and Cyprians and Augustines will arise to defend and illuminate that now benighted country. Should such a result take place, the merit will in a great degree belong to the illustrious founders of the Colonization Society.

Among the striking advantages attending the Colony at Liberia, is the check it has given to the slave trade already, and the probable suppression, ultimately, of that nefarious traffic on a large portion of the western coast of Africa by the gradual extension of the settlements. Before the establishment of the settlements at Liberia, there were several slave factories within a few miles of Monrovia, all of which have been completely broken up. Four or five years since, there was not a single factory from Sierra Leone to Cape Mount, a distance of 100 miles; and 120 miles, from Cape Mount, to Trade Town, the whole of the coast of Liberia. More recently, a factory has been established at Cape Mount, forty-five miles from Monrovia, where the trade is carried on briskly. But it is probable, as soon as the Colony gains more strength, that this nest of pirates, kidnappers and traders in human flesh and human suffering, will be extirpated.

The African chiefs, in the neighborhood of Liberia, have in general voluntarily abandoned the traffic, finding they can procure what articles they want, of European, American, and West India goods, by the sale of their own domestic productions. Some of them have put themselves under the protection of the colony.

To duly appreciate the advantages of this result, it is only necessary to reflect for a moment on the horrors of this nefarious traffic ; and although it has been presented times without number, to the execration of mankind, I may be permited to take a bird's eye view of it. The number of slaves kidnapped in 1824, was 120,000. And the number imported into the single port of Rio for nine years, 1820—8, was 261,964.

In 1820, 15,020	In 1823, 20,349	In 1826, 33,999
1821, 24,134	1824, 39,503	1827, 29,787
1822, 27,363	1825, 26,254	1828, 43,555

Total..........261,964

Walsh's notices of Brazil, vol. 2. p. 178.

Notwithstanding the efforts of the chief maritime powers of Europe, and those of the United States, to suppress this traffic, there have been, from the two towns, Muney and Pangas, 352 cargoes of slaves taken, in little more than a year.

It has been estimated that one third, but say one fifth, perish in the voyage ; and that an equal number die after their landing, of diseases contracted on the voyage, or of grief for their forlorn situation!

To heighten the enormity of this "sin crying to heaven for vengeance," it is ascertained, that in cases of scarcity of provision, the slaves are often remorselessly thrown overboard. On board a vessel some time since, thirty nine negroes became blind, and twelve had lost an eye. They were thrown into the fathomless ocean. A single vessel, the Protector, took on board at Mozambique 807 slaves, of whom 339 died on the voyage.

The Maria Primeira, a Portugese ship, took on board upwards of 500 slaves. This number was reduced to 403 in consequence of extreme crowding, before she was captured, and brought into Sierra Leone. Nearly 100 more died soon afterwards, from diseases contracted on board.—(*Transactions of the London African Association.*)

The following heart-rending picture of the slave trade has been drawn by Sir George O'Meara, who was employed on the coast of Africa, to suppress it.

"Such is the merciless treatment of the slaves, that no fancy can picture the horrors of the voyage. Crowded together so as not to have the power to move—linked one to the other by the leg—never unfettered while life remains, or till the iron shall have fretted the flesh almost to the bone—forced under a deck, as I have seen them, *not thirty inches in height*—breathing an atmosphere the most putrid and pestilential possible—with little food and less water—subject to the most severe punishment, at the caprice or fancy of the brute who may command the vessel—it is to me a matter of extreme wonder that any of these miserable wretches live the voyage through. Many of them, indeed, perish on the passage, and those of them who remain to meet the shore, present a picture of wretchedness language cannot express."

April 26, 1832.   Yours, &c.   M. C.

—◄◄◄❈◇❀►►—

Letter, from the Hon. James Madison, to the Secretary of the Society, dated Montpelier, December 29, 1831.

DEAR SIR: I received, in due time, your letter of the 21st ult. and with due sensibility to the subject of it. Such, however, has been the effect of a painful rheumatism on my general condition, as well in disqualifying my fingers for the use of the pen, that I could not do justice "to the principles and measures of the Colonization Society in all the great and various relations they sustain to our own country and to Atrica," if my views of them could have the value which your partiality supposes. I may observe in brief, that the Society had always my good wishes, though with hopes of its success less sanguine than were entertained by others, found to have been the better judges; and, that I feel the greatest pleasure at the progress already made by the Society, and the encouragement to encounter remaining difficulties afforded by the earlier and greater ones already overcome. Many circumstances at the present moment seem to concur in brightening the prospects of the Society, and cherishing the hope that *the time will come, when the dreadful calamity which has so long afflicted our country and filled so many with despair, will be gradually removed and by means consistent with justice, peace and the general satisfaction*: thus giving to our country the full enjoyment of the blessings of liberty, and to the world the full benefit of its great example. I never considered the main difficulty of the great work as lying in the deficiency of emancipations, but in an inadequacy of asylums for such a growing mass of population, and in the great expense of removing it to its new home. The spirit of private manumission as the laws may permit, and the exiles may consent, is increasing and will increase; and there are sufficient indications that the public authorities in slave-holding States are looking forward to interpositions in different forms that must have a powerful effect. With respect to the new abode for the emigrants, all agree that the choice made by the Society is rendered peculiarly appropriate by considerations which need not be repeated, and if other situations should not be found eligible receptacles for a portion of them, the prospects in Africa seem to be expanding in a highly encouraging degree.

" In contemplating the pecuniary resources needed for the removal of such a number to so great a distance, my thoughts and hopes have been long turned to the rich fund presented in the western lands of the Nation, which will soon entirely cease to be under a pledge for another object. The great one in question is truly of a national character, and it is known that distinguished patriots not dwelling in slave-holding States have viewed the object in that light, and would be willing to let the national domain be a resource in effecting it.

" Should it be remarked that the States, though all may be interested in relieving our country from the coloured population, are not equally so ; it is but fair to recollect, that the sections most to be benefited, are those whose cessions created the fund to be disposed of.

" I am aware of the constitutional obstacle which has presented itself; but if the general will be reconciled to an application of the territorial fund to the removal of the coloured population, a grant to Congress of the necessary authority could be carried, with little delay, through the forms of the Constitution.

" Sincerely wishing an increasing success to the labours of the Society, I pray you to be assured of my esteem, and to accept my friendly salutations."

REV. R. R. GURLEY.

JAMES MADISON.

Extract of a Letter from the Hon. John Marshall, Chief Justice of the United States, dated Richmond, December 14, 1831.

" The great object of the Society, I presume, is to obtain pecuniary aids. Application will undoubtedly be made, I hope successfully, to the several State Legislatures, by the societies formed within them respectively. It is extremely desirable that they should pass permanent laws on the subject, and the excitement produced by the late insurrection makes this a favourable moment for the friends of the Colony to press for such acts. It would be also desirable, if such a direction could be given to State Legislation as might have some tendency to incline the people of colour to migrate. This, however, is a subject of much delicacy. Whatever may be the success of our endeavours to obtain acts for permanent aids, I have no doubt that our applications for immediate contributions will receive attention. It is possible, though not probable, that more people of colour may be disposed to migrate than can be provided for, with the funds the Society may be enabled to command. Under this impression I suggested, some years past, to one or two of the Board of Managers, to allow a small additional bounty in lands to those who would pay their own passage in whole or in part. The suggestion, however, was not approved.

" It is undoubtedly of great importance to retain the countenance and protection of the General Government. *Some of our cruizers stationed on the coast of Africa would, at the same time, interrupt the slave trade—a horrid traffic, detested by all good men, and would protect the vessels and commerce of the Colony from pirates who infest those seas.* The power of the government to afford this aid is not, I believe, contested. I regret that its power to grant pecuniary aid is not equally free from question. On this subject, I have always thought, and still think, that the proposition made by Mr. King, in the Senate, is the most unexceptionable, and the most effective that can be devised.

" The fund would probably operate as rapidly as would be desirable, when we take into view the other resources which might come in aid of it ; and its application would be, perhaps, less exposed to those constitutional objections which are made in the South than the application of money drawn from the treasury and raised by taxes. The lands are the property of the United States, and have heretofore been disposed of by the government under the idea of absolute ownership."